THE AMERICAN CHURCH

BOOKS BY VERGILIUS FERM

THE AMERICAN CHURCH
of the
Protestant Heritage

Edited By
VERGILIUS FERM

*Compton Professor and Head of The Department of Philosophy
in The College of Wooster*

PHILOSOPHICAL LIBRARY
New York

PRINTED IN THE UNITED STATES OF AMERICA

TABLE OF CONTENTS

76496

LIST OF CONTRIBUTORS

JOHN R. WEINLICK, B.D., M.A., Ph.D.
Professor of Historical Theology in the Moravian Theological Seminary (Bethlehem, Pennsylvania)

VERGILIUS FERM, B.D., M.A., Ph.D.
Compton Professor and Head of the Department of Philosophy in The College of Wooster

JOHN CHRISTIAN WENGER, M.A., Th.D.
Mennonite Bishop and Professor of Theology and Philosophy in Goshen College Biblical Seminary (Goshen, Indiana)

CLIFFORD MERRILL DRURY, B.D., S.T.M., Ph.D., D.D.
California Professor of Church History, San Francisco Theological Seminary (San Anselmo, California)

WALTER HERBERT STOWE, B.D., S.T.D.
Editor-in-Chief, *Historical Magazine of the Protestant Episcopal Church* (New Brunswick, New Jersey); President and Editor of Publications, the Church Historical Society, Philadelphia; Historiographer, the Diocese of New Jersey

MILTON J. HOFFMAN, M.A., D.D.
Professor of Church History, New Brunswick Theological Seminary, New Brunswick, New Jersey

EDWIN T. BUEHRER, M.A., B.D.
Minister of the Third Unitarian Church, Chicago, Illinois; Formerly, Editor of *The Journal of Liberal Religion*

MERVIN M. DEEMS, Th.M., Ph.D.
Professor of History of Early Christianity and Missions in the Chicago Theological Seminary, and the Federated Theological Faculty of the University of Chicago

ROBERT G. TORBET, B.D., M.A., Ph.D.
Until recently, Professor of Church History in The Eastern Baptist Theological Seminary; now Associate Editor of *Baptist Leader* and Editor of the Uniform Lesson Publications

W. E. McCULLOCH, D.D.
Associate Editor, *The United Presbyterian*

WILLIAM EUGENE BERRY, Ph.D.

Professor of Religion and Greek, Emeritus, Earlham College (Richmond, Indiana)

KARL A. OLSSON, M.A., Ph.D.

Professor and Chairman of the Historical Division of North Park Theological Seminary of the Mission Covenant Church, Chicago, Illinois; Member of the Corps of Chaplains, United States Army

DESMOND W. BITTINGER, M.A., Ph.D.

President, McPherson College (McPherson, Kansas)

DAVID DUNN, M.A., S.T.B., D.D.

Henry and Emma Meily Heilman Professor of Church History and Dean of the Theological Seminary of the Evangelical and Reformed Church (Lancaster, Pennsylvania)

ELMER T. CLARK, B.D., M.A., S.T.D., LL.D., Litt.D.

Editor of *World Outlook* (New York City)

ROBERT CUMMINS, M.A., M.Th., S.T.D., D.D.

General Superintendent of The Universalist Church of America (Boston, Massachusetts)

PAUL H. ELLER, B.D., M.A., Ph.D.

Professor of Church History in The Evangelical Theological Seminary (Naperville, Illinois)

LeROY EDWIN FROOM

Field Secretary of the General Conference of Seventh-day Adventists; Professor of the History of Prophetic Interpretation, Seventh-day Adventist Theological Seminary (Washington, D. C.)

RONALD E. OSBORN, M.A., B.D.

Professor of Church History, the School of Religion, Butler University (Indianapolis, Indiana)

EARL WEST, M.A., B.D.

Minister of the Irvington Church of Christ, Indianapolis, Indiana

CHARLES EWING BROWN, D.D.

Formerly, Associate Professor of Church History in Anderson College; for many years Editor of *The Gospel Trumpet,* Anderson, Indiana

I

EDITOR'S PREFACE

I

EDITOR'S PREFACE

What we have sought to do in this cooperative volume is somewhat as follows:

Each contributor has attempted to present the European background of the Protestant group about which he is writing, giving the major emphasis upon the American development of the church. Each expositor, too, has tried to make plain the characteristic features of the denomination in terms of its chief doctrines, confessional bases, its theological developments, its type of polity, its larger organizational constructs, its pioneer leaders, its conspicuous theologians and other pertinent data such as American headquarters, schools, journals, and the like —all of which will make clear the pattern of the church.

It may be noted that each contributor has intimate acquaintance "from the inside" of the particular Protestant group about which he is writing, either by way of long and sustained membership or by special studies, or by both. The expositions are chiefly historical although each has felt free to make his own tempting observations and evaluations.

It would, of course, be impossible to include all Protestant groups in a volume of limited size such as this and at the same time present the subjects in a kind of story form. Some omissions are excusable on the ground—so far as the editor is concerned—that such groups were included in another recently published volume. [1, 2] Some readers looking at the array of American denominations might wish to distinguish churches of the Protestant heritage from so-called "sects" or "cults". Such a distinction (often based on the assumption that the latter claim a revelation unique from the main Protestant stream or by reason of a numerical minority in comparison with the

larger churches and therefore "do not belong") is here ignored
as altogether out-moded. Even the prophets of the bigger Protestant denominations acted on the assumption that theirs was
the true revelation of interpretation of some norm (Scripture,
confession). Moreover, those who have claimed "special"
revelation, many of them, affirm, not without justification, that
their own revelatory interpretations are not afar from the heritage that is the Protestant succession, even though amplified.
All denominations like to believe that theirs is the church which
stems truly from the soil of primitive times. And so—such line
between "church" and "sect" or "cult" is here dropped, without apology. It is, moreover, in keeping with a more charitable outlook toward those in historic disagreements with "orthodoxy" not to indulge in classifications which now have odious
meaning.

The justification of such a volume as this may be the justification of any similar type of volume. We need, from time
to time, fresh appraisals by fresh interpreters, certainly by those
not bound too much by the temptation of giving "official" reporting. The church historian like any historian has the same
old facts to look at; but the vantage point of his own experience and circumstance, his own particular training, studies
and contacts, may well give to those facts the kind of clothing
needed to set them off in full splendor of attractiveness, insight and meaning. As such, I am sure, students of the field
will welcome another volume of exposition and interpretation.

Then, too, with "mergers" and "federations" now filling
the air, it is of signal importance that an understanding is
had of historic divergencies and developments, particularly on
American soil. Any Protestant union will not come through
sheer organizational cooperatives; union can only come through
a unity of understanding of common agreements and of differences. And it is well that there are variations of group
species since we continue to be human beings of individual differences, culturally, economically, socially and even spiritually.
All that we may wish for is that we may have the charity that

comes from understanding and then work toward whatever good that can come by unified effort. At least, if we may realize that we are of the twentieth rather than the sixteenth century and desperately try to live *our* way of life as did those who struck out so fearlessly in earlier centuries in living out theirs and reshape our faith for our times as they did for theirs— we have come a long way towards a better destiny. This book, while it looks back, I trust, looks forward toward those on-coming currents which make history. The future is now much more important than ever—both for us who now live and certainly for those who come after—with the mammoth tides of transitions sweeping over the entire landscape of the mid-twentieth century.

My thanks goes to all of the contributors who have accepted the invitation to join in this cooperative volume. Correspondence and planning with them have been, without exception, a pleasant contact. And my appreciation, no less, goes out to the publisher, Dr. D. D. Runes, for making this venture realizable. There are no books without the concrete support of a friendly publisher.

The College of Wooster   Vergilius Ferm

Wooster, Ohio

---

1 *Religion in the Twentieth Century* (New York, 1948). In this volume appear the accounts of such essentially Protestant groups as: The Church of the New Jerusalem, The Church of Jesus Christ of Latter-Day Saints, the Salvation Army, Christian Science, Jehovah's Witnesses—not to omit mention of the general currents of thought, such as Conservative Protestantism, Liberal Protestantism, the borderline group of Anglo-Catholicism and others.

2 I had hoped to include the Pentecostal Churches in this volume. After much correspondence in seeking a representative writer my request was finally met with a reply from a general superintendent expressing "regrets" to the effect that in their group there was "no one . . . even slightly interested in writing the essay . . ."

[3]

II
THE MORAVIAN CHURCH

II

THE MORAVIAN CHURCH

JOHN R. WEINLICK

The Bohemian Brethren

THE MORAVIAN Church is one of the two Protestant bodies which antedate the Reformation, the other being the Waldensian Church. When Luther posted his *Ninety-five Theses* in Wittenberg in 1517 the Bohemian Brethren had already been organized for sixty years and numbered four hundred churches and two hundred thousand members.

Moravian roots go back to John Hus (1373?-1415) whose fearless preaching against the evils of the church during the late medieval period brought about his condemnation at the Council of Constance. His death at the stake in 1415 plunged Bohemia into bitter civil war which lasted for about twenty years. Finally, in 1457, some of the followers of Hus organized themselves under the name of Unitas Fratrum (Unity of the Brethren).[1] In establishing themselves as an independent church, the Brethren were indebted not only to the teachings of Hus, but also to those of Peter Chelcicky (1390-1456). For two centuries, despite severe repression, they played a significant rôle in the religious life of Bohemia, Moravia, and Poland. They were renowned for their simple, Godly lives, their use of the Scriptures, their hymn singing, their schools. They gave to the world, among others, the renowned educator John Amos Comenius (1592-1670) who was one of their bishops.

The Thirty Years' War and the Counter-Reformation brought an end to the organized life of the Brethren, their membership being absorbed into the Roman Catholic, Lutheran, and Reformed churches, the three bodies recognized by the treaty of Westphalia. Nevertheless, the traditions of

[7]

the church were secretly kept alive by the more loyal adherents. This era of Moravian history has been designated as the time of the "Hidden Seed," a term coined by Comenius who never lost hope for the resuscitation of his church.

The Renewed Moravian Church

In the meantime Protestantism in general had arisen and flourished, and was old enough to have lost some of the vitality of its beginning. A revival in the form of German Pietism came in the late sixteenth century. Count Nicholaus Ludwig von Zinzendorf (1700-1760) was a product of Pietism, and it was through him that the church of the Bohemian Brethren became the Renewed Moravian Church. Beginning in 1722, a nucleus of Brethren, nominally Roman Catholic, migrated to the Count's estate in eastern Saxony. There they built Herrnhut (Lord's Watch) which immediately attracted evangelical Christians from all over Germany and beyond. Herrnhut was destined to become within a few years the home community of a world wide program of evangelization.

Two ideals dominated Zinzendorf's concept of Christian service, the preaching of the Gospel to primitive peoples and the gathering of earnest Christians within the various Protestant state churches into an interdenominational fellowship for the nurture of vital spiritual life. Under the impulse of the former the first missionaries went from Herrnhut in 1732 to work among Negro slaves on the island of St. Thomas in the West Indies. The same motive with respect to the American Indians was part of the reason for the Moravians coming to Georgia in 1735. Unsuccessful in Georgia, the Brethren came to Pennsylvania in 1740. Bethlehem, which they founded the following year, became the mother community of the Moravians in America.

The second phase of the Count's program was likewise pursued with zeal. In much of Protestant Europe, particularly among Lutherans, and to a lesser extent among the Reformed, the Brethren helped to bring vitality into the churches through the pattern of the Pietist society. This has kept the Moravians few in number, for Zinzendorf, a devout Lutheran, tried his best to keep his movement within the state churches as an interchurch society, "congregation of God in the Spirit," as he called it. Despite him, however, the Moravians became a denomination within about twenty years after the founding of Herrnhut. Yet, along side of the denomination, the societies remained, with the result that Moravianism on the Continent is two things, a church and an interchurch society, the latter known as the Diaspora.[2]

The American Moravian Church

In England and America, Moravian development, like that of other churches, has been along denominational lines. But even in these two countries the society or diaspora ideal has retarded the organization of congregations and numerical growth. Also, the Moravian Church in America was slower than most in emancipating itself from European control and outlook. Administration was centered in Germany until the middle of the nineteenth century, and American Moravians were handicapped by policies laid down by those who failed to appreciate fully the needs and opportunities of an expanding new world.

During the colonial period American Moravian centers, patterned after Herrnhut, were closed communities known as settlement congregations.[3] Such places were Bethlehem, Nazareth, and Lititz in Pennsylvania, and Salem (now Winston-Salem) in North Carolina. These communities were characterized by strictly regulated behavior and by the division of the congregation into "choirs," that is age and sex groupings. There were the Married Couples, the Single Brethren, the Single Sisters, the Older Boys, the Older Girls, the Younger Boys, and the Younger Girls. Frequent prayer services, song services, love feasts, the use of instrumental music, were conspicuous features of Moravian worship in the early days. For about twenty years in Bethlehem, while the community was establishing itself, a communal economy prevailed. From these centers of intensive religious life missionaries went forth to the Indians, as well as to the heathen across the seas, and evangelists itinerated among the European settlers, particularly among the Germans. To the settlement came the children of many non-Moravians to be educated in the church's boarding and parochial schools.

The over-all effect of European control, closed communities, diaspora rather than denominational outlook, and the emphasis upon foreign missions, all of them the result of Zinzendorf's influence, was to leave the American church on the side lines as far as growth was concerned. By the end of the colonial period the Moravians had established only about thirty congregations in Pennsylvania, New Jersey, New York, and Maryland, and five or six in North Carolina. Their missionaries had done extensive work among the Indians of the Atlantic seaboard and westward into Ohio, but advancing white civilization crowded this work out of the picture within about a century.

During the first half of the nineteenth century growth was slow, though geographically the Moravians extended themselves considerably by establishing a few new centers in Ohio, Indiana, and Illinois. Near the middle of the century the tide turned. The decade from 1847 to 1857 saw constitutional changes in the denomination which culminated in the autonomy of the respective provinces throughout the world. Free to direct its own affairs, except that it was obligated to assume its share of support of foreign missions, the American church launched out on a program of home missions, directed largely toward German and Scandinavian immigrants. Among the latter the effort was confined to a few communities in Wisconsin. Among the Germans in the West, congregations were established or attempted in Michigan, Wisconsin, Minnesota, Iowa, Missouri, Kansas, Illinois, and North Dakota. In the East congregations were formed in New York City and Utica in the same state. Similar origins account for the churches in Elizabeth, Riverside, Palmyra, and Egg Harbor City in New Jersey. In nearby Philadelphia the Moravians failed in their efforts to establish permanent work among the Germans, but subsequently succeeded in having two more churches among older American stock, in addition to the one Philadelphia congregation organized by Zinzendorf in 1742. Unsuccessful attempts were made to organize congregations among German immigrants in a few New England industrial centers in the mid-nineteenth century. Near the end of the century the Moravians extended their work to Alberta and Saskatchewan among German Russians. The background for much of this home mission work in America was the diaspora program in Europe, through which the Moravians had established a point of contact.

The South, not receiving the flood of immigrants, as did the North, was not subject to the same influences. The home mission awakening there came late in the century, and the greater part of the growth of the Moravian Church South centers around the more recent development of the city of Winston-Salem.

There are in the United States and Western Canada 150 Moravian churches, of which about thirty were in existence before 1850. By the end of that century the number of congregations had more than tripled to reach the hundred mark. The remaining third of present day Moravian churches have been organized in the twentieth century. From 1860 to 1900 the membership grew from 8,187 to 22,949. Since 1900 the membership has more than doubled to reach its present total of 48,033.[4]

Doctrine

The Moravian Church holds to those evangelical teachings which are the common possession of Protestant Christians. It subscribes to that universally accepted creed of Christendom, the Apostles' Creed. Because the Brethren have never attempted to formulate a distinctive Moravian creed, and because they emphasize that a life-centered faith is more important than a creed-centered one, some outsiders have the misconception that Moravians disregard doctrine. Though Moravians have never formulated their teachings in a specific creed, they do hold to the necessity of defining theological positions. Besides acknowledging the Apostles' Creed, as above stated, the Moravian Church recognizes that in the various confessions of Protestant churches the chief articles of the Christian faith are set forth. The *Book of Order* states the Moravian position in part as follows:

Foundation of Our Doctrine

1. The Holy Scriptures of the Old and New Testaments are and remain the only rule of our faith and life. We regard them as God's Word, which He spake to men of old time through the prophets, and at last through the Son and His Apostles, to instruct them unto salvation through faith in Christ Jesus. We are convinced that all truths that declare the will of God for our salvation are fully contained therein.

2. We hold fast to our genuine Moravian view, that it is not our business to determine what the Holy Scriptures have left undetermined, or to contend about mysteries impenetrable to human reason. We would keep steadily in sight the aim set before us by the Apostle Paul, Ephes. 4:13,14, that we "may all attain unto the unity of the faith, and unto the knowledge of the Son of God, unto a full-grown man, unto the measure of the stature of the fulness of Christ; that we may be no longer children, tossed to and fro, and carried about with every wind of doctrine." At the same time, we would never forget that every human system of doctrine remains imperfect, for as the same Apostle says, I Cor. 13:9 "We know in part."

Substance of Our Doctrine

1. We hold every truth revealed by God as a precious treasure, and sincerely believe that such a treasure must not be given up, even though we could thereby save our lives. Luke 9:24. But this holds good especially of

the doctrine which the Moravian Church has from the beginning regarded as its chief doctrine, and to which it has, by God's grace, ever held as a precious jewel: That Jesus Christ "is the propitiation of our sins: and not for our's only, but also for the whole world." I John 2:2. . . .

2. With this our chief doctrine the following facts and truths, clearly attested by the Holy Scripture, stand in essential connection, and therefore, with that chief doctrine form the main subjects in our knowledge and preaching of salvation:—

a. The doctrine of the Total Depravity of human nature. . . .

b. The doctrine of the Love of God the Father to fallen humanity. . . .

c. The doctrine of the real Godhead and the real Humanity of Jesus Christ. . . .

d. The doctrine of our Reconciliation with God and our Justification before Him through the Sacrifice of Jesus Christ. . . .

e. The doctrine of the Holy Spirit and the working of His grace. . . .

f. The doctrine of Good Works as the fruit of the Spirit. . . .

g. The doctrine of the Fellowship of Believers with one another. . . .

h. The doctrine of the Second Coming of the Lord in glory, and of the Resurrection of the dead until life or unto judgment. . . .

3. While we do not present these truths and our apprehension of them in a strictly formulated Confession, our understanding of the chief content of Christian doctrine has, in a special way, found expression in what the Church has solemnly professed year by year for more than a century in the "Litany for Easter Morning."[5]

Worship

Moravians have a liturgical form of worship, following to a modified degree the ancient Church Year.[6] Common is the use of a litany for the Sunday morning service and various liturgies for the high points of the year and for special occasions, such as Advent, Christmas, All Saints' Day, Thanksgiving, Missionary, Patriotic, Schools and Colleges, etc. The sacraments are Baptism and the Lord's Supper, the latter being observed about six or seven times a year in accord with the church seasons and certain commemorative occasions in the life of the denomination and the local congregations. The absence of an altar indicates a leaning toward the Reformed interpretation of the Holy Communion, though no attempt is made to define the precise meaning of the Scripture with reference to it.

Children are baptized and later admitted to communicant membership by the Rite of Confirmation, after a period of catechetical instruction. Members of other evangelical churches are received by the Right Hand of Fellowship. Adults not previously baptized are admitted to membership by Adult Baptism, after subscribing to a confession of faith. Baptism is administered either by pouring or sprinkling, and, of course, according to the Trinitarian formula.

The church uses the common hymns sung everywhere, but features the chorale type of hymn. Visitors of Moravian churches seem to be impressed with the dignified simplicity of the services. Particularly worshipful are the Communion services, the Christmas Eve Vigils, and the Easter dawn services on God's Acre. Love feasts, consisting of the distribution and partaking of coffee and buns in the church during the singing of congregational hymns and choir anthems, are common in the older congregations. Symbolic of Christian fellowship, they are sometimes held as a service preparatory to the Lord's Supper, and sometimes as independent services.

Polity

Moravians have the three traditional orders of ministry, deacons, presbyters, and bishops. The episcopate was received from the Austrian Waldenses in 1467 and passed on to the Renewed Moravian Church in 1735 by a surviving bishop of the Bohemian Brethren, who was at the same time a clergyman of the Reformed Church.[7] Bishops are not governing bishops, but are regarded mainly as spiritual leaders. Their one distinctly episcopal function is to ordain ministers. However, more often than not, a Moravian minister who possesses the qualifications for the bishop's office also has other qualities of leadership, and invariably bishops occupy executive positions of the denomination.

Government is a combination of the conferential and synodal form, with the synods (legislative assemblies) being the highest authority, and an executive board known as the Provincial Elders' Conference administering affairs of the church during the intersynodal periods.

The Moravian Church in America is divided into two provinces: the Northern, with headquarters in Bethlehem, Pennsylvania; and the Southern, with headquarters in Winston-Salem, North Carolina. (The division is purely geographic and has no connection with the Civil War.) Between the two provinces there is complete cooperation on all matters of common interest, including a free exchange of ministers, most of whom receive their training at Moravian College and Theological Seminary in Bethlehem. Each province publishes its own church paper. Otherwise both use the same denominational literature, such as church school materials, mission publications, popular inspirational and educational booklets, hymnbooks, etc. Both support the same foreign mission enterprises. The official journal for the North is *The Moravian,* a weekly, and for the South it is *The Wachovia Moravian,* a monthly.

The Northern Province, being very scattered, is subdivided into Eastern, Western, and Canadian districts, each having its synod and a District Executive Board. In the Provincial Synod representation is pretty evenly divided between lay and clerical delegates, while in the District Synod the ratio is about two to one in favor of the laity. In the North synods are held every five years and in the South every three years. The local congregations are governed by a board of elders and a board of trustees, under the supervision of the denominational executives.

Above the provinces, of which, besides the two American, there are the British, the Continental,[8] and several mission provinces, is the Unity or world wide Moravian Church, held together by the General Synod and the General Directory. The former is composed of elected delegates from the provinces, while the latter is an ex-officio body made up of some of the provincial executives. However, the international aspect of the Moravian Church is more fraternal than administrative. The theoretical schedule of a general synod every ten years has been disrupted by the two World Wars. Yet in numerous ways the Moravians have a strong sense of belonging to a fellowship that transcends national boundaries. Undergirding this is the common heritage of nearly five centuries of history and a common mission enterprise.

Missions

When the first Moravian missionaries left Herrnhut in 1732 the only other Protestants in the field were a handful of men sent out by the Danish-Halle Mission, beginning in 1705. Not until William Carey left England for India in 1795 did the foreign mission movement get under way among Protestantism in general. Moravians, therefore, rank with the Pietists of Halle as the pioneers in this field of endeavor. They have distinguished themselves for their specialization in service to primitive peoples.

Moravian mission fields with the dates of their beginnings are as follows: West Indies, 1732; Africa, 1736; Surinam, 1738; North America (Indians), 1740; Labrador, 1771; Nicaragua, 1849; British North India, 1853; Alaska, 1885; Honduras, 1930. For seventy years the church worked among the aborigines of Australia, until in 1920 the field was turned over to the Presbyterians.

Up to the time of the first World War American Moravians united with their Brethren in Europe in common support and administration of mission work. Since then the fields have been apportioned among the home provinces, with the Americans assuming responsibility for the missions in Nicaragua, Honduras, Alaska, and the one remaining field among the Indians, a tiny mission in southern California.

While Moravians in the home churches of Europe and America number only 72,245, those on the mission field number 181,383, for a total of 253,628.[9] In other words, the ratio of home members to mission members is less than one to two. It is to be noted, however, that in Europe, both on the Continent and in Britain, much support is received by friends of the Moravian Church in other denominations.

Schools

The schools maintained by the Moravians in America, with their locations and dates of founding are the following: Moravian Preparatory School, 1741; Moravian Seminary and College for Women, 1742; and Moravian College and Theological Seminary, 1807; all in Bethlehem, Pennsylvania; Linden Hall Academy and Junior College, Lititz, Pennsylvania, 1746; and Salem Academy and College, Winston-Salem, North Carolina, 1771. Moravian Preparatory School, operated by the Bethlehem congregation, is the sole survivor of the parochial schools once common among the Moravians. Moravian Seminary and College for Women, Linden Hall, and Salem are for women, while Moravian College and Theological Seminary is for men. Nazareth Hall, a boys' academy at Nazareth, Pennsylvania, was in existence from 1759 to 1929. In comparison with the Americans, the Moravians in Europe have a much more extensive educational work. Before the upheavals of recent years the

Brethren on the other side of the Atlantic were operating more than twenty schools on the elementary and secondary levels.

Pioneer Leaders

Count Zinzendorf was, of course, the outstanding figure in the history of the Moravian Church. Though he was in America only fourteen months, between November 1741 and January of 1743, his influence prevailed here as well as in Europe.

Next in importance was Augustus Gottlieb Spangenberg (1714-1792), who though lacking the genius of Zinzendorf, far surpassed him in administrative ability. He was head of the church in America for most of the years between 1744 and 1762, with headquarters in Bethlehem. A graduate of the University of Jena, he was highly regarded for his learning. His exposition of Moravian theology, entitled *Idea Fidei Fratrum,* written in 1788 and translated into seven languages, had a wide circulation in Europe. His biography of Zinzendorf is one of the important primary sources of Moravian history.

Outstanding missionary of the American Moravian Church was David Zeisberger (1721-1808) with a record of sixty-two years of service among the Indians of Massachusetts, Connecticut, New York, Pennsylvania, Ohio, Michigan, and eastern Canada. His linguistic gifts gave him fluency in several Indian tongues, and out of his experiences came prodigious literary work in the field of Indian lore.

Other distinguished leaders were Peter Boehler (1712-1774), known to many for his influence upon John Wesley; David Nitschmann (1696-1772), first bishop of the Renewed Moravian Church and founder of Bethlehem; John Ettwein (1721-1802) who guided the Moravians through the problems of the Revolutionary War. Prominent in the development of the church in America were several lineal descendants of Zinzendorf, especially members of the deSchweinitz family. The name which stands out in the story of the Moravian Church in the South is that of Bishop Edward Rondthaler (1842-

1931). Before the time of his assuming leadership there in 1877, this section of the church had been in an arrested state of development. Obviously, any attempt to select those who have done most to advance the development of a denomination involves arbitrary decisions, and each writer would have his own list of great Moravians.

The Character of
The Present Day Moravian Church

The Moravian Church today represents average Protestantism. Because of the small size of the denomination there is, perhaps, a deeper sense of fellowship among the membership than in most churches. The title of one of its publications, *The Moravians A World Wide Fellowship,* aptly expresses the spirit of Moravianism. On social problems and what the church should do about them, there is the usual range of Protestant opinion, with a decided bent, however, toward the conservative side. Moravians place greater emphasis upon remaking individuals than upon remaking society, believing that the latter will follow in the wake of the former. Earlier leanings toward pacificism have been generally abandoned.

Moravians have a good record of interchurch cooperation. The denomination was a charter member of the Federal Council of Churches of Christ in America in 1909, and became a charter member of the Federal Council's successor, the National Council of Churches, in 1951. Likewise, the Moravian Church became a charter member of the World Council of Churches at Amsterdam in 1948. On the local level Moravians are active in ministerial associations, in united youth activities, in city councils of churches. Two favorite mottos among Moravians are "Christ and Him Crucified remain in our confession of faith," "In essentials unity, in non-essentials liberty, in all things charity."

NOTES

[1] This is still the official title of the church. The term Moravian arose only after 1722, because many of those who had a part in the revival of the Unitas Fratrum came from Moravia. In Germany the common designation of the church is "die Bruedergemeine." The term "Herrnhuter" is also well known. Many in various countries refer to adherents of the Moravian Church simply as "Brethren."

[2] On the Continent the membership of the Moravian Church has for many years been about ten thousand, while the Diaspora membership has been as high as 75,000-100,000.

[3] "Resettlement Congregation" is a term applied to a Moravian community in which the civil, economic, and religious life were all under the control of the church. There were four such communities in America and fifteen in Europe. Under modern conditions the system has broken down, and all of the settlements in America, and most of them in Europe, are now organized like other municipalities.

[4] Appendices, *Moravian Daily Texts,* a devotional manual, published annually, Bethlehem, Pennsylvania.

[5] *Book of Order of the Moravian Church in America* (Bethlehem, Pennsylvania, 1938), pp. 9-11.

[6] To what extent the Moravian Church follows the church year can be readily seen by an examination of its hymnal, *Hymnal and Liturgies of the Moravian Church* (Bethlehem, Pennsylvania, 1923).

[7] This surviving bishop of the Bohemian Brethren was Daniel Ernest Jablonski (1660-1741), a grandson of Comenius. After the virtual extinction of the Unitas Fratrum, Comenius and others saw to it that the episcopal succession was maintained by the consecration to the episcopacy of Brethren who were at the same time clergymen of the Reformed Church in Poland. Jablonski at the time he ordained David Nitschmann, the first bishop of the Renewed Church, was court preacher in Berlin.

[8] The Continental Province includes the congregations in Germany, Switzerland, Holland, and Denmark, and the Diaspora work in these and other countries on the Continent.

[9] Appendix, *Moravian Daily Texts* (Bethlehem, Pennsylvania, 1952) (statistics for January 1, 1951), p. 258.

BIBLIOGRAPHY

WALSER H. ALLEN, *The Moravians, A World Wide Fellowship* (Bethlehem, 1940).

Book of Order of the Moravian Church in America (Bethlehem, 1938).

J. H. CLEWELL, *History of Wachovia in North Carolina* (New York, 1902).

Daily Texts of the Moravian Church, Bethlehem, published annually, now in its 222nd year.

ADELAIDE L. FRIES, *Customs and Practices of the Moravian Church* (Bethlehem, 1949).

EDMUND DeSCHWEINITZ, *The History of the Church Known as the Unitas Fratrum* (Bethlehem, 1885).

THE MORAVIAN CHURCH

J. TAYLOR HAMILTON, *A History of the Church Known as the Moravian Church, or the Unity of the Brethren or the Unitas Fratrum, during the Eighteenth and Nineteenth Centuries* (Bethlehem, 1900).

J. E. HUTTON, *A History of Moravian Missions* (London, 1922).

———, *History of the Moravian Church* (London, 1909).

J. M. LEVERING, *A History of Bethlehem, Pennsylvania, 1741-1892* (Bethlehem, 1903).

HARRY EMILIUS STOCKER, *A Home Mission History of the Moravian Church in the United States and Canada* (Bethlehem, 1922).

PERIODICALS:

The Moravian, a weekly published by the Christian Education Board of the Moravian Church, Bethlehem, Pennsylvania.

The Wachovia Moravian, a monthly published by the Christian Education Board of the Moravian Church, Winston-Salem, North Carolina.

III
THE LUTHERAN CHURCH IN AMERICA

III

THE LUTHERAN CHURCH IN AMERICA

Vergilius Ferm

In the midst of his sudden popularity as he fearlessly protested against the "abuses" of the mighty Church, Martin Luther (1483-1546) turned the same voice of protest against his own followers. Thousands had flocked to his banner. His name had become the theme and conversation of the hour: "nine tenths of all Germany were on [his] side"; "no books but his were sold in Worms, and his picture was everywhere to be seen, often with the Holy Ghost hovering over his head"; "the people thought him sinless and infallible and attributed miraculous power to him".—Yet the voice was raised in solemn protest:

"I beg that my name may be passed over in silence, and that men will call themselves not Lutherans but Christians. What is Luther? My teaching is not mine . . . How does it happen that I . . . have the children of Christ called after my unholy name? Not so, dear friends! Let us root out party names and call ourselves Christians, for it is Christ's gospel we have."[1]

He was, at this juncture, a prisoner of his friends at the Wartburg (1521). But events moved swiftly from the months and days preceding the glamorous event of the Diet of Worms (1521) through the following eight years to the Diet of Spires of 1529 from which time the name Protestant began to stick. German political history was being transformed by the new movement: city after city, state after state, embraced Lutheranism in a day charged with theological and civil politics. In spite of his warning, Lutheranism became a party—even with the help of Luther himself!

The fuse had been lit in Wittenberg on October 31, 1517. The Mother Church had been defied by an insignificant priest and university professor on the sensitive question of indulgences (their abuse) and this defiance had unwittingly but logically involved the whole traditional ecclesiastical system. Explosions were set off in rapid fire showing forth how vast was the network of combustible sympathy and revolutionary opinion. German politics was ready to strike against foreign tyranny and welcomed the protestors who were of their own flesh and blood. Luther had no idea that events would lead him directly into the fearful wrath of ecclesiastical excommunication (1521); he had taken his sacramental ordination seriously and never did succeed to cast off its holy mantle altogether. The proceedings of the Diet of Worms proved to be a shock to greater self-examination of how far he had really gone in fearful heresy. And now (1521) he was warning his followers lest they depart too sharply from the truths still inherent in an erring Church. His Catholicism he took with him when he was forced out; emphasizing, as he thought, what had been there but only dimmed by time and changing circumstances. Had his Church reconsidered some of its fathers, such as Augustine, Luther's protesting Catholicism would not have been so revolutionary. But the Church of the sixteenth century had moved too far into an accumulated traditional rigidity.

Ready for him were the times. Progressive forces, religious, social and political, were waiting to be touched off by some fuse. All the elements of Protestantism were present before his own protest, some of them not even ripe for the Reformer. Once a leader of protest was established and things began to move with momentum—out cropped sympathizers of the greatest variety. Lutheranism became solidified not only as a party against Rome but as a party against alleged radicals who would depart too far from a tradition which held conservative views and practices worthy of perpetuation even under revision. The Lord's Supper still offered a mystical presence and those who saw it only as a memorial were, in the view of the German

Reformer, moving too far to the left. The priesthood of all believers did not nullify certain rights and privileges of the clergy even if divested of sacramental sanction of office. Salvation by faith did not permit the license of an untempered religious experience to become normative; such salvation must never be detached from the soteriology linked with Christian history. The Word of God became the essential norm but it was a Word of God not divorced from the written Record. Social reforms were logically and ethically in order but not in terms of radical socialism. Liberalism in education was sought but there was to be no room for the kind of sanctified humanism which carried the disease of self-righteousness and merits.—So went the German Reformation.

Out of his imprisonment at the Wartburg, Luther's first task was to suppress the radicals from Wittenberg but which ended in the sad affair of the Peasants' War. Aligned now with the aristocracy, the Reformer alienated a large section of the proletariat. The Anabaptists represented the disinherited class, the oppressed and the uneducated. Lutheranism moved in the direction of the middle-class conservative party and could then bid for political power and become an established type of church. It is tantalizing to speculate upon the rôle of Lutheranism in subsequent events in Western history had Luther and Desiderius Erasmus (1466?-1536) come to terms. The record clearly reveals that the Reformation began to alienate from its ranks many of the contemporary intellectuals who were repelled by the dogmatic finality of the Reformer and by the deliberate unwillingness to seek mutual understanding.

Solidification of Lutheran forces came naturally by political alignments, by active efforts of organization of forces now under the ban of the Mother Church, in translation into the vernacular of the Scriptures (the herculean effort of Luther at the Wartburg), in hymn compositions, in simple catechisms for instruction and in directives for church discipline.

Both by reason of lack of temperament and the multitudinous involvements which took his time and energy, Luther himself left no legacy of systematic theology and defined polity[2] (as did Calvin). To this more systematic task his right-hand man and lieutenant, Philip Melanchthon (1497-1560), fell heir; developing theology and systematizations provoked bitter internal controversies. Philippists (followers of Philip Melanchthon) tended toward compromise with both the Roman and Reformed groups and with current humanism. Stricter Lutherans (anti-synergists[3], particularly Gnesio-Lutherans) stood irreconcilably against any alleged compromises, winning their struggle in what came to be expressed as normative confessional Lutheranism in the *Formula of Concord* (1580).

The two great contemporary Reformers, Huldreich Zwingli (1484-1531) and John Calvin (1509-1564) assimilated the views of Luther although giving each his own emphasis. There was no original intention of the Reformers to break with Luther; rather, it was through a complex of circumstances, temperaments and egocentricities of leaders plus the resistance of German Lutheranism (and later of independent Anglicanism) which forced a break from a possible unified Protestantism. Doctrinally, the differences between early Reformed ideas and Luther's were small and few. Calvin created no ideas foreign to the common heritage; rather, he shaped the fundamental doctrines of the German Reformer to a sterner logic choosing his base of cosmic theocentrism to that of Luther's soteriological Christocentrism. Zwingli's and Luther's break at Marburg (1529) was tragic enough in that both sought a measure of conciliation (a German and Swiss Protestant alliance); and yet each of them could not overcome the temperamental and experiential differences nor the political considerations which lay back of the Conference. Fuel was added to the fire in their break on the nature of the eucharist by subsequent harsh words which could never be retracted once in print. The great compromiser, Martin Bucer (1491-1551) who had tried unsuccessfully to mediate between Luther and Zwingli on their conflicting views of the sacrament, unwittingly found in his associate Calvin in Strassburg — who had joined him there on his invitation—a disciple of his own views which were destined to formulate a type of Protestantism distinct from Lutheranism and create a major split in the trunk of the Protestant tree. Swiss Protestantism of the heritage of Zwingli followed the triumphant leadership of Calvinism after 1549.

It may well be argued that both Anglicanism and Lutheranism in their conservative features and development sought to preserve their affinity with the Mother Church of Catholicism in holding fast what both regard as essential Catholic Christian views while protesting against the alleged aberrations of doctrines and practices of ecclesiastical traditionalism. But this, too, was characteristic of Calvinism. It is a mistake, in other words, to judge primitive Protestantism too strongly as anti-Catholic in spirit. The Reformers (including Luther) and the English Church were too close to Rome in time. What is more: the Augsburg Confession of 1530[4] was, for example, a definitely conciliatory document to show forth loyalty to the genuine old Catholic faith (while rejecting certain Roman developments and practices). The politically minded Zwinglians and the revolutionary Anabaptists were marked for heresy in this first Protestant Confession of Faith; and loyalty to the ancient creeds (ecumenical) was emphasized (explicitly or implicitly).

Melanchthon who had prepared the Confession of 1530 was consciously conciliatory—too much so even for Luther (then under the ban). A more vigorous position and defense came in the *Apology* a year later when Melanchthon smarted under the failure of Catholic appreciation.[5] These two Confessions became basic testimonies of Lutheranism.

To them were added the more uncompromising and developed tenets of the faith (contrasting Protestant and Roman positions) in the so-called *Schmalkald Articles* affirming the Lutheran emphasis on the Word and the two sacraments as means of grace against enthusiasts who would proclaim indiscriminate grace—Articles directed by Luther in 1537; the *Catechisms* of Luther (1529), simple and irenic expositions of the faith and a model for Calvin's *Institutes* (in the original edition of 1536); and the *Formula of Concord,* a confessional declaration commemorating the fiftieth anniversary of the Augsburg Confession written by second generation Lutherans in the light of the developed controversies involving original sin, synergism, the Lord's Supper, faith and works, predestination —in the spirit of concord amidst theological and political tensions. Pure doctrine from then on became the norm and Lutheran orthodoxy was settling in its foundations. Not all Lutheran groups in the generations which followed were willing to carry theology into such finality, content with the simpler forms of earlier expressions.[6] The *Book of Concord* includes the whole of these confessions; those strictly confessional Lutherans who subscribed to it (together with the ancient ecumenical creeds included in it) were committed to a creed of more than six hundred pages. (One might tempt the remark: thus out-Catholicizing Catholicism!) Theology henceforth for such Lutherans became a committed theology in the light of which any heresy might be made translucent.

The Lutheran Reformation, following Luther, became Christocentric in emphasis; the Scriptures were taken as the sole rule of faith and practice—with the preaching of the Word as a means of grace; the Augsburg Confession of 1530 was acknowledged as the common Protestant creed (with large areas of later generations of Lutherans understanding that Confession to have been properly interpreted and developed in the other symbolical books of the church as contained in the *Book of Concord;* the principles of justification by faith and the priesthood of all believers were taken to be central affirmations; emphasis was given to the doctrines of human depravity and of sin and to the corollary doctrine of Divine grace in salvation (as opposed to any human merits whatsoever); the sacramental status of baptism and the Lord's Supper as means of grace were affirmed; and (though obscured from time to time) the (Lutheran) doctrine of the church continued to be held, *viz.,* that the church is wherever the Word is truly taught and the sacraments properly administered although the real or true church is invisible and known only to God.

The polity of Lutheranism developed in great variety: from the simplicity of congregationalism to the hierarchy of the episcopacy. The Lutheran Reformers permitted their churches to become subjects to secular rulers who then took over the privileges formerly held by bishops. Following the Peasants' Revolt (1526 on) territorial Lutheran churches multiplied. Supreme ecclesiastical power was lodged in the hands of civil magistrates in Germany who appointed ministers and superintendents. Beyond Saxony and provinces as far as Prussia, independent and sovereign cities became Protestant, Lutherans competing with other Reformers during the life-time of both Luther and Melanchthon with the German territories becoming predominantly Lutheran.

* * * * * *

Before England broke with Rome and before the tide of Calvinism, the Church in Sweden separated from Rome (1523). Under Olavus Petri (1493-1552)—a student at Wittenberg when Luther was becoming Protestant—the church of Sweden was aligning itself with Protestantism, declaring itself Lutheran in doctrine and confession (by 1593).

After much struggle Lutheranism took hold in Denmark. Christian II (nephew of the elector of Saxony and brother-in-law of Charles V) was favorable to the Reformation, espousing Lutheranism when he lost his crown and became a refugee in Saxony. His successor, Christian III, secured Hans Tausen (d.1561), a disciple of Luther, to become preacher in Copenhagen and by 1536 Lutheranism became established in that country. In Norway Lutheranism became the state religion in 1537. Lutheran polity in the Scandinavian countries developed in the form of the episcopacy.

* * * * * *

Lutheranism settled into formal orthodoxy when its confessional standards were drawn together in 1580 and later became affected by the religious movement known as pietism. Pioneer promoters in the cause of German pietism were the Anabaptist Caspar von Schwenckfeld (1490-1562), the Lutheran Johann Arndt (1555-1621), mystic and writer of widely read devotional books, John Gerhard, Christian Scriver and John Valentine Andrea. Philipp Jakob Spener (1635-1705) led the movement about 1675 as a reaction against the cold and formal orthodoxy of the day in the direction of a warm piety and puritan way of life. August Hermann Francke (1663-1727) guided the movement at Halle, stressing those doctrines which promoted piety and philanthropic and missionary zeal. It was under the influence of this school that the "father of the Lutheran Church" in America planted Lutheranism anew in Pennsylvania. Pietism exerted an enormous influence also in Scandinavia.

A plan to consolidate Lutheran and Reformed churches by a union under one government and worship without touching doctrinal differences, the so-called "Evangelical Union" of 1817, was inaugurated in Prussia under king Frederick William III (1797-1840). This plan developed bitter controversies. The party of opposition became known as "Separatists" and "Old Lutherans" who insisted upon "pure doctrine" as the sole basis of any union. Johannes Grabau (1804-1879) led a group of some thousand exiles and set sail for America in 1839, organizing themselves as the "Synod of Exiles from the Lutheran Church of Prussia" and settled in and near Buffalo, New York; later this group became (1845) the Buffalo Synod of Lutherans, continuing the controversies with fellow conservative and confessional American immigrants (the Missourians) on doctrines relating to the church, ministry and ordination.

* * * * * *

Colonial America saw the influx of Lutheran immigrants as early as 1637 from Sweden, settling at Fort Christina (Wilmington), Delaware. Old Swedes' Church (1699) at Wilmington and Gloria Dei Church in Philadelphia (1677, 1700) are now historic shrines. These Lutherans were episcopal in polity and, after the Revolution when English speaking ministers were sought, looked to the Church of England for leaders; in time they became affiliated with the Episcopal Church. John Campanius (d.1683) was an early Lutheran minister at Fort Christina, a translator of Luther's Smaller Catechism in the dialect of the Delaware Indians.

Lutherans came to the Hudson colony as early as 1643, sent by fellow Lutherans in Holland. They were not allowed to organize in Peter Stuyvesant's domain in New Amsterdam. William Penn who visited Germany in 1671 and 1677 promoted German immigration. A Frankfort company purchased land where in 1685 Germantown was founded. Palatinates settled later in New York, Pennsylvania and the Carolinas. Salzburg Lutherans found refuge from persecution in their home, the duchy of Salzburg, in Ebenezer near Savannah, Georgia (1734). This colony under the leadership of Johann Bolzius (b. 1703) was visited by the evangelists John Wesley and George Whitefield.

A new wave of Lutheran immigration to Pennsylvania began in 1720. The threat (1741) of Zinzendorf, the Moravian, to take over Lutheran colonists prompted two Lutheran leaders in Europe to give concrete support to these colonists to help maintain Lutheran loyalty by sponsoring and providing Lutheran leadership. The two men were Friederick M. Ziegenhagen (1694-1776) of London and Gotthelf Francke (d. 1769) at Halle. With the commission (1742) of Henry Melchior Muhlenberg (1711-1787) as a foreign missionary to America, the Lutheran Church in America was launched the same year as an organized American Protestant denomination.

Muhlenberg has been called the "patriarch of the Lutheran Church" in America. Six years after his arrival he organized the first Lutheran synod of America, known through the years as the Ministerium of Pennsylvania. He organized churches, trained and ordained ministers, wrote liturgies, church constitutions and edited an American hymnal (1782). Detailed

accounts of his missionary work are set forth in the famous
Halle Reports which furthered the sympathetic relationship
with his sponsors at Halle.[7] His motto was: *ecclesia plantanda*:
the church must be planted. With him Lutheranism in eastern
America took on at the start the characteristics of German pietism of the school of Spener and Francke. He fraternized with
other denominations. The Anglicans he considered "best
friends"; so also the evangelists Tennent and Whitefield. Following him were Lutheran leaders who published their own
catechisms independent of the traditional catechisms of Luther
with departures in doctrine. Agreements were emphasized
among other Protestants and doctrinal differences were not
stressed. It was an era of good feeling prompted by the pioneering spirit. The orthodoxy which characterized an earlier
period of European Lutheranism was noticeably absent.

In 1820 there was organized the first united church of Lutheran groups in America, called the General Synod. A conspicuous leader emerged in the person of Samuel Simon
Schmucker (1799-1873), son of a pioneer Lutheran minister.
In the history of American Lutheranism his name is indelibly
linked with the rise and development of an indigenous type
of Lutheranism later known as "American Lutheranism."
Schmucker was the first theological professor in the Gettysburg
Theological Seminary where he taught for a quarter of a century; he aided in the establishment of the General Synod; he
founded a classical school which later became Gettysburg College; he framed model constitutions for churches and district synods; he published the first English text of Lutheran systematic
theology (*Elements of Popular Theology,* 1834); he edited
Luther's Catechism with free interpretations; he prepared
hymn-books and liturgies; he stressed religious pietism and was,
by nature, irenic. In 1838 he sought to unite Protestants in a
plan of union, *Appeal to the American Churches*. He defended
an American type of Lutheranism free from the scholasticism
of an earlier day and was ready to revise the Augsburg Confession when pressed to do so.

A change was coming over the American scene in the 1840's with waves of immigration bringing in their wake an incoming tide of European Lutherans of the conservative school. All Protestant churches in America in the middle of the nineteenth century were becoming self-conscious of their European rootage and began to reassert their own denominational distinctions. In 1855 the crisis between the two Lutheran schools came to a head in the publication of the *Definite Synodical Platform,* a recension of the Augsburg Confession, circulated anonymously for adoption by district synods. The furor of the controversy which followed only revealed how great the reaction was on the part of the newly arrived "Old Lutherans" against the diluted form of Lutheranism (as they thought) which had been evolving on independent American soil. Schmucker lost his leadership and the General Synod many of its members. A competing synod in the eastern states was organized in 1867 which called itself the General Council.

Conspicuous leader in the movement for a genuinely confessional type of Lutheranism in eastern America was Charles Porterfield Krauth (1823-1883), a former pupil under Schmucker. The Ministerium of Pennsylvania was now conscious of the historic Lutheran symbols as the basis for any genuine Lutheranism. Krauth was professor in the competing theological seminary at Mt. Airy (Philadelphia), newly founded. His *magnum opus, The Conservative Reformation and its Theology* (1871) became the standard theological text for the immediate generations which followed in this formidable section of American Lutheranism. Krauth wrote prolifically in matters touching doctrine, polity and liturgy. Thus the church of the heritage of Muhlenberg became divided into competing camps, with a mild liberalism fostered at Gettysburg and conservative confessionalism at Philadelphia.

The breach was ultimately healed in a formal way in the formation of the United Lutheran Church in America (1918) uniting these two groups with the United Synod of the South (breach from Civil War days when the southern synods were read out of the General Synod in 1861 as "given to the cause of treason and insurrection"). Conservatism won the day. The United Lutheran Church acknowledged the unaltered Augsburg Confession and at the same time gave recognition to the other symbolical books of Lutheran confessionalism as "in the harmony of one and the same pure Scriptural faith."

The Prussian Plan of Union of 1817 produced a ringing protest on the occasion of the tercentenary celebration of the Reformation in the form of the celebrated Ninety-five Theses published by Claus Harms (1778-1855). These theses condemned the alleged spirit of rationalism and denounced the proposed union of Lutheran and Reformed churches and sounded a trumpet call to all true Lutherans to remain steadfast to their distinctive heritage and confessional position. The contemporary theologian Friedrich Daniel Ernst Schleiermacher (1768-1834) raised his voice against the reactionary movement but at the same time deplored the coercive intrusion of the state upon Protestants not ready for the step. (Schleiermacher defended an Evangelical Church with a presbyterian system to include both Lutheran and Reformed.) The literature of the period reveals the issue squarely joined between Symbolists and Anti-Symbolists, *i.e.,* how far a real Lutheran is pledged to the symbolical books. Dogmatic treatises and editions of the symbolical books were issued in great numbers; debates and discussions filled the air.

It was in such weather that the two settlements, important in the history of Lutheranism in America, were founded. In a new wave of emigration to America which was then in its beginning, to the land of opportunity and religious freedom, the one group (already mentioned) came and settled near Buffalo; and the other in and near St. Louis, Missouri. They were German "Separatists" and "Old Lutherans". The year of the migration for both was 1839. From Saxony by way of the Gulf of Mexico and up the Mississippi came five vessels with emigrants dissatisfied with ecclesiastical and civil conditions at home and loyal to their church and opposing the inroads of "rationalism" and "unionism". Martin Stephan and the Walthers were the religious leaders of these "Missourians" as they came to be known. Karl Ferdinand Wilhelm Walther (1811-1887) became the strong leader of the group as it planted its colony, becoming the first president of its Lutheran synod (the "German Ev. Lutheran Synod of Missouri, Ohio and Other States"), founder of two vigorous journals (*Der Lutheraner,* 1844 and *Lehre und Wehre,* 1853), champion of unequivocal loyalty to all the historic symbols of Lutheranism, father and organizer of a theological seminary (Concordia), designer of model church constitutions and author of numerous theological articles and treatises.

The Missouri Lutherans represented the most conservative wing of Lutheranism in America through the years. Their own parochial school system protected by an inner doctrination the genius of their group; their isolation from other Lutherans was open and unequivocal, without apology; their opposition to any form of unionism followed as a conclusion in the strict syllogism of their own premises; their loyalty to the Scriptures meant for them a loyalty to the letter as well as the spirit. They continued to avow openly in strict agreement with the confessions the assertion that the Roman pontiff was anti-Christ; in a controversy on predestination their leaders taught the doctrine of man's election to salvation on the basis of the merits of Christ (not in view of faith in those merits which smacked of synergism nor because of the arbitrary will of God to election); they opposed membership in secret orders and lodges (as did other Lutheran synods for ministers) on the part of both laymen and ministers; and they practiced discipline seriously, even the right and necessity of excommunication.

The Bavarian Lutheran church leader, Wilhelm Löhe (1808-1872), a strong confessionalist, gave impetus and aid to the establishment of German Lutheranism in the Middle-West. He was instrumental in establishing a Lutheran theological seminary at Fort Wayne, Indiana. He helped to direct his followers into the organization of the Missouri group and later (1854) in disputes with that group formed an independent body, the Iowa Synod. His pupils established the Lutheran Wartburg Seminary in Dubuque, Iowa. Löhe's interest in liturgy was strong (his own liturgy forming the basis of the "Common Service of the American Lutheran Church").

Another group in America organized in Wisconsin in 1850, representing the Church of Prussia in theology and polity, becoming a strictly confessional Lutheran body, was the Lutheran Joint Synod of Wisconsin and Other States. A union was effected in 1892 of three synods: Wisconsin, Minnesota and Michigan. It joined with the Missouri group and others in a larger Conference (the Synodical Conference). Dissenting from this group (after 1926) was the Protestant Conference (Lutheran), most of the churches being located in Wisconsin. Strictly confessional the Conference stressed spiritual poverty, searching self-examination, critical appraisal of other Christians and the cultivation of Lutheran classical hymns.

The Swedish Lutherans fraternized in the Mid-West with members of the General Synod but eventually found the General Council more congenial to their conservatism. New Sweden in Iowa (1848), Andover, Illinois (1850) were early Mid-West Swedish colonies. The Synod of Northern Illinois (1851) included various nationalistic groups. Swedes and Norwegians joined in 1860 in organizing the Scandinavian Lutheran Augustana Synod, the Norwegians withdrawing in 1869. The Lutheran confessional statements placed emphasis on the unaltered Augsburg Confession "understood through their development in the other symbolic writings of the Lutheran Church."

The pioneer Swedish emigrants to America, however—including those who joined to form the organization of "Augustana" Lutherans — were, many of them, of the free-church spirit, a movement then current in Sweden which stressed pietism, Biblical simplicity and regenerated living. Lars Paul Esbjörn (b.1808) has been called the founder of the Swedish Lutheran Church in America. He was a pietist, a translator of the devotional works of Johann Arndt and a liberal. He came to America in 1849 expressly to become acquainted with the free church system. Settling in Andover he helped to organize the Synod of Northern Illinois and in the work of the General Synod. After a professorship at Illinois State University and at Augustana Theological Seminary he returned to Sweden and the state church.[8] Olof Olsson (1841-1900) who came to America from Sweden in 1869 founded the celebrated colony at Lindsborg, Kansas and in 1876 became professor in the Swedish Lutheran Seminary (Augustana Theological Seminary, Rock Island, Illinois) and president of that institution. He, too, represented a free spirit at the time when orthodoxy was closing in, even expressing willingness to make minor changes in the Augsburg Confession. Although under suspicion he walked discreetly among his more conservative brethren who were in the majority. Later generations of Augustana Lutheran ministers came under the influence of their systematic theological teacher, Conrad Emil Lindberg (1852-1930), whose *Dogmatik* (1898, Eng tr., *Christian Dogmatics,* 1922) became their standard of systematic theological thought, following the trend of Lutheran confessionalism.

In 1918 when the great merger of Lutherans took place[9] the Augustana Synod demurred. Only in latter days has this group of Lutherans shown a decided tendency to lift its own isolationism, partly because of the displacement of a foreign nationalistic consciousness and its thorough Americanization and the wider contacts with other academic institutions which its teachers have been making particularly in graduate studies.[10]

Norwegian Lutheranism in America became expressed in a variety of groups. The first Norwegian colony was founded in Rochester, New York, in 1825. Later, in 1834-37 the first colony in the Mid-West was established on Fox River, Illinois. The "Haugeans" were a pioneer group, organized under the leadership of Elling Eielsen (d. 1883, follower of Hans Nielsen Hauge, a lay preacher who had inaugurated a revival in Norway) who emigrated to America in 1839. In 1846 this organization became the first Norwegian Lutheran Synod in America. In 1853 the Norwegian Synod was organized in Wisconsin. Many Norwegian immigrants joined other Lutheran groups, Swedish, German and Danish. The Eielsen synod demanded evidences of conversion as prerequisite to membership, relaxing its stricter requirements in 1875 and calling itself later Hauge's Norwegian Evangelical Lutheran Synod. (Eielsen continued a minority group in the older organization, adhering to the Augsburg Confession and congregational in polity with churches found in Wisconsin, Iowa, the Dakotas and Minnesota.)

The Norwegian Synod (1853) developed conservatism even to the extent of cooperation with the Missouri Lutheran Synodical Conference. Those who dissented from this development were known as the "Anti-Missouri Brotherhood". In 1887 fellow Norwegians called for a merger of groups which in 1890 became "the United Norwegian Lutheran Church in America" with a further union in 1917. The new name of the church became: The Evangelical Lutheran Church (1946) adhering to the unaltered Augsburg Confession and Luther's Small Catechism as confessional bases. Two dissenting groups from the main body developed: the Norwegian Lutheran Free Church in 1893, a free association organized in 1897 over a dispute on the control of the Augsburg Seminary in Minneapolis. This group formed a conference with independent Norwegian Lutheran churches in Minnesota and Wisconsin, the Church of the Lutheran Brethren of America, in 1900, affirming the Augsburg Confession and Luther's Small Catechism and practising strict discipline. The other dissenting group was organized in 1918 (Norwegian Synod of the American Ev. Lutheran Church) in protest against the union of 1917, becoming in 1920 a member of the Lutheran Synodical Conference and adhering to the traditional confessional books and fraternizing with the Missouri group.

Immigration of Danes began about 1864. Eight years later the "Kirkelig Missions Forening" was organized at Neenah,

Wisconsin and thus began the Danish Lutheran Church in America. In 1894 after divisions the church was organized as the Danish Ev. Lutheran Church in America; with another group (Association) a united church, United Danish Ev. Lutheran Church in America, was formed in 1896 with the Augsburg Confession and Luther's Small Catechism as standard confessions. (Its educational institution: Dana College [Blair, Nebraska] and Trinity Theological Seminary.) The original group maintained its name and organization with the two confessional standards. In Des Moines, Iowa (Grand View) this latter group conducts its theological seminary.

Finnish Lutherans in America date back to about 1850 when these people emigrated from their mother country, many seeking to practice their own indigenous life in the northern Michigan copper country. Their churches were organized about 1867 in Hancock and Calumet, with a synod founded in 1890 (Suomi Synod, or Finnish Ev. Lutheran Church of America) and a college and seminary at Hancock in 1896. The Lutheran confessions were affirmed. An opposition group called the Finnish Ev. Lutheran National Church of America was organized in 1898 in Ironwood, Michigan, giving support to the Missouri Concordia Seminary and affirming the Lutheran confessions. Another group, the Finnish Apostolic Lutheran Church of America under the leadership of Salomon Korteniemi organized their church in 1872 (the name came later). They had been fraternizing with Lutherans in Calumet, Michigan. The Augsburg Confession was the recognized Lutheran symbol. Origin of this group dates back to a revival under Lars Levi Laestadius (1800-1861), a Swedish Lutheran state minister, who taught personal-encounter type of Christianity, religious experience, the doctrine of absolution attended upon open confessions. These Finns were also known as Laestadians.

About 1870 Icelandic immigration began with early settlement in Milwaukee, Wisconsin, with a colony and a church founded in 1874 in Shawane county, Wisconsin. A migration followed later to the Dakotas. In Canada at Lake Winnipeg,

Manitoba, a large colony developed; another at Pembina county, North Dakota; and another in Lynn and Lincoln counties in Minnesota. The Icelandic Evangelical Lutheran Synod in North America, international in scope, was organized in 1885, affirming the Augsburg Confession and Luther's Small Catechism as normative Lutheranism. Jon Bjarnason Academy in Winnipeg is maintained. With the Norwegian and the United Lutheran churches they maintained close cooperation becoming a constituent of the United Lutheran Church.

The congregational form of polity has been characteristic of the Lutheran churches in America. With the coming of large mergers, however, there has been some vocal whispering among certain groups toward a revival of the European tradition of the episcopacy with leadership assuming more delegated power.

A merger of organizational Lutheran groups occurred in 1930. The American Lutheran Church joined together the Ev. Lutheran Joint Synod of Ohio and Other States (org. 1918); the Ev. Lutheran Synod of Iowa and Other States (org. 1854) and the Lutheran Synod of Buffalo (org. 1845). This body acknowledges all the Lutheran symbolical books. The American Lutheran Conference is a federation of five Lutheran bodies (1930): the American Lutheran Church; the Augustana Lutheran Church; the Ev. Lutheran Church of America (Eielsen Synod); the Lutheran Free Church; and the United (Danish) Ev. Lutheran Church in America. This federation which guarantees sovereignty to each group affirms the Lutheran confessions "as the true presentation of the pure doctrine of the Word of God and a summary of the faith."

The Ev. Lutheran Synodical Conference of North America was organized in 1872 by synods holding stricter doctrines and closely committed to the historic Lutheran confessions. The bodies now joined to this Conference are: the Lutheran Synod of Missouri, Ohio and Other States now legally known as Lutheran Church—Missouri Synod; the Ev. Lutheran Joint Synod of Wisconsin and Other States; the Slovak Ev. Lutheran Synod of America (organized in 1902 in Pennsylvania and in fully declared accord with the Missouri Lutherans in doctrines and polity) ; the Norwegian Synod of the American Ev. Lutheran Church; and the Negro Mission.

A National Lutheran Council took rise in 1918 as a cooperative agency in the circumstances of war and peace. Its periodical *The National Lutheran* has served to promote cooperative efforts among eight participating Lutheran bodies: the American Lutheran Church; the Augustana Lutheran Church; the Evangelical Lutheran Church; The Danish Lutheran Church; the Finnish Suomi Synod; the Lutheran Free Church; the United Ev. Lutheran Church (Danish) ; and the United Lutheran Church.

Four Lutheran bodies participated in the organization of the World Council of Churches: the United Lutheran Church; the American Lutheran Church; the Augustana Lutheran Church; and the Danish Ev. Lutheran Church in America.

In 1951 at the organization of the National Council of the Churches of Christ in the United States of America at its meeting in Cleveland, Ohio, three Lutheran bodies became charter members: the Augustana Lutheran Church, the Danish Ev. Lutheran Church and the United Lutheran Church in America.

*　*　*　*　*　*

Lutheranism in America[11] has maintained, perhaps as few other denominations in this country, a uniqueness of character and a self-consciousness marking it as a distinct Protestant group. This characteristic has come about by reason of numerous factors. The persistent use of a foreign tongue and the self-consciousness of the fatherland of generations of immigrants have, only until about three decades ago, maintained a socio-religious isolationism in large areas of American Lutheranism. Consciousness of confessional norms has served to give unity in a common platform of creed as over against the winds of doctrine which have come and gone throughout the Protestant scene where confessionalism was less strong. The liturgical heritage from European and state churches has, perhaps, done more to consolidate forces in this church than may on the surface be apparent. This liturgical emphasis in worship, in the endeavor to express a Common Service, with rootage in a kind of Protestant classicism has bound Lutherans in America together somewhat in the same way that the *Book of Common Prayer* has held together Episcopalians of whatever private schools of opinion or degree of conservatism. (This does not imply that all Lutherans have had identical liturgies.) The Lutheran Church from its earliest beginning in Europe has been characteristically a liturgical church.[12]

Moreover, theological seminaries in Lutheran America have been kept under strictest observation by repeated proving tests so that a minimum of departure of theological views could be noted and publicly disclaimed. Ordination vows on the part of candidates for the ministry have followed only after searching examination of doctrinal views and subscription to the norms taken seriously. Publishing houses have been conscious of the *Nihil Obstat* of church officers and delegated committees with only a lessening of this consciousness in recent years in the recommended bibliographical lists of books other-than Lutheran.

Lutheranism in America has produced no conspicuous theological movements of thought except to welcome, at least guardedly, the movements of European Lutheran theological thought which appear not too far removed from the essential tradition, *e.g.*, the Lundensian theology. The tendency has been to turn scholars of the church away from the fields of strict theology and Biblical critical studies to areas less hazardous such as historical studies, liturgics, Bible translations, parish methods, and the like. In recent years Lutheranism, as in the case of many other Protestant denominations, has taken special interest in liturgical forms and emphases and in organizational promotion which, it is evident, leaves the ideological field much as it has been—except for the ever-present minority voices which call for development in theological thought and adaptations to changing cultures and newer insights from other fields of inquiry.

Isolationism from other Protestant churches, thus, has many causes, partly cultural, partly linguistic and social, but conspicuously because of a logical consistency of loyalty to the European heritage of a normative Lutheranism which continued in the stream of immigration. Time and circumstance bring many changes. Lutheranism in America—from the pews and slowly up to the pulpits—is giving evidence of some stir toward catholicity[13] which may be gaining more momentum than can be estimated at short range and even by those in the traditional circles. As its record shows, American Lutheranism is still the Church of the Reformation in that, while it is Catholic in its emphasis upon venerable confessions and its reverence for traditionalism (not to mention again the Catholic heritage in Luther even when he became a full-fledged Protestant), it is at the same time highly conscious of its Protestantism in the continuing consciousness of those elements singled out by Luther as worthy of persistent emphasis. In this sense Lutheranism has remained unique—certainly in America—while other of the Protestant groups have gone on to lead the way to adventure in territories of thought and practice with the risk of departure from tradition.

NOTES

I am indebted to my friend, Armin G. Weng, Ph.D., president of the Chicago Lutheran Theological Seminary, who has given this essay a critical reading, particularly in the area of factual statements. Any judgments of interpretation, however, are chargeable solely to myself.

1 Arthur Cushman McGiffert, *Martin Luther: The Man and his Work*, p. 215.

2 The Lutheran Church has no distinctive form of organization.

3 Synergism is the view that the gift of Divine grace does not cancel out the cooperation of man's will in conversion and salvation. In his controversy with Erasmus, Luther maintained that man had nothing to do with his salvation: it was a matter of Divine grace alone. In the first edition of the *Loci Communes* (1521), Melanchthon had affirmed the same view. In later editions of this work, however, as well as in the edition of the Augsburg Confession of 1540 (known as the *Variata*) Melanchthon declared himself for synergism. Synergism thus became associated with Melanchthonian Lutheranism. In the *Formula of Concord* it is declared that the work of conversion is altogether that of the Holy Spirit but in such a manner that the human will impelled by God by its own nature cooperates at the moment the Spirit operates. Traditional Lutheranism became very sensitive to this doctrine, fearful lest the merits of man

overshadow the full grace of God in salvation as Luther had declared in his controversy with the Catholic merit system.

4 The Confession of 1530 is known as the "unaltered" or *Invariata* Confession.

5 In 1540 came the altered Augsburg Confession which provoked strict Lutherans to demur particularly on the tenth article dealing with the sacrament of the altar.

6 *E.g.,* the unaltered Augsburg Confession and Luther's Small Catechism.

7 His sons became national figures: Peter (1746-1807) ordained in 1768 by the Lutheran Ministerium of Pennsylvania and in 1772 by the Episcopal bishop of London, was a major-general under Washington in the American Revolution, also a U. S. senator; Frederick (1750-1801), a Lutheran minister in New York, was speaker of the first and third Congress; and Gotthelf Henry Ernst (1753-1815), also a minister, became known as a scientific student of American flora.

8 Tuve Nilsson Hasselquist (b. 1816) was another early leader in the Swedish Lutheran Church in America. In Sweden he had been sympathetic with the free churches and continued his pietistic emphasis. Although theologically conservative he was a free spirit and influential (professor and president at Augustana, 1863-1891) and editor of the widely circulated Swedish periodical (later called) *Augustana.*

9 *See ante,* p. 35.

10 These, of course, are not the only considerations.

11 The National Lutheran Council reported in November, 1951 its compilation of 6,103,784 Lutherans in the United States. *Newsweek,* November 12, 1951, p. 64.

12 When Luther offered to the Protestant Church of Germany its first liturgy he kept close to Roman liturgical practice. His *Formula Missae* (1523) was succeeded by his *Deutsche Messe* (1526) which dropped certain Roman elements. Later developments show great liturgical variations in Lutheranism. Luther's principle of making necessary changes with the least possible disturbance has, on the whole, been followed by Lutherans. The Church of Sweden, in form, deviated little from Roman usages while the Lutheran Church of Holland has practically no liturgy, even lacking altars.

13 That is, a newer type of Protestantism which is a protest against the traditional form of Protestantism, showing a freer and more comprehensive spirit, more horizontal in outlook than vertical (traditional).

BIBLIOGRAPHY

ROLAND H. BAINTON, *Here I Stand* (New York, 1950).

CONRAD BERGENDOFF, *Olavus Petri and the Ecclesiastical Transformation in Sweden* (New York, 1928).

EDGAR M. CARLSON, *The Reinterpretation of Luther* (Philadelphia, 1948).

VERGILIUS FERM, *The Crisis in American Lutheran Theology* (New York, 1927).

———, ed., *What is Lutheranism?* (New York, 1930).

———, ed., *An Encyclopedia of Religion* (New York, 1945).

———, *A Protestant Dictionary* (New York, 1951).

———, *Cross-Currents in the Personality of Martin Luther, A Study in the Psychology of Religious Genius* (Yale University Library, 1923).

ALBERT HYMA, *Luther's Theological Development from Erfurt to Augsburg* (New York, 1928).

THE LUTHERAN CHURCH IN AMERICA

HENRY EYSTER JACOBS, *A History of the Evangelical Lutheran Church in The United States* (New York, 1893).

————, ed., *The Book of Concord or The Symbolical Books of the Evangelical Lutheran Church* (Philadelphia, 1911).

HUGH T. KERR, ed., *A Compend of Luther's Theology* (Philadelphia, 1943).

JAMES MACKINNON, *Luther and the Reformation*, 2 vols. (New York, 1925-).

ARTHUR CUSHMAN MCGIFFERT, *Martin Luther: The Man and his Work* (New York, 1917).

J. L. NEVE, *History of the Lutheran Church in America* (Burlington, 1934).

RICHARD NIEBUHR, *The Social Sources of Denominationalism* (New York, 1929).

WILHELM PAUCK, *Heritage of the Reformation* (New York, 1950).

JOSEPH SITTLER, *The Doctrine of the Word* (Philadelphia, 1948).

PRESERVED SMITH and CHARLES M. JACOBS, eds., *Luther's Correspondence and Other Contemporary Letters* (Philadelphia, vol. 1, 1913; vol. 2, 1918).

GEORGE M. STEPHENSON, *The Religious Aspects of Swedish Immigration* (Minneapolis, 1932).

WILLIAM WARREN SWEET, *The Story of Religions in America* (New York, 1930).

ABDEL ROSS WENTZ, *The Lutheran Church in American History* (Philadelphia, 1923).

IV
THE MENNONITES

IV

THE MENNONITES

John Christian Wenger

European Background

THE MENNONITES are of two separate and independent ethnic origins, Swiss and Dutch. The Swiss Mennonites, at first called simply Brethren but nicknamed Anabaptist, were founded in January, 1525, by a Zurich patrician and scholar named Conrad Grebel. Young Grebel, who had studied for six years in the universities of Basel, Vienna and Paris, was led from Catholicism to evangelical faith by the leading reformer of German-speaking Switzerland, Ulrich Zwingli. But Grebel separated from Zwingli because he felt Zwingli was proceeding too mildly and slowly in his Reformation program. Grebel insisted on an abrupt separation of church and state, on the abolition of infant baptism, and on an ethic of absolute love, including the complete rejection of the military for Christians. The Swiss cantons, especially Zurich and Bern, felt themselves compelled to take vigorous measures against this radical religious movement, since they felt certain it would lead to political ruin. A long line of martyrs extending from 1525 to 1614, imprisonment, galley sentences, forcible deportations, brandings, etc., continued until the eighteenth century, and forcible baptisms occurred even in the early nineteenth century. Grebel himself died in 1526 after many imprisonments, and left no significant writings; yet his biographer has been able to present a clear picture of his life, activity and program.[1]

There are today about 2,000 baptized Mennonites in Switzerland, about 3,000 in France, 50 in Luxembourg, and several thousand in South Germany, all of Swiss extraction basically.

But the bulk of the Mennonites who descend from Grebel's "Brethren" are found in the United States east of the Mississippi, and in Ontario.[2] The most conservative group of American Mennonites, the Old Order Amish, still sing from the Swiss Brethren hymn book of 1564, the *Ausbund*.[3] The Mennonites of North America who are of Swiss ethnic origin would total over 100,000 baptized persons; converts are usually baptized between the ages of twelve and eighteen, depending largely on the particular group or congregation involved.

The Dutch portion of the Mennonite brotherhood was founded by Obbe Philips in the years, 1533-34; his followers were called Obbenites at first. In 1536 a Roman Catholic priest named Menno Simons (1496-1561) united with the Obbenites and ultimately the group adopted the appellations Mennist or Mennonist in recognition of his strong leadership. Menno served as the outstanding elder of his group for almost twenty-five years and wrote a score of books and booklets which were ultimately published as his *Opera Omnia*.[4] The Dutch Mennonites migrated into North Germany and the Danzig area in the sixteenth century, and from Danzig to South Russia in the latter eighteenth century. As in Switzerland, the Dutch Mennonites were severely persecuted during the sixteenth century, about two thousand of them perishing as martyrs.[5] Both Obbe Philips and Menno Simons taught the *shunning* of excommunicated persons but the Dutch Mennonites abandoned the practice later.

The Mennonites of Holland now number 45,000 baptized members. Those who lived in Russia were largely of Dutch ethnic origin, but were German as to language and culture; also included in Russia were a number of Swiss Mennonite congregations. Even today many of the Mennonites of North Germany are of Dutch extraction. All the Mennonites of Germany, Swiss and Dutch, now total 7,000 baptized members. The Mennonites thrived in Russia beyond those of all other European lands. However, the organized church life of the Russian Mennonites has been broken in the years, 1918-48. Thirty-five thousand made their way across the Russian frontier during the Second World War but 70 per cent of them were forcibly repatriated, only to be cruelly scattered over Siberia.

The Swiss Mennonites suffered a major division in 1693. Hans Reist was the leading elder of the mother body. Jacob Ammann was the schismatic elder who formed the conservative *Amish* group. The Mennonites, who were less severe than the Amish in their cultural nonconformity to the contemporary society, were sometimes called *Knöpfler* (those who wore buttons), while the Amish, who shunned buttons in favor of the older hooks-and-eyes, were labelled Häftler. But Ammann's main point of difference from the Mennonites was his introduction of shunning, a breaking of all social fellowship with excommunicated persons.

The Russian Mennonites had several schisms which are represented in America today. In 1812 a small group in South Russia who wished to practice a stricter discipline withdrew from the main body, and because of their numerical smallness acquired the name *Kleingemeinde,* which they now recognize as their official title. In 1860 another group, somewhat influenced by revivalism, withdrew from the main body also, and ultimately secured one-third of the Mennonites of Russia for their *Mennonite Brethren* (M.B.) group. In 1869 still another group, this time in the Crimea, withdrew from the *Kleingemeinde* and formed the *Krimmer Mennonite Brethren* (K.M.B.), also a revivalist movement. There was Baptist influence both in the M.B. and K.M.B. groups and both adopted immersion as their mode of baptism; affusion (pouring) had been the Mennonite mode from 1525.

American Immigration

European Mennonites have come to North America in several major waves of immigration. The first permanent settlement was made in the Pennsylvania Quaker village of Germantown, now a part of Philadelphia, in 1683. But American immigration did not begin seriously for the Mennonites before 1710.

During the following sixty years several thousand persons, mostly Swiss Mennonites (only a few dozen Swiss Amish families immigrated) settled in eastern Pennsylvania in two major settlements.[6] The Conestoga and Pequea valleys, fifty or sixty miles west of Philadelphia, and both in Lancaster County now, became the original locations of the Lancaster Mennonite Conference; while the Franconia Conference has its center at Souderton, Pennsylvania, thirty miles north of Philadelphia, in a district partly in Bucks and partly in Montgomery county. For a time in the latter eighteenth century the Germantown congregation was weak numerically and without a minister and its pulpit was supplied by various ministers from the Franconia Conference. The present baptized membership of the Lancaster Conference is 15,000, and of Franconia, 5,000. During the eighteenth and nineteenth centuries a series of conferences was established in Virginia, Ontario, Ohio, Indiana, and states farther west. The conferences west of Pennsylvania were composed partly of settlers from Pennsylvania, and partly of later immigrants from Europe. The eighteenth century Mennonite immigrants came to America to escape persecution and to better themselves financially.

The second wave of immigration began after the time of Napoleon and continued for several decades. Several thousand Swiss Amish settled in western Pennsylvania, Illinois, Iowa, etc. This wave of immigrants also included some Swiss Mennonites who settled in Wayne County, Ohio, and Adams County, Indiana. The nineteenth century Amish immigrants were less conservative in discipline than the Pennsylvania Amish of the eighteenth century.

The third, fourth and fifth waves of immigration all consisted of Mennonites from Russia, mostly of Dutch extraction but including some Swiss. Twenty thousand left Europe in the 1870's, twenty thousand in the 1920's and ten thousand following the Second World War. Those who came from Russia in 1874 and the following years settled in Minnesota, Nebraska, Kansas, South Dakota, and Manitoba.[7] The Russian Mennonites who crossed the Atlantic after the First World War settled largely in western Canada, but 6,000 settled in Paraguay and Brazil. The immigrants of the mid-twentieth century divided about evenly between Paraguay and Canada, only a few hundred locating in the United States.

Major Bodies

Prior to 1800 there were two kinds of Mennonites in North America, the Mennonites and the Amish.[8] In 1812 a layman, John Herr, organized a small group in Lancaster County, Pennsylvania, which is still independent. These *Reformed Mennonites,* being socially exclusive and strict in discipline, now number about 1,000. They are somewhat portrayed in Helen R. Martin's novel, *Tillie, A Mennonite Maid* (New York, 1904).

The main body of Mennonites meanwhile continued to grow and had no major division until 1847 when a progressive minister of the Franconia Conference, a man named John H. Oberholtzer, withdrew to form a more progressive conference in eastern Pennsylvania. His group was sometimes called New Mennonites while the parent body was dubbed Old Mennonites; the latter are officially known as the *Mennonite Church,* however. In 1860 Oberholtzer sought to create an all-Mennonite General Conference allowing each member congregation to have whatever particular rules and regulations it desired, while the General Conference would stand only for basic Mennonite principles. The phrase which would describe this General Conference is, "In essentials unity; in non-essentials liberty." But Oberholtzer's vision was not favorably received by the (Old) Mennonites. The consequence was the creation of a second major type of Mennonites, a body less strict in discipline and more free to accommodate itself to American Protestantism. Many of the Mennonite immigrants of the 1870's from Russia united with Oberholtzer's 1860 General Conference.

These two bodies, the Mennonite Church with 70,000 members, and the General Conference Mennonite Church with 52,000 members, constitute well over half of all the Mennonites of North America. Seven other groups run in size from five to twenty thousand members each, and eight others each have two thousand members. Here is a brief description of all the groups of American Mennonites, including all bodies of one thousand members or more.

1) *The Mennonite Church,* 70,000 members. Main line (Swiss) Mennonites who settled in Pennsylvania in the eighteenth century, and progressive nineteenth century Amish Mennonite immigrants who merged with the Mennonites around 1920. This group historically had an untrained lay ministry, but now has some seminary-trained ministers. They have musical instruments in their homes but not in their churches. During the latter nineteenth century they adopted Sunday schools, began to hold evangelistic meetings, set up mission boards, started to operate church academies (later, colleges, seminaries and Christian primary schools), etc. They now have a publishing house, foreign missions (South America, Africa, India, Japan, etc.), and home missions in many of the larger cities of the United States. These changes from the "old order" occasioned the secession (1870-1900) of the so-called Old Order Mennonites who rejected Sunday schools, missions, higher education, etc. The Mennonite Church has almost 600 congregations, 175 bishops, 800 ministers and 400 deacons. About 90 per cent of the members live in the United States.

In addition to baptism (by affusion) and the Lord's Supper (they practice close communion), the group also observes feet washing (John 13) as an ordinance. Each woman member wears a religious veil or "devotional covering" during worship (I Cor. 11). Fashions are shunned, and all ministers and some laity wear a garb. The basic authority of the group is vested in its 16 district conferences of North America. These conferences are composed of all the ordained bishops, ministers and deacons. The bishops are the disciplinary officers and are charged with upholding the standards set by the district conferences. Since 1898 the group also has its "Mennonite General Conference" which has been basically advisory, but which is growing in influence and prestige. This is by far the largest body of Mennonites, and in comparison with the others, is moderate in discipline. Theologically the Mennonite Church is evangelical and conservative.

Prior to 1940 the three most influential leaders of this group were: 1) John F. Funk (1835-1930), founder in 1864 of the first significant religious periodical of the group, the *Herald of Truth* (also published in German as the *Herold der Wahrheit*); 2) Daniel Kauffman (1865-1944), editor for almost forty years of the *Gospel Herald,* the organ of the denomination and successor of the *Herald of Truth,* and author and/or editor of many doctrinal works such as *Bible Doctrine* (1914) and *Doctrines of the Bible* (1928); and 3) John S. Coffman (1848-99), the first great evangelist of the Mennonite Church and pioneer promoter of higher education.

2) *The General Conference Mennonite Church.*[9]

The chief founders of this second-largest Mennonite group were John H. Oberholtzer (1809-95) and Daniel Krehbiel (1822-88). Mention was made above of Oberholtzer's secession in 1847 from the (Old) Mennonite Church. In 1861 Oberholtzer's General Conference represented eight congregations and 800 members. Today the group has two hundred congregations and 52,000 members. Many of the strongest congregations of the General Conference Mennonite Church are those of the "Russian" Mennonites in Minnesota, Nebraska, South Dakota, Kansas, Oklahoma, California, and Canada, as well as the Swiss congregations in eastern Ohio, in eastern Indiana, etc.

The government of this group is strictly congregational. The general conference meets every three years to hear reports from the boards of Missions, Education, Publication, Peace and Emergency Relief, and any special committees. Neither General Conference nor the six district conferences of the group have any authority to control the standards or discipline of the constituent congregations. Yet it is assumed that on a few major Mennonite beliefs there will be more or less unanimity; these major beliefs would include the doctrine of love and nonresistance, the rejection of all oaths, opposition to secret societies, and the practice of believer's baptism. But there is no longer any religious garb of any sort. The congregations generally have organs or other musical instruments in their churches. Feet washing as a religious rite is optional, being observed in some congregations and not in others. There is little distinction between the General Conference Mennonites and many other Protestants except on the matter of the oath and nonresistance. Theologically they are not entirely homogeneous; as a whole they are theologically conservative with but traces of liberalism and neo-orthodoxy. They have perhaps been more influenced by twentieth-century Fundamentalism than the (Old) Mennonites. The General Conference Mennonites practice open communion, and take a more cooperative attitude toward other Christian denominations than most Mennonite groups.

3) *The Mennonite Brethren*[10] are a Mennonite group who originated in Russia in 1860 as a revivalist movement, partly under Baptist influence. It was this latter fact which accounted for their adoption of immersion as their mode of baptism. They have a strong emphasis on conversion as a "definite religious experience," on nonresistance and opposition to militarism, on missions and evangelism, and on Bible study and spiritual life. They are much opposed to any formalism whatever, including the catechetical instruction of children. They began to migrate to Kansas in 1873, and by 1887 had 1,200 members in North America. Their 20,000 members today are organized in five district conferences: Ontario, Northern, Central, Southern and Pacific. One of their leading ministers is P. C. Hiebert, for many years chairman of the all-Mennonite relief organization, the Mennonite Central Committee.

4) *The United Missionary Church*[11]. This body of Mennonites, composed of four or five schismatic American Mennonite groups, was formerly known as the Mennonite Brethren in Christ. They are the Holiness or Methodistic Mennonites, stress-

ing emotional conversions, personal testimonies, and the so-called second work of grace in which the individual believes that he is permanently relieved of his inner proneness to sin, *i.e.,* the Adamic nature of depravity. This group has also adopted immersion, although their strongest leader, Elder Daniel Brenneman (1834-1919) of Indiana, who had been baptized as an (Old) Mennonite, was never rebaptized. Every trace of a religious garb has been discarded, but feet washing is still observed as a church rite, and membership in secret orders is not permitted. This group has probably won more non-Mennonites into its fold than any other group. It is most strongly represented in Ontario, Pennsylvania, Ohio, Indiana and Michigan. There are 15,000 baptized members.

5) *The Old Order Amish*[12] are the extreme traditionalists of the Mennonite family. As was indicated above they arose in Switzerland in 1693 under the leadership of Elder Jacob Ammann, who inaugurated the practice of shunning (*Meidung*). The Amish of America were basically one group until about the middle of the nineteenth century, although they are strict congregationalists having neither general nor district conferences. But about 1850, earlier in some communities and later in others, some of the Amish began to build church buildings and to make other departures from the time-honored traditions of the group. These progressives, who about seventy years later largely merged with the (Old) Mennonites, took the name Amish Mennonites in the nineteenth century but were often dubbed "church Amish" or "high Amish" in contrast with the conservatives who clung to the older customs and regulations and therefore came to be known as Old Order Amish. The latter attempt even today to keep their mode of life as near to that of 1700 as possible. The men wear beards and leave their hair grow much longer than is currently conventional. Their drab clothing is home-made and is fastened with hooks-and-eyes rather than buttons. The women wear large bonnets and plain dresses of solid colors, never figured. They generally have no telephones or electric lights or modern plumbing in

their homes. The automobile is also considered to be of the "world," so the Amish drive with horse and buggy. Sunday schools are not accepted in their church life, and every part of their services must be conducted in the German language following their Swiss forebears. Their martyr-hymns are sung to ancient tunes which were never printed until recently.[13] The Amish generally stick rather close to the soil, and really excel as master farmers. Fifteen thousand strong, the Amish are found mainly in Pennsylvania, Ohio, Indiana and Iowa.

The above five groups are the only ones having 15,000 or more members each, and are four main types: The General Conference Mennonites, and to a certain extent the Mennonite Brethren, are more culturally accommodated to American Society than are the (Old) Mennonites. The Amish are the strict conservatives, and the United Missionary Church is somewhat Wesleyan in its doctrine of sanctification. But there is basically a fifth type, the Christian communal Mennonites known as Hutterites or Hutterian Brethren.[14]

6) *The Hutterian Brethren.* Soon after Grebel founded the Swiss Brethren movement in Switzerland in 1525, some Brethren refugees found their way to Moravia where they hoped to find an asylum from persecution. At Nikolsburg a group of two or three hundred Brethren began to pool their resources to care for other refugees. The spring of 1528 the entire group were ordered to leave the community unless they were willing to attend the services of the established church. They left. At their first encampment they chose "ministers of temporal needs" (deacons) who spread a garment on the ground and everyone put on it all his financial resources. (The New Testament pattern they sought to follow was Acts 4:34, 35.) The leader of these communistic Anabaptists was Jacob Wiedemann. They settled at Austerlitz in Moravia where they were joined in 1529 by a Swiss Brethren minister named Jacob Huter. In 1531 the group divided into a stricter and a more lenient party and the stricter party located at a village called Auspitz where they at once set up their first *Bruderhof,* an estate for com-

munal living. In 1533 Huter became the leader and efficient organizer of the Auspitz group. But in 1536 he was apprehended as a heretic and burned at the stake in his native Tirol. Indeed it is estimated that a thousand Anabaptists were executed in the Tirol and in Gorizia by 1531. Nevertheless in the latter part of the sixteenth century the Hutterian Brethren, or Hutterites, as these followers of Huter are called, thrived. In 1618 they were estimated at 70,000. Severe persecution which resulted in emigration and scattering reduced their numbers to two thousand by 1631. After a forced conversion to Roman Catholicism there was finally an edict of toleration in 1781 and fifty Hutterites promptly located in Russia. The first *Bruderhof* in Russia, however, was not set up until 1857. In less than twenty years thereafter fear of compulsory military service drove the Hutterites to migrate from Russia to South Dakota (1874-75). They were treated so roughly during the First World War (two of their boys died of the abuse received because they refused military service) that most of them migrated to Canada. They now number about 8,000 in Canada, 400 in U.S.A., 700 in Paraguay, and 200 in England.

Those in England and Paraguay employ the name, Society of Brothers, having been founded by Dr. Eberhard Arnold (1883-1935) of Germany in 1920. Arnold united with the Alberta Hutterites in 1930. These German neo-Hutterian Brethren fled from Germany to escape Nazi persecution in 1937. From England, whither they had fled, many migrated to Paraguay in 1940 because of the critical attitude of some of the British toward the Germans in their midst. They have recently published an English translation of their doctrinal teachings and standards.[15]

The remaining small bodies of Mennonites require but brief mention.

7) *The Old Order Mennonites* are composed of various local groups who withdrew from the (Old) Mennonite Church when it adopted Sunday schools, evangelistic meetings, the use of English in place of German, missions and evangelism,

and higher education. Included among their founders were Jacob Wisler of Indiana, 1871, Abram Martin of Ontario, 1889, and Jonas Martin of Lancaster County, Pennsylvania, 1893. These groups have had trouble holding together and in some communities have had at least two divisions in the twentieth century. Their total membership is 5,500.

8) *Manitoba Mennonites.* Independent from the above but also rather conservative are five independent bodies of "Russian" Mennonites found mostly in Manitoba: 1) The Sommerfelders with 4,000 members; 2) the *Kleingemeinde* with 2,000 members; 3) The Rudnerweide Mennonites with 2,000 members; 4) the Chortitz Mennonites with 2,000 members; and 5) the Old Colony Mennonites with 2,000 members in Canada and 5,000 members in Mexico whither they migrated from Manitoba.

9) *The Conservative Amish Mennonites* are a body of former Old Order Amish who have deviated more or less from the "Old Order" by building church buildings, adopting the use of English more or less, driving automobiles, etc. They number about 5,000 and exist as a conference since 1910.

10) The *Church of God in Christ, Mennonite,* commonly called "Holdemans," was founded by an (Old) Mennonite layman named John Holdeman (1830-1900) of Medina County, Ohio. Holdeman thought he had a number of special revelations from God including a call to be a minister. His followers practice "shunning" or avoidance (*Meidung* in German), and all the men must wear beards. His followers are scattered over many states and provinces: Ohio, Michigan, North Dakota, Florida, Kansas, New Mexico, Alberta, Manitoba, Oklahoma, and California, as well as Mexico. There are 5,000 members.

11) The *Evangelical Mennonite Brethren,* 2,000 in number, were founded by two Russian Mennonite immigrants, Isaac Peters (1826-1911), ordained as an elder in Russia in 1867, and an 1874 immigrant to Henderson, Nebraska, and Aaron Wall (1833-1905), ordained as an elder at Mountain Lake, Minnesota, in 1876. For a time their followers were organized as

the Nebraska-Minnesota Conference, and until 1914 were affiliated with the (Old) Mennonite General Conference. Later they employed the name, Defenseless Mennonites, a name already held by another group of Mennonites. In 1937 they finally began to call themselves the Evangelical Mennonite Brethren. They resemble the (Old) Mennonites somewhat, but are probably more free to discard Mennonite forms of worship or standards of discipline than are the (Old) Mennonites.

12) *Evangelical Mennonite Church,* 2,000 strong, formerly known as Defenseless Mennonites. Their founder was an Old Amish bishop named Henry Egly of Geneva, Indiana, about the year 1865. Egly had an "awakening" experience and took half his congregation with him into his new group. This body of Mennonites resembles the General Conference Mennonites except for three points: a) their special emphasis on "experimental" Christianity, b) their doctrine of Holy Spirit "baptism" as an event subsequent to conversion and c) their teaching on divine healing.

Negotiations are at present under way for a merger of the Evangelical Mennonite Brethren and the Evangelical Mennonite Church.

13) *American Mennonite Brethren,* 2,000 in number, formerly Krimmer Mennonite Brethren, described above. Their founder in Russia in 1869 was Jacob A. Wiebe (1836-1921). The group migrated to Marion County, Kansas, in 1874 where they founded the village of Gnadenau. They are now located in Kansas, South Dakota and a few other states and provinces including Alberta and Saskatchewan. In many respects this group resembles the larger Mennonite Brethren body.

14) The *Kleingemeinde,* mentioned several times above, which originated in Russia in 1812 under the leadership of Claas Reimer and Cornelius Janzen, migrated to Manitoba in the 1870's. They closely resemble the (Old) Mennonites except that they have largely retained the use of German in their homes and church life, and they practice shunning. They now have 2,000 members.

15) Apart from a few unaffiliated congregations the chief remaining division is the *Reformed Mennonite Church,* a strict group which withdrew from the (Old) Mennonites in 1812 and inaugurated the practice of shunning. Their members are restrained from listening to the sermons of any but their own ministers. They have only 1,000 members.

Basic Agreements

All Mennonite groups hold an evangelical and conservative attitude toward the Scriptures. All subscribe to the doctrine of absolute love and nonresistance, and officially oppose service in the military. All also refuse the swearing of any kind of an oath. All believe in the principle of separation from the world, but the practical applications of the doctrine make them unable to merge into one larger group. All oppose membership in secret orders. All practice believers' baptism only, and the two main bodies, (Old) Mennonites and General Conference Mennonites, both employ affusion; some of the smaller groups have adopted immersion. All believe in church discipline but its extent and severity varies from group to group. Since 1920 the all-Mennonite relief organization, the Mennonite Central Committee, has carried on an extensive ministry of relief and reconstruction around the globe.

Leaders, Writers and Writings

To date the Mennonites have produced no outstanding writers.[16] In the largest group, the (Old) Mennonite Church, the three persons who have done the most to mold the group by literature are John F. Funk (1835-1930), Daniel Kauffman (1865-1944) and John Horsch (1867-1941). Funk and Kauffman served as editors of the church organ of their group, and Kauffman also wrote many books and booklets to indoctrinate the members of the church.[17] Horsch probably wrote more extensively than any other Mennonite, both scholarly and popular articles and books.[18] Harold S. Bender has also produced works of scholarly merit on Anabaptist and Mennonite history.

The outstanding writers of the General Conference Mennonite Church were John H. Oberholtzer (1809-95), editor and author; Daniel K. Cassel (1820-98), historian;[19] and C. Henry Smith, Ph.D. (1875-1948), the "dean of American Mennonite historians."[20]

The Mennonite groups are not creedal bodies, although their several confessions of faith have had considerable weight during past centuries. The various confessions of faith, as well as their catechisms, all teach the same basic doctrines.[21] The official confession of the Mennonite Church is that of the Dordrecht (Dutch) Mennonites of 1632.[22] The confession of the General Conference Mennonite Church was originally written by Cornelis Ris of Hoorn, Holland, in 1766.[23]

The first scholarly journal published by Mennonites was the Dutch *Doopsgezinde Bijdragen* (1860-1919). This was succeeded in 1927 by *The Mennonite Quarterly Review,* published by The Mennonite Historical Society, Goshen, Indiana. This society also collaborated with the (Old) Mennonite Publishing House, Scottdale, Pennsylvania, in the publication of *Studies in Anabaptist and Mennonite History,* a series of scholarly monographs. The most significant publication of the General Conference Mennonites is *Mennonite Life,* published by Bethel College, North Newton, Kansas, since 1946.

The best description of the Mennonites and their history is that of C. Henry Smith, revised, 1950, by Cornelius Krahn, Th.D., *The Story of the Mennonites.*[24] The most reliable reference work on the Mennonites is the three-volume German encyclopedia, *Mennonitisches Lexikon.* At this writing a comparable American work is being prepared, *The Mennonite Encyclopedia.*[25] Various monographs have also been prepared on special topics such as nonresistance[26] and nonconformity to the world.[27]

NOTES AND BIBLIOGRAPHY

1 H. S. BENDER, *Conrad Grebel* (Goshen, Ind., 1950).

2 C. H. SMITH, *The Story of the Mennonites,* third ed. (Newton, Kansas, 1950).

3 J. C. WENGER, *Glimpses of Mennonite History and Doctrine* (Scottdale, Pa., 1947), p. 135.

4 Dutch (1681); English (Elkhart, 1871). A new translation to be published soon by Mennonite Publishing House, Scottdale, Pa.

5 *See* T. J. VAN BRAGHT, *Martyrs' Mirror* (Dutch, 1660), (Scottdale, Pa., 1950).

6 C. H. SMITH, *The Mennonite Immigration to Pennsylvania in the Eighteenth Century* (Norristown, Pa., 1929).

7 C. H. SMITH, *The Coming of the Russian Mennonites* (Berne, 1927).

8 The best portrayal of the Amish is by J. W. YODER, *Rosanna of the Amish* (Huntingdon, Pa., 1940).

9 H. P. KREHBIEL, *History of the General Conference of the Mennonite Church of North America,* Vol. I (Canton, Ohio, 1898); Vol. II (Newton, Kansas, 1938).

10 JOHN H. LOHRENZ, *The Mennonite Brethren Church* (Hillsboro, Kansas, 1950).

11 J. A. HUFFMAN, *History of the Mennonite Brethren in Christ Church* (New Carlisle, Ohio, 1920).

12 JOHN A. HOSTETLER, *Annotated Bibliography of the Amish* (Scottdale, Pa., 1951).

13 J. W. YODER, *Amische Lieder* (Huntingdon, Pa., 1942).

14 JOHN HORSCH, *The Hutterian Brethren, 1528-1931* (Goshen, Ind., 1931).
A. J. F. ZIEGLSCHMID, *Die aelteste Chronik der Hutterischen Brüder* (Philadelphia, 1943).
————, *Das Klein Geschichtsbuch der Hutterischen Brüder* (Philadelphia, 1947).

15 PETER RIDEMAN, *Account of Our Religion, Doctrine and Faith . . . of the Brothers Whom Men Call Hutterians* (England, 1950). (Translated from the German by Kathleen E. Hasenberg, M. A. The original German edition was 1565.)

16 H. S. BENDER, *Two Centuries of American Mennonite Literature* (Goshen, Indiana, 1929).

17 H. S. BENDER, "Daniel Kauffman . . .," *Mennonite Historical Bulletin,* V, 1 (Scottdale, Pa.), (March, 1944).

18 *John Horsch Memorial Papers* (Scottdale, Pa., 1947). (Bibliography of Horsch's writings, 77-100).

19 Author of *History of the Mennonites* (Philadelphia, 1888); *Geschichte der Mennoniten* (Philadelphia, 1890); etc.

20 *See The Mennonite Quarterly Review,* XXIII, 1 (January, 1949), 4-21 (Goshen, Indiana). (Bibliography of his writings, 16-21).

21 J. C. WENGER, *Doctrine of the Mennonites* (Scottdale, Pa.). Contains reprints of three historic confessions and three catechisms.

22 *Ibid.,* 75-85.

23 CORNELIS RIS, *Mennonite Articles of Faith* (Berne, Indiana, 1925).

24 Mennonite Publication Office, Newton, Kansas, 1950. Note the bibliography, pp. 821-833.

25 The printer is Mennonite Publishing House, Scottdale, Pa.

26 MELVIN GINGERICH, *Service for Peace* (The Mennonite Central Committee, Akron, Pa., 1949); GUY F. HERSHBERGER, *The Mennonite Church in the Second World War* (Scottdale, Pa., 1951).

27 J. C. WENGER, *Separated unto God* (Scottdale, Pa., 1951). Note the bibliography on pages 88-94.

V

THE PRESBYTERIAN CHURCH IN AMERICA

V

THE PRESBYTERIAN CHURCH IN AMERICA

CLIFFORD MERRILL DRURY

THE PRESBYTERIAN Church takes its name from the Greek word for elder, *presbuteros,* which is found in the New Testament. Also in the New Testament is the word *episcopos,* or bishop. The two words are used as synonyms. The government of the Apostolic Church appears to have been quite democratic. The rise of bishops as distinct from elders began in the second century. Today the Presbyterian form of church polity occupies a mid-way position between episcopacy and congregationalism.

In the Presbyterian polity, churches are governed by elected representatives or elders who form the session over which the minister presides as the Moderator. A group of churches and ministers within a certain area compose the Presbytery. Three or more Presbyteries form a Synod which in the United States usually follow State boundaries. Three or more Synods are needed to establish a General Assembly which in the United States represents the highest judicatory of the Presbyterian Church.

Among the basic principles of Presbyterian polity are the following two: the parity of the ministry and equal representation of clergy and laity at all church courts. Every installed Presbyterian pastor of the Presbyterian Church, U.S.A. is technically the "bishop" of his congregation. The youngest ordained minister in the denomination is on the same ecclesiastical level as he who holds the office of Moderator of the General Assembly. There are no questions of doctrine, polity, or discipline which are reserved for the exclusive right of the clergy to settle. Representations of clergy and laity at all of the church judicatories are provided on a basis of equality.

The Protestant Reformation, which was launched by Martin Luther in 1517, divided into the Lutheran and the Reformed branches in 1529. The great French theologian who did his best work at Geneva, Switzerland, John Calvin (1509-1564), became the intellectual leader of the Reformed branch. His *Institutes of the Christian Religion* appeared in 1536 when Calvin was in his twenty-seventh year. The work was subsequently enlarged and revised. Calvin's *Institutes* provided the clearest and most comprehensive statement of the Reformed faith produced during the Reformation and remains to this day as one of the standard Protestant works in the field of theology.

Calvin developed in his writings the Presbyterian ideal of church government. He insisted upon the independence of the church from secular government even though he was unable to achieve this ideal in the church-state of Geneva. His philosophy of Presbyterian polity prepared the way for the separation of church and state as it is practiced today in the United States.

The Presbyterian form of Government first took root in France with the Huguenots. The first Presbyterian national Synod of France met in Paris in 1559 and adopted a Confession of Faith, which was Calvinistic in theology, and a Book of Discipline, which was Presbyterian in polity. The Huguenots of France endured many persecutions under the Guises during the years 1521 to the signing of the Edict of Nantes in 1598. There were eight distinct Wars of Religion. The Massacre of St. Bartholomew took place in 1572 at which time, according to conservative estimates, some 70,000 Protestants were killed.

The Protestant Church of Holland was and is for the most part Presbyterian. Here, also, the Protestants suffered. Persecutions extended over a period of nearly sixty years ending in 1581 with the *Apology* of William the Silent. The Dutch Reformed Church of today is a recognized branch of the Presbyterian family.

John Knox (1513 or 1515-1572) became the great leader of the Reformation in Scotland which became the headquarters of Presbyterianism. The first General Assembly of Scotland met in Edinburgh in 1560. For about one hundred years the Presbyterian Church of Scotland struggled against the repeated efforts of the rulers of England to impose the episcopal form of church government upon it. The final settlement came in 1690 from which time the Presbyterian Church of Scotland has had a continuous history.

The Presbyterian Church took root in the ten northern counties of Ireland, known as Ulster, during the reign of James I of England. Soon after James became king of England in 1603, he invited colonists from Scotland to settle on lands in northern Ireland which had been confiscated because of a rebellion. The Scotch responded so enthusiastically that they soon became the dominant group there. For the most part these Scotch-Irish Presbyterians were more evangelistic and less liturgical in the expression of their faith than were their brethren in the mother country. Most of the first Presbyterians to migrate to America were from North Ireland. They left an indelible impression upon the growing Presbyterian Church in the colonies.

The Puritan, or the purifying party, in the Church of England started during the reign of Queen Elizabeth. Many of the members of this party preferred the Presbyterian form of Government. The Separatists, or the Pilgrims, for the most part chose the congregational method of governing the church. Prior to the establishment of the Commonwealth Government under Oliver Cromwell, in 1649, many of the English Presbyterian Puritans migrated to America.

The Presbyterian "family" in the United States has eleven subdivisions, six of which belong to the main Presbyterian group in which the Presbyterian Church, U.S.A., with about 2,500,000 members, is the largest single unit. Five bodies belong to the descendants of the Covenanter or the Seceder branches of the Presbyterian Church of Scotland, among which the United Presbyterian Church with nearly 300,000 members is the largest unit. The combined membership of the first group of six denominations numbers about 3,200,000 while the five smaller bodies add up to 325,000. This brings the combined

Presbyterian membership in the United States, according to 1950 statistics, to over 3,500,000.

Presbyterian Beginnings in The American Colonies

Contrary to popular opinion, the beginnings of Presbyterianism in the American colonies came from England rather than from Scotland or North Ireland. The Puritan movement in England, which started during the reign of Queen Elizabeth, contained within itself a strong Presbyterian element. There is some evidence to indicate that some Presbyterian-Puritans settled at Jamestown, Virginia, at the time this colony was founded in 1607 or shortly thereafter. The Rev. Alexander Whitaker, who arrived at Jamestown in 1611, is reported to have organized "an informal Congregational Presbytery."[1] Since he appointed "four of the most religious men" to aid him in governing the church, it appears that he had adopted the Presbyterian form of polity in the local church. Whitaker expressed his non-conformist views by writing: "Here neither surplice nor subscription is spoken of."[2] Nansemond County, Virginia, is reported to have had three non-conformist parishes by 1641.[3] Governor William Berkeley, who took office in Virginia in 1642, was unsympathetic to these non-conformists and harried them out of the colony. Some of the ejected colonists moved north into Maryland where Presbyterianism appears to have been rooted as early as 1657.

A similar situation developed in New England where the dominant party was the Congregationalist. Cotton Mather states that about 4,000 Presbyterians arrived in New England before 1640.[4] Since no presbyteries were then in existence in this country, the main point of difference between the Presbyterians and the Congregationalists was the government used in the local congregations. The Presbyterians ruled through elders while the Congregationalists governed by majority vote of all members. Since the Congregational party was dominant in New England, again the Presbyterians had either to conform or migrate.

As early as 1640 a Presbyterian church was formed at South-old, Long Island, by a colony of New Englanders. In 1644 the Rev. Richard Denton, a Presbyterian, established a church at Hempstead, Long Island. Some of these early churches did not remain Presbyterian. The oldest Presbyterian church with a continuous history now a part of the Presbyterian Church, U.S.A., is that formed at Jamaica, Long Island, on June 3, 1672. Other Presbyterians followed, pushing down into New Jersey, Maryland, and Pennsylvania. Thus, the Middle Colonies began to be the center of Presbyterianism even before the coming of the Scotch and the Scotch-Irish.

In the meantime the Westminster Assembly had met in London during the years 1643-1648 which gave to Presbyterians everywhere their five basic standards: the Confession of Faith, the Longer and the Shorter Catechisms, the Directory of Worship, and the Form of Government. During the Commonwealth Government, 1649-1660, Presbyterianism was the recognized religion of England. For a few years the Presbyterian-Puritan migration to America actually went into reverse.

The restoration of the monarchy in 1660 brought fresh persecutions of the Presbyterians, especially in Scotland and North Ireland, which greatly stimulated migration from these countries to the American colonies. Political and economic conditions in North Ireland after 1702 added further incentives to the Presbyterian migration. A common estimate is that between 1705 and 1775 about 500,000 Scotch-Irish came to America. Although most of them settled in the Middle Colonies, yet by the time of the Revolutionary War the Scotch-Irish were more widely diffused through the thirteen colonies, especially on the frontier, than was any other single religious group.

The Church Becomes Organized

In 1683 the Rev. Francis Makemie, known as "The Father of American Presbyterianism" arrived at Rehoboth, Maryland. Makemie was a member of the Presbytery of Laggan in North Ireland. According to a tradition of long standing, Makemie organized six churches in Maryland sometime before or about 1700. He seems to have been the leading figure in the organization of the first Presbytery in 1705 or 1706—the exact date is in doubt because the first page of the original records is lost.[5] Makemie was the first Moderator. A church building erected at Rehoboth, Maryland, in 1706, two years before Makemie died, is still being used by the Presbyterian Church at that place.

Of the seven charter member ministers of that first Presbytery, two came from Delaware, one from Philadelphia, Pennsylvania, and four from Maryland. The Presbytery had no name—it was just "The Presbytery." In 1716 the Presbytery had so grown that its members voted to divide it into four presbyteries and organize a synod. The Synod, also without a name, was organized in 1717 with 19 ministers, 40 churches, and about 3,000 communicants. By this time the Presbyterian churches in Long Island, New York, and New Jersey were included.

At its first meeting the Synod established the Pious Fund which was an omnibus benevolence agency designed especially for the care of widows and orphans of deceased ministers but which also included other causes. In 1759 this Fund became a chartered organization with its own self-perpetuating Board of Directors (which made it independent of the Presbyterian Church) under the name of The Presbyterian Ministers' Fund. This was the first charter granted a Life Insurance Company in America.

Shortly after the organization of the Synod, a controversy arose in the Church regarding credal standards. The Scotch and Scotch-Irish favored the adoption of the Westminster Confession of Faith; the English did not. After some debate, the Synod in 1729 passed the Adopting Act which required each minister to subscribe to the Westminster Confession of Faith "as being in all the essential and necessary articles, good forms of sound words and system of Christian doctrine." This is a pivotal date in the history of Presbyterianism in the United States. It meant the formal acceptance by the Presbyterian

Church in America of the doctrine, polity, and worship of the Westminster standards.

The Adopting Act made a few important changes in the original Westminster documents, one being to deny to civil magistrates "the power to persecute any for their religion." This Act was, therefore, not only the Magna Charta of American Presbyterianism, it was also the first official declaration by any organized church in the colonies of the principle of the separation of Church and State.

A separate branch of the Presbyterian Church took root in New England. Sometime between 1726 and 1729, Londonderry Presbytery was organized entirely independent of the Synod in the Middle Colonies. Because of missing original records, the story of Presbyterianism in New England during the eighteenth century is confused. From the evidence at hand we know that the Church had many difficulties. A Synod of New England was formed in 1775 which led a precarious existence for about seven years. In 1809, the New England Presbyterians, then reduced to the Presbytery of Londonderry, joined the main body of Presbyterians in the United States.[6]

The New Side—Old Side Schism of 1741-1758

The Presbyterian Church was greatly affected by the First Great Awakening which started about 1735. This was the American counterpart of the contemporary Wesley-Whitefield revival in England. Indeed, George Whitefield was the coordinating element not only between England and America but also between the colonies. He made seven itinerating trips to the American colonies.

The outstanding Presbyterian leader in this Awakening was Gilbert Tennent, the son of William Tennent, founder and sole faculty member of the Log College. William Tennent opened his school for the training of a Presbyterian ministry in a log cabin on the banks of the Neshaminy in Bucks County, Pennsylvania, about 1735. Some fifteen young men, including four of Tennent's sons, received their theological training in this embryo theological seminary. The eloquent Gilbert was graduated from Yale, evidently before the Log College was established. After the death of William Tennent in 1746, some of the alumni of the Log College founded the College of New Jersey which, after some perambulating, settled in Princeton and in time became Princeton University.

Several of the graduates of the Log College joined the New Brunswick Presbytery where they demonstrated a strong evangelistic spirit. Some of the Presbyterian clergy were critical of the Log College. They would have no part in the revivals that were a part of the Great Awakening. By 1740 a sharp line of demarcation divided the Church into two almost equal parts known as the Old Side and the New Side, the latter being the Log College or the revival party. A scathing sermon by Gilbert Tennent delivered in 1740 on "The Danger of an Unconverted Ministry" hastened the climax. The Synod in 1741 expelled New Brunswick Presbytery. In 1745 New Castle and New York Presbyteries united with New Brunswick to form the Synod of New York. The remaining part of the Church became the Synod of Philadelphia. Thus the first schism to rend the Presbyterian Church in America centered not in doctrine but rather in issues connected with the First Great Awakening.[7]

The two Synods remained apart until 1758 when a union was effected to make the Synod of New York and Philadelphia. During the years of division the Old Side barely held its own in the number of its ministers—actually the number decreased from 24 to 23. The New Side, on the other hand, increased from 22 to 72.

The work of the famous missionary to the Indians, David Brainerd, a New Side Presbyterian, falls within this period. This zealous and devoted missionary died in 1747 after only about three years' active service. Jonathan Edwards edited and published Brainerd's Journal which became one of the great missionary textbooks of all time.

The division of 1745-1758 was not altogether an evil as certain important points of Presbyterian polity were settled in the plan of union which remain operative to this day. The authority of the presbytery to ordain was upheld. A higher judicatory can establish standards for ordination but the individual presbytery is given the right to interpret those standards and even to make exceptions should it so desire. A second important point settled in 1758 was that no minister should labor outside the bounds of his presbytery without permission.

From 1758 to the organization of the first General Assembly in 1789, the Presbyterian Church enjoyed a steady growth. The convening officer of the first Assembly was Dr. John Witherspoon, President of the College of New Jersey (now Princeton University) and the only clergyman to sign the Declaration of Independence. The organization of a General Assembly was made necessary by the growth of the church and the difficulties of travel. The original Synod of New York and Philadelphia was divided into four—New York and New Jersey, Philadelphia, Virginia, and the Carolinas. The Church then boasted of having 177 ministers, 419 congregations, and 16 presbyteries.

The Second Great Awakening and Its Effects

The westward movement of the population over the mountains into the Mississippi River Valley began in earnest after the Revolutionary War. The 1790 census reported 200,000, or about 5 per cent of the total population of 4,000,000, were then living west of the mountains. Presbyterian missionaries joined in this westward migration. As early as 1766 two Presbyterian ministers, the Rev. George Duffield and the Rev. Charles Beatty, had itinerated into the Ohio Valley. In 1781 the Presbytery of Redstone was organized in western Pennsylvania.

About 1800 a great spiritual stirring took place on the frontier in Kentucky and Tennessee. This revival, often marked by emotional excesses, swept eastward over the mountains into the older settlements. A parallel spiritual quickening arose in the colleges under the leadership of such men as Timothy Dwight of Yale. Among the many results of this Second Great Awakening was the birth of organized missionary endeavor on the part of the American churches.

In 1802 the Presbyterian General Assembly appointed its Standing Committee of Missions which represented the first official action on the part of any of the Protestant churches of America to promote national missions. This Committee became a Board of Missions in 1816. Upon the establishment of the Board of Foreign Missions in 1837, the earlier Board was known as the Board of Domestic Missions until 1870 when the name was changed to the Board of Home Missions. In 1923 the Presbyterian Church reorganized its benevolence agencies combining some twenty organizations into four—among the latter of which was the Board of National Missions. In 1952 the Presbyterian Church observed the 150th anniversary of the establishment of the Standing Committee of Missions, the ancestor of the present Board of National Missions.[8]

Also in 1802 the Synod of Pittsburgh organized the Western Missionary Society as an agency to conduct home missionary work within its boundaries. This Society in 1831 enlarged its activities to include the foreign field by appointing missionaries to India. The name was then changed to the Western Foreign Missionary Society. In 1810 the American Board of Commissioners for Foreign Missions was established. This became an interdenominational agency in which the Presbyterian Church cooperated until 1837.

One of the unfortunate results of the Second Great Awakening, as far as the Presbyterian Church was concerned, was the Cumberland schism of 1810. The Cumberland Presbytery, organized in 1802, of the Synod of Kentucky began to ordain men who did not possess the educational qualifications prescribed by the Church. Upon investigation, the Synod of Kentucky found that some of the men thus ordained were "not only illiterate, but erroneous in sentiment." The Synod in 1806 dissolved the Presbytery. However, in 1810 the Rev. James McGready and two others organized an independent Cumberland Presbytery. This Presbytery, using the frontier techniques of the Methodists and the Baptists, had a remarkable growth. By 1829 the original Presbytery had expanded to seventeen with a membership of about 170,000. A General Assembly was organized in 1829.

Another important development associated with the westward movement of the population and the Second Great Awakening was the Plan of Union effected in 1801 between the Presbyterian General Assembly and the General Association (Congregational) of Connecticut. Later other branches of the Congregational Church joined. This plan was designed to promote cooperation between Presbyterian and Congregational ministers and churches on the frontier. The two denominations had much in common. Both had accepted the Westminster Confession of Faith. Both were trying to supply ministers to the large number of new communities springing up on the frontier, especially in western New York and in the Ohio River Valley. This Plan of Union created what might be called federated churches with the two denominations, Presbyterian and Congregational participating. The operation of the plan was successful in many frontier communities and did much to eliminate denominational competition and to provide ministers to weak congregations.

Old School—New School Schism of 1837

The Presbyterian Church suffered a serious division in 1837 when the denomination divided into two sections each claiming to be the continuing Presbyterian Church. The Old School party had about five-ninths of the strength of the church while the New School had the balance.

Three main reasons contributed to the schism. The first centered about polity. The Old School party was critical of the operations of the Plan of Union which brought federated churches with a hybrid polity into the Presbyterian fold. Such churches were often called "Presbygational." The General Assembly of 1837 by a margin of only six votes declared the Plan of Union of 1801 to be unconstitutional. The next step logically followed—the presbyteries formed under the peculiar provisions of the Plan of Union were also unconstitutional. Since the Old School was in the majority in that Assembly, three Synods located in western New York were excommunicated.

A second point of polity affected the benevolence funds of the Church. The New School party advocated cooperation with the Congregationalists in the American Board of Commissioners for Foreign Missions and in the American Home Missionary Society. The Old School demanded benevolence agencies under the control and direction of the General Assembly. The Assembly's Board of Missions, which evolved out of the Standing Committee of Missions, was prepared to conduct national missions. After excluding the New School party, the Assembly of 1837 took over the Western Foreign Missionary Society of the Synod of Pittsburgh and made it the Presbyterian Board of Foreign Missions.

The other two main reasons which led to the division of 1837 involved doctrine and social issues. The New School party was accused by the Old School of being too liberal in doctrine. Also, the New School was more sensitive to social issues, including especially the slavery question. Many of the New School favored abolition. The "disinterested benevolence" emphasis of the New England brand of theology, which was held by many New School leaders, provided fertile soil for a developing social consciousness.

The controversial slavery issue retarded the growth of the New School. Even though the majority favored a positive stand against slavery, the presence of a strong southern minority in the Assemblies for about ten years prevented this branch of the Church from making a public anti-slavery statement. In 1857 the New School Assembly took action which condemned the holding of slaves by church members. As a result, representatives from some 21 presbyteries located in Missouri, Virginia, Kentucky, Tennessee, and Mississippi severed their connection with the New School Assembly and organized the United Synod of the Presbyterian Church on April 1, 1858.

The Old School Assembly was able to avoid the controversial issue until 1861. The crisis came in the meeting of the General

Assembly that year which opened its sessions in Philadelphia on May 16th, about five weeks after the Confederates had opened fire on Fort Sumter. Ten southern states had already voted to secede from the Union and the eleventh, North Carolina, followed the others on May 20th. The General Assembly of the Old School was the first national meeting of any of the Protestant churches following the outbreak of hostilities. The whole nation waited to hear what the Presbyterians would say and do.

The opening prayer by the venerable Dr. Gardiner Spring of New York carried a petition for the preservation of the Union. A few days later Dr. Spring introduced a set of Resolutions which, in essence, called upon the church to support the Government. Then the debate started. The opponents of the Spring Resolutions expressed their horror at the sacrilege of taking the church into politics. Prominent leaders such as Dr. Charles Hodge of Princeton, realizing that an acceptance of the Spring Resolutions by the Assembly would alienate the Southern element, strove earnestly for an indefinite postponement of the vote. Hodge held that it was wise to withhold comment at that time in order to preserve the unity of the church. Dr. William C. Anderson, pastor of the First Presbyterian Church of San Francisco, and the great-grandfather of Dr. Harrison Ray Anderson, the Moderator of the Church in 1951-52, led the fight for the Spring Resolutions. After days of debate, the Assembly on May 29th adopted the Spring Resolutions with some changes.

Commissioners from 47 presbyteries, formerly in connection with the Old School Assembly, met at Augusta, Georgia, on December 4, 1861, and organized the Presbyterian Church in the Confederate States of America. The United Synod, representing the Southern branch of the New School, and the Confederate Church joined under the name of the latter in 1864. After the Civil War the name of the denomination was changed to "The Presbyterian Church in the United States." The Southern Presbyterian Church, as it is often called, published its statistics for the first time in 1866. These show that the Church then had 10 synods, 48 presbyteries, 850 ministers and licentiates, 1,309 churches, and 80,532 members. A large part of the Synod of Kentucky of the Old School (North) changed its allegiance to the Southern Church in 1869 and a part of the Synod of Missouri did likewise in 1874. Some of the churches in the border areas which at first joined in the secession movement returned to the Northern Church.

The Presbyterian Church in the United States reported having 673,000 members in 1950. The denomination is largely confined to the south-eastern part of the United States having only a scattering of churches north of the Mason-Dixon line. However, it is strong in Texas and has good work established in Oklahoma, Arkansas, and Missouri.

Various efforts have been made to unite the Presbyterian Church in the United States with the Presbyterian Church in the United States of America, the latter being formed by the union of the two northern branches of the Old School and the New School in 1869. However, to date the Southern church has been hesitant to enter a union partly because of differences in doctrinal emphasis and partly because of divergent views between the North and the South in regard to the treatment of the Negro. The sentiment is growing in the Southern Church in favor of union.

Presbyterians Unite

Following the Civil War, the two northern branches of the Old School and the New School drew together. The three major reasons which had precipitated the schism of 1837 had one by one been removed. The Congregational Church abrogated the Plan of Union in 1832 and the New School Presbyterians had established their own denominational agency to handle their national missions funds. The doctrinal issues that once seemed so important had passed with the rise of a new generation. The Civil War had settled the slavery issue. A union of the two Assemblies was consummated in 1869.

The reunited church grew rapidly increasing from 446,561 members in 1870 to over a million in 1900. Union with the Cumberland Church took place in 1906. The Cumberland Church, which began with one presbytery in 1810, had grown to 114 presbyteries by 1906. At the time of the reunion with the Mother Church, the Cumberland Presbyterians were scattered through twenty-four states being especially strong in Kentucky, Illinois, Missouri, Arkansas, and Texas.

Since the Cumberland Church was historically not as "creedal" as was the Mother Church, certain changes were made in 1903 in the Westminster Confession of Faith by the Presbyterian Church, U.S.A., in order to remove some objections on the part of some of the Cumberland Presbyterians and also to give expression to some widely held convictions on the part of members of the Mother Church. An unofficial condensation of the Westminster Confession of Faith was made by the Assembly of 1903 which is known as the "Brief Statement of the Reformed Faith." This Brief Statement, by vote of the General Assembly, is now included in the Presbyterian Hymnal. These revisions to the Confession of Faith and the preparation of the Brief Statement helped to consummate the union of 1906. However, the two Cumberland synods in Tennessee refused to enter the union. They carried on as the continuing Cumberland Presbyterian Church. In 1950 this body had about 80,000 members.

Since the Cumberland Church had many churches in the South, the union of 1906 made the Presbyterian Church, U.S.A., once more a truly national body for the first time since 1861. Therefore, while it is proper to speak of the Presbyterian Church, U.S., as the Southern Presbyterian Church, the Presbyterian Church, U.S.A., is not a regional body. The Presbyterian Church, U.S.A., now has organized work in each of the 48 states.

The Cumberland Presbyterian Church had about 20,000 Negro members before the Civil War. Following the War, the Negroes with a new race consciousness sought separate churches and an entirely independent ecclesiastical organization. The

Colored Cumberland Presbyterian Church started in 1869 when presbyteries for Negro ministers began to be formed. A General Assembly was established in 1874. This Church has experienced little growth having but 30,000 members in 1950.

A second union with another Presbyterian body took place in 1920 when the Welsh Calvinistic Methodist Church joined with the Presbyterian Church, U.S.A. This union brought in 6 synods, 16 presbyteries, 150 churches, 100 ministers, and about 15,000 members. The Calvinistic Methodist Church arose in Wales as a result of the Wesley-Whitefield revival. These churches accepted the Calvinistic theology of Whitefield but took over some of the methods of Wesley. The denomination became Presbyterian in polity. The Welsh language was used in its services. The church was planted in this country prior to 1869. Colonies of Welsh settled in western New York, Ohio, Pennsylvania, Wisconsin, and Minnesota. The Welsh Presbyterians maintained the separate existence of their six synods for a time after the union of 1920. During the years 1934-36, these synods were absorbed into the collateral synods of the larger body.

The Fundamentalist-Modernist Controversy

For several decades after 1910 the Presbyterian Church was disturbed by theological controversy. About 1910 a series of twelve small volumes known as *The Fundamentals* appeared which were conservative in doctrine and premillennial in outlook. Financed by two wealthy laymen of Los Angeles, about 3,000,000 copies of these booklets were distributed. Dr. Harry Emerson Fosdick, a Baptist minister but at the time a guest preacher in the First Presbyterian Church of New York City, became a key figure in the controversy when his sermon on "Shall the Fundamentalists Win?" was printed and widely distributed. In 1924 the General Assembly invited Dr. Fosdick either to become a Presbyterian or to abandon the pulpit of the First Church of New York. He chose to do the latter.

In the meantime, the 1923 General Assembly set forth five

doctrines as being "essential." Regardless of the content of these doctrines, many ministers of the Church felt that this method of selecting certain docrines as being essential was tantamount to altering the creedal standards of the Church by methods not in accord with Presbyterian polity. Consequently 1,293 ministers signed a protest which was known as the Auburn Affirmation. This denied the right of the Assembly to amend through a legislative act the Constitution of the Church.

The conservative group, critical of Princeton Theological Seminary, opened Westminster Theological Seminary in Philadelphia in 1929 and in 1933 established the Independent Board for Presbyterian Foreign Missions. The Assembly of 1934 ordered all Presbyterians to withdraw from the Independent Board. Several ministers declined to do so. They were censured by their respective presbyteries in 1935, which action was confirmed by the General Assembly of 1936. Consequently the Orthodox Presbyterian Church (at first and for a short time known as the American Presbyterian Church) was organized. This body in turn suffered a division in 1939 when the Bible Presbyterian Church was formed. Each of these two denominations now have from 5,000 to 8,000 members.

The Presbyterian Church in the United States of America

The Presbyterian Church has long been known as a college building church. The 1951 Report of its Board of Christian Education listed 44 colleges and a boys' academy as being endorsed by or closely related to the Presbyterian Church. In addition the Church has nine recognized seminaries, including one, Louisville, which is a joint undertaking with the Southern Presbyterians. There are two seminaries for the training of Negro ministers—one at Lincoln University in Pennsylvania and the other at Johnson C. Smith University in North Carolina. The other six seminaries are Princeton, Bloomfield, Western at Pittsburgh, McCormick at Chicago, Dubuque, and San Francisco at San Anselmo, California. The Church also conducts three lay training schools for professional workers.

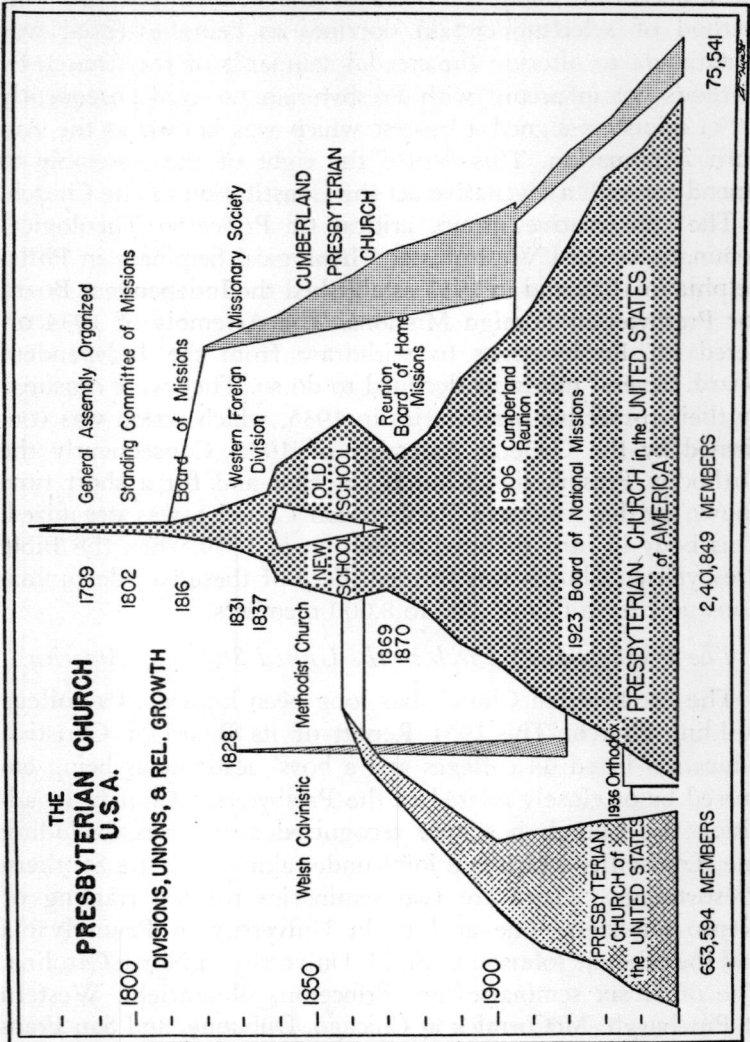

THE
PRESBYTERIAN CHURCH
U.S.A.

DIVISIONS, UNIONS, & REL. GROWTH

1789 General Assembly Organized

1802 Standing Committee of Missions

1816 Board of Missions

Western Foreign Missionary Society
Board of Missions
Division

1831
1837

NEW OLD
SCHOOL SCHOOL

1869
1870

Reunion
Board of Home
Missions

1906 Cumberland Reunion

CUMBERLAND PRESBYTERIAN CHURCH

1923 Board of National Missions

PRESBYTERIAN CHURCH in the UNITED STATES of AMERICA

1828 Methodist Church

Welsh Calvinistic

1936 Orthodox

PRESBYTERIAN CHURCH of the UNITED STATES

1800

1850

1900

653,594 MEMBERS

2,40,849 MEMBERS

75,541

From *Presbyterian Panorama*, Copyright 1952, by Hermann N. Morse, published by the Presbyterian Board of Christian Education, Philadelphia.

[86]

Following the union of the Old and New Schools in 1869, the Presbyterian Church gradually became top-heavy with organization as a separate board or committee was established for each new recognized need. By 1922 the Church had fourteen boards, four permanent committees, and a special committee on military chaplains. The Assembly of 1922 voted to consolidate these administrative units into the following four major boards—National Missions, Foreign Missions, Christian Education, and Pensions. In 1946 the Assembly established a Council on Theological Education and directed that a portion of the benevolent funds of the Church should be used to support the recognized seminaries.

The membership of the Presbyterian Church, U.S.A., has increased at a faster ratio during the past 150 years than has the nation's population. The following statistics tell the story:

	Presbyterian Membership	*Total Population*
1800	20,000	5,308,483
1850 (O.S. & N.S.)	347,051	23,191,876
1900	1,007,689	75,994,575
1950	2,447,975	150,697,361

Whereas the population of the country increased about fifteen times between 1800 and 1900, the membership of the Presbyterian Church increased fifty times. If the statistics of the denominations which branched off from the Mother Church also be considered, the statistics would be even more striking. Since 1900 the comparative ratio has been more nearly equal. During the past fifty years the population has increased about 20 per cent while the Presbyterian Church has grown about 24 per cent.

In 1951 the Presbyterian Church had 37 synods in continental United States, 27 of which conform almost exclusively to state borders and are known by the names of the states they occupy. The others are regional synods and of these four are composed of Negroes and one is for people of German descent. Presbyterianism is numerically strong today in such states as New Jersey, New York, and Pennsylvania—the area once known as the Middle Colonies which was the cradle of Presbyterianism in America—and in such other states as Ohio, Michigan, Indiana, Illinois, Iowa, and California. The total membership of the Church in these nine states at the end of 1950 was over 1,440,-000 or about three-fifths of the total membership of the denomination.

The official headquarters of the Church are in Philadelphia and New York. Dr. Eugene Blake, the Stated Clerk, has his office in Witherspoon Building in Philadelphia, while Dr. Glenn Moore, the General Secretary of the General Council, has his office at 156 Fifth Avenue, New York City. The official journal of the Church is *Presbyterian Life* which, in May, 1951, boasted a paid subscription list of 450,000, making it the "largest Protestant magazine in Christendom."[9]

NOTES

[1] CHARLES A. BRIGGS, *American Presbyterianism* (New York, 1885), p. 87.

[2] *Ibid.*

[3] EDWARD MACK, "Our Presbyterian Heritage in Eastern Virginia," *Union Seminary Review* (Richmond), July, 1924.

[4] COTTON MATHER, *Magnalia Christi Americana* (Hartford, 1855), p. 80.

[5] The original record book of the first presbytery is in the archives of the Presbyterian Historical Society, Witherspoon Building, Philadelphia, Penna.

[6] ALEXANDER BLAIKIE, *A History of Presbyterianism in New England* (Boston, 1882), gives a good review of the complicated story of New England Presbyterianism.

[7] LEONARD J. TRINTERUD, *The Forming of an American Tradition* (Philadelphia, 1949), gives the finest and most detailed account of Colonial Presbyterianism.

[8] CLIFFORD M. DRURY, *Presbyterian Panorama* (Philadelphia, 1952) is the official history of the Board of National Missions published on the occasion of its Sesquicentennial. Much of the material used in the balance of this chapter is drawn from the author's book here mentioned.

[9] *Presbyterian Life,* June 23, 1951, p. 17.

BIBLIOGRAPHY

CHARLES AUGUSTUS BRIGGS, *American Presbyterianism* (New York, 1885).

CLIFFORD M. DRURY, *Presbyterian Panorama* (Philadelphia, 1952).

LEFFERTS A. LOETSCHER, *A Brief History of the Presbyterians,* [Pamphlet] (Philadelphia, 19......).

B. W. MCDONNOLD, *History of the Cumberland Presbyterian Church* (Nashville, 1888).

ROBERT ELLIS THOMPSON, *A History of the Presbyterian Churches in the United States* (New York, 1900).

LEONARD J. TRINTERUD, *The Forming of an American Tradition* (Philadelphia, 1949).

ANDREW C. ZENOS, *Presbyterianism in America* (New York, 1937).

VI

*THE PROTESTANT EPISCOPAL CHURCH
IN THE UNITED STATES OF AMERICA*

VI

THE PROTESTANT EPISCOPAL CHURCH IN THE UNITED STATES OF AMERICA

WALTER HERBERT STOWE

THE PROTESTANT EPISCOPAL CHURCH In The United States Of America, commonly known as "The Episcopal Church" or "The American Episcopal Church," is a self-governing branch of the Anglican Communion, which the Lambeth Conference of 1930 defined as a

> Fellowship within the One, Holy, Catholic, and Apostolic Church, of those duly constituted Dioceses, Provinces, or Regional Churches in communion with the see of Canterbury.[1]

These Churches are bound together, not by a central legislative or executive authority, but by voluntary allegiance to a common faith and order as set forth in the Book of Common Prayer, under the primacy of the Archbishop of Canterbury. Each national Church can revise or adapt the Prayer Book to meet its own needs, particularly in the spheres of discipline and worship, provided the substance of faith and order "be kept entire." The Archbishop of Canterbury is "first among equals" —the meaning of primacy—and has no pretensions to spiritual supremacy, temporal supremacy, or infallibility; and no such claims are acknowledged by the autonomous Churches.

In the expansion of the Anglican Church into a world-wide Communion of some 40,000,000 members, the American Episcopal Church has been the trail blazer: 1) It was the first autonomous Church to be organized outside the British Isles; 2) it was the first to have a valid, free, democratic, and purely ecclesiastical episcopate—that is, an episcopate both free of state control and free from civil functions or powers; 3) it was the first to prove that a Church of Anglican origin could not only survive but thrive without being established or supported by the state; and 4) it was the first to introduce into the government of the Church the direct representation of the laity.[2]

The Church of England

Christianity came to the island of Britain probably in the third century, for its bishops were in attendance at Church councils on the European continent in the early part of the fourth century.[3] Following the withdrawal of the Roman legions about 410, the invading Angles and Saxons, who were pagans, drove what survived of the Church into western England and Wales.

The first efforts for the re-conversion of what is now England came not from the east and south, but from the west and north—from the Celtic monks whose propagating center was the famous monastery at Iona, founded in 563 by St. Columba, which was a light of the western world. Although Christ-like in their lives, with a burning zeal and love of souls, these Celtic missionaries were deficient in the gifts needed for parochial and diocesan organization. This need was provided from Rome.

In 597, St. Augustine and a band of forty monks, sent by Gregory the Great, Bishop of Rome, arrived in Kent, and the see of Canterbury—the mother church of the Anglican Communion—was established.

Augustine was unable to win acknowledgment of his authority from the Celtic churchmen, but beginning with the Councils of Whitby (664) and Hertford (673), Roman customs and usages, especially the observance of Easter, won out over Celtic practices. Henceforth, papal claims to spiritual supremacy over the Church, and, in the reign of John, temporal supremacy over the state, were made increasingly effective in England.

The medieval idea of a nation being like a single coin, one face being the state and the other the Church, has been carried over into modern times in England; and, however foreign or illogical to Americans, it must always be taken into account if church-state relationships in that country are to be understood.

Although it is dangerous to simplify history, it is not unfair to say that the sixteenth century witnessed to the fact that *Ecclesia Anglicana,* as it was termed in Magna Carta of 1215, was not to be dominated by Roman Catholicism; the seventeenth century, that it was not to be dominated by Calvinism; the eighteenth century, that outside of England, Wales and Ireland, it was not to be dominated by the state; and the nineteenth century, that it was not to be dominated by any doctrine of Biblical infallibility.

The Reformation in England was very different from that on the Continent, where it was in reality a revolution. In contrast to the Continental Reformation, there was in England a constitutional reformation *before* there was a doctrinal reformation: in fact, the latter was half a generation later than the former. Freedom of the Church of England from papal control was attained under Henry VIII, maintained under Edward VI, lost under Mary, and finally regained under Elizabeth. But the principle of continuity with the pre-Reformation English Church was jealously guarded throughout the upheavals of the sixteenth century, and out of the crisis the Church of England emerged as a *National Catholic Church.*[4]

"Anglicanism" is a result of the Reformation. It is the form which the Catholic Church in England took after it had been reformed in the reigns of Henry VIII, Edward VI, and Elizabeth. It is the type of Christianity which we find in the national Church after the "Elizabethan Settlement," and which has been evolving ever since through four centuries of history . . .[5]

The famous "Elizabethan Settlement" was not another sharp reaction like that under Edward. It was a deliberate compromise, providing the legal setting and secular framework within which Anglicanism could develop as a *via media*. This characteristic note of Anglicanism was struck early in the Queen's reign by legislation which declared in effect that the Church of England was both Catholic and Reformed. Reflecting the sovereign's temperate mind and moderate policy, the Church was neither to revert to Rome nor to advance to meet Protestant Geneva. Yet because this Settlement embodied the deepest traits and tendencies of a great people, it was far more than a temporary remedy invented by statecraft. It gave outward shape to what has since been recognized as essential in the nature of Anglicanism—loyalty to a Catholic past in creeds and polity, and glad appropriation of the fruits of reform not only in freedom from papal control but in the central place assigned to the Scriptures and in definite changes in doctrine and ritual. . .[6]

In 1549, the Anglican Church gave to the Christian world the Book of Common Prayer, which, with its subsequent revisions, is one of the greatest mediums of public worship and devotion in Christendom. In 1611, it gave the King James or Authorized Version of the Bible—the most influential single book in the English language, and one used among almost all English-speaking Protestants throughout the world.

The seventeenth century was at once the "golden age" of Anglican literature, made illustrious by the Caroline Divines, and the era of Anglicanism's greatest defeat, humiliation, and recovery. Identified with the king and the doctrine of the divine right of kings, it suffered defeat with Charles I in the Civil War, and then was driven underground during the Commonwealth and Protectorate of Cromwell. With the Restoration of Charles II in 1660, episcopacy was re-established under the leadership of Archbishop Laud's disciples; and the Puritans, whether Presbyterians or Independents (Congregationalists and Baptists), withdrew from the Church of England, henceforth to be known as Nonconformists.[7]

The attempt of James II to restore Roman Catholicism as the established religion ended with his flight. Under William and Mary, the Church of England became more aggressive both at home and abroad, and the turn of the century witnessed the establishment of two great missionary societies—the Society for Promoting Christian Knowledge (1699), commonly called the S.P.C.K.,[8] and the Society for the Propagation of the Gospel in Foreign Parts (1701), commonly called the S.P.G. or the Venerable Society[9]—both of them founded by the Rev. Dr. Thomas Bray,[10] and both of which are doing effective work all over the world a quarter of a millennium later.

It is to the S.P.G. that the American Episcopal Church owes most, under God, "for her first foundation and a long continuance of nursing care and protection."

The Anglican Church in Colonial America

The continuous history of American Society begins with the foundation of Jamestown, Virginia, in 1607. The continuous history of the Episcopal Church in America begins at the same time, in the same place, and with the same event. As they say in the radio commercials, no other denomination can make that claim.[11]

This is true enough, but it would be misleading if one assumed from it that Anglicans emigrated to the American colonies in large numbers, or that they were even in a majority in any place outside of Virginia. As a matter of fact, Anglicans were a minority—and an unpopular one—in practically all of the colonies.

In Britain, after the Toleration Act of 1689, religious persecution largely ceased, but the rigid economic and social caste system remained. To improve their economic and social status was reason enough for emigration, whether from Great Britain or from the European Continent. But relatively few Anglicans emigrated, presumably because their economic and social status was satisfactory to them, and there were no Anglicans at all to come from the Continent.

Immediately following the settlement of Jamestown, Robert Hunt, chaplain to the new colony of Virginia, conducted public worship from the Book of Common Prayer, and celebrated the Holy Communion under "an old saile," according to the Anglican rite. A rude log church was among the first buildings erected in the new settlement. The actual establishment of the Anglican Church in Virginia is usually dated from 1619, and it remained the established church until 1784.[12]

When the eighteenth century opened, the Church was still pathetically weak. The turning point came with the founding of the S.P.G., and with the landing at Boston on June 11, 1702, of its first missionaries—George Keith[13] and John Talbot.[14] Technical establishment had come in the four lower counties of New York by the Vestry Act of 1693. Establishment followed in Maryland in 1702; in South Carolina, by acts of 1704 and 1706; and in North Carolina in 1715. But only in Virginia and Maryland was the revenue from taxation sufficient for the support of the clergy. In the other colonies, whether with or without establishment, the S.P.G. had to supplement the salaries of most of the clergy.

During the ensuing four score years, the Venerable Society established work in all of the colonies outside of Virginia and Maryland, maintained over 200 central stations, and supported in whole or in part 353 missionaries, usually with a stipend of £40 to £50 sterling per year for each.[15] It initiated and sustained work of Christianization and education among Indians[16] and Negroes,[17] which, among the former, was continued in Canada when the Mohawks migrated there during the Revolutionary War.

Educationally, the S.P.G. supported many schoolmasters in a time when public schools were unknown, established scores of parochial libraries, and gave thousands of volumes to the libraries of Harvard, Yale, and King's College (now Columbia University), over none of which did it have any control, although King's College had been founded under Anglican influence.

Dr. Thomas Bray and his associates, independently of the S.P.G., founded upwards of fifty lending libraries, and sent 34,000 books and tracts to America in a day when libraries were few indeed and when a book was a cherished treasure.

The letters and reports of these missionaries and schoolmasters to the Society and to the Bishop of London total 50,655 manuscript pages. According to Professor Frank J. Klingberg, an authority on them, they are "the most important single source for an understanding of American character, the processes of Americanization, and the broad story of American culture."[18]

Nevertheless, despite the growth and progress which the first seventy-five years of the eighteenth century witnessed, the Anglican Church in America was a "maimed" church: it was hamstrung in the full exercise of its spiritual powers by the dominance of the state over the mother Church of England, for it was compelled to function without a bishop and without diocesan organization for 177 years.

All of the Anglican colonial churches were supposed to be under the jurisdiction of the Bishop of London, but this relationship was largely nominal. He had no effective control over them except to refuse to license clergymen. Various bishops of that see, beginning with Henry Compton, tried to overcome the handicap by appointing commissaries in the various areas, but being presbyters and not bishops, they were resented, and their efforts were largely nullified. Thus the leadership which a bishop is intended to exercise—in planning and executing the strategy of church expansion, in encouraging worthy clergymen, and in disciplining unworthy clergymen—was almost entirely lacking.

Under Anglican polity and practice, only a bishop can confirm and ordain. Confirmation was never administered in America until after the Revolutionary War; consequently, the Church's sacramental life was at a low ebb, and the principal means of promoting growth in the number and quality of its communicants was denied it.

In order to fulfill its mission, the Church needed to become indigenous. To accomplish this a native ministry was essential. Beginning with the "Dark Day" at Yale College in 1722, when its president, Timothy Cutler, and two of its tutors, Daniel Brown and Samuel Johnson, declared themselves convinced of the necessity of Anglican orders, the colonial Church was increasingly successful in recruiting a native ministry—but at tragic cost. Not only did every candidate have to travel 3,000 miles to London at a heavy charge of approximately £100 sterling, but one out of every five never returned alive, dying either of disease (usually of smallpox, which was endemic in London) or in shipwreck.

The English bishops were willing and anxious to consecrate bishops for America, who should have no civil functions or powers, and who should have no jurisdiction except over Anglicans. But Parliament was adamant in its refusal. Its reasons are clear enough: 1) The parliamentary leaders were religiously indifferent, in a century notorious for deism and latitudinarianism; 2) they suspected that American bishops might increase the sense of colonial independence; 3) the American laymen in the colonies where the Anglican Church was established, were lukewarm if not hostile, fearing that they would have to share with a bishop their control over the Church; and 4) the dissenters both in the colonies and in England raised loud and bitter protests against American bishops, and would not believe Anglican pleas that such bishops would have no civil functions or powers, and no jurisdiction over others than Anglicans. This last factor was the most powerful with Parliament.

Thus the Anglican Church in America was the victim of state control over the Church of England, and its true destiny, like that of the thirteen colonies, could only be achieved by independence of King and Parliament.

The Revolutionary War precipitated the most critical period in the history of the Episcopal Church in America.[19] As Bishop

William White, who lived through it, used to say about that period fifty years later, it was "approaching annihilation."

The Anglican clergy were placed in a cruel dilemma. Every one of them, before ordination both as deacon and as priest, had had to take a special oath of allegiance to the king, which the ministers of no other church in America had had to take.[20] The Book of Common Prayer, which they were bound to use, had prayers for the king and the royal family. The ranks of both clergy and laity were split between loyalists and Whigs: the former believed they must use the Prayer Book unaltered, and therefore closed their churches by the score; the latter believed they were justified in omitting prayers for the king, and kept their churches open as far as hostilities permitted.

Most of the S.P.G. clergy and thousands of the flower of the laity left the country for Great Britain, Canada, or other parts of the empire, never to return. Ordinations practically ceased for a decade, 1776-1785. The Church throughout the South was disestablished, the S.P.G. by 1785 withdrew all financial support, and in the period of its greatest weakness the Church was called upon to support itself.

The tenuous connection with the Bishop of London was broken, and the war left, not an Episcopal Church, but an aggregation of separate congregations, which were the victims of bitter prejudice and "loss of face," and which had no bishops, no constitution, no state or national organization.

The Organization of the American Episcopal Church

To achieve full ecclesiastical independence, to organize an autonomous church, and to attain unity among the separated congregations, three steps were imperative without delay: 1) American bishops must be obtained; 2) a constitution must be framed; 3) the Book of Common Prayer must be adapted to its American environment. It required seven years of persevering, and sometimes contentious effort to accomplish all this.[21]

The process of national organization was initiated by the appearance on August 6, 1782, of a notable pamphlet, *The Case of the Episcopal Churches Considered.* It was written by

William White (1748-1836),[22] a young priest thirty-four years old, who was then rector of Christ Church and St. Peter's, Philadelphia, and chaplain of the Continental Congress. He was destined to be the chief architect and the most influential bishop of the Episcopal Church. His primacy of forty-one years was the longest, and his epsicopate of forty-nine years was the second longest, in its history. Practically every proposal set forth by White in this pamphlet, except that dealing with the perpetuation of the ministry, was incorporated into the Church's constitution, and remains an integral part of it to this day.

White's overall thesis was that the Church should first be organized on a diocesan and national basis, and only then should bishops, if possible, be obtained. The Connecticut clergy, on the other hand, maintained that no national organization should be attempted until bishops were on hand to participate and lead in it. Most of them were converts to the Church, and they were furious at the idea of continuing the ministry without ordination by bishops, and they rejected White's assumption that bishops "cannot at present be had." This latter assumption White based on the ground that the British government would not make peace for many years with the infant republic. In less than four months this assumption was proved wrong, for on November 30, 1782, the preliminary articles of peace were signed in Paris.

On March 25, 1783, five months before the signing of the definitive treaty of peace, ten of the Connecticut clergy gathered secretly in Woodbury, and chose Samuel Seabury (1729-1796)[23] as their bishop, supplied him with testimonials, and requested him to sail for England for consecration.

Seabury spent over a year in England at his own expense seeking episcopal orders, but the Archbishop of Canterbury and his colleagues refused on three grounds: 1) the law forbade the consecration of a bishop who was not a British subject and who could not take the oath of allegiance to the crown; 2) the prime minister, William Pitt, refused to move a change in the law for fear of offending the American government; and 3) the laity had had no part in Seabury's election, and doubt was expressed as to his being properly received and supported as a bishop in America.

Seabury then turned to the bishops of the proscribed Scottish Episcopal Church, and on November 14, 1784, he was consecrated to the episcopate in Aberdeen by Bishops Kilgour, Petrie and Skinner.

Meanwhile, the first interstate meeting looking towards the union of the Episcopal churches had met on May 11, 1784, in New Brunswick, New Jersey, attented by both clergy and laymen. This meeting issued a call for a large meeting to convene in New York in October. This second interstate meeting adopted seven "Fundamental Principles," and called on churchmen in the various states to organize dioceses and to send deputies to the first "general convention," which was appointed for September, 1785.

To the General Conventions of 1785 and 1786, without benefit of the presence of Bishop Seabury or of any deputies from New England, belongs the credit of securing two American bishops in the English line of succession, of drafting the preliminary constitution, and of setting forth the *Proposed Prayer Book*.

In 1786, Parliament passed an act authorizing the Archbishops of England "to consecrate persons being subjects or citizens out of his Majesty's dominions," without requiring them to take the oaths of allegiance and supremacy to the king. But the English bishops did not like some items in the proposed constitution and in the *Proposed Prayer Book* of the embryo Church in America. Changes to satisfy them were made; the General Convention of 1786 signed the testimonials of two bishops-elect—Dr. White of Pennsylvania and Dr. Samuel Provoost (1742-1815) of New York, and on February 4, 1787, they were consecrated in London by the Archbishops of Canterbury and York and two other English bishops.

But the threat of continuing disunity was very real. The

churchmen in New England objected strenuously to the preliminary constitution and the *Proposed Prayer Book,* and resented the aspersions cast on the validity of Bishop Seabury's orders by the General Convention of 1786. Two factors among others saved the day. The *Proposed Prayer Book* was unpopular among the laity of the South as well as of the North, and it was patent that that work would have to be done over. Bishop Seabury, a High Churchman, and Bishop White, a Low Churchman, were both men of good sense; both were opposed to the idea of schism; and they got along famously together.

The General Convention of 1789 was the greatest in the history of the American Episcopal Church. It framed a sound constitution, it revised the Prayer Book to general satisfaction, and it achieved national unity. In its first session, it opened the door for the New England churchmen to attend the second session by declaring unanimously that Bishop Seabury's orders were valid, and by amending the constitution to meet the major objections of Bishop Seabury and his clergy. The latter thereupon signed it, and took their seats in the second session. The first House of Bishops was made up of Seabury and White. Provoost, the latitudinarian, was absent because of illness.

The constitution as finally adopted provided for a General Convention, meeting triennially, as the supreme legislative body of the Church, made up of a House of Bishops and a House of Clerical and Lay Deputies. Thus the laity were given a direct voice and vote in the counsels of the Church. On the state level, each diocese was to have an annual convention, composed of all the clergy and representatives of the laity elected by the parishes, and to be presided over by the bishop.

The new Prayer Book, as the manual of doctrine and worship, retained the Apostles' and Nicene Creeds, but omitted the Athanasian Creed; the historic ministry of bishops, priests and deacons; the historic sacraments; and the Bible as "containing all things necessary to salvation." But in matters of discipline and worship it was considerably revised to suit American needs. It served for a century before it was revised again.

In fulfillment of an agreement with the Archbishop of Canterbury that three American bishops would be consecrated in the English line before White and Provoost would participate in an American consecration, James Madison (1749-1812) of Virginia was consecrated in 1790 by Archbishop Moore and Bishops Porteus of London and Thomas of Rochester.

The American college of bishops now consisted of four—Seabury, White, Provoost and Madison. On September 17, 1792, all four united in consecrating Thomas John Claggett (1742-1816) as first bishop of Maryland. Since then the American succession has been continuous. By the end of 1951, a total of 510 bishops had been consecrated in the American succession.[24]

Revival, Rapid Growth and Expansion

The closing years of the eighteenth century show the lowest low-water mark of the lowest ebb-tide of spiritual life in the history of the American Church.[25]

The recovery of the Episcopal Church during the twenty years following its autonomous organization was so painfully slow that many despaired of its survival. This was due to several factors, the worst being the low estate of religion and education generally. Another was that the bishops had to retain the rectorship of a parish or the presidency of a college to support themselves, and therefore had little time for visitations outside their parishes. A third was the fear of prelacy, which caused the first group of bishops to be over-cautious.

Nevertheless, beginning about 1800, young and able priests were doing such effective work that when some of them were elevated to the episcopate, the turning of the tide became immediately visible. Their consecration was at once a symbol of the revival already under way and a promise of energetic leadership in accelerating that revival.

The period, 1800-1840, was both an era of great bishops and of the development of the most important institutions of the Church of today—Sunday schools, Bible and Prayer Book and tract societies, periodicals, theological seminaries, colleges, boarding schools for boys and girls, organizations of women, and missionary societies.

The consecration in 1811 of John Henry Hobart[26] (1775-1830) of New York and Alexander Viets Griswold[27] (1766-1843) of the Eastern Diocese, which included all of New England except Connecticut, gave to the episcopate two very different men, each of whom was just the right one for his particular jurisdiction. In them were personified the two schools of thought—High Churchmanship and Evangelicalism—which have been the most influential in the Church unto this day.[28]

Hobart was Bishop White's son in the faith and the apple of his eye, but whereas White was almost a lone survivor of eighteenth century Low Churchmanship, Hobart was already a thorough-going High Churchman when he stepped on the stage of history. Magnetic, versatile, physically and intellectually vigorous, a hardy controversialist, he gave to High Churchmanship a characteristic American color.

Like the English Laudians, he was no Calvinist; he believed episcopacy to be of the *esse* of the Church; he had a "high" view of the sacraments, and was the first American bishop to urge upon his clergy, in season and out, the use of confirmation, and was energetic in his travels to administer it. It became the primary agency of conversion to the Episcopal Church. Although a strict constructionist in the use of the Prayer Book, he was no "high and dry" churchman. In a day when read sermons were the rule, he was an extempore preacher of great power, combining an emotional warmth with doctrinal assurance. Like a great military strategist, he believed that the best defense was to attack, and not only the whole state of New York but the entire Episcopal Church felt the vigor of his personality.

The General Theological Seminary was founded by the General Convention in 1817.[29] After its removal to New York City in 1821, Hobart championed it, and it largely reflected his churchmanship, as it still does. In 1822, Geneva (now Hobart) College was founded by him in Geneva, New York.

Griswold was a pioneer Evangelical, but he was much more gentle than most of his colleagues and successors. His wisdom, humility and benign leadership disarmed much of the Puritan prejudice and bitterness against the Church, and evoked from an old Congregationalist the tribute: "He is the best representative of an apostle that I have seen, particularly because he does not know it."

The Evangelicals were Calvinists; justification by faith was a basic doctrine. With them the Bible came first, the Church second; episcopacy was not of the *esse* but of the *bene esse* of the Church. The sacraments were not as highly regarded by them as by the High Churchmen, although they too administered confirmation with increasing regularity. However, in contrast to eighteenth century Low Churchmanship, personal conversion of a strong but controlled emotional character was stressed, and confirmation was looked upon as the sign and seal of such conversion. They held, with Anglican Evangelicals, in contrast to the Methodists, that schism is a sin. They were liberal constructionists in the use of the Prayer Book, and encouraged extra-Prayer Book services such as informal prayer meetings. Their view of the relation of the Church and Bible was the Achilles' heel of the Evangelical position, and Biblical criticism was to reveal it.

What non-Episcopalians have difficulty in understanding is why, when two such pugnacious schools of thought battle for supremacy, the Episcopal Church is not rent in twain. The answer is threefold: 1) Both schools believe that schism is a sin, and must not be allowed to happen; 2) however strongly convinced of the rightness of their respective positions, each possesses a basic humility and realization that it does not have a monopoly of the truth; 3) the truth will prevail, and, under the doctrine of tension, God the Holy Spirit will resolve the conflict by leading all schools into a larger room of truth. In other words, each school learns from the other, and if the underlying unity is broken, disaster results to the schismatics, as was proved later by the schism of the Reformed Episcopal group in the 1870's.

The Church's revival in the South began in South Carolina under the leadership of Theodore Dehon (1776-1817), who was made bishop in 1812. In 1790 an effort had been made to organize a diocese in North Carolina, but it failed, and the Church languished there until 1817, when a diocesan organization was effected. In 1823, John Stark Ravenscroft (1772-1830), a convert to the Church, became its first bishop and a power in the state until his untimely death.

Not content with disestablishing the Church in 1784, the Virginia legislature in 1802 confiscated the glebes, and the Episcopal Church was well nigh prostrated. Its revival was led by "young reformers," of whom William Holland Wilmer (1782-1827) was the chief. They secured the election of Richard Channing Moore (1762-1841), an eloquent and persuasive preacher, as the second bishop of Virginia. Within ten years, the Church's recovery was so substantial that the Virginia Theological Seminary was established, and immediately became the leading Evangelical school for the training of the clergy, which it is to this day. By 1829, episcopal assistance had become necessary, and William Meade (1789-1862) was made assistant bishop, and in 1841 succeeded Moore as diocesan. Meade is generally considered to have been the greatest of Virginia bishops.

New Jersey was a diocese without a bishop for thirty years. In 1815, John Croes (1762-1832), of Polish ancestry and a convert to the Church, was consecrated as its first bishop, and during his episcopate he strengthened foundations he had as a priest done much to lay. His successor, George Washington Doane (1799-1859), was the greatest of New Jersey bishops. He was Hobart's successor as the leader of the High Churchmen, and a pioneer in the higher education of women.

The disestablishment of the Congregational Church in Connecticut in 1818 presented an opportunity which the Episcopalians seized by electing the next year Thomas Church Brownell (1779-1865) as the third bishop of that diocese. In 1823, he secured a charter for Washington (now Trinity) College, of which he was president until 1831.

The time required to recover the lost ground on the eastern seaboard delayed too long the expansion of the Church across the Alleghenies, whither emigrants had been streaming before the close of the Revolutionary War. In 1821, the Domestic and Foreign Missionary Society had been organized, but its efforts for fifteen years were feeble. Meanwhile, some intrepid missionaries, without support from any missionary society, had been moving into the Ohio valley and planting the Church where they could.

Philander Chase (1775-1852), a born missionary, had been converted at Dartmouth College by reading the Book of Common Prayer, and brought most of his family over with him. In 1819, the expansion of the Church over the mountains received recognition by his consecration as first bishop of Ohio, where in 1824 he founded Kenyon College. In 1831 he resigned that jurisdiction, and in 1835 accepted election as first bishop of Illinois. There he founded Jubilee College, which, however, has not survived.

James Hervey Otey (1800-1863) was a pioneer missionary and schoolmaster in Tennessee, and in 1834 became its first bishop. Although he is formally listed as a diocesan bishop, he was one of the greatest missionary bishops the Southwest ever had. He journeyed on horseback through Florida, Louisiana, Mississippi, Arkansas and Indian Territory, in addition to the unfailing discharge of his duties in Tennessee.

In 1830, the Episcopal Church was still a small affair. It could count but 12 bishops in 20 dioceses, 600 clergy, and 30,000 communicants—mostly confined to the Atlantic seaboard. In the ensuing decade the number of clergy and communicants practically doubled. By 1840, for the first time in its existence, its influence began to be felt somewhat generally in the community.

During the century, 1830-1930, its rate of increase in communicants was almost five times that of the population of the United States. In 1930, it had 152 bishops; 105 dioceses, of which 32 were missionary districts; 6,300 clergy and 8,250 parishes and missions; 500,000 Sunday school scholars; and almost 2,000,000 members, of whom over 1,260,000 were communicants. It was a going concern wherever the flag of the United States was unfurled, and it had several flourishing foreign missionary districts. Whereas in 1830 only one out of every 415 persons in the United States was a communicant of the Episcopal Church, in 1930 that ratio had improved to one communicant out of every 97 persons in the total population.[30]

For forty years, 1890-1930, the rate of growth in relation to the total population was considerably lessened by the great increase in immigration from Continental Europe, none of which was Episcopalian.[31] With the practical cessation of immigration during the decade 1930-40, an immediate improvement in the ratio of communicants was visible. In 1950, that ratio was one communicant among every 91 persons of the total population; in the United States it had 2,500,000 members, of whom 1,640,000 were communicants. Its baptisms were totalling over 100,000 per year; its confirmations, over 85,000 per year; its church schools numbered 62,000 teachers and 540,000 scholars; and annual contributions amounted to over $80,000,000.[32] But World War II had seriously interfered with the recruiting of the ministry. Although the theological seminaries were full to overflowing, the Church was still having difficulty in manning its congregations.

Bishop Thomas M. Clark of Rhode Island, writing his *Reminiscences* in the 1890's and looking back over sixty years, assessed some of the causes for the rapid growth, beginning in the 1830's, of the Episcopal Church, to which he was a convert and in which in 1836 he had been ordained:

Several causes combined to excite an interest in the Episcopal Church, especially in New England, where the breaking up of the established *regime* was more conspicuous than anywhere else. The rigid yoke of New England puritanism had become intolerable, but in seeking relief from the iron bonds of Calvinism a large proportion of both ministers and people had cast aside some of the fundamental doctrines of the Christian faith. There ensued a movement toward the Episcopal Church by those who wished to throw off the shackles of a harsh and complicated creed, and by others who, having sought for freedom in their own inherited domain, found themselves floating off into the wide sea of indifference and unbelief, and still were not prepared to deny entirely the divinity of the Being from whom the Christian Church takes its name. The breadth of this Church attracted the former, and its stability gave confidence to the latter.

The simple service of the old Puritan worship was becoming barren and wearisome, as the original fervor which inspired it died out, and the short prayer and the long prayer, with two or three of Watts' hymns, and perhaps a chapter from the Bible once on the Sunday, did not quite satisfy the average worshipper. There was a growing desire on the part of many persons to participate in the forms of worship that had existed in the ages all along, strengthened by the feeling that it did not seem expedient to depend entirely upon the intellectual ability or the spiritual mood of the minister to formulate the devotions of the congregation . . .[33]

Also, he adds, the organization and government of the Episcopal Church "attracted considerable attention . . . because of its inherent fitness and conformity to the general order of things—the constitution of the civil government and of all other societies and corporations."[34]

Resentment against the institution of new and unscriptural tests of communion by many religious bodies—anti-masonic, anti-slavery, total abstinence, and the like—"induced a certain amount of emigration toward the Episcopal Church, while some of the ministers of various denominations looked thitherward as a field for greater independence and freedom."[35]

The Church itself adopted a more aggressive and effective missionary policy. The General Convention of 1835,[36] one of the greatest in the Church's history, overhauled the Domestic and Foreign Missionary Society, and set forth two simple but revolutionary principles to be acted on in the future: 1) Every baptized member of the Church was declared to be a member of the missionary society, and 2) bishops would be sent to the frontier by the whole Church and not wait until they were asked for. Jackson Kemper[37] (1789-1870) was then and there elected for the Northwest, and in 1838 Leonidas Polk[38] (1806-1864) was consecrated for the Southwest.

Although plagued by the lack of enough men and money for his immense field, Kemper made a remarkable record. He began his episcopate with one clergyman and no church building in Indiana, and with one church building and no clergyman in Missouri. When in 1859 he resigned his missionary jurisdiction to serve the rest of his life as diocesan of Wisconsin, he could report to the General Convention of that year a very different state of affairs in his original area of responsibility: In Missouri, a bishop and 27 clergy; in Indiana, a bishop and 25 clergy; in Wisconsin, himself and 55 clergy; in Iowa, a bishop and 31 clergy; in Minnesota, a bishop and 20 clergy; in Kansas, 10 clergy, who were to have their own bishop five years later; in Nebraska, 4 clergy, with Joseph C. Talbot as his successor in a new jurisdiction of the Northwest. Moreover, two theological seminaries had been established under the leadership of James Lloyd Breck (1818-1876): Nashotah House in 1842 in Wisconsin, and Seabury Divinity School in 1858 in Minnesota. The latter in now Seabury-Western Theological Seminary in Evanston, Illinois.

Polk had been converted while a cadet at West Point under the preaching of Charles P. McIlvaine (1799-1873), silver tongued orator and intellectual leader of the Evangelicals, who in 1832 had succeeded Chase as bishop of Ohio. Polk began his episcopate as both a domestic and foreign missionary bishop, for Texas was then not a part of the United States. In 1841 he accepted his election as first bishop of Louisiana. He was the prime mover in founding the University of the South, Sewanee, Tennessee, for which the present site was obtained and $500,000 raised. Polk laid the cornerstone of the first building on October 9, 1860. On the urgent pleading of Jefferson Davis, Polk accepted a general's commission in the Confederate army, and was killed at Pine Mountain, near Marietta, Georgia.

It was also in this notable decade, 1830-1840, that the first missionaries of the Episcopal Church were sent abroad—to the Near East, China, and Liberia. Since then missionary work has been undertaken in every state and territory under the American flag; in Japan, Latin America, and the Philippines. In Southern Brazil there are now three missionary districts, and one each in Mexico, Cuba, Haiti, and the Dominican Republic.

Two principles have governed this Church's missionary policy abroad: 1) To cooperate and not to compete with other branches of the Anglican Communion in the foreign field; and 2) to recruit native ministries and to organize autonomous churches as rapidly as wise administration will permit. In 1887, the *Nippon Seikokwai,* or the Holy Catholic Church in Japan, was organized. It is now entirely under the control of Japanese bishops, clergy, and laymen. In 1912, the *Chung Hua Sheng Kung,* or the Holy Catholic Church in China, was formed by a union of English, Canadian and American districts in one Church. Only native Chinese bishops and clergy remain at the present time to administer it, and to bring it through the present travail.

Theological Developments

The objects of the Oxford Movement (and for the most part still operative) were: 1) To vindicate the Catholic position of the Church of England; 2) to reassert its identity with the pre-Reformation Church in England; 3) to insist on the continuity of its apostolic succession; 4) to exalt episcopal order; 5) to emphasize the importance of the sacraments; 6) to enhance the ideal of the priesthood.[39]

The Oxford Movement, which began in 1833, made little impression in America, for some unexplainable reason, until the 1840's, but from then on it has profoundly affected the Episcopal Church.

The objects of the movement had been in considerable measure anticipated by Bishop Hobart and his followers, but paradoxically, Hobartian High Churchmanship has been such a severe brake on Anglo-Catholicism, which developed out of the Oxford Movement, that it has never in its advanced types mustered the power in America which it possesses in England. John Henry Hopkins, Jr., was later to assert that "the greatest enemy of true Catholicism in the American Church was not the Evangelical party, but the old High Church faction."[40] The movement not only split the High Church school into two groups, but it placed such a strain on the loyalty of the Evangelicals that, a generation later, the Low Church wing of that school seceded to form the Reformed Episcopal Church.

The decade of the 1840's saw party strife reaching regrettable proportions in several American denominations, and the Episcopal Church did not escape, although it was spared for the time being from the sin of schism. The Evangelicals squared off for battle, led intellectually by Bishop Charles P. McIlvaine of Ohio. Not content with an academic battle, the legislative councils of the Church were torn with partisan maneuvering. The General Convention finally rendered a verdict of "toleration," but not until stark tragedy, in particular the suspension of Bishop Benjamin T. Onderdonk, had been inflicted on the Church.

Many converts to the Episcopal Church had been reared in very narrow forms of Protestantism. Once having grasped the "church idea," some completely lost their balance, and under the impact of the *Tracts for the Times,* they were swept into the totalitarian concept of the Church as represented by Roman Catholicism. Between 1818 and 1855—approximately a generation—thirty clergymen of the Episcopal Church seceded to Rome. Of these, four had seceded prior to the Tractarian period, and four who seceded returned to the Episcopal Church; thus the permanent loss directly due to the first stage of the movement was twenty-two.

Meanwhile, William Augustus Muhlenberg (1796-1877), a convert from Lutheranism and the greatest presbyter of his generation, was reflecting on ways and means of breaking down the social snobbery which afflicted the Episcopal Church. The famous Muhlenberg Memorial of 1853, presented to the House of Bishops, sought to widen the ministrations of the Church to reach the common people more effectively, especially with respect to a greater degree of liturgical freedom. Not much resulted from it at the time, but many of its proposals were prophetic, and some were adopted years later.

The Civil War was another crucial test of the unity of the Episcopal Church. When the Southern states seceded, Southern churchmen organized in 1861 the *Protestant Episcopal Church in the Confederate States of America.* If their premise be granted, namely, that a new nation had been founded, Southern churchmen were quite justified on Anglican principles in establishing a separate national church. But the outcome of the Civil War nullified the premise, and the grave question was, "Will the Southern dioceses return to union with the General Convention of the Protestant Episcopal Church in the United States of America?" It was a powerful testimonial to the strength of the "church idea," and to the belief that schism is a sin, that all of them did return immediately. In contrast, reunion among the Methodists was not achieved until 1939, and the Presbyterians and the Baptists are still divided.

The explosive point of the intellectual revolution of the nineteenth century was the publication in 1859 of Darwin's

Origin of Species, and great was the distress and turmoil in all churches.[41] The very next year, Anglican circles were particularly wrought up by the book, *Essays and Reviews,* with the publication of which the Broad Church Movement may be dated.

The Evangelicals, already sorely beset by the Tractarians, were now under attack from a more fatal quarter. Their intellectual position was never very strong, and one of their fundamental principles was particularly vulnerable. This was that "Scripture had an antecedent character" in relation to the Church. If, as Biblical criticism asserted, the Bible is not infallible, then the Evangelical position was undermined.

Potentially, the High Churchmen had a stronger position than the Evangelicals in that they held the authority of the Church to be primary, since members of the Church wrote the Bible, and the Church had determined which books were inspired and which were not, thus fixing the canon of Scripture. But the High Churchmen joined forces with the Evangelicals in denouncing Biblical criticism, because the latter raised embarrassing questions as to the Person of Christ.

The Broad Church school sought to adapt the Church's doctrines to the findings of science and Biblical criticism. Its principal leader in America was Phillips Brooks (1835-1892), the greatest preacher the Episcopal Church has produced. By 1868 he had determined to come to grips with the intellectual revolution, and in his great ministry in Trinity Church, Boston, he did. In the stronghold of Unitarianism, he never became a Unitarian; on the contrary he converted thousands from Unitarianism. All his preaching was centered in the gospel that "God is love," and he perceived that the doctrine of the Trinity is the necessary intellectual expression of that gospel.

Beginning in 1889, under the leadership of Charles Gore (1853-1932) and the *Lux Mundi* school, Anglo-Catholicism was delivered from obscurantism, and the reality of Democratic Catholicism was demonstrated by showing that a believer in the Catholic faith did not have to hide his head in the sand in the face of new knowledge.

Just when the Evangelicals made their intellectual adjustment it is impossible to date, but by the end of the first decade of the twentieth century practically all theological seminaries were teaching the assured results of Biblical criticism and accepting the findings of science.

Contemporaneous with the intellectual revolution, which was stirring up the Church from without, was the Ritualistic Controversy, which was shaking the Church from within.

The first Tractarians were not at all concerned with ceremonial, or with what is popularly called "ritual." But their Anglo-Catholic successors sought to give visual expression, by means of ceremonial, ornaments, music and architecture, to the teachings of the Oxford Movement. The laity, who had been largely indifferent to the theological battles of the earlier generation so long as they were on an academic plane, were now thoroughly aroused by the changes taking place before their eyes in their houses of worship.

As a matter of fact, ritualism was introduced into the American Church by William Augustus Muhlenberg, who was not an Anglo-Catholic, but who, having used it as a matter of course in Lutheranism, desired it in the Episcopal churches under his pastoral care.

The Ritual Controversy in its acute stages lasted from 1868 to 1874, and occupied a good deal of time in three sessions of the General Convention. Under the leadership of James De Koven (1831-1879) of Wisconsin, who dominated the great debate in the General Convention of 1871, the attempt "to strike at the doctrine of the Real Presence" was defeated; but in 1874 the so-called "ritual canon" was passed. It was practically a dead letter from the moment of its adoption, and in the general revision of the canons in 1904, this canon was quietly dropped in its entirety.

The Reformed Episcopal Church

Evangelical men had contended for the right to act and live—yes, to live and act as freely as any other in this Church of ours, and this right they had secured. They were in full possession of it, and that was enough. I felt that as under civil government there could be various parties, while all could be good citizens, so under our ecclesiastical system there could be divers schools, and yet all could be good Christians. Only let these schools enjoy their inalienable rights, and then all could dwell together in harmony and peace.[42]

Beginning in the 1860's, the Evangelical school, for the reasons already given, was in a ferment. Some became High Churchmen; a larger number became Broad Churchmen; the majority retained their Evangelical beliefs in the spirit expounded above by Heman Dyer, one of their ablest presbyters; but a militant minority became the Low Church wing, who seceded in 1873 to found the Reformed Episcopal Church.[43]

In the winter of 1867, during the annual meeting of the Evangelical societies in Philadelphia, the Low Churchmen were in open rebellion against the leadership of the veteran Evangelicals—Bishops Charles P. McIlvaine of Ohio, John Johns of Virginia, Alfred Lee of Delaware, Manton Eastburn of Massachusetts, and such presbyters as Alexander H. Vinton, John Cotton Smith, Richard Newton and Heman Dyer.

The more prominent leaders of the Low Churchmen were George David Cummins (1822-1876), assistant bishop of Kentucky, Charles E. Cheney of Chicago, Franklin S. Rising, secretary and agent of the American Church Missionary Society (organized by the Evangelicals in opposition to the official Domestic and Foreign Missionary Society of the Church), and Stephen H. Tyng, Jr., of New York City. Rising was killed in a steamboat explosion in 1868, and the younger Tyng did not, when the test came, secede.

The demands of the Low Church crystallized along four lines:

1) That they should be allowed to preach everywhere and anywhere without regard "to false interpretations of canonical law." This would involve changes in the canon "against intrusion," which forbade a minister to officiate in another man's parish without the latter's consent.

2) That non-episcopal ministers should be allowed to preach and celebrate the Holy Communion in Episcopal churches, which would require modification of the canons forbidding such actions.

3) The Book of Common Prayer must be radically revised. The Low Churchmen contended that the Anglican reformers and their successors had retained errors in the Prayer Book which must be expurgated. In August 1868, a pamphlet appeared, entitled *Are There Romanizing Germs in the Prayer Book?*, written by Franklin S. Rising, but without his name attached. The answer to the question was an emphatic "Yes," and included a bill of particulars as to the revision needed in the Ordinal, the office of Institution, of Baptism and the Holy Communion, and even the Catechism.

4) Ritual as then being practiced must be suppressed.

In 1867, the younger Tyng had been convicted under the canon against intrusion, and had been admonished by Bishop Horatio Potter of New York. In 1869, Cheney was convicted of making unauthorized changes in using the Prayer Book, and was suspended. When he ignored the sentence, he was tried again on charges of contumacy and deposed by Bishop Henry J. Whitehouse of Illinois.

By the end of 1870, the radical Low Churchmen were contemplating the extreme step of founding a new church if the General Convention of 1871 denied them what they asked. They fully expected that there would be a large exodus of laymen. But the General Convention of 1871 did not give them what they demanded. All it gave them was a Declaration from the House of Bishops that in the office of Baptism of Infants "the word 'regenerate' is not there so used as to determine that a moral change in the subject of baptism is wrought in the recipient." This was far from satisfying Bishop Cummins and his associates.

On November 10, 1873, Bishop Cummins wrote his diocesan, Bishop Benjamin Bosworth Smith of Kentucky, announcing his withdrawal from the Episcopal Church. Three days later he issued a circular letter, calling for a meeting of likeminded people the next month in New York. No doubt was left in the letter as to the purpose of the meeting:

> The purpose of the meeting is to *organize,* and not to discuss the expediency of organizing. The verbatim reprint of the Prayer Book of 1785 is in the press, and will be issued during the month of December.[44]

On December 2, 1873, eight clergymen, including Bishop Cummins, and nineteen laymen met in response to the call. Five of the eight clergymen had been deposed from the ministry of the Protestant Episcopal Church at various times prior to the meeting. The organization of the new Church was effected by the following resolution:

> *Resolved,* That we whose names are appended to the call for this meeting, as presented by Bishop Cummins, do here and now, in humble reliance upon Almighty God, organize ourselves into a Church, to be known by the style and title of *"The Reformed Episcopal Church,"* in conformity with the following *Declaration of Principles,* and with the Right Reverend George David Cummins, D.D., as our Presiding Bishop.[45] [Italics in the original.]

The *Declaration of Principles* contained as its heart the *Proposed Prayer Book* of 1785, which was never officially authorized for use in the Protestant Episcopal Church. Although Bishop Cummins had praised this book in his call, it was not exempt from fundamental changes by the first General Council of the Reformed Episcopal Church, not only in phraseology but also in doctrine.

The Catechism was left out entirely; the Preface to the Ordinal was omitted; so also were such words as "priest," "sacrament," "mysteries," "altar," "Holy Communion of the Body and Blood of Christ." In the Baptismal Office, "regenerate" in all its forms was deleted. Episcopacy was recognized and adhered to, "not as of divine right, but as a very ancient and desirable form of church polity"; and the episcopate was considered to be merely an office, and not a separate order, a bishop being only first among his fellow presbyters.

The number of seceders, both clerical and lay, from the Protestant Episcopal Church was disappointing to the founders of the new Church. Charles D. Kellogg, one of the laymen present at the organization meeting, writing some years later for the standard *History of the Reformed Episcopal Church* stated:

> It did seem surprising to the laymen, not quite a score in number, who assembled in the Y.M.C.A. parlors in New York City, on that memorable second of December, 1873, that of the hundreds who with them for years had longed and prayed for some sign of effective resistance to the encroachments of sacerdotalism and its concomitant errors, so very few were ready to respond when the door of escape from them was so graciously opened. . . .[46]

According to the *Hand Book of the Reformed Episcopal Church, 1901*, that Church had 64 churches, 99 clergymen, and 10,000 communicants. Fifty years later, according to the *Yearbook of American Churches 1951*, it had 71 churches and 8,928 members; and 66 Sunday schools, with a total enrollment of 5,234 pupils, officers and teachers. There are four bishops, but the total number of ordained clergy is not given.

The Episcopal Church From 1875 to 1950

About the beginning of the last quarter of the nineteenth century, the social gospel began to receive increasing emphasis, initially characterized by the building of parish houses, church hospitals, orphanages, homes for the aged, and settlement houses. This quickened consciousness and sensitivity to the needs of a rapidly changing religious, social and industrial order, received significant expression during the first five decades of the twentieth century.[47]

After years of careful preparation and the raising of an initial sum of $8,000,000 under the able leadership of Bishop William Lawrence (1850-1941) of Massachusetts, The Church Pension Fund was established in 1917. This enables aged and disabled clergymen to receive a pension, not as charity, but as deferred salary. It was the first soundly based pension system on such a scale in America, and its methods have been widely followed by other churches both at home and abroad— particularly, by other branches of the Anglican Communion, including the mother Church of England.

The General Convention of 1919 was the greatest since that of 1835, for two reasons: 1) By launching the Nation-wide Campaign in that year, it materially raised the standard of the Church's giving for benevolences as well as for local parish support; and 2) by creating the National Council, with an elected Presiding Bishop as its head, and with missions, religious education, and social service coordinated under it, the Church had an executive agency such as it had never had in its history.

The Prayer Book of 1789 served the Church for a century without important changes. The need for enrichment and greater flexibility, in the light of new liturgical knowledge and rapid social change, resulted in a limited revision in 1892. A generation later, in 1928, after fifteen years of painstaking work, the Book of Common Prayer was thoroughly revised and enriched, with the result that the Church now has the finest manual of worship and devotion it has ever had.

When the Church became autonomous in 1789, church music was largely confined to the singing of the psalms. During the nineteenth century, church music in general and hymnody in particular made great strides. The *Hymnal of 1892,* which was something of a companion volume to the Prayer Book revised that year, was supplanted by the *New Hymnal of 1916.* Although this latter book marked a great advance in the Church's music, it had serious limitations as a congregational hymnal. *The Hymnal 1940,* adopted by the General Convention of that year, has received high praise both at home and abroad, and is generally considered to be the finest hymnal for congregational use which this Church has thus far possessed.

In 1934, in the midst of the nation's worst economic depression, the Forward Movement was authorized to "reinvigorate the life of the Church and to rehabilitate its work." Its mission was the stimulation of the spiritual life and the development of personal devotion, operating through established channels, especially the parishes. Its publications have circulated in the millions, and have done much to strengthen personal religion.

As far back as the middle of the nineteenth century, the Episcopal Church had interested itself in the cause of Christian reunion. It initiated the *Chicago-Lambeth Quadrilateral* of 1888, which was originally adopted by the House of Bishops during the General Convention of 1886, and accepted with some modifications by the Lambeth Conference two years later. This declaration proposed four points as a basis for unity: the Holy Scriptures as the Word of God; the Apostles' and Nicene Creeds as the rule of faith; the two sacraments of Baptism and the Holy Communion; and the episcopate as the central principle of church government.

The General Convention of 1910 appointed a commission to arrange for a World Conference of Faith and Order. Charles Henry Brent (1862-1929), first Missionary Bishop of the Philippine Islands, Chaplain-General of the American Expeditionary Forces of World War I, and then Bishop of Western New York, was the outstanding leader of the first such conference, which was held in 1927 in Lausanne. The second was held in 1937 in Edinburgh, which was immediately followed by another great conference on Life and Work at Oxford. Friendly discussions on reunion in all parts of the world have been stimulated, and a World Council of Churches has been organized.

Conclusion

At "half past fifty," Christianity all over the world is in a life and death struggle with secularism. While secularism, strictly speaking, is a philosophy of life which rejects all forms of religious faith and worship, it possesses in Communism, its apotheosis, attributes of religious zeal and devotion, rising at times to fanaticism, and proclaiming science as its messiah. All fear of God has been thrown off by millions of people, and in its place man is creating a world in which fear of the future, of man for man, is more terrifying than any fear of the hereafter which the fire and brimstone preachers in their palmiest days were able to generate.

In this struggle, the American Episcopal Church, along with all other American Churches, has both a national and an international responsibility. To an Anglican, as to an American Episcopalian, the word "Protestant" is an adjective, signifying that the Church always stands under judgment and is always in need of reform. We hope that it is apparent to readers of this essay that the Episcopal Church is conscious of standing under judgment and of always being in need of reform. Its very controversies, its Evangelical Movement, its Oxford Movement, its Broad Church Movement, and all that followed in their train are testimonies to its consciousness of always being in need of reform.

We hope, also, that it is clearly evident that this Church, with all its faults, is infinitely stronger today than it was at the end of the Revolutionary War, and therefore better able today to discharge its responsibilities to America and the world than it was in the former time. Since God in His wisdom elected to save this Church from "annihilation," it would appear that it has certain values to contribute to America and the world, which no other Church was quite able to supply. Perhaps its example of unity in diversity, its respect for authority combined with freedom of the individual, its doctrine of tension (*i.e.,* in case of controversy, not splitting up into sects, but of waiting patiently for the Holy Spirit to reveal the truth) are three such values.

The genius of the Anglican Communion in general, and of the American Episcopal Church in particular, is its stress on "balance," and is well summed up in some lines of Robert Bridges from his *Testament of Beauty*:

> We sail a changeful sea through halcyon days and storm,
> and when the ship laboureth, our steadfast purpose
> trembles like as the compass in a binnacle.
> Our stability is but balance, and conduct lies
> in masterful administration of the unforseen.

NOTES

[1] J. S. HIGGINS, *The Anglican Communion Today* (Philadelphia, 1947), p. 6. For other references on the Anglican Communion *see below,* the Bibliography.

[2] WALTER H. STOWE, "The Trail Blazer in the Expansion of the Anglican Communion," *The Historiographer, 1946* (Philadelphia, 1946), pp. 3-12.

[3] For this section, *see* HENRY O. WAKEMAN, *An Introduction to the History of the Church of England from the Earliest Times to the Present Day* (London, 7th ed., 1904), 505 pp.

[4] For the Reformation period, *see* P. M. DAWLEY, *Highlights of Church History: The Reformation* (Philadelphia, 1949); *also,* the Bibliography *below.*

[5] J. T. ADDISON, *The Episcopal Church in the United States, 1789-1931* (New York, 1951), p. 5.

[6] *Ibid.,* p. 8.

[7] R. S. BOSHER, *The Making of the Restoration Settlement: The Influence of the Laudians, 1649-1662* (New York, 1951), pp. 309.

[8] S. C. McCULLOCH, "The Foundation and Early Work of the S. P. C. K.," *Historical Magazine of the Protestant Episcopal Church,* XVIII (1949), 3-22.

[9] F. J. KLINGBERG (editor), "The S. P. G. 250th Anniversary Number," *Historical Magazine of the Protestant Episcopal Church,* XX (1951), 117-240.

[10] J. W. LYDEKKER, "Thomas Bray (1658-1730): Founder of Missionary Enterprise," *Historical Magazine . . .,* XII (1943), 186-214.

[11] W. W. MANROSS, "The Church in Virginia," *Historical Magazine . . .,* XVI (1947), 132.

[12] G. MacLAREN BRYDON, *Virginia's Mother Church* (Richmond, 1947), p. 67.

[13] *See* "The Rev. George Keith Number," *Historical Magazine . . .,* XX (1951), 343-487.

[14] *See* E. L. PENNINGTON, *Apostle of New Jersey: John Talbot, 1645-1727* (Philadelphia, 1938), pp. 217.

[15] *See* C. F. PASCOE, *Two Hundred Years of the S. P. G.* (London, 1901), pp. 849-856.

16 See F. J. KLINGBERG, *Anglican Humanitarianism in Colonial New York* (Philadelphia, 1940), pp. 11-120.

17 *Ibid.*, pp. 121-186; *also*, F. J. KLINGBERG, *An Appraisal of the Negro in Colonial South Carolina* (Washington, 1941), pp. 180.

18 F. J. KLINGBERG, "Contributions of the S. P. G. to the American Way of Life," *Historical Magazine . . .*, XII (1943), 220-221.

19 See WALTER H. STOWE, "The Critical Period in the History of the American Episcopal Church," *Historical Magazine . . .*, XX (1951), 243-251.

20 See WALTER H. STOWE, "A Study in Conscience: Some Aspects of the Relations of the Clergy to the State," *Historical Magazine . . .*, XIX (1950), 300-323. The oath is on p. 303.

21 For this section, *see* "The Development of the Church's Constitution," *Historical Magazine . . .*, VIII (1939), 177-303.

22 WALTER H. STOWE (editor), *The Life and Letters of Bishop William White* (Philadelphia, 1937), pp. 306.

23 See "The Bishop Seabury Number," *Historical Magazine . . .*, III (1934), 121-225; E. E. BEARDSLEY, *Life and Correspondence of the Rt. Rev. Samuel Seabury, D.D.* (Boston, 1881), pp. 498; W. J. SEABURY, *Memoir of Bishop Seabury* (New York, 1908), pp. 453.

24 *Living Church Annual, 1952* (New York, 1951), pp. 366-385.

25 L. W. BACON, *A History of American Christianity* (New York, 1897), p. 231.

26 JOHN MCVICKAR, *The Early Life and Professional Years of Bishop Hobart* (2 vols., New York, 1836). A 20th century biography of Bishop Hobart is much needed.

27 JOHN S. STONE, *Memoir of the Life of the Rt. Rev. Alexander Viets Griswold, D.D.* (Philadelphia, 1844), pp. 620; *also,* W. W. MANROSS, "Bishop Griswold and the Eastern Diocese," *Historical Magazine . . .*, IV (1935), pp. 13-25.

28 For these two schools of thought, their leaders, and their later developments, *see* E. C. CHORLEY, *Men and Movements in the American Episcopal Church* (New York, 1946), pp. 501; GEORGE E. DEMILLE, *The Catholic Movement in the American Episcopal Church* (Philadelphia, 2nd ed., 1950), pp. 219; A. C. ZABRISKIE (ed.), *Anglican Evangelicalism* (Philadelphia, 1943), pp. 283. For biographical sketches of other leaders mentioned in this section, see *Dictionary of American Biography.*

29 See "The General Theological Seminary Number," *Historical Magazine . . .*, V (1936), 145-264.

30 *Living Church Annual, 1952*, p. 28.

31 See WALTER H. STOWE, "Immigration and the Growth of the Episcopal Church," *Historical Magazine . . .*, XI (1942), 330-361.

32 *Living Church Annual, 1952*, pp. 22-23.

33 THOMAS M. CLARK, *Reminiscences* (New York, 2nd ed., 1895), pp. 32-33.

34 *Ibid.*, p. 34.

35 *Ibid.*, p. 35.

36 See WALTER H. STOWE, "A Turning Point: The General Convention of 1835," *Historical Magazine . . .*, IV (1935), 152-179.

37 See "The Bishop Kemper Number," *Historical Magazine . . .*, IV (1935), 129-244.

38 See "The Bishop Polk Number," *Historical Magazine . . .*, VII (1938), 303-418.

THE PROTESTANT EPISCOPAL CHURCH IN THE U. S. A.

39 W. H. STOWE, *The Essence of Anglo-Catholicism* (New York, 1942), p. 12. For this whole section, *see above,* the references given under Note 28.

40 GEORGE E. DEMILLE, *op. cit.,* p. 98.

41 *See* W. H. STOWE, *The Intellectual Revolution and the Anglican Communion* (Philadelphia, 1947), pp. 22.

42 HEMAN DYER, *Records of an Active Life* (New York, 1886), pp. 371-372.

43 *See* E. C. CHORLEY, *op. cit.,* pp. 393-424; ANNIE D. PRICE, *A History of the Reformed Episcopal Church, 1873-1902* (Philadelphia, 1902), pp. 308.

44 *Journal of the First General Council of the Reformed Episcopal Church* (New York, 1873), pp. 6-7.

45 *Ibid.,* pp. 7-8.

46 ANNIE D. PRICE, *op. cit.,* p. 288.

47 For more detailed treatment of the period, 1901-1931, *see* J. T. ADDISON, *The Episcopal Church in the United States, 1789-1931* (New York, 1951), pp. 293-378.

BIBLIOGRAPHY

I. THE ANGLICAN COMMUNION

WILLIAM R. CURTIS, *The Lambeth Conferences* (New York, 1942), pp. 355.

J. MCLEOD CAMPBELL, *Christian History in the Making* (London, 1946).

JOHN S. HIGGINS, *The Anglican Communion Today* (Philadelphia, 1947), pp. 41.

WALTER H. STOWE, "The Trail Blazer in the Expansion of the Anglican Communion," *The Historiographer,* Vol. I, No. 6 (Philadelphia, 1946).

J. W. C. WAND, (editor), *The Anglican Communion: A Survey* (London, 1948), pp. 353.

II. THE CHURCH OF ENGLAND

HENRY BETTENSON (editor), *Documents of the Christian Church* (New York & London, 1947), pp. 457.

ROBERT S. BOSHER, *The Making of the Restoration Settlement: The Influence of the Laudians, 1649-1662* (New York, 1951), pp. 309. [The standard work on the period.]

POWEL M. DAWLEY, *Highlights of Church History: The Reformation* (Philadelphia, 1949), pp. 48.

PERCY DEARMER, *Everyman's History of the Prayer Book* (Milwaukee, American Edition, 1931), pp. 268.

LEONARD ELLIOTT-BINNS, *The Reformation in England* (Duckworth, 1937), pp. 244.

CYRIL GARBETT, *The Claims of the Church of England* (London, 1947), pp. 304.

C. F. PASCOE, *Two Hundred Years of the S. P. G., 1701-1900,* 2 vols., (London, 1901).

NORMAN SYKES, *The Crisis of the Reformation* (Unicorn Press, 1938), pp. 176.

H. P. THOMPSON, *Into All Lands: The History of the Society for the Propagation of the Gospel in Foreign Parts, 1701-1950* (London, S. P. C. K., 1951).

HENRY O. WAKEMAN, *An Introduction to the History of the Church of England from the Earliest Times to the Present Day* (London, 7th edition, 1904), pp. 505. [A standard history.]

THE AMERICAN CHURCH

A. T. P. WILLIAMS, *The Anglican Tradition in the Life of England* (London, 1947), pp. 128.

III. THE PROTESTANT EPISCOPAL CHURCH IN THE UNITED STATES OF AMERICA INCLUDING THE COLONIAL PERIOD

NOTE: Several works referred to in the Notes are not repeated here. For special periods, consult the footnote references.

J. THAYER ADDISON, *The Episcopal Church in the United States, 1789-1931* (New York, 1951), pp. 400. [The latest standard history, which carries the story down to later times than most.]

C. RANKIN BARNES, *The General Convention: Offices and Officers, 1785-1950* (Philadelphia, 1951), pp. 148.

G. MACLAREN BRYDON, *Virginia's Mother Church* (Richmond, Virginia, 1947), pp. 571. [Vol. I, 1607-1727; Vol. II is in the press.]

E. CLOWES CHORLEY, *Men and Movements in the American Episcopal Church* (New York, 1946), pp. 501. [Invaluable for the history of thought, controversies, and leaders of the Episcopal Church.]

ARTHUR L. CROSS, *The Anglican Episcopate and the American Colonies* (New York, 1902), pp. 368.

GEORGE E. DEMILLE, *The Catholic Movement in the American Episcopal Church* (Philadelphia, 2nd ed., 1950). [The standard work on the subject.]

Dictionary of American Biography, 20 vols. (New York, Scribner's, 1928-43). [Contains biographical sketches of most of the Americans mentioned in this essay.]

Historical Magazine of the Protestant Episcopal Church, edited by Walter H. Stowe (New Brunswick, N. J., 1932 to date). [21 vols. have been published to date. Indispensable for the latest researches in the history of the Episcopal Church. Consult the Notes above for special references.]

WILLIAM W. MANROSS, *A History of the American Episcopal Church* (New York, 2nd ed., 1950), pp. 404. [A standard history, recently revised.]

————, *The Episcopal Church in the United States, 1800-1840: A Study in Church Life* (New York, 1938), pp. 270.

ALEXANDER C. ZABRISKIE (editor), *Anglican Evangelicalism* (Philadelphia, 1943), pp. 283. [The standard work on the subject.]

IV. THE REFORMED EPISCOPAL CHURCH

A. M. CUMMINS, *Memoir of George David Cummins, D. D., First Bishop of the Reformed Episcopal Church* (New York, 1878), pp. 544. [The author was the wife of Bishop Cummins.]

Journal of the First General Council of the Reformed Episcopal Church, Held in the City of New York, December 2, 1873 (New York, 1873), pp. 26.

ANNIE DARLING PRICE, *A History of the Formation and Growth of the Reformed Episcopal Church, 1873-1902* (Philadelphia, 1902), pp. 308.

VII
THE REFORMED CHURCH IN AMERICA

VII

THE REFORMED CHURCH IN AMERICA

Milton J. Hoffman

For purposes of clarity it will be best in this brief sketch to divide the history of the Reformed Church in America into three periods: 1628-1664, a period of beginnings, ending with England's conquest of New Amsterdam and changing the name to New York; 1664-1771, the period when politically the Church was under English control, and ecclesiastically under the control of the Classis of Amsterdam; 1771 to the present, the period without any foreign restrictions either politically or ecclesiastically.

Period One

In 1609 Hendrik Hudson, an Englishman, in the employ of the Dutch East India Company, in the hope of finding a north-western passage to the East Indies sailed up the river which has ever since borne his name. As the result of this venture trading posts were established at Fort Orange, now Albany, and at Manhattan, now New York. By 1628 there were a sufficient number of Dutch and Walloons in New Amsterdam to form a church. This was done under the leadership of Rev. Jonas Michaelius. This first church was composed of about fifty communicant members. They accepted and were guided by the doctrinal standards and rules of church government formulated at the famous Synod of Dortrecht in 1618-1619.

It should be emphasized that the motive which led to colonization was not to escape religious persecution. Holland was then the refuge for the religiously oppressed people everywhere. The ventures were economic and commercial, the enterprising Dutch hoping to profit from a lucrative fur trade with the Indians. In justice it must be said that the religious welfare of the colonists was not neglected. When the English took over New Amsterdam, thirty-six years after the founding of the first church, there were thirteen churches with eight ministers in active service. The West India Company (successor to the East India Company) had sent over fifteen ministers in all. There were churches in New York, Brooklyn, Harlem, Staten Island, Jersey City (Bergen), Kingston (Esopus), and Albany.

Period Two

Though the Anglican Church naturally became the established church of the colonies, the Dutch Church was allowed considerable liberty. In fact, the slow growth (there were only one hundred churches at the end of this period) of the church is not due primarily to any governmental opposition, but rather to the stubborn insistence on the part of many to retain the use of the Dutch language in public worship, and to the rather arbitrary control of the Classis of Amsterdam which made it impossible to educate and ordain a native ministry.

In fact, this period may be described as a century of conflict—a conflict not about doctrine, but rather about the issue whether or not the Reformed Church should remain exclusively Dutch, or building on its Dutch heritage adapt and adjust itself to a new country and to new possibilities. In 1736 farsighted leaders on this side urged the formation of a Coetus—an organization designed for fraternal conference on the state and wants of the churches, and, in emergencies, empowered to ordain ministers. In 1747 the Classis of Amsterdam gave reluctant approval. Strange as it may seem, opposition came not so much from the Netherlands as from ultra Dutch ministers here. These were determined to keep the church Dutch, and so organized a counter-movement called the "Conferentie." Unfortunately, feeling between the two groups became quite bitter, especially when the Coetus group took the lead in the revival movements of the time, and in making plans for the founding of a college and theological training school. No one was more zealous in this respect than Rev. Theodorus Jacobus Freylinghuizen, who, as a young man in Germany, had come strongly under Pietistic influences.

This unhappy period came to an end in 1771 when the Rev. Dr. John Henry Livingston returned, an ordained minister, from his studies in Utrecht where he had distinguished himself by his learning, piety and statesmanship. During his student days he had discussed the problems of the American Church with Dutch Church Leaders, and as a result before he left he had worked out with the Classis of Amsterdam and "Plan of Union" which, immediately after his return was submitted to a representative gathering of both groups here, and unanimously ratified. This left the Church, now happily united, free to train and ordain her own ministers, while maintaining cordial relationship with the Mother Church.

Period Three

The securing of ecclesiastical independence was soon followed by the thirteen colonies securing their political independence from England. This then is the period in which a free church lives and works in a free land. At the same meeting at which the "Plan of Union" was adopted there was much discussion about the necessity of proceeding at once with the founding of a theological seminary. The eight years of bitter struggle for national independence inevitably delayed the realization of long cherished hopes. In 1784 the General Synod took the first bold steps in providing for theological training when it elected Dr. John Henry Livingston as Professor of Theology, and Dr. Hermanus Meyer as Professor of Languages. Lack of financial resources made the venture precarious, but the action of Synod remained in force. In 1810 Dr. Livingston came with his students from New York, where the school had been located, to New Brunswick, New Jersey, becoming at the same time President of Rutgers (originally Queens) College, and head of the theological department. This has been the home of the Seminary ever since. This Seminary has served the denomination loyally and well. Nearly 1500 young men have received their training for the ministry here.

The Church caught the tempo and spirit of the new day. In New Jersey, along the Hudson and Mohawk Rivers new churches were founded. By 1830 the use of the Dutch language in public worship had practically ceased. Missionary societies were organized in the churches. The twenties and thirties witnessed the formation of Synod's Boards—Education, Foreign and Domestic Missions. A Church paper, *The Christian Intelligencer,* began a notable career. The quickening of spiritual life expressed itself in ambitious missionary undertakings in Japan, China and India.

The year 1847 marked the beginning of expansion westward. In that year began a veritable stream of emigration from the Netherlands. That there were social and economic reasons behind this emigration no one would deny. But the strongest drive was religious. This seems peculiar in the light of Holland's traditional glory—religious liberty. As an aftermath of the French Revolution when for nearly two decades the Netherlands was a part of France with Louis, Napoleon's brother, reigning as King in The Hague, the Dutch Republic became in 1815 the Kingdom of the Netherlands with William I as King. This occasioned momentous changes. The cabinet included a Minister (Secretary) of Religion. The heretofore democratically elected church judicatories were now more or less under state control. At the meeting of the General Synod, for example, the king's representative was always present. Then too the State demanded more latitude theologically. The form of subscription required for the ordaining of a minister was liberalized. All this produced a reaction. The first sign of open revolt and secession came in 1834. Once started the fires soon spread. Because such conduct was defiance of state as well as church, fines, arrests and imprisonment of seceding ministers soon followed. The people who followed their leaders often shared their fate. Naturally these people looked for a safe haven, and America beckoned them. Rev. Dr. A. C. Van Raalte led a large colony to western Michigan in 1847. That same year Rev. H. P. Scholte founded a similar colony in Central Iowa calling his refuge "Pella." Of hardships, especially in Michigan, there were many, but here they found the freedom once denied them. Here was good land for the asking. Their letters home stimulated thousands to follow them.

The Reformed Church in the east welcomed these immigrants, and assisted them in many ways. Within three years there were a dozen new churches in Michigan. These were invited to come into the fellowship of the Reformed Church. Nothing could have been more natural. Dr. Van Raalte made careful investigation. He found the Church in the east true to the faith. That Church stood exactly by the same truth the newcomers stood for. Their form of church government and doctrinal standards were the same. In fact this Church held exactly the position held by the Church in the Netherlands prior to 1815. So here was their spiritual home, why start another denomination? Hollanders in Iowa joined this fellowship a little later.

This union has greatly strengthened each section, in fact, it largely made the Reformed Church in America what she is today, a small, but very significant religious influence in the nation's and the world's life. The Church was greatly enriched by the coming of thousands of German immigrants, members of the *Reformierte Kirche* in Germany. This group sponsored a noteworthy educational enterprise in German Valley, Illinois. From the original centers in Michigan and Iowa, and also due to continued immigration the Church expanded into Illinois, Wisconsin, Minnesota, North and South Dakota, Kansas, Nebraska, and Colorado. Within recent years the Classis of California was organized.

In early days the bond among the people of the churches so recently come from the Netherlands was a Dutch religious weekly, *De Hope*. About thirty years ago this paper was discontinued. A religious periodical, *The Leader*, largely took its place. A few years ago *The Christian Intelligencer* and *Leader* were combined into *The Church Herald* with a weekly circulation of 40,000.

The Dutch character of the Reformed Church in America, particularly during the early years, is apparent in its polity, doctrinal standards, liturgy and zeal for education, especially for a well trained ministry.

The earliest immigration to this country took place during the time that the Netherlands was making heroic efforts, commonly called the Eighty Years War, for political independence from Spain, which implied also spiritual independence from Rome. It was during these years that five Synods, two held in Germany (Wesel, 1568 and Embden, 1571) and three within the Netherlands, Dordrecht, 1574, Middleburgh, 1581 and The Hague, 1586, evolved a form of church government, adopted a liturgy and required on the part of ministers subscription to the Belgic Confession prepared by Guido de Bres in 1561, and the Heidelberg Catechism, the work of Kaspar Olevianus and Jacharias Ursinus, completed in 1562. The Belgic Confession corresponds in essentials to similar confessions, *e.g.,* the Swiss, French, and later the Westminster Confession. The Heidelberg Catechism has well been called "the most sweet-spirited and experiential of the expositions of Calvinism."

The polity evolved by these Synods was essentially democratic—the local church elects elders and deacons who in turn call a minister and together constitute the consistory. Churches in near geographical proximity organized themselves through delegated representatives into Classes. The Classes in each Province organized themselves into Provincial Synods. These in turn through delegates from each Synod formed the General Synod.

Obviously the most outstanding Synod was that held at Dordrecht 1618-1619. The Arminian controversy made this Synod imperative. After months of deliberation the Canons of Dort were adopted. To tell the story of this Synod and to discuss the Canons would require a good sized volume. The Canons are alike an expression and a defense of Calvinism as interpreted by the Dutch mind. Their basic contention, though often referred to as the five points of Calvinism, is that in the matter of salvation God is the primary factor. Predestination and election mean that the initiative and the glory are not ours but God's. These Canons became the third item in the doctrinal standards of the Reformed Church in Holland.

Naturally when the first Dutch church was organized in New Amsterdam, now New York, the formulas of unity — Belgic Confession, Heidelberg Cathechism and Canons of Dort —binding on the churches in Holland became binding here. In other words, the new church and all other Dutch churches to be later organized were as Dutch in liturgy and doctrine as if they had been located in Holland instead of the new world, and in essentials that is true today. For example, every minister in the Reformed Church in America subscribes to a form of which the following constitutes one paragraph:

> We, the underwritten, in becoming ministers of the Word of God within the bounds of the Classis of..............., do by this our subscription, sincerely and in good conscience before the Lord, declare that we believe the Gospel of the Grace of God in Christ Jesus as revealed in the Holy Scriptures of the Old and New Testaments, and as truly set forth in the Standards of the Reformed Church in America and that we reject all errors which are contrary thereto. We promise that we will exert ourselves to keep the Church free from such errors.

In the matter of Liturgy, though basically in accord with the liturgical practices of the Church of Holland, conditions in the new world demanded no little variation so as to adjust to new situations. Its corporate character is its basic characteristic; that is to say, that in worship the whole body of Christ's people join. There are many fixed forms for example for Holy Communion, Baptism and Ordination. However, for the regular service of worship great freedom is enjoyed. Many churches still have in the pews, *The Liturgy of the Reformed Church in America,* a book of 138 pages. In this volume are suggested Scripture readings for the Church year, for example, for the season of Advent, the death and resurrection of our Lord, and the season of the mission of the Holy Comforter. Then follow orders of morning and evening worship. The greater part of the liturgy is comprised of the various "Offices"—Baptism; Communion; Marriage; Burial of the dead; Installation of ministers and missionaries, elders, deacons and other lay workers; Laying of a Corner Stone; Dedication of a Church; the final office being that for Church discipline. It has in order the three creeds of the Church—Apostles', Nicene and Athanasian. Prayers, corporate and personal, make up the closing section of thirty-eight pages.

As has already been intimated the organization of the Reformed Church in America resembles that of the mother Church. The local church elects its governing body, the consistory, composed of elders and deacons. The consistory calls a minister, usually with advice and consent of members of the church. The minister automatically becomes president of the Consistory. Local churches in geographical proximity organize themselves through the ministers and delegated elders into a classis, of these there are forty-three. Classes on a regional basis organize themselves into a Particular Synod of which there are five,—the Synods of Albany, Chicago, Iowa, New Jersey and New York. The highest judicatory is the General Synod to which the various classes send delegates, the number being determined by the total membership of each classis. This body meets annually, usually in June.

The powers of each body are carefully set forth in the Constitution which was adopted in 1833. Prior to this time the church was governed by the Rules of Church Government prepared at the Synod of Dort in 1619, though certain explanatory articles were added from time to time better adapting these rules to American conditions. These rules were translated into English in 1792. The Constitution is in fact a fusion of the Rules of Dort, explanatory articles and amendments as they existed prior to 1833. The Constitution has been amended from time to time. A general revision requiring several years of study was completed in 1916. The first incorporation of the church took place in 1819 under the name, "The Reformed Protestant Dutch Church." In 1869 the Legislature of the State of New York approved an action adopted by the General Synod in 1867 in changing the name to "The Reformed Church in America."

The total communicant membership is 187,256. There are 767 fully organized churches. During 1950 these contributed to benevolences approximately $2,700,000. For congregational purposes they spent $8,296,357.00.

The mother Church in Holland has been severely criticized for refusing to relinquish control of the colonial Dutch churches in this country. Some of this criticism is deserved. One aspect of this control is often overlooked. The mother Church feared greatly that lowering standards of ministerial training would ultimately mean not just a lowering of church standards all along the line, but might result in churches going out of existence entirely. Hence she encouraged, sometimes demanded, that candidates for the ministry receive their training in Holland, or at least go there for ordination, for that would allow careful examination of a candidate's fitness intellectually as well as spiritually.

It became perfectly obvious to the leaders of the churches here that something would have to be done to assure proper ministerial training. Domine John Frelinghuysen, son of Theodorus Jacobus, became the spearhead of this movement which resulted in the securing of a charter for Queens College (later Rutgers University) in 1766. In the quaint language of the day the charter expressed the purpose of the founding of a college for "Study in the learned languages and in the liberal arts, and in the philosophical sciences; also that it may be a school of the prophets in which young Levites and Nazarites of God may be prepared to enter upon the sacred ministerial office."

For nearly two centuries this, one of the earliest colonial colleges, has responded to this purpose. In fact, the New Brunswick Theological Seminary, the oldest theological training school in this country, founded in 1784, would have languished for lack of students, particularly during the nineteenth century, had it not been for Rutgers College, which became the State University of New Jersey in 1925.

This determination to secure properly trained ministers is likewise the reason for the founding in 1784 of the Academy in Schenectady, New York. Domine Dirck Romeyn, then the pastor of the First Dutch Church in that village, was largely responsible for this effort. The Academy grew into Union College which has the distinction of being the first college to declare in its act of incorporation for complete freedom in religious thought. It set out to answer "the loud call for men of learning to fill the several offices of the Church and State." While never under the control of the Reformed Church scores of her graduates, especially in the early years, entered New Brunswick Theological Seminary for their ministerial training.

This significant emphasis was equally characteristic of the pioneers in the Middle West. While most of his people were still living in log houses, the Rev. Van Raalte was urging the necessity of education. Ten years after their arrival an Academy was started which in 1866 became Hope College. Of the anchor which became the seal of the college, the Rev. Van Raalte said, "This is my Anchor of Hope for my people in the West".

Again, the primary drive behind the founding of the college was adequate ministerial training. The college added a theological department which a few years later became a separate institution called the Western Theological Seminary which together with Hope College gives rare distinction to Holland, Michigan where both have their home.

As population increased the Reformed Church established academies in Orange City, Iowa; German Valley, Illinois; Harrison, South Dakota, and Cedar Grove, Wisconsin. The coming of High Schools gradually crowded out church related academies, so that only the first two mentioned are still in operation. In 1916 the Reformed Church received from the Baptists the campus and buildings of Central College in Pella, Iowa. This institution has added greatly to the educational forces of the Reformed Church. In 1928 the General Synod approved a petition made by certain western classes that the Academy at Orange City be expanded into a Junior College. In 1950 the General Synod approved establishing there of a full four year college. Some of our churches in California are urging a collegiate institution on the West coast.

The Reformed Church has always been missionary minded. In early years home missions were of local or classical concern. In 1831 the General Synod organized what became known as the Board of Domestic Missions. This board did for church extension, church and parsonage building what the Board of Education founded the same year did for academies, colleges, and seminaries. Unfortunately for too long a time the Board of Domestic Missions took too narrow a view of its task in that it limited its activities to areas where there were Dutch or German settlements. It did, however, establish and continue, with the aid of the Women's Board of Domestic Missions organized in 1882, work in Jackson County, Kentucky, Indian work in Winnebago, Nebraska and Dulce, New Mexico, work among colored people at Brewton, Alabama, as well as cooperative work in the province of Chiapas, Mexico. Just now a vigorous effort is being made to help the thousands of emigrants into Canada organize churches. Within a year or two there will undoubtedly be a Classis of Ontario.

There are those within and outside the Reformed Church who feel that she has over extended herself in her foreign missionary activity. In the early years of the nineteenth century such efforts were interdenominational. But intense missionary interest was not content with anything less than the denominational promotion of foreign missions. Hence, in 1832, the

Board of Foreign Missions was organized. Work was begun or continued in India, China and Japan. This board received valiant support from the Women's Board of Foreign Missions, organized in 1875. In 1893 work was begun in the Persian Gulf area largely independent of the official boards, but later directed by them. Hundreds of churches have undertaken to support a foreign missionary, or if unable to assume full responsibility to take on a share of such personal support. This has had most beneficent results in that personal contacts have created a sense of urgency and dedication, so that more of the benevolent funds of the church go to Foreign Missions than to any other cause.

Though Dutch in origin and generally loyal to Dutch traditions, the Reformed Church in America has always cherished the ecumenical mind and spirit. Many of her sons have gone into the ministry of other communions, and ministers from other communions have received a warm welcome to her pulpits. In fact not a few of those who made major contributions to our church life came from other denominations. It is safe to say that in scores of our churches, especially along the eastern seaboard, less than 25% of the membership have a Reformed Church background. This Church was a charter member of the Federal Council of Churches of Christ in America, and now a member of both the National and World Council of Churches.

The Christian Reformed Church

This article may give the impression that the Reformed Church is the one denomination that has sailed on smooth and untroubled seas. Anyone who has this opinion does not know the Dutch. This church has had its share of strife and contention, of schisms, some temporary, others permanent. Only those who have lived through language controversy days know what strife that can create. The Coetus-Conferentie strife in the eighteenth century was such a struggle.

In 1822 a small group of ministers succeeded in taking some twenty Reformed Churches with them into an organization which they called the "True Dutch Reformed Church." The reason they alleged to justify this secession was that the Reformed Church harbored Hopkinsian ideas, was lax in discipline, encouraged intercommunion, and did not emphasize sufficiently the doctrine of election and predestination. The General Synod carefully examined all these complaints, and found them groundless and false. That secession soon withered, and would have died out but for a serious situation which arose among the Michigan churches.

Any unbiased study of the Union of 1850 between the new pioneer churches in Michigan with the long established Reformed Church in the East must conclude that that union was unanimously endorsed and heartily welcomed from both sides. But very shortly after this Union voices were raised in Michigan against it. It must be remembered that these people had seceded from the Church in the Netherlands. It is a pity that among some people the spirit of secession grows by what it feeds on.

The following charges made by one of the seceding churches under date of April 7, 1857 summarize pretty well the supposed grievances:

1. Instead of using only the versification of the Psalms some 800 hymns were introduced contrary to church order.
2. Inviting men of all religious views to the Lord's Supper, excepting Roman Catholics.
3. Neglecting to preach the Heidelberg Catechism regularly, to hold catechetical classes, and to do house visitation.
4. And what grieves our hearts most in all of this [so reads the letter] is that there are members among you who regard our secession in the Netherlands as not strictly necessary, or think that it was untimely.
5. Dr. Wyckoff of Albany who invited us to join the Reformed Protestant Dutch Church assured us that if at any time we regretted this act of union we could be by ourselves again.

This storm might have blown over or become localized but

for the fact that pamphlets issued by the secessionists of 1822 found their way to Michigan, and added fuel to the fire. Personal letters from these same secessionists did no end of harm. As a result some half dozen churches took the road to secession. They established fraternal relations with what was left of the 1822 movement and called themselves by the same name. The numbers of seceding churches remained small. However, by 1876 they were able to begin a theological training school in Grand Rapids, Michigan.

In the early eighties the storm over masonry and secret societies of all kinds broke over the churches in the Middle West. During the seventies the General Synod of the Reformed Church had often to wrestle with this problem. The final conclusion reached was that this was a matter of individual conscience. The Synod would not say that a mason could not be a Christian, and so could not be a member of the Reformed Church. Pulpits everywhere took up the issue. A pamphlet war followed. The net result was that scores of ministers and hundreds of families seceded from the Reformed Church, and joined, and in joining greatly increased the strength of the True Dutch Reformed Church, whose name was later changed to the "Christian Reformed Church."

This is not the place to stoke old fires dead or slumbering. Let it be said that those who boasted that a church, whose grounds for secession, to say the least, were highly questionable, could not possibly meet with the favor of God, and so was doomed to a languishing death have not been vindicated. The Christian Reformed Church is today one of the fastest growing religious bodies in America. Her college and theological training school, called Calvin College and Seminary, located in Grand Rapids, Michigan, is an institution of which any denomination might be justifiably proud. This Church has promoted an aggressive missionary program largely among people of Dutch extraction both in the United States and Canada. Her Indian Mission work deserves the highest praise.

In recent years her missionaries have gone to China, Africa, Ceylon and South America.

Her religious journalism is of a high order. The Church maintains two weekly publications, one in Dutch, *De Wachter,* and the other in English, *The Banner.* The Faculty of Calvin College and Seminary publishes monthly *The Calvin Forum.* The "Back to God Hour" is one of the best national radio programs. Her uncompromising Calvinism, though keeping her out of both the National and World Council of Churches, has not saved her from internal strife. Wherever possible she maintains her own Christian schools, though welcomes children from other communions.

The total communicant membership is 88,827. There are twenty classes. There are 367 congregations and 271 ministers. Eighty-seven churches are without ministers. With 111 students enrolled in Calvin Seminary the matter of vacancies will soon be solved.

BIBLIOGRAPHY

MAURICE G. HANSEN, *Reformed Churches in the Netherlands* (1884), published by the Board of Publication of the Reformed Church in America. (Abr. R. C. A.).

Centennial of the New Brunswick Theological Seminary, 1784-1884, published by the Board of Publication, R. C. A.

EDWARD TANGORE CORWIN, *The Reformed Church, Dutch,* Vol. VIII, American Church History Series (New York, 1895).

———, (compiler), *Digest of Synodical Legislation of the R. C. A.,* published by the Board of Publication, R. C. A. (1906).

WILLARD DAYTON BROWN, *The Reformed Church in America, a History,* published by the Board of Publication, the R. C. A. (1928).

VARIOUS WRITERS, *Tercentenary Studies Reformed Church in America, 1628-1928,* published by the Board of Publication, R. C. A.

W. H. S. DEMAREST, *History of Rutgers College, 1766-1924,* published by the Rutgers Press.

Minutes of the Classis of Holland, 1848-1858. English Translation. Published by the Grand Rapids Printing Co.

Semi-Centennial Volume Theological School and Calvin College, 1876-1926.

Yearbook (1951) of the Christian Reformed Church, published by the Christian Reformed Publishing House.

VIII
UNITARIANISM

VIII

UNITARIANISM

Edwin T. Buehrer

UNITARIANISM, AS an organized movement in both Britain and America, dates back officially to May 25, 1825, but its origins go much further into the past than is commonly realized. Nor is Unitarianism properly designated primarily as a form of anti-Trinitarianism. It derives its name from the fact that it has rejected the concept of the triune God, (Father, Son and Holy Ghost) ; but anti-Trinitarianism is only one of the aspects of its structure of beliefs that distinguish a Unitarian from a believing member of some orthodox or liberal Christian denomination.

In his conflict with the more conservative Congregationalists of New England, William Ellery Channing (1780-1842) was not nearly so passionately or eloquently anti-Trinitarian as he was anti-Calvinist; and though he consistently exalted Christ as someone more than a mere human being, he did deny his saviourhood. But Channing also exalted the dignity of man. His concept of human dignity, his insistence on the right of the common man to help fashion his own destiny, made the great Boston preacher one of America's outstanding reformers. He fought for temperance, for the improvement of prison conditions, for better working conditions and minimum wages for labor, for public education and for the emancipation of the slaves. The type of Unitarianism which Channing and his younger contemporary, Theodore Parker (1810-1860), preached so eloquently during New England's flowering, and its Indian summer, the Unitarianism which Thomas Jefferson admired, and commended to all young Americans, the kind which

Ralph W. Emerson (1803-1882) set forth in his sermons, lectures and essays, was the glorification and extension of liberal thought and action in every area of life. It is thus that no matter how far back one reaches into history, wherever prophets and pioneers have moved beyond the traditions of their own religion or culture, wherever they have sought new frontiers of intellectual and spiritual adventuring, there, a Unitarian would say, are the antecedents of his faith.

The prophetic emphasis on morality over ceremony, as exemplified by Amos, Hosea, Micah and Isaiah are, in this sense, Unitarian. The later Old Testament emphasis on the "one true God", uncorrupted by the alloy of polytheism—or even the tri-theism of early Christian theology—is Unitarian. Unitarians find in the ancient Christian scholar, Origen, a kindred spirit. Living in an age when Christianity was spreading far and wide, and establishing its system of theology, Origen's creative mind labored unceasingly over a long span of years; and it is impossible to assess his great influence. He rejected the miraculous, and he assumed that God was without corporeal existence. He accepted the prevailing Trinitarian theology, involving the Logos; and he assumed without question that there was never a time "when He (Christ) was not", an assumption which Arius and his followers questioned. There was, however, in Origen's thought a seed of heresy which began to grow, and which Arius carefully nourished. Christ, said Origen, is "the second God", a duplicate of God—and of another substance or essence. He was therefore subordinate to God; and it was this differentiation which foreshadowed Unitarianism and provided a soil and a climate in which the Arian position could be stated and debated at the Council of Nicea. Origen advocated reason, tolerance and cultural adjustment, and it is significant that he was never made a saint; it is also significant that it was not Origen (185?-254?), but St. Augustine (354-430) who once said: "I would not believe the gospel if the authoritarianism of the Catholic Church did not compel me," for Origen believed that a faith which does not express itself in ethical living is invalid. Origen has been called the first Christian liberal—a prophet voice heralding the ultimate coming of Humanism. No wonder Arius quoted him in support of his own anti-Trinitarianism.

Fourth century Arianism, though not Unitarian in the modern sense, suggests how, 1,600 years ago, Unitarianism rather than Trinitarianism might have emerged from these early debates out of which our Christian dogmas eventually came. The doctrine of the Trinity was not specifically established until after the Council of Nicea, 325 A.D., at which Arius, the most eloquent and the most persistent dissenter was ruthlessly overridden. Arius represented the teachings of Origen and Lucian—that Christ was a created being, not of the substance of God, and not, therefore, eternal. Superior to men, the Son remained nevertheless a creature, and less than God. At Nicea, however, Christ was declared to be "God of God, very God of very God . . . consubstantial with the father." Arius called such teaching polytheistic, and though he was crushed, the intimation that Christ was man, not God, haunted the minds of intellectuals through the centuries.

There was another, but similar, heresy known by the dread name of Pelagianism. Pelagius' (d.C. 420) heresy was the denial of original sin. His was the prophetic utterance that the doctrine of human depravity undermined the human will, and insulted God. Pelagianism agitated Christian councils for a century with the assertion of greater moral responsibility for the individual, through a higher freedom of the will than was taught or accepted by the church. The full weight of St. Augustine's influence was brought to bear against this dangerous heresy, and inasmuch as the doctrine of the church was deeply entrenched after Nicea, the heresy was routed. A thousand years of relatively undisturbed Trinitarianism and predestinationism prevailed. In turning its back on Origen, Arius and Pelagius, however, and accepting Tertullian, Cyprian, and Augustine, Christianity turned its back upon tolerance,

secular culture and rational thinking, and embraced dogmatism, legalism and sacramentalism. Christianity preferred Tertullian's delight in the torture of the damned to the Univer-
salistic faith of Pelagius. Africanism and Latinism were asserted
over Hellenism for the hand of Christianity, but the Greek
spirit continued to re-inspire the struggle for a more liberal
religious philosophy. Ironically enough, it remained for a lonely Spanish theologian and churchman, Claudius, of Turin,
to be called an Arian in the year 820—a living link, as it were,
between ancient and modern Unitarianism, and suggesting, if
not proving, that there must have been others who merely
whispered their heresies, or kept them quietly to themselves.
It is therefore no mere historical coincidence that many of the
heresies of ancient Christianity were the theological "straws
in the wind" of a Unitarianism in the future. The non-conformists, though not liberal in our sense, were sufficiently independent of Aristotelian or Augustinian authoritarianism to
ask un-admitted questions. They lifted lone voices; they would
not, with Tertullian (b.C. 160) believe a thing "because it
was absurd". They were the men whose inquiring minds moved
in the direction of the Renaissance, hardly knowing what they
were doing.

The fourteenth century brought John Wycliffe (1320-1384).
He was a man of the Renaissance who substituted the authority of Scripture for the authority of the Pope. "If there were
one hundred popes", said he, "and all the friars were cardinals,
their opinions should carry no weight in matters of faith, except it be based on Scripture." Out of such independence of
mind and non-conformity came the Reformation. The fifteenth
century brought the printing press which made possible a wider
distribution of the Bible; the sixteenth century brought Lutheranism with an orthodoxy not far removed from Catholicism,
but with the insistence on the precious right of private judgment. More than Luther could possibly have realized did his
assertion of "the priesthood of the believer" carry his point
beyond his own authoritarianism of the Scripture. It inspired

Michael Servetus (1511-1553) to publish in 1531 his *Errors of the Trinity;* and as early as 1535 the "poor, scattered and scorned" Anabaptists fled from Holland to England, there—under Henry VIII—to be burned for their Arianism. Luther and Calvin, in their recoil from Catholic dogma, long avoided the term "Trinity", but they also recoiled from anything less than the deity of Christ; and for Protestantism, no less than for Catholicism, Arianism was regarded as "the great sin". Erasmus, himself—subtle and indirect, rather than pointed and out-spoken—became "that cursed anti-Trinitarian".

The first and immediate effect of the Reformation was the release it brought from the frightful pressure of mediaeval authoritarianism. It made a tradition of the right of private judgment, it modified the sacramental system, and it eventuated in a simplified body of belief; and with these doors to religious freedom slightly ajar, it is not to be wondered that Unitarian leaders and communities emerged. A contemporary of Servetus and of Calvin (1509-1564) was Francis David (1510-1579), who became the father of Unitarianism in Transylvania. A Lutheran at the age of 46, he was won over to Calvinism, and later converted to Unitarianism. His zeal made him a popular debater—with exponents of a more conservative faith—under the friendly protection of king Sigismund. It was because of the latter's sympathy with the Unitarian cause that the churches obtained the legal standing and protection necessary to their existence. In 1568 the king issued one of the most remarkable edicts in the long history of the growth of religious toleration. He decreed that:

> preachers shall be allowed to preach the gospel everywhere, each according to his own understanding of it. If the community wish to accept such preaching, well and good; if not, they shall not be compelled, but shall be allowed to keep the preachers they prefer. No one shall be made to suffer on account of his religion, since faith is the gift of God.[1]

It is true, of course, that this great advance into the frontiers of religious liberalism was halted; it is also true that this decree antedated Thomas Jefferson's famous Statute of Religious Freedom in Virginia by more than two hundred years. Nor did Sigismund live long enough to defend and establish the freedom he so boldly proclaimed. And Francis David was caught up in the wave of persecution which followed the king's death; even so, he ranks with Servetus as one of the great Unitarian martyrs in history.

Younger contemporaries of Servetus and David, were the Socinus brothers, Laelius (1525-1562) and his nephew, Faustus (1539-1604). The younger Socinus arrived in Poland in 1579. Under his leadership the Unitarian movement spread until it included some three hundred churches. A catechism was published in 1605, stressing moral action rather than correctness of belief, and rejecting Trinitarianism. As in Transylvania, however, so also in Poland, religious liberalism was ahead of its time, and statutes were prepared for its suppression. There were anti-Trinitarian leaders and fellowships in Italy, Spain, and England; indeed, there was never a time after the Reformation when such expressions of religious liberalism did not exist. It is to be remembered however, that Socinianism, though clearly anti-Trinitarian, did promote the "worship of Christ". A more radical concept of Jesus' nature could not have gained any kind of foothold whatever. Be this as it may, Unitarianism was a heresy to be reckoned with throughout the seventeenth century, and into the eighteenth. John Biddle, the "first Unitarian of England" was born in 1615, and educated at Oxford. His society of "mere Christians" disappeared, but it planted the seeds from which a hardier plant of liberalism could grow.

This brings us to the story of Theophilus Lindsey. Born in 1723, he graduated from Cambridge University, with honors, and was ordained a clergyman in the Church of England. At the age of fifty he withdrew from the Church, being unable to accept the Thirty-Nine Articles of Religion. In 1774 he erected his Essex Street Chapel, the first Unitarian meeting house in England. His influence was far-reaching, and was carried to America by William Hazlitt, father of the distinguished essayist. It was Hazlitt who, in 1784, persuaded James Freeman, the young minister of King's Chapel in Boston, to omit from the Prayer Book Trinitarian references and prayers to Christ, and thus to transform his church into the first Unitarian Church on the new continent. Benjamin Franklin often attended services there, though he never joined. Lindsey's junior by ten years was the famous scientist and preacher, Joseph Priestly (1733-1804). Priestly served several dissenting churches, taught in dissenting academies, and then, in 1780, went to the new meeting house in Birmingham where he spent eleven years. Eventually, feeling the restrictions upon him, he moved to America and established a Unitarian church in Philadelphia. Here Thomas Jefferson came under his influence, and the two became warm, life-long friends.

A discussion of Unitarianism in America would be incomplete without emphasis upon the influence of science and philosophy on the thinking of the early political and intellectual leaders of our American life. Priestly himself was more distinguished as a scientist than as a theologian; and it was John Newton and John Locke rather than Martin Luther or John Calvin who inspired his thinking. These were the men who—along with Francis Bacon, Harvey, Kepler, Galileo, Descartes. Pascal, Huyghens, Boyle, Leibniz and Spinoza—moved Prof. Whitehead to call the seventeenth century "The Century of Genius". Unable, under the influence of such minds, to accept the teachings of Christian orthodoxy, the intellectuals of the eighteenth and early nineteenth centuries moved in the direction of Deism. Jefferson was deeply influenced. So also were Tom Paine, Benjamin Franklin, James Madison and many others including even George Washington. In New England, during the "flowering", Congregational ministers, particularly, influenced by philosophy and science, began to question the doctrine of Calvinism which stemmed from the preaching of Cotton Mather. It was, therefore, not Cotton Mather's God of wrath to whom the authors of the Declaration of Independence appealed; it was "nature and nature's God"—the God of Deism.

Unitarianism is thus at every point an integral part of a very broad current of history. American liberalism did not create the American Revolution, but the revolution helped to crystallize liberalism, giving form and direction to scattered ideas, and compelled the intellectual leaders of the times to state their philosophy in practical and understandable language. The development and organization of Unitarianism in America started with and ran parallel to the rise of the great democratic experiment; and its beginning can no more be explained without that experiment than can our liberal democratic tradition be explained without the philosophy of John Locke and the disciplined philosophical mind of Thomas Jefferson. Revulsion against the spiritual and emotional orgies of the Great Awakening moved some people out of the church altogether, and sent the more intelligent and critical members seeking other sources of religious satisfaction. The churches of the Pilgrim fathers were non-dogmatic in theology, and congregational in polity; and non-conformity was invited in the very nature of things. The "tribunal of last appeal" was always the "tribunal of truth". In Sprague's *Annals of the American Pulpit* there are recorded the lives of forty-nine ministers of known Unitarian belief settled in Congregational churches during the eighteenth century. Jonathan Mayhew (1720-1766) was probably the first to openly oppose the doctrine of the Trinity. Eventually Harvard University was "infected", with Joseph Willard the first anti-Trinitarian on the faculty. He corresponded with friends of Voltaire in France, as well as with Priestly, before the latter left England for America. The historian, Joseph H. Allen, says that there was not a strict Trinitarian among the Congregational clergy in all of Boston. In 1805 Henry Ware (1764-1845) was appointed Hollis Professor at Harvard, then in rapid succession four others—five appointments in two years —which made Harvard "exceedingly and dangerously liberal".

So serious had the situation become that the famous Dr. Lyman Beecher of Boston observed that

> All the literary men of Massachusetts were Unitarian; all the trustees and professors of Harvard College were Unitarian; all the elite of wealth and fashion crowded Unitarian churches; the judges on the bench were Unitarian, giving decisions by which the peculiar features of church organization so carefully ordered by the Pilgrim Fathers had been nullified, and all the power had passed into the hands of the congregation.[2]

At last came the time when someone had to give the movement voice and leadership. That leader was William Ellery Channing, and the occasion was the installation of the Rev. Jared Sparks in the church in Baltimore in 1819. His sermon was a spiritual call to arms against Calvinism—the doctrine which had long inspired some of the most eloquent preaching in the very churches to which all the laymen and ministers of that congregation belonged. The entering wedge had been driven, and inevitably the churches were divided, with substantial portions of the congregations desirous of retaining the older pattern of theological thinking, and the majorities—in most instances — ready and eager to abandon their former Trinitarian beliefs. Eventually a legal decision was called for, and the Massachusetts Supreme Court ruled that the church in Dedham should become the property of the Unitarians. The decision affected more than a hundred churches in Eastern Massachusetts which, within a radius of thirty-five miles of Boston, considered themselves Unitarian. Steadily, now, ministers and congregations took their courage into their hands, and on May 25, 1825, organized themselves into the American Unitarian Association, incorporated by the State of Massachusetts, with headquarters in Boston. By an astonishing coincidence the British Unitarian Association was organized on the same day. Already there was a thriving church in Washington, D.C., ready to join the new denomination. In 1830 churches were established in Cincinnati and Louisville, and a year later a congregation was gathered in Buffalo. Three years after that there was one in St. Louis. It was the St. Louis congregation which helped in the founding of Washington University. It was not until 1860 that Unitarianism reached the Pacific coast. In that year Thomas Starr King, then only thirty-five years of age, went to San Francisco to organize a new church. By the end of the century there was a Unitarian membership of more than 40,000.

The question is often asked: Why has the Unitarian movement, so closely in accord with the modern temper, so eager to adapt itself to modern science and culture, so sensitive to social problems and inequalities—why has it not attracted to itself a stronger numerical following in America? Space does not permit a lengthy attempt to answer this question, but one observation may provide the clue. Unitarianism was never a missionary program; it was an intellectual movement which left many of the traditional beliefs of orthodox Christianity—out of which it emerged—abandoned on the roadside of history. It was thus a pioneering venture in a sense quite different from the highly charged emotionalism of Christian evangelicalism. Unitarianism was an orderly, doctrinal separation which resulted from an intellectual conflict, with the new denomination seeking only freedom to go its way. Looking back from the perspective of our own mid-century it is no wonder, therefore, that almost immediately a new form of conservatism developed. Even Channing and Theodore Parker, radical though they seemed and were in their day, did not greatly alter their ideas about the divine inspiration of the scriptures, miracles, or the doctrine of immortality. In their acceptance of these beliefs as in their polity, they remained Congregationalists. They rejected predestinationism and the deity of Jesus, but they never quite outgrew their habit of referring to Jesus in the familiar language of "Jesus Christ". Indeed, some of their colleagues often added the phrase, "our Lord and Saviour". There may still be found today, a Unitarian "Church of the Saviour", and a "Church of the Messiah".

For all such theological overtones, however, these original Unitarians placed their confidence in the power of the mind, and their hope in the integrity of human personality. Channing regarded himself as "poor material" for a reformer, but on this account, he added that the work of reform was good for him; and every social front was his fighting front. Through his passionate preaching he was the perennial source of inspiration for such pioneers of social service as Wendell Phillips, Horace Mann, Dorothea Dix, and many others. It needs also to be recorded that Channing was obviously disturbed at the complacency of the ministers and leaders of the denomination which he so conspicuously helped establish; moreover, as late as 1853, eleven years after Channing died, and while Parker was still filling the Boston Music Hall with thousands of eager listeners, the American Unitarian Association committed itself officially to the belief in "the divine origin and authority of the religion of Jesus Christ, through the miraculous interposition of God as recorded by divine authority in the gospels."[3] Channing had seen it coming, and it seemed to him an ignominious failure to move forward with the accumulated knowledge and experience of the modern world. Shortly before his death, and only sixteen years after the founding of the denomination, he wrote to his distinguished British colleague and friend, Dr. James Martineau:

> Old Unitarianism must undergo important modifications . . . It began as a protest against the rejection of reason,—against mental slavery. It pledged itself to progress as its life and end, but it has gradually grown stationary, and now we have a Unitarian orthodoxy.[4]

For a decade this situation prevailed, with the denomination losing its zest, its fire. Unitarianism had become old, fearful, conservative and deeply entrenched before it had really come into its own as something unique in religious history. Moreover, a biennial conference was called in New York in 1865 to persuade Unitarians to drop controversy, and to devote their united hearts and souls to "the positive truth, the positive faith, and the positive work of the gospel of Jesus Christ." With orthodoxy firmly in control, and the liberal elements defeated, the younger members and leaders, bereft of Channing and Parker, set about to organize a protest, and, if necessary, a rump conference. Emerson was interested, and so was Lucretia Mott, a Hicksite Quaker and Unitarian. They organized themselves into The Free Religious Association with the two-fold purpose of promoting religious liberalism in America and, if possible, to redeem the Unitarian church from orthodoxy. That was in 1866. The F.R.A. as an autonomous movement declined in the 1880's, but it did not disband until its major purposes were achieved. Its membership consisted of a great variety of liberals and radicals who never learned to work well together; but it had the most eloquent preachers, and its annual meetings for a decade commanded more newspaper space than did the meetings of the American Unitarian Association. Its leaders entered eagerly into a consideration of the implications of Darwinism for religion; and one of its ablest leaders, Dr. Minot Savage, claimed to be the first preacher in America to speak of Darwin's contribution to scientific thinking, and the emergence of life and of man on earth, as an asset rather than a liability to religious thought and experience.

The crowning achievement of the F.R.A. was the convening of the Parliament of Religions at the Chicago World's Fair in 1893. The Parliament was designed to stimulate a wider interest in all world religions, and to introduce studies in comparative religion into the curricula of the theological seminaries of the major denominations. Moreover, the liberalizing of the Unitarian fellowship progressed so rapidly that in 1882 Dr. Savage introduced an amendment to the constitution of the Unitarian National Conference which virtually secured freedom of thought within the denomination. The amendment stated that while the constitution embodied the views of a majority of Unitarians, it was distinctly understood that there was no authoritative test of Unitarianism, and that none would be excluded from its fellowship "who, while differing from us in belief, are in general sympathy with our purposes and practical aims."[5] With the door thus opened for the inclusion of the most unorthodox ministers, the F.R.A had at last accomplished its purpose. Not only was Unitarianism saved from its mid-nineteenth century orthodoxy, but it was prepared to bring forth and nourish an even more startling expression of liberalism, namely a form of religious Humanism which no longer regards itself necessarily as either theistic or Christian.

There are churches in the denomination, and particularly in the Middle West, whose ministers find their inspiration in a frank acceptance of the structure and grandeur of the physical universe, and its emerging life, including the developing life of man. Finding their authority, not in an ancient church —or in an ancient book, tradition or creed—but in scientific method and human experience, these ministers find, also, friendly acceptance and warm fellowship in the Unitarian denomination. Most Unitarian clergy and laymen do not regard themselves as Humanists; but it is probably not an overstatement to say that there are strong, positive Humanist characteristics and attitudes in almost every Unitarian minister. The American Humanist Association, though completely independent of official Unitarianism, was organized by Unitarian clergymen; and finds its continuing support in those whose philosophy and purpose are closely allied with Unitarianism. Humanism is not nature worship, or natural mysticism, although there are Humanists who feel themselves closely identified with the total structure and life of the world. Humanism does not involve the worship of man as an individual, or of society as a collective entity; but it is man-centered, rather than God-centered, in the sense that every problem men confront is frankly accepted as a human problem, every tragedy as a human tragedy, and every joy a human joy. The Humanist finds no verifiable experience of a supernaturally revealed truth, or of a love that transcends human love. He does not see in the vast structure of the world any evidence of self-awareness, or an awareness of the presence of man on earth. Some of the most dynamic and eloquent preachers in the Unitarian denomination are Humanist preachers; and some of the most active and progressive churches are Humanist churches; nor is there any outspoken desire in the Unitarian denomination to exclude them —or a technique for doing so even if the desire were existent.

Unitarianism has recently experienced a steady and substantial growth in numbers, having doubled its membership during the first half of the present century. It enjoys, today, a numerical strength of eighty thousand, the greatest in its history. Its president, usually though not necessarily, a clergyman, is elected by The American Unitarian Association, consisting of ministerial and lay delegates who meet annually in Boston. The A.U.A. also elects its Board of Directors who convene quarterly to conduct the affairs of the denomination.

The Unitarians have recently—by an overwhelming vote of their 355 active churches and delegates, adopted a proposal for a federation, or merger, with the Universalist denomination. A joint commission is now drafting the terms of the federation which will in turn be submitted for a future referendum in both denominations. A hymnal, jointly prepared, has been in use since 1937. There is a denominational journal, *The Christian Register,* which has a circulation, and an influence, far beyond the bounds of the denomination.

NOTES

[1] HARRY B. SCHOLEFIELD, *Unitarianism—Some Past History and Present Meanings* (Boston, 1950), p. 14.
[2] JOSEPH HENRY ALLEN, *A History of Unitarians* (New York, 1894), p. 194.
[3] STOW PERSONS, *Free Religion*—An American Faith (New Haven, 1947), p. 6.
[4] STOW PERSONS, *op. cit.,* p. 12.
[5] STOW PERSONS, *op. cit.,* p. 155.

UNITARIANISM

BIBLIOGRAPHY

JOSEPH HENRY ALLEN, *A History of Unitarians* (New York, 1894).

JOSEPH L. BLAU, editor, *Cornerstones of Religious Freedom in America* (Boston, 1949).

FRED GLADSTONE BRATTON, *The Legacy of the Liberal Spirit* (New York, 1943).

The Works of William Ellery Channing, issued by The American Unitarian Association (Boston, 1903).

HENRY STEELE COMMAGER, *The American Mind* (New Haven, 1950).

————, *Theodore Parker—Yankee Crusader* (Boston, 1947).

G. W. COOKE, *Unitarianism in America* (Boston, 1902).

OCTAVIOUS B. FROTHINGHAM, *Recollections and Impressions, 1822-1890* (New York, 1891).

ARTHUR CUSHMAN MCGIFFERT, *A History of Christian Thought,* 2 vols. (New York, 1932).

HENRY B. SCHOLEFIELD, *Unitarianism—Some Past History and Present Meanings* (Boston, 1950).

EARL MORSE WILBUR, *A History of Unitarianism* (Cambridge, 1950).

IX

THE CONGREGATIONAL CHRISTIAN CHURCHES

IX

THE CONGREGATIONAL CHRISTIAN CHURCHES

Mervin M. Deems

I

The closing decades of the sixteenth century in England witnessed a curious religious situation which in spite of church-state control also exhibited some fluidity. Many individuals and groups believed that the Reformation had not been carried to its logical conclusion. Some of these people actually separated from the Established Church, while others remained within it voicing their protests. As far back as Mary's reign (1553-1558) separate, "gathered" communions met secretly and independently. Other groups of émigrés on the Continent also helped to create a pattern. There is no clear connection between these early "churches" and later Congregationalism. But before Robert Browne comes upon the scene there were evidently several independent congregations in London such as the Plumbers' Hall group, Mr. Pattensen's fellowship, a congregation under John Browne ("the Brownings"), and another under Richard Fitz. There also may have been other Separatist groups which migrated to Scotland. At least one of the London congregations had a covenant whereby the subscribing member subjected himself to God's Word, united himself with the body of Christ and repudiated "the church of the traditioners". Nevertheless it is impossible further to identify these groups save to say that Congregationalism (*i.e.,* as polity) was a means to an end. According to Albert Peel:

> It ought to be realized too, that in the fluid condition
> of religious life and ecclesiastical organization between
> 1560 and 1580 it is more or less futile to attempt to

fix exact and definite labels to men, churches, and even movements, to dub them Puritan, Separatist, Presbyterian, Congregational, Non-Conformist, as if each of these were classes that excluded and did not overlap the others.[1]

Elizabeth's insistence upon uniformity turned many Puritans into Separatists for the feeling grew that the queen had no right to "compell anie man to believe any thing contrary to God's word." Cambridge University became a center of Puritanism, and in spite of the driving out of Thomas Cartwright, remained so, as Robert Browne affirmed in his *True and Short Declaration.*

All that we can safely say about these backgrounds of Congregationalism is that before 1580 revolt, if necessary from political and religious authority, by the gathering together of covenanted groups on the basis of the Scriptures was in the very atmosphere.

II

Both Robert Browne (1550, 1556?-1633) and Robert Harrison, products of Cambridge, were endeavoring to further the reforming of the church. Both of them, learning of kindred spirits in Norfolk, moved to Norwich where, apparently, Browne convinced Harrison that even the bishops were wrong, and a church along Congregational lines was formed of Christian believers under covenant with God in 1581. Promptly the little group found itself persecuted and most of the members with Browne and Harrison moved to Middelburg, Zealand, where Browne wrote his *Treatise of Reformation without Tarying for Anie,*[2] and his *Booke Which Sheweth the Life and Manners of All True Christians,*[3] works which were widely read. According to Browne, "he is a Christian which is redeemed by Christ vnto holiness & happines for euer & professeth the same by submitting him self to his lawes & governmet". This is as true of the magistrate as of the common citizen. A church is composed of people living a godly life, under covenant with

God and subject to the government of God and Christ. Magistrates, ruling the commonwealth, have no power or authority over the church, nor can genuine religion ever be forced. But Browne did not teach separation of church and state. Each church, for purposes of teaching and guiding, has a pastor, teacher, and elders, who, after the consent of the people, ordain and "pronounce them, with prayer and imposition of handes, as called and authorised of God". Ultimately Browne and Harrison disagreed and the former returned to the Established Church, but the influence of his writings was extensive and persistent, especially in London, where the Congregational movement continued under the leadership of John Greenwood, Henry Barrowe and John Penry all of whom suffered martyrdom for their beliefs. Francis Johnson, pastor of the church of which Greenwood was teacher, was imprisoned but again pressure forced most of the group out of the country and they finally settled in Amsterdam, about 1595. Their Confession of Faith of the following year provides for a "Ministerie of Pastors, Teachers, Elders, Deacons, Helpers", and "that . . . every Christian Congregation hath povvre and commandement to elect and ordeine their ovvn ministerie . . ."[4] Again the Separatist group had trouble. Francis Johnson, while still in prison, had married a well-to-do widow of London whose dress was not always to the liking of some of his parishioners. As Knappen puts it, "Stays became literally great bones of contention",[5] and Johnson, in the controversy, parted company with his brother and father among others.

In contrast to the Anabaptist principle of separation of church and state these groups, although Separatist, maintained the importance and prestige of the magistrate.

III

Early in the seventeenth century a Separatist group at Gainsborough under John Smyth moved to Amsterdam and joined with the congregation there. Another part of the original Gainsborough church, meeting, for the convenience of its members, at Scrooby in the home of William Brewster (1560?-1644) also removed at first to Amsterdam under Richard Clifton and John Robinson (1575?-1625) and then, noting with concern the trouble in *that* communion, went on to Leyden. Clifton, however, remained in Amsterdam, with Robinson becoming pastor of the church. Here in Holland the little English group remained eleven years, but life was hard, customs strange, and their children were growing up in a foreign country. Besides they wished to live under English law, and even entertained the missionary hope that they might propagate the gospel in some part of the new world. Toward this end they appealed to the London-Virginia Company for the right to settle somewhere along the coast of Virginia and, to show they were not rebels, they sent on ahead the Seven Articles in which they admitted the right of the King to appoint bishops, civil overseers, or officers to oversee the churches,—an Erastian document if ever there was one![6]

Thereupon the little band returned to England and in the fall of 1620 set forth in the Mayflower for the new world, their minister reluctantly remaining behind. According to Edward Winslow, John Robinson gave some farewell advice to the group including the immortal words that "the Lord had more truth and light yet to break forth out of his holy Word".[7] Two months later they anchored off Cape Cod and, since they were beyond the limits of their patent, drew up the Mayflower Compact by which they covenanted (with one another and their God) and combined themselves into a civil body politic. Thus the first official document of these Englishmen reflected Congregational principles and polity, though it was not a religious statement. The Plymouth colony, the Pilgrims, barely survived the rigors of their first New England winter, yet these heroic souls gave to this nation its heritage of Thanksgiving Day. And if we may believe Cotton Mather, by 1642 there were a dozen ministers, some of whom were "stars of the first magnitude."[8]

In the meantime a colony of Puritans had come out to Salem under John Endicott late in 1628. That winter, many of the colony falling ill, Dr. Samuel Fuller, a deacon in the Plymouth church, was sent for, and thus direct news of the Separatist group was obtained. Both groups were Calvinist in theology and Fuller made such a good impression that Endicott wrote to Governor Bradford that "Gods people are all marked with one and ye same marke", and hoped "that we may, as Christian breethren, be united by a heavenly & unfained love".[9] The following summer, at Salem, two ministers, Samuel Skelton and Francis Higginson, were elected pastor and teacher respectively, the latter with three or four others laying their hands on Skelton, "using prayer therewith", and then hands were laid on Higginson. Later, elders and deacons were set aside and Governor Bradford and other representatives of the Plymouth church participated in the ceremonies. The covenant of the Salem church, remarkable for brevity and clarity, ran as follows:

> We Covenant with the Lord and one with an other; and doe bynd our selves in the presence of God, to walke together in all his waies, according as he is pleased to reveale himself unto us in his Blessed word of truth.[10]

Thus from the very beginning of Congregationalism over here certain principles and procedures may be observed, 1) a church is composed of Christians gathered under covenant with God and each other; 2) each church elects its officials and ordains them; 3) neighboring churches participate in the special services of setting apart, or dedication, or ordination of such officers. The details of meetings in these early days are not always clear but the general pattern of autonomy and fellowship is already formed. This is not surprising since Puritan and Separatist alike believed they were copying New Testament models in planting their churches. Before the end of the century Plymouth and Massachusetts Bay were united in the same church-state.

IV

Space will not permit the detailed delineation of other settlements around Massachusetts Bay and in the Connecticut River valley. In general the colonists flourished and waves of immigrants sought hopefully a new life on these shores. In 1631 Massachusetts Bay decided that only church members might vote, and the minister, who had oversight of church membership, promptly advanced in importance even over the magistrate. This electoral restriction was not removed until well into the nineteenth century.

Because of the success of the Presbyterians in England in the decade of the 1640's and the fear that Presbyterianism would be foisted upon New England—a fear strengthened by the fact that here and there were colonists with Presbyterian or semi-Presbyterian sympathies—and because many were denied the right to vote, the General Court of Massachusetts Bay asked the churches to come together in synod to discuss such matters as membership and baptism. The Cambridge Synod, which began sitting in 1646 and which produced the Cambridge Platform of 1648, was the result. Here for the first time New England Congregationalism defined its faith and polity. Its faith was the same as that announced in the Westminster Confession. In polity the Platform provided for the autonomy of the local church, but also strongly advocated "church-communion" (*i.e.,* fellowship between churches). It designated church officers as pastor, teacher, elders, and deacons, and maintained to magistrates the right to interfere. The Cambridge Platform of 1648 might be called the Great Charter of Congregationalism.

From the custom of the clergy meeting with the general Court arose the Ministers' Convention in Massachusetts, and by the beginning of the eighteenth century there were five district associations. These had only advisory powers but in Connecticut, by the Saybrook Platform of 1708, these associations became Standing Councils and, in Fairfield County, a Consociation. Such Presbyterianism was repudiated in Massachusetts. Yet New England Congregationalism was largely a product of its ministers, among whom there were giants in those days. One can only mention in passing John Cotton (Boston), Richard Mather (Dorchester), John Davenport (New Haven), and Thomas Hooker, who moved his congregation from Newtowne (later Cambridge) to Hartford.

With the passage of time changes occurred. Elders dropped out, deacons taking over their functions without their authority. Pastor and teacher coalesced into pastor; synods disappeared, but associations and (later) conferences emerged, but ultimately retained only advisory powers. The Sacraments were and are baptism and the Lord's Supper.

Theologically Congregationalism tried to adjust growing disinterestedness of the second and third generations by the Half-Way Covenant, which satisfied no one, but which permitted grand-children of godly grandparents to be baptized though their parents had not acknowledged publicly a religious experience. Then, in the Great Awakening the churches had their spirits heartened and their life strengthened by the preaching of Jonathan Edwards (1703-1758), with his emphasis upon responsibility, George Whitefield (1714-1770), Samuel Hopkins (1721-1803), who stressed "disinterested benevolence", Nathanael Emmons (1745-1840), Timothy Dwight (1752-1817) and others. Emmons particularly held to the democracy inherent in Congregationalism and opposed the forming of associations in Massachusetts holding that "Associationism leads to Consociationism; Consociationism leads to Presbyterianism; Presbyterianism leads to Episcopacy; Episcopacy leads to Roman Catholicism; and Roman Catholicism is an ultimate fact."

Nevertheless, an excellent argument may be made that Congregationalism, as it fashioned slowly its polity, and formed its concepts of church and church-estate, prepared the way for those discussions and protests which led to the Revolutionary War.[11] The Congregational clergy played a prominent part in arousing the people against England, in sustaining their spirit in the dark days of an apparently lost cause, in serving as chaplains, and finally, when the war was won, in lending their wisdom to constitutional conventions.

V

"The Congregationalists have the longest record of missionary endeavor of any of the American churches", according to William Warren Sweet.[12] It is not only long, it is impressive. One of the reasons why the Leyden pilgrims wanted to come to these shores was to spread the gospel. During the second session of the Cambridge Synod, in 1647, John Eliot preached to the Indians in the presence of the Assembly. Others who carried on the work among the aborigines were David Brainerd, and the Mayhews who, for five generations, preached to the Indians at Martha's Vineyard. When New England Congregationalists began to move westward in great numbers a keen missionary interest had already been expressed in the General Association of Connecticut of 1774. But the War and the subsequent decline in religion resulted in the delay in founding societies. However, in 1798 the Connecticut Missionary Society was formed, and in the following year a similar society was organized in Massachusetts, with New Hampshire and Vermont following in that order. These state societies promoted home missions and ultimately turned over their work to the interdenominational American Home Missionary Society, founded in 1826. The early state organizations, whose beginnings paralleled a second wave of revival from Maine to Rhode Island, published missionary periodicals and also encouraged the founding of Bible societies. Under the American Home Missionary Society the "Illinois Band" of Yale Divinity School students came out to Illinois in 1828, planting churches and founding Illinois College. Fifteen years later the "Iowa Band" of nine Andover students came out to that state and in addition to churches established Iowa College (now Grinnell).

In the meantime the Connecticut type of Congregationalism

was leading directly toward cooperation with the Presbyterians as both denominations pressed westward. Before the end of the eighteenth century the Presbyterian General Assembly and the General Association of Connecticut were exchanging delegates who even had the right to vote. In 1801 both bodies adopted the Plan of Union which was designed to aid in a reciprocal relationship the ministers and newly planted churches in the territory stretching from western New York to Michigan and Iowa. Doubtless the greater centralization of the Presbyterians resulted in the absorption of many Congregational churches, but at a crucial moment in the westward trek of thousands the Plan of Union provided an important basis for joint religious endeavor which was to have its effect for years to come. It largely came to an end when the "Old School" Presbyterians voted it down in the General Assembly of 1837, though the "New School" continued to cooperate until the Congregationalists in the Western Convention of 1846 recommended abandonment of the Plan. Both denominations cooperated, however, in the work of the American Home Missionary Society, which extended to the Pacific coast[13] until 1861 when the Presbyterians withdrew.[14]

Just as Congregationalists led in missions to the Indians and in home missions, so they instituted the first Board of Foreign Missions in America. Samuel J. Mills had already dedicated his life to missions when he founded a society called "The Brethren" at Williams College. The objective of the society was "to effect, in the persons of its members, a mission or missions to the heathen."[15] When Mills and others went on to the newly founded Andover Seminary he took the society with him, where other kindred spirits united in promoting its objectives. But when Mills, Adoniram Judson, Samuel Nott, and Samuel Newell desired to go out to the foreign field there was no agency to send them. They therefore petitioned the General Association of Massachusetts, which instituted the American Board of Commissioners for Foreign Missions, formally chartered in 1812. In addition to work in foreign lands this Board also had oversight of missions to the Cherokees, Choctaws and other American Indian tribes. At first completely Congregational the American Board later included eight commissioners from the Presbyterians and one from the Dutch Reformed. But by 1870 it was again denominational.

Another important missionary endeavor was that of the American Missionary Association, organized by combining a number of small antislavery societies, at Albany in 1846. In addition to work among negroes and Indians it carried on foreign missions in lands from Africa to Hawaii, but its major emphasis was upon schools and churches in the southern states. Before the end of the century it had transferred its foreign work to the American Board and assumed responsibility for Congregational work among the Indians and Eskimos. Perhaps the chief contribution of this Society has been its important work in connection with institutions of learning for negroes. Atlanta, Howard, Fisk, Talladega, Dillard, Tougaloo and Tillotson are only a few of the institutions which have felt the impress of its spirit.

VI

Congregationalists have been known generally for their educated ministry. Within a decade of its planting Massachusetts Bay Colony established Harvard College to train ministers to replace, in time, those who had come over (largely from Cambridge) in the early years. Yale was founded in 1701 and Dartmouth in 1770. Williams, Bowdoin, Middlebury, and Amherst followed, but each was governed by a Board of Trustees, not by the denomination as such. Andover was the first Seminary established by the Congregational churches in 1808 and was followed by Bangor in 1814. As they went west Congregationalists planted colleges from the Alleghenies to the Pacific in order to train teachers for western schools, and to help spread culture on the frontier. Seminaries were also founded, the Chicago Theological Seminary, 1855, being the most unique since its Board of Directors is elected by and responsible to the

Congregational churches of sixteen middle western states whose representatives meet triennially in convention. Many of the colleges established by the denomination in the nineteenth century have lost their denominational color but they were set as lighthouses of learning and religious influence in a wilderness.

VII

The nineteenth century was to prove climactic for Congregationalism. We have already noted the activity of the denomination in missions and in education. We have now to observe the coming to birth of a national consciousness. To be sure the century began with the Unitarian separation, caused principally by growing divergence between liberals and Edwardean conservatives, and culminating in the struggle for the Chair in Divinity at Harvard. When this went to Henry Ware (1805), Andover Seminary was founded in protest. But the movement was accelerated by the preaching of William Ellery Channing (1780-1842), especially his sermon at the ordination of Jared Sparks in Baltimore, in 1819. The division grew slowly but increased in momentum with the decision of the Massachusetts Supreme Court in the Dedham case, that a church exists in connection with a society, and consequently only that part of the church membership recognized by the society has right to the property. As a result the Unitarians took over almost one hundred churches, yet the movement was centered largely in and around the Boston area, and made practically no headway in Connecticut.

Another who disagreed with the Edwardean theology was Horace Bushnell (1802-1876), minister of the North Congregational Church in Hartford. In his *Discourses on Christian Nurture* (1846) he advanced the idea that a child born into a Christian home should naturally grow up to be a Christian and "never know himself as being otherwise". The beneficent influence of Bushnell came down the years liberalizing a Calvinism which was already out of date and unreal.

It took a long time for Congregationalism to become national in organization. This was because there have always been Congregationalists who viewed any attempt at national cohesion with suspicion, fearing overhead control. But as members and churches east and west began to sense their unity nationalization was as inevitable as tomorrow's sun. Michigan set the pace calling together representatives of churches of the northwestern states in 1846, and six years later New York Association invited every Congregational church to be represented by pastor and delegate at a convention which met at Albany and which was noteworthy. It dealt with the Plan of Union, aided church extension (Congregational Church Building Society organized 1853), began collecting statistics (first Year Book issued, 1854), and encouraged the extension of the denomination in the western states. We have already seen how the Chicago Seminary was maintained by a Triennial Convention. This convention with the General Association of Illinois began looking toward a national gathering of representatives, and such a meeting was held in Boston, 1865. This body approved a statement of faith (Calvinistic, but liberal), and a formulation of polity (autonomy of the local church, fellowship of the churches, a non-hierarchical ministry). The success of this Council led directly to the forming of the National Council at Oberlin in 1871, which provided for a permanent triennial council which, at Kansas City in 1913, became biennial.

We are now in a position to see the entire structure of American Congregationalism. The local church is an autonomous body, but it belongs to an Association of Congregational churches and ministers which meets usually twice a year, and to which the local church sends pastor and delegates. The Association follows more or less county lines. Next comes the State Conference (the old General Association) meeting annually to which churches of the Associations send ministers and delegates. The national body, the General Council, meets biennially and, generally speaking, its delegates are on the basis of one for every 1000 church members (churches of over 1000 members are limited to one delegate; churches of fewer than 1000 members are grouped into units), and alternate between minister and layman. Usually a Conference has a superintendent, but he is responsible to the Conference, and enjoys no authority by virtue of his position. Thus Congregationalism is a delicate structure maintaining a nice balance between autonomy of the "gathered-covenant" church (over which there can be no authority imposed) and, no less, a fellowship of churches and ministers in Association, Conference and General Council. Two sentences from the Kansas City Statement adopted by the National Council of 1913 illustrate this:

> We hold to the autonomy of the local church and its independence of all ecclesiastical control. We cherish the fellowship of the churches, united in district, state and national bodies, for counsel and cooperation in matters of common concern[16].

Having accomplished a national organization Congregationalists held their first International Council in London in 1891.

VIII

From anti-slavery interests the Congregational churches moved to a concern over the critical area of industrial and social relationships. Washington Gladden, George A. Gordon, Newman Smythe, Henry Churchill King, Graham Taylor, Arthur E. Holt and others, through sermons and books attempted to apply a Christian gospel to a difficult time. A decade before the close of the nineteenth century The Chicago Theological Seminary established a Department of Social Training under Graham Taylor. In 1907 Washington Gladden (1836-1918) stirred the National Council with his address on "The Church and the Social Crisis", but it was not until the Oberlin Council of 1934 that a Council for Social Action, responsible to the national body, was established. This Council is now engaged in studying carefully the application of what it believes to be the Christian gospel to our complex social relationships.

IX

Ever since Congregationalism came to a realization of its national unity it has been a proponent of church union. It has never thought of itself as the only true Church, but rather as a part of the churches of Christ. It has cooperated fully with national and international Protestant organizations. Since it is essentially a creedless denomination it has sometimes been accused of having no belief. No charge could be wider of the mark since Congregationalists deeply cherish faith in God, Christ, the Holy Spirit, the guidance of the Scriptures, and the Church of Christ. The Kansas City Statement put this matter concisely and because it has received wide acceptance I quote it in full:

> We believe in God the Father, infinite in wisdom, goodness, and love; and in Jesus Christ, his Son, our Lord and Saviour, who for us and our salvation lived and died and rose again and liveth evermore; and in the Holy Spirit, who taketh of the things of Christ and revealeth them to us, renewing, comforting, and inspiring the souls of men. We are united in striving to know the will of God as taught in the Holy Scriptures, and in our purpose to walk in the ways of the Lord, made known to us. We hold it to be the mission of the Church of Christ to proclaim the gospel to all mankind, exalting the worship of the one true God, and laboring for the progress of knowledge, the promotion of justice, the reign of peace, and the realization of human brotherhood. Depending, as did our fathers, upon the continued guidance of the Holy Spirit to lead us into all truth, we work and pray for the transformation of the world into the kingdom of God; and we look with faith for the triumph of righteousness and the life everlasting.[17]

If this is considered carefully one may find the depth of man's confrontation by God, the presence of the living Christ and his Spirit, the openness of soul which expects and receives fresh and new insights and truth, the sense of responsibility which every Christian must have for his world, "and the life everlasting".

Congregationalism's unique characteristics of full local autonomy and firmness of fellowship between Congregational churches, its freedom from slavery to a creed, and its reiterated declarations of interest in Christian unity have resulted in the denomination's leadership in matters ecumenical. In 1925 the Evangelical Protestant Churches were received as a Conference (on conference level) by the National Council.

Before the beginning of this century negotiations regarding union were begun with the churches of the Christian connection. This denomination was itself the result of a union of small bodies of Virginia Methodists, Vermont Baptists, and Kentucky Presbyterians,—all calling themselves "Christians". For the moment nothing came of the negotiations between the Congregationalists and the Christians, but in 1931 the Christian General Convention and the Congregational National Council united at Seattle to form what is now the General Council of the Congregational Christian Churches. This was a union at the top. When, recently, the same sort of merger was attempted with the Evangelical and Reformed Church, a small group of Congregationalists, organized to oppose the merger, successfully (but how tragically!) threw the matter into the courts, where it is now being reviewed. But the great majority of Congregationalists probably believe that they can maintain their local autonomy and yet further the cause of unity among Protestants. Some of those who most vociferously champion the "church of the Pilgrim fathers" seem curiously unaware that Congregationalism has evidently possessed a rare talent in churchmanship, namely, the ability (through reception of more truth and light breaking forth out of his holy Word) to meet new challenges with fresh inspiration, and to adjust itself and its message accordingly. Thus when young people's work was desperately needed Francis E. Clark (1852-1927) founded in Portland, Maine, in 1881 Christian Endeavor,—a society which became international some years later. But the danger of modern Congregationalism is that its pardonable pride in the accomplishments of the Pilgrims and Puritans may prevent its contributing to a united Protestantism those very qualities in which it has gloried in the past.

The Congregational Christian Churches, according to latest available statistics, number over 5,600 churches and more than 1,204,000 members in this country, but their influence in many areas of American life has been out of all proportion to their numbers.

NOTES AND BIBLIOGRAPHY

Space prevents any attempt at Bibliography of Congregationalism, not to mention Puritanism. But one must mention in passing,

GAIUS GLENN ATKINS and FREDERICK L. FAGLEY, *History of American Congregationalism* (Boston and Chicago, 1942).

HENRY MARTYN DEXTER, *The Congregationalism of the Last Three Hundred Years as Seen in its Literature* (New York, 1880).

The textual notes follow:

[1] ALBERT PEEL, *The First Congregational Churches* (Cambridge, 1920), p. 13. *See* also the same author's *The Brownists in Norwich and Norfolk about 1580* (Cambridge, 1920).

[2] *Old South Leaflets,* Vol. iv, No. 100 (Boston, n. d.).

[3] Extracts may be found in WILLISTON WALKER, *The Creeds and Platforms of Congregationalism* (New York, 1893), pp. 18-27.

[4] For this Confession of Faith of 1596 *see* WILLISTON WALKER, *op. cit.,* pp. 41-74.

[5] M. M. KNAPPEN, *Tudor Puritanism* (Chicago, 1939), p. 314.

[6] WILLISTON WALKER, *op. cit.,* p. 89ff.

[7] Quoted by WALTER H. BURGESS, *The Pastor of the Pilgrims* (New York, 1920), p. 240.

[8] COTTON MATHER, *Magnalia Christi Americana* (Hartford, 1855), p. 61.

[9] WILLIAM BRADFORD, *History of Plymouth Plantation* (Boston, 1856), p. 264.

[10] WILLISTON WALKER, *op. cit.,* p. 116.

[11] ALICE M. BALDWIN, *The New England Clergy and the American Revolution* (Durham, N. C., 1928). Attention should also be directed to PERRY

MILLER'S *Orthodoxy in Massachusetts* (Cambridge, 1933) and *The New England Mind* (New York, 1939).

12 WILLIAM WARREN SWEET, *Religion on the American Frontier, 1783-1850.* Vol. iii, *The Congregationalists* (Chicago, 1939), p. 43.

13 *Cf.,* COLIN BRUMMITT GOODYKOONTZ, *Home Missions on the American Frontier* (Caldwell, Idaho), 1939.

14 FREDERICK KUHNS, "End of Joint Missionary Work by Presbyterians and Congregationalists", *Journal of the Presbyterian Historical Society,* Dec. 1950, pp. 249-269.

15 Quoted in *Memorial Volume of the First Fifty Years of the American Board of Commissioners for Foreign Missions,* 4th ed. (Boston, 1861), p. 41.

16 *The National Council of Congregational Churches of the United States* (Boston, 1913), p. 341.

17 *Ibid.,* pp. 340, 341.

X

BAPTIST CHURCHES IN AMERICA

X

BAPTIST CHURCHES IN AMERICA

ROBERT G. TORBET

THE PEOPLE called Baptists can name no single leader or founder. They can point to no distinctive creed. Nor can they refer to a certain organization to which all belong. As a matter of fact, they are not entirely in agreement as to their origin. There are some who seek to establish a continuity of Baptist churches from New Testament times to the present. Others contend that historical evidence is insufficient to support such a view. However, it is possible to point to numerous groups, often regarded as heretical by the Medieval Church, which bore witness to one or more of the principles held by modern Baptists. The latest of these were the Anabaptists, known today as Mennonites. They represented a left wing of the Reformation and were distinguished by their rejection of the covenant idea of the church with its practice of infant baptism and its connection with the state. They are the nearest of kin among the spiritual ancestors of the Baptists.

European and British Backgrounds

It is the judgment of many Baptists today that their history as a denomination may be traced more properly to a refugee congregation of English Separatists in Amsterdam, Holland. They became Baptists in 1609 under the leadership of their pastor, John Smyth, an Anglican clergyman who had become a Puritan, then an Independent. After a careful study of the Scriptures concerning who are the rightful members of the church, he took the next step and became a Baptist. Rejecting the covenant idea by which infants are baptized into the church, he accepted the principle of believer's baptism. After baptizing himself, he administered the ordinance to about forty persons. Within a comparatively short time, a part of this church returned to England under the leadership of Thomas Helwys. It became the source of one stream of Baptists known as General Baptists, so-called because they were Arminian in theology, emphasizing that the atonement is for all. A second stream came into existence in 1638 under the leadership of John Spilsbury, a former Congregationalist. These were known as Particular or Calvinistic Baptists because they taught that the atonement is limited to those predestined to be saved. By 1641, this congregation restored immersion as the scriptural mode of baptism, a practice which eventually became universal among all Baptists.

Typical of the freedom enjoyed by Baptists, each group carried on its own work and maintained separate organizations in the British Isles. It was not until 1891 that they were merged in the Baptist Union for Great Britain and Ireland. Their influence upon their times was significant in three respects. First, they exerted a strong pressure in behalf of religious liberty which played a part in the winning of tolerance for nonconformists by the State Church and the Government. Second, they provided a training ground in democracy for the underprivileged peoples who found spiritual refuge in their midst.[1] Third, they gave rise to the modern foreign missionary enterprise of Protestantism in the work of William Carey, whose zeal was responsible for the organization of the Baptist Missionary Society at Kettering in 1792[2].

Baptist Developments in America

Baptist beginnings in America are dated from the establishment of a Baptist church at Providence, Rhode Island, in 1639 by Roger Williams, a Separatist minister who had established a new colony dedicated to religious liberty, after he had been driven out of Massachusetts Bay Colony. The Newport church, founded by John Clarke in the same colony, disputes the claim of the Providence church to being the first in America.

In the years that followed, severe persecution in New England discouraged any large growth of Baptists, although a sprinkling of churches was to be found there prior to the beginning of the Great Awakening in the late 1720's. The freer atmosphere of the Pennsylvania Colony allowed the organization of the first association of Baptist churches in America in 1707 when five small congregations organized the Philadelphia Baptist Association. This body, with its Calvinistic Confession of Faith, set a pattern for early American Baptists.

During the Great Awakening, the number of Baptists increased as evangelists and made a strong appeal for personal religion. It was not long before Baptists, like Presbyterians and Methodists, were divided over the emphasis of the revival into Old Lights or Regulars and New Lights or Separates. The latter group encouraged emotionalism, and insisted upon a freedom of the individual to be led by the Holy Spirit. Accordingly, its members were opposed to organization or authority. Separate Baptists grew in number, particularly in New England and the Southern Colonies, as the era of revivals continued. Two factors, however, eventually united the two groups. One was the common cause of winning religious liberty, in which they both engaged during the American Revolution. The other was the foreign missions' enterprise which Baptists undertook in 1814 when they organized the General Missionary Convention of the Baptist Denomination in the United States of America in response to the plea of Luther Rice for support of Adoniram and Ann Judson in Burma.

This Triennial Convention, as it was called, was the first step in the development of a denominational consciousness among American Baptists. The trend was furthered by the organization in 1824 of a General Tract Society, later called the American Baptist Publication Society, and of the American Baptist Home Mission Society in 1832. These were national societies which were to function separately from the autonomous local churches and their associations. The hope of unity was blasted, however, by certain dissatisfactions which stemmed from a feeling that the home agency was failing to evangelize southern territory and from a clash of points of view concerning slavery. By 1845 a schism occurred in the Triennial Convention when the southerners withdrew to form their own Southern Baptist Convention. The new body was fashioned after a pattern of organization which caused the Convention to function for the churches through boards for home and foreign missions, education, and publication. This represented a more centralized polity than that which was continued in the North, where the churches functioned only through separate agencies or societies.

The Triennial Convention was renamed the American Baptist Missionary Union; it is known as the American Baptist Foreign Mission Society. In the 1870's, the women of the North organized their own societies, the Woman's American Baptist Foreign Mission Society and the Woman's American Baptist Home Mission Society. Support for these various agencies was raised by separate appeals to the churches.

To avoid the confusion and duplication of effort which resulted from this practice, the Northern Baptist Convention was organized in 1907 at Washington, D. C. This was in reality a corporation with restricted powers, to which the churches sent representatives annually, and with which the national societies, the state conventions, and city mission societies were affiliated by voluntary action. Each of the agencies remained intact, relinquishing only a degree of self-determinism in the co-operative plan of raising and distributing funds with a unified budget. Because it represented a cross between the society and convention methods of Baptist polity, tensions arose in some circles where fear of centralization was felt most keenly. During the first half century of the Convention's existence, changes were made from time to time in its structure in the interest of efficiency and to allay such criticisms. In 1950 its name was changed to the American Baptist Convention, and the office of general secretary was created.

At the mid-century, the Convention was composed of 6,768

local Baptist churches, each of which is autonomous and constitutes the basic unit of Baptist polity. The total membership was 1,561,073[3]. The churches are united in local areas into associations which serve for purposes of fellowship, co-operative service, and counsel with respect to ordination and other matters. Thirty-four state conventions carry on the main co-operative work of the churches in intra-state home missions, in education, and in the raising of funds to support the national societies. Sixteen Baptist city societies conduct home mission and church extension service in metropolitan areas. The education program is carried on through thirteen theological seminaries, three training schools for girls, eleven academies, six junior colleges, and twenty-nine colleges and universities including ten for Negroes. The care of children is met through eighteen homes, while the aged are provided for in twenty-two institutions. Six hospitals minister to the sick.

The American Baptist Home Mission Society conducts work in thirty-four states, Alaska, Central America, Cuba, El Salvador, Haiti, and Puerto Rico. It maintains missions and schools for the Indians and Negroes. The Woman's American Baptist Home Mission Society supplements these services by its program of assigning single women to Christian centers, bilingual churches, hospital visitation and Christian friendliness work among Indians, Negroes, and Orientals in this hemisphere.

Foreign mission stations are maintained by the American Baptist Foreign Mission Society and the Woman's American Baptist Foreign Mission Society in Burma, Assam, India, China, Japan, the Congo, and the Philippines.[4] Baptists have rendered most successful service to underprivileged peoples in these countries. Their policy has been to develop national leadership and self-supporting churches, a strategy which has proved its worth during the stress and confusion of two world wars with the accompanying upsurge of anti-Caucasian feeling.

The Southern Baptist Convention has grown from three

hundred churches of 352,950 members in 1845 to 27,788 churches of 7,079,889 members in 1950. Within a single generation, Southern Baptists have gained four million members. This has been due to a number of factors: 1) a scattering and multiplying of southerners north and west; 2) their hold upon the allegiance of rural people, even those who move to town; 3) their churches "are centers of social life for their members"; 4) laymen have a large part in the church program; 5) their social emphasis is broadening without a relinquishing of the simple biblical preaching which appeals strongly to the rank and file of Americans.[5]

The Convention functions through five denominational boards, for home and foreign missions, Sunday school work, education, and ministerial relief. Home mission stations are maintained throughout the South, in Alaska, Cuba, Costa Rica, Panama, and the Canal Zone. The Home Mission Board also conducts work jointly with Negro Baptists. It carries on an extensive program in behalf of migrants, Indians of the Southwest, underprivileged of the Appalachian and Ozark Mountain ranges, and of small congregations in need of church buildings.

Foreign mission work is maintained in twenty-two countries and three continents. Although Southern Baptists spent nearly eight million dollars in 1949 and supported 700 foreign missionaries, its record, in comparison with its huge membership of over seven million members, ranks third "among the denominations in the number of missionaries sent overseas." The American Baptist Convention, with only one and a half million members, has 550 missionaries, while the Presbyterian Church, U.S.A. with two million members supports 1,300 missionaries.[6]

The greatest achievement of the Southern Baptist Convention is probably the work of its Sunday-School Board, which provides literature for over four and a half million pupils in nearly twenty-six thousand Sunday schools. A solidarity of denominational teaching and loyalty is maintained through this means as well as through the training program of the five theological seminaries which are supported and controlled by the Convention. In addition, Southern Baptists support thirty colleges, twenty-three junior colleges, eight academies, twenty-nine hospitals, and twenty orphanages.[7]

Baptists of the North and the South hold their basic principles in common. The Southerners, however, are more insistent upon close communion, localism in church polity, and aloofness from inter-denominational associations. They also represent a more faithful adherence to revivalism as the main type of evangelism. They view with considerable suspicion the more liberal social and economic points of view held by many Baptists in the North, although they are undergoing considerable change in social outlook at the present time. Southern Baptists generally look with disapproval upon the American Baptist Convention's membership in the National Council of the Churches of Christ in the United States of America and in the World Council of Churches.

In spite of these differences, however, the two conventions co-operate along with the two conventions of Negro Baptists in the Baptist World Alliance, which was organized in 1905 as a purely advisory body of Baptists throughout the world. It meets every five years for fellowship and discussion of themes of mutual interest, and to safeguard the principle of religious liberty. In 1950 nearly fifty thousand persons were in attendance at the Congress meeting in Cleveland; they represented approximately eighteen million Baptists.[8] Headquarters of the organization are in Washington, D. C.

Baptists of North and South, both Caucasian and Negro, also co-operate in the Baptist Joint Committee on Public Affairs which was organized in 1938 to enable Baptists to be more alert in behalf of issues involving the preservation of religious liberty and separation of church and state. Through its executive director, Dr. Joseph M. Dawson, the Baptist point of view on such issues is kept before the Government and the public.

Negro Baptists number approximately seven million. They

are organized in two major conventions: the National Baptist Convention of the United States of America, Incorporated, and the National Baptist Convention of America. They are thus divided because of a division which occurred in 1915-16 over a dispute concerning control of property and publications. The latter body, although the smaller (2,645,789 members in 10,851 churches), by court action retained the original name and so dates its origin from 1895. The former body is the larger (4,445,605 members in 25,350 churches), and was incorporated in 1915 under the laws of the District of Columbia.[9] Both organizations share a polity very similar to that of other Baptists. They conduct missions in Africa and help needy churches and schools in the United States. Their significance in American life is much greater than becomes evident to the casual reader of Baptist history. Their story needs yet to be told adequately. Suffice it to say that their churches have provided an important segment of the American public with Christian instruction and an opportunity to develop first hand, through their own church life, the benefits of democracy. For in their churches, American Negro Baptists have enjoyed, as nowhere else, a complete freedom to be themselves and to experience the growth that comes from participation in a democratic group life. This is all the more impressive when one remembers that one-half of the total number of Negroes in America are Baptists.

Smaller Baptist Bodies

The emphasis upon personal religion and individual experience which is inherent in Baptist teaching often has expressed itself in a variety of ways and has given rise, at times, to small, but vocal groups who maintain a separate identity, although their differences from the main bodies are slight. This right to dissent has been guarded carefully by Baptists. It has been enjoyed particularly in America where religious freedom is allowed and where economic prosperity makes possible the luxury of many sects and churches. It is not surprising, then, to discover that the sixteen million Baptists in the United States are divided into twenty-three distinct denominational bodies, nineteen of which contain in their combined membership only one-quarter of a million communicants. This tendency for the greatest bifurcation to take place among the smallest number of people is equally evident in American Protestantism in general where 198 of the 241 denominations represent only a little more than four per cent of the total Protestant church membership.[10]

This multiplicity of Baptist bodies reflect cultural, social, and doctrinal differences. The smaller groups fall into three general categories. The first is composed of those who represent the Arminian or Freewill theology. Since the greater number of Baptists in the United States have been Calvinists, Freewill Baptists have been in the minority, although they were among the earliest in America. The General Six-Principle Baptists first appeared in Providence, Rhode Island, in 1670 where they established a church upon the six foundational teachings laid down in Hebrews 6:1-2, namely: repentance from dead works, faith toward God, baptism, the laying on of hands, the resurrection of the dead, and eternal judgment. They, like their English counterpart, regarded the laying on of hands by the elders after baptism as a sign of the reception of the gifts of the Holy Spirit. Today, there are less than three hundred members in three churches.

A second Arminian body, called the Original Freewill Baptists, was organized in 1729 in Virginia and North Carolina. They claimed to be descended from the congregation of Thomas Helwys, pastor of the first congregation of General Baptists in seventeenth century England. They practiced ceremonial foot washing, anointing of the sick with oil, plural eldership, and a conference type of organization which had considerable authority over the churches. In 1870 they formed a General Association in which all of their local associations were represented. They have dwindled in number to less than forty thousand in 580 churches scattered throughout Illinois, Kentucky, Tennessee, Missouri, Arkansas, and Nebraska.

Another group which claims the same origin are called the Regular Baptists. This usage of the term is not to be confused with an earlier application of it to the main bodies of Baptists who were Calvinistic in contrast to those who were Arminian. Since about 1890, the term has been applied to those who are for the most part Arminian, although a few lean toward Calvinism. They practice close communion and foot washing. They have declined noticeably in membership in recent years, totalling now little more than seventeen thousand in about 266 churches.

By far the largest and most prominent body of Freewill Baptists are those who arose in New England in 1780 under the leadership of Benjamin Randall, a farmer-preacher of New Hampshire who reacted vigorously against the Calvinistic teaching of his day. His followers developed a rather extensive work of Sunday schools, churches, temperance and missionary societies. By 1910 their fifty-one associations and 1,586 churches held property valued at more than three million dollars. In 1911, they merged with the Northern Baptist Convention, which indicated a blurring of theological distinctions between Calvinistic and Arminian Baptists.

A second general category of small Baptist bodies is composed of those which represent the extremes of Calvinism. Called hyper-Calvinists, they opposed all human efforts to influence men to receive the gospel on the grounds that conversion was entirely an act of God. Hence, they avoided emotionalism and frowned upon Bible societies, missionary societies, Sunday schools, and temperance societies. Being a frontier people, their antipathy to evangelism on biblical grounds was reinforced by a suspicion that the East was controlling the finances of the churches as it did of the nation.

The most interesting example of the hyper-Calvinists are known as the Two-Seed-in-the-Spirit Predestinarian Baptists, a group which was organized in the 1820's by Elder Daniel

Parker of Virginia to oppose missions and Sunday schools. He based his dislike for Methodist teaching and all forms of missionary effort on a theory that two seeds entered the life stream of mankind through Eve. The good seed was imparted by God; the evil, by Satan. By this explanation, he justified his doctrine that some are predetermined to be saved while others are to be lost. He and his followers regarded foot washing as an ordinance and refused to recognize a paid ministry. As extreme forms of Calvinism have declined in popularity, the membership of this group has diminished to a mere two hundred in sixteen churches.

The spearhead of the antimission crusade was the Primitive Baptists, who were variously called by such names as Old School, Hard Shell, or Antimission. They have never been organized formally as a denomination. Although they favor evangelistic preaching they represent a protest against such organized efforts of evangelism as Bible societies, Sunday schools, state conventions, and theological seminaries. They are also opposed to all secret societies. Foot washing is practiced as an ordinance. Although they enjoyed a rapid growth in the 1840's, particularly in the South and in Illinois and Indiana, their numbers have decreased by nearly half, to a little more than sixty-nine thousand. Of all Baptists they are perhaps the most strictly orthodox.

The extreme Calvinistic Baptist sects have been strongest in the southern states where a Scotch-Irish Presbyterian population became prominent during the latter part of the eighteenth century. These people seem to possess a reluctance to change, which may explain the presence of anti-organizational and antimissionary attitudes in territory of the strongly organized and missionary-minded Southern Baptist Convention. Their influence has not lingered in the North where Baptists have become steadily less Calvinistic in emphasis.

A third category of small Baptist groups describes those who are dissatisfied with the major conventions. Such is the American Baptist Association, whose members are sometimes called Landmarkists because of their concern to maintain pure Christianity. This they attempt to do by adhering faithfully to the old apostolic order of church polity, which they interpret to be found only in churches of the Baptist pattern. They began in 1905 as the Baptist General Association. It was a protest move against organized conventions which they felt threatened the prerogatives of the local church. In 1924 they organized under the present name at Texarkana, Arkansas-Texas.

They are committed to an exclusively local view of the church which rules out any other units of church life. They oppose "alien immersion;" that is, they refuse to recognize as valid for membership in a Baptist church immersion which was administered by a non-Baptist. They are strictly close communion, even limiting observance of the Lord's Supper to the members of the local church. Moreover, they deny that paedobaptist congregations are churches in the New Testament sense of the word, and they refuse to recognize paedobaptist clergymen as true ministers of the gospel.

Landmarkists are chiefly in the South, the Southwest, and the Southeast, with a scattering of churches in California, Idaho, Colorado, Kansas, Massachusetts, and Pennsylvania. During the past fifteen years, they have enjoyed a striking increase in membership to 313,817 and 2,460 churches.[11] Their membership is shifting rapidly from rural to urban areas, probably due to population moves to war-industry centers. Their current growth may be explained by a combination of strongly fundamentalist doctrines, which include an emphasis upon the imminent return of Christ, with a pronouncedly authoritarian type of preaching which appeals to many in times of world unrest.

A second group of Baptists to oppose policies and teachings of a major convention is the General Association of Regular Baptist Churches (North). Organized in 1933 when fifty churches withdrew from the Northern Baptist Convention (now called the American Baptist Convention) because of dissatisfaction with denominational connectionalism and the presence of theological liberalism in that body, the new association was intended to be a fellowship with a minimum of organization. The moderately Calvinistic New Hampshire Confession of Faith was adopted, with a premillennial interpretation of the final article. The General Association of Regular Baptists interpret the word "Regular" to designate themselves as being in conformity to biblical Christianity as interpreted within the context of Fundamentalism.

Reluctant to develop agencies of their own, they channel their missionary funds through "approved" mission boards and designate "approved" schools in which their candidates for the ministry may be trained. The Association remains aloof from the National Council of Churches of Christ in the United States of America and the World Council of Churches on the grounds that these organizations represent theological, social, and economic liberalism. Its membership totals 80,000 members in 521 churches.[12]

A sect of Baptists which do not fall into either of the previously mentioned classifications is the Seventh-Day Baptists. They trace their history back to an English Sabbatarian Baptist named Stephen Mumford, who organized in 1671 in Newport, Rhode Island, the first church to bear that name in the Colonies. It appears, however, that there were already in existence in New England at the time some thirty other Seventh-Day Baptist churches, although they were not so named. Eventually, other centers were established in Philadelphia and New Jersey. Today there are 62 churches with 6,430 members in twenty-nine states. They claim that their adherence to the seventh day as the Sabbath has influenced ten other Protestant denominations, among which are the Seventh-Day Adventists.[13]

The Seventh-Day Baptists have their own missionary society, publishing house, and three schools located at Milton, Wisconsin, Alfred, New York, and Salem, West Virginia. This sect is not to be confused with the German Seventh-Day Baptists, who were led by John Conrad Beissel, an immigrant from the Palatinate, to Germantown, Pennsylvania, in 1728.

Characteristics of Baptists in America

Baptists belong to the left wing of American Protestantism. They emphasize the primacy of the Bible in their faith and polity, and cherish belief in the prerogative of the individual conscience to interpret the Bible with the help of the Holy Spirit. This explains why Baptists are not credalists. A second cardinal principle is acceptance of the supreme Lordship of Jesus Christ, the Savior, which prompts them to reject the idea of a human priesthood beween man and God. Because of their concept of the church as a fellowship of confessing disciples who have received believer's baptism by immersion, they refuse to baptize infants. Theirs is a democratic type of Christianity which is non-ecclesiastical and which expresses itself in a congregational form of church government. Convinced that vital religion is a personal matter between man and God, Baptists uphold the principle of religious liberty and separation of church and state.

The basic unit of church life among Baptists is the local congregation. Its autonomy in all matters pertaining to its functioning is a recognized principle of Baptist polity. But equally important is the associational principle by which churches in a reasonably close proximity unite in local associations and state conventions for fellowship, mutual counsel, and cooperative service. National conventions have come into existence to carry on more effectively the educational and missionary work of the denomination. These organizations meet periodically to receive reports from established committees, boards, societies, or institutions, and to make recommendations. They have not, however, any authority to enforce their decisions. Thus the independence of the local church is protected without losing the benefits of joint association and cooperative planning. Although there are occasional abuses of this free church life, Baptists generally have learned to use their democracy wisely.

Although the majority of Baptists in the United States share the same basic principles of faith and polity, there are variations in point of view and emphasis among them. These are often the product of cultural and social differences. The point of view and outlook which are characteristic of various sections of the country frequently are reflected in the predilections, interests, and methods of thought and work which mark one convention from another.

For example, the American Baptist Convention is composed mainly of people who practice open communion, who do not object to fraternal relations with other denominations in the National Council of Churches of Christ in the United States of America, and who are willing for their convention to be a constituent member of the World Council of Churches. In these matters, Baptists of the North manifest more of a cosmopolitan outlook than their brethren of the South. By the same token, leaders of the American Baptist Convention reflect a more progressive point of view with respect to social and economic issues. This is due to the fact that the pressures of urban and industrial problems were felt earlier in the North and the East than in the South and Southwest. Hence, social Christianity has influenced the American Baptist Convention sooner and more pronouncedly than it has affected the thinking and practice of the Southern Convention.

As frontier conditions receded more rapidly in the northern states, particularly in the East, revivalism lost its favored position as the chief method of evangelism in favor of a broadening interpretation of the term "evangelism" so as to include a variety of methods. Although the word describes the primary motivation of their enterprise, the missionary program of Northern Baptists is interpreted to include a larger service to men and women than might be included in the traditionally narrow use of the word "evangelism." Here again one sees that enlarging view of the application of the gospel to the whole of man which springs from a growing consciousness of human needs in modern life.

Southern Baptists, on the other hand, reflect to the present their predominantly rural culture. They still give prominence to revivalism, that method of evangelism which was so successful in winning frontier America to Christ, with its heart-warming emotional appeal for personal decision and its zealous exhortation backed by a simple faith in the authority of the Bible message. This democratic appeal of the Baptists to a people who valued their individualism has virtually made of the South a Baptist Bible Belt. Only the Methodists come close to sharing their numbers and influence. Through a careful plan of Sunday school instruction and the widespread distribution of Baptist literature, the Southern Baptist Convention has developed a Baptist consciousness and solidarity which has made for such great strength. A certain provincialism, however, has caused Southern Baptists to regard with a good deal of suspicion any participation of their fellow Baptists in the ecumenical movement. At the same time, there has developed amongst them a sense of destiny—to forget the Mason-Dixon Line and spread their churches throughout the entire country.

Most Southern Baptists practice close communion and close membership; whereas Northern Baptists are generally for open communion, but close membership except in scattered churches where persons from paedobaptist denominations are received upon profession of faith, without being required to be rebaptized.

As we have observed earlier, there is in the Southern Baptist Convention a survival of revivalism which colors its program of evangelism and missions. There is also a greater degree of theological agreement among Baptists in the South than there is in the North. In fact, as theological dissension has developed within the American Baptist Convention, there has been a drift of the Fundamentalists in the direction of the Southern Baptist Convention. By the same token, there is some indication that the more progressive element among

Southern Baptists is looking toward the American Baptist Convention for a natural affinity and fellowship. The differences between the two conventions are not on major doctrinal matters, nor are the lines sharply drawn. They are rather the reflection of the difference which exists between the broader interpretation of the application of the gospel to both society and individual and the narrower interpretation of its application primarily to the individual.

Although there does not seem to be the possibility of union of the major bodies of Baptists in the United States in the foreseeable future, there is the hope of something even more important. That is the development of better understanding between Baptists of varying backgrounds and cultural influences. This is being achieved gradually by at least three factors: 1) the lessening of sectional tensions which are coming about as Americans travel more widely and come to view the problems of each area with greater sympathy and understanding; 2) the participation of the major Baptist conventions in the Baptist Joint Committee on Public Affairs and in the Baptist World Alliance; 3) the passing of students north and south for their theological training, which is developing broader understanding among ministers.

The Influence of Baptists on American Life

Although Baptists have not given primary place to social and political reform, largely because of their view of separation of church and state, they, nevertheless, have exerted a marked influence upon life in the United States. This has been true partly because of their sheer strength of numbers and partly because of their emphasis upon holy living which is expected of all who profess to be converts of Christianity.

From the outset, their congregational form of church life and their democratic spirit made a strong appeal among the early settlers. Like the teaching of the Methodists, Baptist principles found easy lodgement in frontier communities and lonely cabins. The evangelistic zeal of farmer-preachers and stalwart missionaries like John Mason Peck and Isaac McCoy bore fruit in the planting of churches and Sunday schools across the country. Baptists shared with the Methodists and the Presbyterians in the spread of evangelical Christianity to the far West. They shared also a Puritan pattern of life which, because of their large membership among the common people, did much to develop a sturdy fiber of national morality.

Although Baptists were not in the lead among Protestants in the establishing of church schools, they did found academies, colleges, and theological seminaries which were distinctive in that they did not set up credal barriers to admission. One of the earliest co-educational institutions was organized at Lewisburg, Pennsylvania, in 1846. It was a Baptist academy out of which developed the University of Lewisburg, now known as Bucknell University. A university for poor boys of Philadelphia was established in 1886 by Dr. Russell Conwell and the Grace Baptist Church of which he was pastor in that city. It is known today as Temple University. Baptists have been ardent supporters of unsectarian public education because they believed that all children should have the benefits of schooling and because they felt that tax support of sectarian instruction would be a violation of separation of church and state. On occasions, they have refused government funds to support their own denominational institutions rather than to impair the cause of religious liberty.[14]

It has been generally conceded by historians that Baptists were largely responsible for the achievement of religious liberty in the United States. Through the efforts of such men as Dr. John Clarke, Roger Williams, Isaac Backus, and John Leland, the Baptists of colonial New England and Virginia made a heroic struggle for religious freedom "which culminated victoriously in the omission of any religious tests or restrictions when the Constitution of the United States was being framed."[15]

Their consistent support of the principle of religious liberty and the separation of church and state has placed Baptists in the forefront in the current opposition to the use of tax funds for the support of church institutions and sectarian efforts. It is their conviction that just as "the state has no right to interfere with the religious beliefs and practices of individuals or congregations," just so "the church on its part, has no claim upon the state for financial support."[16] The application of this principle led to the practice of voluntary church support in Christian polity, which has done much to free the churches from secular control.

Baptists' practice of democratic polity undoubtedly influenced the trend in government and political thought, especially on the frontier. Their influence was felt most plainly in such states as Kentucky, Indiana, and Illinois, and Texas where they were most numerous. By their recognition of the worth of the redeemed individual, Baptists gave to democracy a foundation which was spiritual rather than materialistic.

Baptists have made their greatest contribution to American life by their ministry to the common people and in behalf of the common people. By their insistence upon religious liberty for all, upon the right of all men to receive the benefits of education and especially of the gospel, and by their special attention to the depressed classes of society, they have touched more of the actual life of America than may ever be indicated by statistical data. Theirs has been the spread of a leaven which has won for them the acclaim of free men.[17]

NOTES

[1] G. M. TREVELYAN, *British History in the Nineteenth Century, 1782-1901* (1922), p. 160.

[2] For a detailed account of British Baptists, *see* A. C. UNDERWOOD, *A History of the English Baptists* (London, 1947) and ROBERT G. TORBET, *A History of the Baptists* (Philadelphia, 1950), chaps. 3-7.

[3] GEORGE F. KETCHAM, ed., *Yearbook of American Churches, 1951 Edition*, p. 234.

[4] Data in the aforegoing paragraphs are based on the *Yearbook of the American Baptist Convention, 1950,* pp. 422-587.

[5] E. P. ALLDREDGE, *Southern Baptist Handbook, 1945,* p. 184; KETCHAM, *op. cit.,* p. 234; CHARLES G. HAMILTON, "What Makes Southern Baptists Tick?" *The Christian Century,* LXVIII, No. 40 (Oct. 3, 1951), pp. 1125-26.

[6] FRANK S. MEAD, *Handbook of Denominations in the United States* (Nashville, 1951), p. 30.

7 MEAD, *op. cit.,* p. 31; TORBET, *op. cit.,* pp. 507-8.

8 *Proceedings of the Eighth Congress of the Baptist World Alliance* (Philadelphia, 1950), pp. 342-43.

9 KETCHAM, *op. cit.,* p. 234.

10 Computed from statistics in KETCHAM, *op. cit.,* pp. 234-39.

11 For brief summaries of the smaller bodies, *see* MEAD, *op. cit.,* pp. 33-40. For more detailed treatment, *see* TORBET, *op. cit.,* chap. 10.

12 MEAD, *op. cit.,* p. 38.

13 *Ibid*; KETCHAM, *op. cit.,* p. 235.

14 ROBERT G. TORBET, *A Social History of the Philadelphia Baptist Association, 1707-1940* (Philadelphia, 1944), chap. 8.

15 TORBET, *A History of the Baptists,* p. 481.

16 *Ibid.*

17 For expanded treatment of this section, *see* TORBET, *A History of the Baptists,* chap. 17.

BIBLIOGRAPHY

ROBERT A. BAKER, *Relations Between Northern and Southern Baptists* (Fort Worth, Texas, 1948).

HENRY COOK, *What Baptists Stand For* (London, 1947).

AUSTEN K. DEBLOIS, *Fighters for Freedom: Heroes of the Baptist Challenge* (Philadelphia, 1929).

GEORGE F. KETCHAM, (ed.), *Yearbook of Churches, 1951 Edition.* National Council of the Churches of Christ in the United States of America, 1951.

W. J. McGLOTHLIN, *Baptist Confessions of Faith* (Philadelphia, 1911).

WILLIAM R. McNUTT, *Polity and Practice in Baptist Churches* (Philadelphia, 1935).

FRANK S. MEAD, *Handbook of Denominations in the United States* (New York and Nashville, 1951).

ERNEST A. PAYNE, *The Fellowship of Believers: Baptist Thought and Practice Yesterday and Today* (London, 1945).

H. WHEELER ROBINSON, *The Life and Faith of the Baptists* (London, 1946).

HILLYER H. STRATON, *Baptists: Their Message and Mission* (Philadelphia, 1941).

ROBERT G. TORBET, *A History of the Baptists* (Philadelphia, 1950).

———, *A Social History of the Philadelphia Baptist Association, 1707-1940* (Philadelphia, 1944).

A. C. UNDERWOOD, *A History of the English Baptists* (London, 1947).

HENRY C. VEDDER, *A Short History of the Baptists* (Philadelphia, 1907).

———, *A Short History of Baptist Missions* (Philadelphia, 1927).

JOHN C. WENGER, *Glimpses of Mennonite History and Doctrine.* Second edition revised and enlarged (Scottdale, Pa., 1947).

W. R. WHITE, *Baptist Distinctives* (Nashville, 1946).

CARTER G. WOODSON, *The History of the Negro Church.* Second edition (Washington, D. C., 1921).

XI

THE UNITED PRESBYTERIAN CHURCH IN AMERICA

XI

THE UNITED PRESBYTERIAN CHURCH IN AMERICA

W. E. McCULLOCH

THE UNITED Presbyterian Church thinks well of its ancestry. Among its forebears were the heroic Covenanters of Scotland, men and women who endured terrible persecution with faith and courage unsurpassed. On occasion of the adoption of the National Covenant in 1638, some indomitable Scotsmen opened the veins in their arms and signed the doctrine with pens dipped in their own blood. The period of suffering, part of which is known as "the killing time," is coincident with the reigns of the Stuart kings, Charles II and James II, from 1660 to 1688. Charles II, determined to force episcopacy on Scotland, declared that "Presbyterianism is not a religion for a gentleman." His judgment in this particular instance is not to be received as an oracle of wisdom.

In Greyfriars Churchyard, Edinburgh, is the Martyrs' Monument, with its inscription: "From May, 1661, to February, 1688, were one way or another murdered or destroyed for the same cause about eighteen thousand, of whom were executed at Edinburgh about one hundred of noblemen, gentlemen, ministers and others—noble martyrs for Jesus Christ."

The reign of Charles II came to its inglorious close in 1685. He was succeeded by his brother, James II, an avowed Roman Catholic. The latter's brief rule ended in the Revolution of 1688, which brought William of Orange to the British throne, along with the establishment of religious liberty. To employ Artemus Ward's famous phraseology, these two Stuart kings "earned their living by making mistakes."

Presbyterianism became the established religion in Scotland in 1690. Scotsmen are said to be clannish, and they are fiercely loyal to their country, but they insist on the right to disagree with one another. This may account largely for the bewilderment which possesses one who undertakes to unravel the entanglements of Scotch-Irish-American church history.

Dissatisfied with the "Revolution Settlement" and the established church, a considerable number formed independent groups which, after a few years, were consolidated into the Reformed Presbyterian Church. Other dissidents organized the Associate Presbyterian Church.

During the years of persecution a goodly number of Scotch people migrated to northern Ireland. They formed societies practically identical in faith and organization with those in Scotland. These Scotch-Irish contributed largely through migration to American Presbyterian churches.

The two Scotch churches, the Reformed Presbyterian and the Associate Presbyterian, sent many of their members to the New World. Settlements were made in eastern Pennsylvania, in New York, in New England, and the Carolinas. They made commendable progress. In the American Revolution they seem to have supported with practical unanimity the cause of the Colonies. Two ministers of the Associate Church, Dr. Mason and Dr. Annan, served as chaplains in the colonial army.

In 1782 these two Presbyterian bodies united in forming the Associate Reformed Presbyterian Church. Complexity rather than unity was the result. A number of the Associate fathers and brethren refused to enter the union and maintained the Associate Presbyterian organization. A small minority of the Reformed group held aloof and in 1798 organized the Reformed Presbytery of North America. In 1833 a division occurred with the result that there are two organizations, the Reformed Presbyterian Church *of* North America, and the Reformed Presbyterian Church *in* North America. Both are known as Covenanters. The former, in 1951, reported 75 congregations, 56 pastors, and 5,339 communicants, with average per member contributions of $77.50. The latter has a membership of 5,242.

The General Synod of the Associate Reformed Presbyterian Church, with six presbyteries in southern states, dates from 1822 when the Synod of the Carolinas withdrew from the Associate Reformed Presbyterian Church. Its chief educational institution is Erskine College, located at Due West, S.C. The College has a Department of Theology with an attendance of 29 students (1951). The church membership (1951) is 26,544. Foreign mission work is in Pakistan and Mexico.

The two larger denominations, the Associate Reformed Presbyterian Church, and the Associate Presbyterian Church, maintained separate organizations until 1858. In that eventful year they came together, through their commissioners, and in Old City Hall, Pittsburgh, Pa., formed the United Presbyterian Church of North America. The combined memberships totaled 54,789 with 49 presbyteries, 484 ministers and licentiates, and 660 congregations. The official figures of the United Presbyterian Church for 1951 record a membership of 219,027. There are 51 presbyteries, 929 ministers and licentiates, and 830 congregations.

The Home Missionary enterprise in America furnishes an amazing record of initiative, courage, self-sacrificing devotion, and stupendous achievement. At the close of the Revolutionary War the population of the country was approximately 4,000,000, practically all of which was east of the Appalachian Mountain range. "Westward the course of empire takes its way" has never had a greater demonstration than the mighty pioneer invasion which, with small beginnings but increasing momentum, pushed its way through the years across the vast stretches of mountains and forests and rivers and prairies and deserts until it reached the shores of the Pacific. The history of American Home Missions is the record of missionaries following pioneers, enduring all the dangers and hardships, ministering in Christ's name to individuals and groups, organizing congregations, building churches and schools and colleges, laying the foundations of intelligence, faith, integrity and character that make a nation truly great.

Prof. Woodburn[1] says that "the Scotch-Irish settlers were the frontiersmen of our history." Theodore Roosevelt describes them as "a shield of sinewy men thrust in between the people of the seaboard and the red warriors of the wilderness:" and he continues, "Full credit has been awarded the Round Head and the Cavalier for their leadership in our history; nor have we been blind to the deeds of the Hollander and the Huguenot; but it is doubtful if we have wholly realized the importance of the part played by that stern and virile people, the Irish, whose preachers taught the creed of Knox and Calvin. These Irish representatives of the Covenanters were in the West almost what the Puritans were in the North and more than the Cavaliers were in the South."[2] Mr. Roosevelt should have used the hyphenated term, Scotch-Irish, but complaint is not in order since he mentions Knox and the Covenanters.

The United Presbyterian Church joined with the other denominations in sending forth its pioneers, missionaries and educators into the great West. Prominent among the early circuit-riders was John Cuthbertson who, in 39 years, is said to have traveled "on horseback about seventy thousand miles, or nearly equal to three times around the world."[3] At the time of the union of 1858 the bulk of United Presbyterian membership was east of the Mississippi River. The First Presbytery of Nebraska was organized in 1863. At the present time (1951) there are 16 presbyteries, 181 congregations, and a membership of 39,415 west of the Father of Waters, 14,913 in the states bordering the Pacific.

Certain distinctive areas of service are worthy of attention. Work among the Negroes of the south was begun in Nashville, Tennessee, in 1863. Ten thousand Negro war refugees were in the city where Gen. Clinton B. Fisk was in command of the Union forces. From this beginning, Freedmen's Missions, as it was designated, has developed into a work that includes churches and schools in Kentucky, Tennessee, Virginia, North Carolina, and Alabama. Knoxville College is one of the finest and most efficient Negro institutions in America. On the occasion of its quarter centennial in 1900, the president, Dr. R. W. McGranahan, received the following message from Booker T. Washington:

> The church with which your college is connected has for a number of years placed the entire Negro race under deep obligations to it for its unselfish, wide and far-reaching work for our people through its schools, colleges and churches.

Approximately 4,000,000 Mountaineers, half of whom are of Scotch-Irish descent, inhabit the Appalachian Range. They were a neglected people until the Protestant churches sent missionaries and teachers among them. For many years United Presbyterians maintained mission stations and schools, under supervision of the Board of American Missions, in the mountainous regions of Kentucky and Tennessee. In each the state authorities finally took over the task of education, and the mission stations, with the exception of a few in Tennessee, were discontinued. The Women's General Missionary Society supports schools and churches in Frenchburg and Ezel, Kentucky. Its schools are attended by more than 800 pupils and have Class A rating with the Kentucky schools.

Twenty-five years ago the United Presbyterian Board of American Missions had under its care 18 missions for aliens, including Italians, Syrians, French and Slovaks. Necessity for this particular kind of work was greatly reduced by the restrictive immigration laws of 1921 and 1924. The policy of mission boards has been to discourage the maintenance of foreign language-speaking congregations and gradually to absorb them into distinctively American churches. Some years ago Dr. Hugh Black of Scotland was a visitor to America and one day while enjoying himself on the golf links he inquired of his dark-eyed, dark-haired caddie, "Are you an Italian?" "No sir," was the prompt and indignant reply, "I'm an American." This is the attitude which American Home Missions has sought from the first to develop and to spiritualize.

If ever pride is justifiable United Presbyterians may be granted approval in their estimate of the Women's General Missionary Society. It is doubtful if there is a more efficient organization of its kind in any denominaton in America. Mrs. H. C. Campbell and Mrs. Mary Clokey Porter were among its organizers and through many years poured their lives into its projects and activities. The Society participates in practically everything that has to do with missionary work at home and abroad; in the foreign fields of India, Pakistan, Egypt, Ethiopia, the Sudan, in America, in behalf of presbyterial missions, aliens, Negroes, Indians, Mountaineers. The Annual Thankoffering is a special feature, the first in 1888 amounting to $5,919.20, that of 1950 totaling $246,461.62. In 63 years the Thankoffering has brought $6,200,802 into the treasury, the same having been distributed among the various projects supported by the Society. Its kindred and cooperating organization, the United Presbyterian Women's Association, maintains three excellent institutions, Columbia Hospital, Home for the Aged, and Orphans' Home. It cannot be forgotten that the Apostle Paul wrote, "Let your women keep silence in the churches; for it is not permitted unto them to speak." Certain social customs and regulations that fitted into the first century of the Christian era are manifestly impossible of observance in the twentieth.

> New occasions teach new duties; Time makes ancient
>   good uncouth;
> They must upward still, and onward, who would keep
>   abreast of Truth.[4]

Any one who has listened to United Presbyterian women deliver addresses in assemblies, synods, presbyteries and other public gatherings, is well aware that not even a superman, should such a creature appear, could compel them to refrain from utterances in the churches.

The wisest in every age have been concerned with the interests of youth. From Cicero, two thousand years ago, came the question; "How can we more essentially benefit our country, than by instructing and giving a proper direction to the minds of our youth?" The words seem strangely fitting to our day. The United Presbyterian Church gives faithful and efficient attention to the welfare of children and youth. Officially it functions through the Department of Bible School-Youth Work of the Board of Christian Education. There is thorough Bible School organization, based on modern methods, for all ages and groups. Part of the curriculum has been evolved in cooperation with the Presbyterian Church, U. S., and the Reformed Church in America, and the literature, prepared by persons expert in their profession, has high rank. There are conferences for teachers of the various grades, adult training schools, vacation Bible schools. The ably edited young people's paper, *The Christian Union Herald,* furnishes material of great value to Bible School and youth pupils and leaders. Youth organizations consist of Pioneers, 12 to 14; Builders, 15 to 17; Fellowship, 18 to 24; Forum, 25 and up. In addition to the National Convention there are presbyterial rallies, summer conferences, caravaning projects, summer work camps, recreation workshops, and other activities which modern leaders have devised for the good of youth.

Until quite recent years the majority of men's clubs in churches have not provided shining examples of spiritual fervor and fruitful service. It has been decisively proved that something more is needed on the program besides chicken dinners, travelogues, trumpet solos, motion pictures, and varying exhibitions of cheap comedy. There must be something of real practical worth with which to challenge the minds and hearts of earnest, red-blooded men. They will respond to appeals that call for labor and sacrifice that promise results of lasting value. The Board of Christian Education has definitely undertaken to provide a working program for men that shall enlist them in the whole denominational enterprise. Organization is congregational, presbyterial, national, and in cooperation with the inter-denominational United Church Men. For a good while this question has troubled the thought and conscience of the church: Why do not men, through organized endeavor, serve as loyally and enthusiastically and effectively as women in the work of the Kingdom of Christ? It is time for men to furnish a satisfactory answer.

This essay deals primarily with the church in America, but it is imperative that a few words be offered concerning work abroad. From early days the United Presbyterian Church has had upon its heart the Great Commission of Christ to evangelize the world. Prior to the union of 1858 the Associate Reformed Church sent Dr. Thomas McCague to begin the work in Egypt. The date is 1854. In 1855 Dr. Andrew Gordon, from the Associate Church, entered India. Through the years that have followed, these two heroic pioneers have been succeeded by hundreds of devoted men and women who have invested their lives in the great task. Work was begun in the Sudan in 1900 by Dr. J. K. Giffen and Dr. H. T. McLaughlin, and in Abyssinia in 1919 by Dr. T. A. Lambie. In these fields there are (1951) 313 organized congregations and 135 mission stations. The church membership is 78,239. The foreign missionary enterprise of today seeks to minister to human life in all its varied needs, notably industrial, educational, physical, spiritual. Among missionaries are evangelists, teachers, agricultural experts, physicians, college and theological professors. The "Romance of Missions" is not a misnomer. The work has a strange, unyielding grip on the souls of the men and women who toil in Christ's name in the distant lands. It must be conceded that they are in the front line of the "mighty army" and many of them seem to have something like fierce delight in conflict with the "principalities and powers, the rulers of the darkness of this world."

Denominational organization is substantially identical with

that of other churches holding the Presbyterian system—General Assembly, Synods, Presbyteries, Congregations. Ministers are designated as teaching elders, members of sessions as ruling elders, and they are on an equality in all matters of government and discipline. There are five Boards—Administration, American Missions, Foreign Missions, Christian Education, Ministerial Pensions and Relief. The Board of Administration is frequently described as the denominational clearing house. It receives and distributes all monies for missionary and educational purposes, supervises the departments of evangelism and stewardship, promotes the annual every member canvass, and plans its programs in cooperation with the four budget Boards. Eleven synods stretch from coast to coast, New York, Pittsburgh, First West, Ohio, Second, Illinois, Iowa, the Plains, Nebraska, California, Columbia. Each has a superintendent of missions under supervision and direction of the Board of American Missions.

United Presbyterian colleges are six in number: Westminster in Pennsylvania, Muskingum in Ohio, Monmouth in Illinois, Tarkio in Missouri, Sterling in Kansas, Knoxville in Tennessee. United Presbyterians find peculiar satisfaction in these institutions, for their past records and present-day achievements are of the order of excellence. Among the graduates of each of these colleges are men and women who love their alma mater as Daniel Webster loved Dartmouth.

A United Presbyterian past professor of Church History declares that "the first Sabbath School in the United States is credited to David Bethuen, a member of the Associate Reformed Church in New York; that in our ancestry is the first theological seminary west of the Allegheny Mountains; that at least fifteen years before Francis E. Clark founded the Christian Endeavor Society, a flourishing young people's society was organized in the United Presbyterian Church at Bellefontaine, Ohio."[5] As regards "the first theological seminary" it was founded by the Associate Church in 1794 and was located at Service, Pennsylvania. It was a two-story log structure. The ground floor served as lecture room and library and the attic housed less than half a dozen students. One professor, the consecrated Dr. John Anderson, conducted for 25 years the various courses of study. In 1821 the seminary was removed to Canonsburg, Pa., in 1855 to Xenia, Ohio, in 1921 to St. Louis, Mo. The Pittsburgh Seminary dates from 1825, established by the Associate Reformed Church. Its first professor, Dr. Joseph Kerr lived without benefit of luxury on a salary of $200 a year. In 1930 the two institutions were merged into the Pittsburgh-Xenia Seminary. With its able faculty of twelve members, its added Department of Christian Education, its new and beautiful Pittsburgh location, it holds high rank among American "schools of the prophets."

The *United Presbyterian* is the Assembly-authorized Adult Weekly paper of the church. Its staff consists of an editor-manager, assistant editor, eight associate editors, and five corresponding editors. It seeks to keep its readers well informed concerning significant world events, religious movements and enterprises, and denominational and inter-denominational news. It provides space for narratives of human interest, letters from subscribers, special articles, and expositions of Bible school lessons and young people's programs. Across its front page each week is printed the denominational slogan, "The Truth of God—Forbearance in Love." Differences of opinion and conviction, when expressed reasonably and in a Christian spirit, are given place in the paper, but personal grievances and controversial material of the torrid zone variety are denied entrance to its columns. Its aim is to offer things enlightening, wholesome, spiritually inspiring.

The headquarters of the United Presbyterian Church is in Pittsburgh, Pa. Its Publication Building, 209 Ninth Street, houses the Boards of Administration, American Missions, Christian Education, the Women's General Missionary Society, and the denominational Book Rooms. In the two presbyteries, Allegheny and Monongahela, corresponding in area with the

Pittsburgh metropolitan district, are more than 80 United Presbyterian congregations.

The immediately preceding generation produced a number of preachers of outstanding pulpit ability. Prominent among them were Doctors W. G. Moorehead, W. J. Reid, Sr., J. K. McClurkin, R. M. Russell. In the judgment of many the church's greatest theologian was Dr. James Harper; its foremost scholar, Dr. John McNaugher; its chief historian, James Brown Scouller; its leading archaeologist, Dr. Melvin G. Kyle.

The United Presbyterian Church joins with other Presbyterian bodies in accepting the Westminster Standards, the Confession of Faith, the Larger and Shorter Catechisms, as the expression of its creed. These were the product of the labors of the leading scholars of Great Britain, through a period of nine years, from 1643 to 1652. That they constitute a truly great statement of Christian doctrine is universally admitted. At the time of the union of 1858 the United Presbyterian Church added to the Westminster Standards the "Articles of the Testimony," 18 in number. In time three of the 'Articles' became known as "distinctives": Secret Societies, Restricted Communion, and Psalmody. Persons who were members of secret, oath-bound societies were not admitted to church membership; Communion was practically of the 'close' variety; and the Psalms were used exclusively in worship. Even from the beginning there was not unanimous agreement that these 'distinctives' should be included in the Testimony. Passing of time and changing convictions eliminated them from creedal declarations.

The United Presbyterian Church has been regarded as one of the more conservative of the Presbyterian groups. But it has amply demonstrated the fact that it is not afraid to move forward when it is convinced that truth makes plain the way. By authority of the General Assembly of 1919 a committee, with Dr. John McNaugher as chairman, began work on a revised statement of faith. It was adopted in final form in 1925, and is known as The Confessional Statement of the

United Presbyterian Church of North America. In the Preamble is the remarkable declaration: This Statement contains the substance of the Westminster symbols, together with certain present day convictions of the United Presbyterian Church. It takes the place of the Testimony of 1858, and wherever it deviates from the Westminster Standards its declarations are to prevail.

That is clear enough to stand by itself without necessity of explanation or exposition. The Confessional Statement is the creed of the church. Its literary qualities are excellent, its clarity is such that "he may run who reads," and it proclaims the great fundamental doctrines of the Christian faith with fervor and power. Its Forty-Four Articles are evangelical in tone and content. It gives strong emphasis to the necessity of individual evangelism and world-wide missionary endeavor, and its conception of the so-called "social gospel" is set forth in Article XXXVIII:

Of The Social Order

We believe that the Divine plan for mankind includes a social order in harmony with the ideals and spirit of Jesus Christ; that the triumph of the Kingdom of God in its present aspect would mean not only its establishment in the hearts of men individually, but a world in which righteousness and brotherhood should prevail; and that a primary duty of the Church is to give positive witness that the Christian principles of justice and love should have full expression in all relationships whatsoever — personal, industrial, business, civic, national and international.

The United Presbyterian Church has followed the groups that formed it in an aggressively militant attitude toward moral and social evils. It demanded the abolition of human slavery. It has fought the liquor traffic consistently and uncompromisingly through the years. It champions clean home life as against the growing tragedies of divorce. Years ago, through its General Assembly, it adopted, along with other evangelical denominations, the Social Creed of the Churches, which stands for the principles of justice and righteousness and fair and charitable dealing as clearly revealed in the Gospel of Jesus Christ.

United Presbyterians have achieved a reputation as liberal givers. For the year ending March 31, 1951, with a membership of 219,027, contributions for all purposes amounted to $10,136,799, an average per member of $46.28.

Commendably peaceful relations among themselves have been maintained by United Presbyterians. Unanimity in judgment and expression is manifestly among things impossible, especially where persons of Scotch-Irish descent are in the field. At times warm winds of recognizable force have swept over the areas of debate, but there have been no destructive tempests. "Let brotherly love continue," is an inspired exhortation that is given practical demonstration.

Relations with other Christian churches have been most cordial and cooperative. Active membership is sustained in the two great interdenominational organizations, the World Council of Churches and the National Council of Churches. There is growing sentiment for organic union with other related bodies, particularly the Presbyterian Church USA, the Presbyterian Church US, and the Associate Reformed Presbyterian Church.

The group spirit is strong, especially where heritage and history have contributed things of lasting worth. What of the years to come? If the United Presbyterian Church maintains unquestioned loyalty to the Word of the living God, if it proclaims faithfully through life and character and spoken testimony the New Testament Gospel of Jesus Christ and him crucified, if it proves itself the foe of all that oppresses and degrades and the friend of all that frees and uplifts, if it regards the world as its parish and keeps a clear vision of the whitened fields—then its future is secure, whether it pursues its course independently, or joins its forces with those of other likeminded Christians in forming a larger unit in the army of the Lord. The records in God's Book of Life are never lost, and loving service has its fruitage through the ages. After all has been said and done, when the reports are all in, the supreme and abiding reward is Christ. There is the familiar yet always heart-moving story that the Lord appeared to Thomas Aquinas, the "Angelic Doctor," in a vision and said, "Thomas, thou hast written many beautiful things about me. What reward wilt thou have?" Thomas replied, "Only Thyself, Lord! Only Thyself!"

NOTES

1 JAMES A. WOODBURN, *The Scotch-Irish Presbyterians of Monroe County, Indiana.*

2 THEODORE ROOSEVELT, *The Winning of the West,* Vol. I. By permission of publishers, G. P. Putnam's Sons.

3 JAMES B. SCOULLER, *History of the United Presbyterian Church of North America,* American Church History Series, XI.

4 JAMES RUSSELL LOWELL, *The Present Crisis.*

5 CLARENCE J. WILLIAMSON, *I am a United Presbyterian.* By permission of the author.

BIBLIOGRAPHY

JAMES B. SCOULLER, *History of the United Presbyterian Church of North America,* American Church History Series, XI (1894).

W. E. MCCULLOCH, *The United Presbyterian Church and its Work in America* (Pittsburgh, 1925).

CLARENCE J. WILLIAMSON, *March On with the United Presbyterian Church of North America* (Pittsburgh, 1933).

Anniversary Committee, R. A. HUTCHISON, Ch., *Seventy-fifth Anniversary of the United Presbyterian Church of North America* (Pittsburgh, 1933).

WILLIAM ADAMS BROWN, *The Church in America* (1922).

S. T. WILSON, *The Mountaineers of the South* (1912).

J. MELDRUM DRYERRE, *Heroes and Heroines of the Scottish Covenanters* (New York, n. d.)

JOHN HOWIE, *Scots Worthies* (New York, 1854).

XII

THE SOCIETY OF FRIENDS IN AMERICA
(QUAKERS)

XII

THE SOCIETY OF FRIENDS IN AMERICA
(QUAKERS)

WILLIAM EUGENE BERRY

QUAKERISM TODAY with its various branches is the resultant of many influences that have affected it in the last 300 years. Yet it still bears the impress of its founder, George Fox (1624-1691), and the early Friends who proclaimed what they considered to be primitive Christianity. A historical treatment seems to be needed that present day Quakerism may be understood.

In the first place, it should be borne in mind that in the seventeenth century there existed a general dissatisfaction with the Church. With its corrupt practices, ritualism, secularism, etc., Christianity seemed to be merely a legalistic, external type of religion which failed to meet the deeper needs of the human heart. Contemporary with this, the mystics Eckhart, (*c.* 1260-1327), Tauler (*c.* 1300-1361) and others were for many persons helping to meet this spiritual need. As a consequence of the current situation there had come into being many small sects and hundreds of so-called "Seekers". These provided the material for the Quaker movement which developed under the preaching and the leadership of the spiritually dynamic person, George Fox, and his immediate followers.

George Fox had spent agonizing years seeking release from despair. Finally this came to him in a wonderful experience of which he writes, "When all my hopes in them (priests) and in all men were gone, so that I had nothing outwardly to help me . . . then; o then, I heard a voice which said, 'There is one even Christ Jesus that can speak to thy condition': and when I heard it my heart did leap for joy . . . For though I read the Scriptures that spoke of Christ and of God, yet I knew him not, but by revelation, as He who had the key did open, and as the Father of Life drew me to His Son by His Spirit."[1] Here we have in a nutshell the whole of the early Quaker faith, the one eternal and universal Principle—as Rufus Jones expresses it, "The inwardly present and creative work of God's own Spirit operating in man was the central Principle of the Quaker movement."[2] Central throughout the centuries has been this conviction that there is in man that which responds to God's Spirit. It has not been a matter of reason, nor of logical proof. It is not an intellectual belief nor a theory, but is known and recognized by experience only.

This marvelous experience seemed to the early Quakers to be a rediscovery or perhaps a recovery of the experience which came to the early Christians in Jerusalem. George Fox writes of it thus, "I was sent to turn people from darkness to light, that they might receive Christ Jesus: . . . I was to turn them to the grace of God, and to the truth in the heart, which came by Jesus; that by this grace they might be taught, which would bring them to salvation . . . These things I did not see by the help of man, nor by the letter, though they are written in the letter, but I saw them in the light of the Lord Jesus Christ, and by His immediate spirit and power, as did the holy men of God by whom the Holy Scriptures were written."[3]

This was the one great message of the new reformation of the Quakers, that there is a continuous revelation of God's will in the soul of man. Fox was convinced of this both by his own experience and by the testimony of the many "Seekers" and finally by texts from the Bible with which he was very familiar. "He met the Calvinistic theory" so universally prevalent, "of a congenital seed of sin in the new-born child by the counter claim that there is a seed of God in every soul. This 'seed' or 'light' . . . was thought of as a capacity of response to divine intimations and openings, a basis of inward communication . . . between God and man and a moral searchlight revealing to man the absolute distinction between right and wrong."[4]

In this early Quakerism no creed was preached. Not even were the Quakers a sect. They were the "seed of God" labeled by their enemies "Quakers".[5] It was an intense fellowship which all might share as they turned to the light of Christ in their own hearts. Fox often speaks of the light of Christ. "Believe in the Light, that ye may become children of the Light" was his constant message.

However, though the Spirit of God had supreme authority, the Scriptures were not neglected. By this Spirit of God in the soul the Scriptures came alive. Quotations from many early writers support this. Richard Hubberthorne says to King Charles II, "Now I know the Scriptures to be true by the manifestation and operation of the Spirit of God fulfilling them in me."[6]

One of the most striking and impressive things about early Quakerism was the fact that Friends actually accepted the implications which their fundamental principle, "that of God in every man", demanded. That each man of whatever race or class or state of society, saint or sinner, friend or enemy, was thus endowed, made them every one a sacred being and therefore to be recognized and treated as such. It brought to Friends a great compulsion to help all men to realize this great truth which they felt must be universal. It sent Quakers all over England and the Continent, to the American colonies, and to distant parts of the world. It also caused Friends to do pioneer work in prison reform, in treatment of the insane, in work for Negroes and American Indians, and in other avenues of human welfare work.[7]

From this fundamental principle there very naturally developed what are called "testimonies". Because all men are equal no special privilege or deference should be recognized. Hence a common speech was used, "thou" in place of the complimentary "you". Hats were not removed. Simplicity in dress and behavior were inculcated. Always the truth was spoken so oaths were not used as though without an oath the lie was expected. Testimony against certain forms of art as "music, the theatre and fiction, came partly from viewing them as untruthful, and partly as superfluities which might distract attention from more important things."[8]

Friends' testimony against war has been continuous. When George Fox was offered a captaincy he refused and was put in a dungeon. He says, "I told them from whence all wars arise, even from the lust, according to James' doctrine and that I lived in the virtue of that life and power that took away the occasion of all wars."[9] "The Quaker testimony concerning war does not set up as its standard of value the attainment of individual or national safety, neither is it based primarily on the iniquity of taking human life. It is based ultimately on the conception of 'that of God in every man' to which the Christian in the presence of evil is called on to make appeal, following out a line of thought and conduct which, involving suffering as it may do, is in the long run most likely to reach the inward witness and so change the evil mind into the right mind." [10] Friends have responded differently to this testimony. It is not an authoritarian creed. The only authority is the Spirit of Christ in the heart. George Fox once said to William Penn soon after he became a Quaker, "Wear the sword as long as thou canst." Friends have been compelled to do what the leadership of the Spirit has seemed to require regardless of consequences.

George Fox died in 1691. Since the beginning of the movement in 1647, preachers of truth had covered England and Ireland, had traveled on the Continent, and had proclaimed the message in the Islands and the Colonies of America. This had been with great persecution with many Friends spending years in prison, having property confiscated, and even giving their lives for their principles. George Fox spent a total of six years in prison. But in spite of opposition, by 1691 there were 50,000 Friends in England and by 1750 an estimated 50,000 in the Colonies. This includes William Penn's Holy Experiment in Pennsylvania. Also by 1691 an organization similar to that of the present day had been perfected, with only enough of organization to perpetuate the movement, with no exercise of authority. It was and still remains completely democratic.

While there are many important writers of the first century of Quakerism who help to interpret to us the movement, as George Fox, Isaac Pennington, William Penn and others, we shall speak of Robert Barclay (1648-1690) particularly about whom Rufus Jones says, "All the controversies of later Quaker history involve Barclay".[11] Barclay was a scholar, a theologian who became converted to Quakerism in 1666. He writes of his experience, "When I came into the silent assemblies of God's people, I felt a secret power among them, which touched my heart, and as I gave way unto it, I found the evil weakening in me and the good raised up."[12] Barclay undertook to express Quakerism in theological form, *i.e.,* to interpret it to the time. Braithwaite says, "It is to Barclay that we owe the most systematic formulation of the Quaker faith,"[13] as it appears in his *Apology for the True Christian Divinity.* He attempts to support Quakerism by the Bible, by reason, and by other Christian writers. Braithwaite says, "Barclay's mind . . . is occupied mainly with two convictions—the current conception of the innate depravity of human nature, from which he was not able to escape, and the conviction, grounded in his own living experience, of the inwardness of religion as the power of a universal and saving Divine life incarnated in Jesus, but, in measure, a living gift of God seeking out all men."[14] Barclay attempts to adjust Quakerism to current theology. He says, "That he hath given to every man a measure of saving, sufficient, and supernatural light and grace."[15] He quotes John 1:9, "That was the true light, which lighteth every man that cometh into the world." In V. 15 he says, "Christ is in all men as in a seed." But he says, "It cannot be any of the natural gifts or faculties of our soul . . . this light is said to 'shine in darkness'", which is "man in his natural state." He considers that man as mere man cannot be saved, but referring to Paul who speaks of the Gentiles who do things according to the Law, he says "There were some relics of the heavenly image left in Adam."[16]

In Proposition XI Robert Barclay presents an excellent discussion of worship as early Friends conceived it. Worship "is neither limited to times, places, nor persons." "In prayers, praises or preachings we aught not to do it in our own will where and when we will." While one day is no more holy than another, as all are holy, it is the duty of all to assemble, "and so met together inwardly in their spirits, as well as outwardly in their persons, there the secret power and virtue of life is known to refresh the soul . . . And no man here limits the spirit of God, nor bringeth forth his own conned and gathered stuff; but everyone puts that forth which the Lord puts into their hearts." "Divers meetings have past without one word; and yet our souls have been greatly edified and refreshed." "This is that divine and spiritual worship." "The witness of God ariseth in the heart, and the light of Christ shineth, whereby the soul cometh to see its own condition." "We enjoy and possess the holy fellowship and communion of the body and blood of Christ."

In Propositions XII and XIII are treated the sacraments of baptism and communion. Quoting Eph. 4:5 and other references he shows that "There is one baptism which is a pure and spiritual thing, not a baptism of water which is outward but a baptism of the Spirit which is inward. Communion" is likewise "inward and spiritual . . . by which the inward man is daily nourished."

Although Barclay seems not to have intended it, there developed from his writing a tendency to regard the Bible which is the product of the Spirit as superior to the Spirit that produced it. Also, a silent and quiet devotion came to take the place of the evangelistic zeal of the first century. While as Rufus Jones says, "The work of translating the Quaker faith into a contemporary system of thought was performed by

Robert Barclay," still Barclay maintained that "experience is everything and system almost nothing."[17]

Another result of Robert Barclay's *Apology* was to so adjust Quakerism to the prevalent Quietism that a Quietistic type of Quakerism developed. Rufus Jones says of Quietism that it was "a deep and widespread movement confined to no one country and . . . limited to no one branch of the Christian Church," and "It was an intense and glowing faith in the direct invasion of God into the sphere of human personality . . . but a faith, at the same time, indissolubly bound up with a fundamental conception of man's total depravity and spiritual bankruptcy." It was accepted that "Nothing spiritual can originate on the level of 'nature' " and "Nothing divine, nothing that has religious value, can originate in man, as man."[18]

This Quietistic point of view prevailed both in English and American Quakerism during the eighteenth century and has had a great influence on Friends even to the present day. Barclay's interpretation of the "Seed of God" was "a supernatural Light superadded to 'man's nature' as a gift of grace purchased by Christ's sacrifice for fallen man." This was perfectly suited to the Quietist way of life and thought. To prepare for spiritual operations one must be "still" and "wait". This "Quakerism of the eighteenth century . . . was corporate rather than individualistic." "Corporate silence . . . a silence prolonged unbroken sometimes for hours . . . came more and more . . . to be exalted as the loftiest way of worship."[19]

John Woolman (1720-1772) is an excellent example of one who "shows the Quietist temper in all the aspects of his religious life, both outer and inner." In his *Journal* "Woolman gives the best and most beautiful account of this quietistic attitude."[20] To illustrate, in Philadelphia Yearly Meeting in 1759 Woolman spent several days "covered with the spirit of supplication." Near the end of the business sessions he says the "way was opened in pure flowings of Divine love for me to express what lay upon me."[21] In all of Woolman's concern against slavery to visit slave owners, and to speak in meetings against slave owning, he exhibited a humility, a self-efface-ment—combined with a "holy boldness". He guarded against "creaturely activity" and often waited for days for the com-pulsion of the Spirit. His gentleness, his humility, his complete dedication to the leadership of the Spirit made his service very effective, not hurried or insistent, always seeking the good of the slave owner as well as the slave.

This century or more of Quietism was still a time of real life though not with the evangelistic zeal of the first century. It was a time of seeking perfection that one might be worthy of divine guidance, worthy of salvation. There was great dis-trust of human reason and human thought and plan, called "creaturely activity" which should be avoided. Many meet-ings for worship were in complete silence for week on week. However, the spiritual life was strengthened by many visit-ing ministers. They came with no preparation but brought a fellowship of spirit and a new courage. This period was mark-ed with a great amount of philanthropic activity with "con-cerns" for slaves, for men in prison, for the American Indians, etc. Quiet guidance of the Spirit in Meetings for Worship seemed to make response to concerns a divine necessity. "By 1780 no slaves were held by Quakers" and Quakers worked for the freeing of slaves by the underground. After the Eman-cipation came, the Friends Freedman Association collected funds to establish schools for Negroes and otherwise render aid to Negroes.[22]

A new period of American Quakerism came through the Evangelical movement which started in England with the Wesleyan revivals toward the end of the eighteenth century affecting Friends in England and America and bringing in a new fervor and zeal comparable to the first century of Quaker-ism. While it stressed the Calvinistic theology it did have an appeal to Friends because it likewise emphasized the necessity of a personal religious experience.[23] With this came a great emphasis on the study of the Bible with a tendency to accept it as final authority in place of the direct first-hand leadership of the Spirit.

This Evangelicalism was accepted by a great many Friends, but there were protests against it in some quarters as it seemed to be a casting aside of the fundamental Quaker principle of Inner Light. Finally in 1828-29 it resulted in the Great Separation which started in Philadelphia Yearly Meeting and spread to New York, Baltimore, Ohio, and Indiana Yearly Meetings. The controversy centered about the person of Elias Hicks who has been described as "one of the most powerful of all itinerant ministers of the time. He was a profoundly mystical type of person, able to sit for long periods in 'a perfect calm' wherein his whole being was 'swallowed up in divine seraphic enjoyment.' "[24] The controversy was only partially theological. The country Friends who had listened to the farmer preacher Elias Hicks for so many years followed him in his overemphasis of the doctrine of Inner Light which he supported to the exclusion of all else. They felt also that the city Friends, who had accepted the evangelicalism of the day, had a domineering attitude in the business of the Yearly Meeting. Rufus Jones says, "This serious honest man was not alone to blame for the misplaced emphasis. Nobody in the Society of Friends had adequately faced the implications and the difficulties involved in the doctrine of inner Light and nobody on the other hand reached any true comprehension of the relation of historical revelation to the Light within the individual soul. Neither party succeeded in getting down through the cooled crust of inherited Quakerism to any fresh springs of water."[25]

As a result of the separation there have come to be two Philadelphia Yearly Meetings, the Orthodox (so-called) and the "Hicksite", now united with other Hicksite Yearly Meetings in what is called General Conference. The Orthodox has emphasized a definite theology, has found religious fellowship with Evangelical churches and used their Sunday School literature in their Bible study. Hicksites on the other hand as depending upon leadership of the Spirit have naturally been more liberal and tolerant toward divergent theological belief.[26]

In connection with the Evangelical Movement in America must be mentioned Joseph John Gurney (1788-1846). He was an English gentleman and an excellent scholar, a great student of the Bible and theologian, accepting the theology of Evangelical Protestantism. He came to America with the concern to restore the Hicksites to a more orthodox position and thus bring about unity. In this he was not successful, but he did give to the Orthodox group a new life and incentive, greatly needed after the disastrous separation. Young Friends saw in him new possibilities. He gave an impetus to education, a new interest in Bible study, and in cultural pursuits without the fear of taking away spirituality by this so-called "creaturely activity." Russell[27] declares that the basis of Quakerism was radically changed so that it became "a *doctrine* quite divorced from experience . . . instead of an *experience* of the inward work of the Spirit."

Joseph Gurney visited the Orthodox Meetings and contributed much to their new life and growth. He gave them a theology, with an emphasis on the authority of the Bible so that some Friends came even to practice sacraments, especially water baptism. Gurney's emphasis on sanctification, an experience of infilling of the Holy Spirit after that of justification caused some to drift into various "holiness" movements. But in spite of these sporadic excesses Gurney's work was valuable and led to a splendid new growth in the Orthodox Meetings which came to be styled "Gurneyite".

In contrast with this teaching John Wilbur (1774-1856) felt a great concern to oppose the "creaturely activity" of the Gurneyites. He over-emphasized the Inner Light as all important and infallible. Russell declares that Wilbur was "in the main as opposed to Hicksism and as thoroughly orthodox as Gurney" but with a different emphasis.[28] This protest of John Wilbur caused some Friends to withdraw and establish what have been called Conservative Meetings. Philadelphia Yearly Meeting Orthodox avoided division by discontinuing correspondence with Wilburite and Gurneyite groups alike, although they did not refuse to accept into membership persons from each group. This practice of Philadelphia Yearly Meeting Orthodox (Arch Street) "of doing nothing that would jeopardize the unity of the Meeting has been the keynote of its subsequent history." The other Orthodox Meetings have thus been deprived of its "steadying conservative influence" and it was deprived of the "stimulus of liberal and progressive movements" of other Yearly Meetings.[29] Wilburite separations occurred also in New England, Ohio, and Iowa Yearly Meetings.

A very small group in Philadelphia Yearly Meeting of very conservative Friends objected to receiving into membership Friends from Gurneyite Meetings. They withdrew and formed a General Meeting, calling themselves "Primitive Friends". This group has now essentially disappeared.[30]

Just before and after the Civil War a great religious awakening spread over the United States with revivalists Charles J. Finney and Dwight L. Moody. Friends were caught in the movement and a number of very effective Quaker evangelists went over Quakerdom, many having come in from other denominations. The revival fervor and activity were particularly effective among the Gurneyite meetings of the Midwest in the Northwest Territory which was opened up in 1787. Friends in great numbers had come in from the Carolinas and Virginia to escape the kind of life dependent upon slave labor. In many communities where Friends started or built up Meetings through the revival movement the membership came to be largely made up of persons without the Friends tradition and type of worship. In some cases the revivalist stayed on as minister to the meeting. Persons with a gift in the ministry were sometimes encouraged to come into the community. Gradually in these Meetings a pastoral plan was developed and objections to a "hireling ministry" died down.

While this Evangelistic influence was spreading over Quakerdom there was also developing a distinctly liberal movement. As Russell says,[31] it was a reaction from the dogmatism of the Evangelical theology and likewise from the rigid Quietistic attitude toward science and thought which were considered to be "creaturely activity". Development of the natural sciences especially with discoveries in geology and biological evolution, new ideas in philosophy, theology, changes in social and political conditions due to the Industrial Revolution, these all tended toward a liberal thinking.

Also connections still remained with the other types of Quakerism in the Philadelphia Orthodox, the Conservative and the Hicksite Yearly Meetings and with English Friends with the literary heritage of early Quakerism, with the "testimonies for peace, women's ministry, a non-sacerdotal ministry and non-sacramental worship, the equality of men and women in the church, and faith in inward spiritual guidance." All these had their influence. Russell says, "The history of the Society from 1881 onwards is an account of a slow reaction toward the original Quaker basis of life and worship."[32]

We see by this very brief presentation what has happened to the early Quaker Principle which Rufus Jones speaks of as a mutation which he describes as "a unique and unpredictable variation in the process of life. . . Something 'emerges' that was not there before." "The birth of the Society of Friends is one of the mutations."[33] It was an experience of direct, actual contact of man and God, the inwardly present and creative work of God's own Spirit operating in man.

Organization

Since Quakerism has been intrinsically a leadership of the Spirit and a fellowship in worship and service, organization and authority have seemed of little importance. This may seem to many a weakness.

The local membership is called a Meeting (with a tendency in some areas to call it a church). The official title is Monthly Meeting as Salem Monthly Meeting of Friends. The Monthly Meeting business session is a fellowship in worship. There is no chairman but a Clerk sits at the head of the Meeting with

a Recording Clerk. Concerns may be presented by the Clerk
or any other member. All members, young and old, ministers,
elders, have equal participation. Each may express his opinion though no one insists on his solution. Gradually the real
solution emerges often different from anyone's original idea.
Yet it is not a compromise but a true solution that will remain. Such a meeting is a success when Friends yield to the
leadership of the Spirit in true fellowship. Time is often taken
in quiet waiting for Divine Guidance. When finally the Clerk
feels that the Meeting is united he may state the "sense of the
Meeting". If acceptable it is thus recorded. If no solution comes
the question is delayed for future action.[34] One important function of the Meeting has been to consider the "concern for
service" which a member may present. If the Meeting unites
a "minute for service" is granted. The group serves as a test
of individual concerns.

Various interests of the Meetings are the particular care of
standing committees such as missionary, public morals, peace
and service, religious education, education, evangelistic, etc.
These same departments of work are in the Quarterly and
Yearly Meetings.

Also each Meeting has a "select body" which meets monthly
particularly concerned with the spiritual life of the Meeting.
Once a year a careful "report on the Spiritual Condition" of
the Meeting is prepared, which is sent on to the Quarterly and
Yearly Meetings. This "select body", called in the Five Years
Meeting "Meeting on Ministry and Counsel", is composed of
ministers and elders. Ministers are those who have been recorded as having a gift in the ministry as finally approved by
the Yearly Meeting. Elders are persons of deep spiritual dis-
cernment who have been appointed by the Monthly Meeting.

A Quarterly Meeting composed of two or more Monthly
Meetings in a given area is an intermediary between the
Monthly Meeting and the Yearly Meeting. The Yearly Meet-
ing is the highest legislative body. All members of the Monthly
Meetings may participate in Yearly Meeting business, which

is handled the same as Monthly Meeting business. "It has power to decide all questions of administration, to counsel, admonish, or discipline its subordinate meetings, to institute measures and to provide means for the promotion of truth and righteousness,and to inaugurate and carry on departments of religious and philanthropic work."[35]

An important part of the Yearly Meeting session is the reading of "epistles" from other Yearly Meetings, both American and Foreign. An "epistle" is carefully prepared by a committee expressing the special concerns of this session and encouraging all to have renewed confidence and trust in the goodness and creative leadership of God.

Most Yearly Meetings have an Executive Secretary or Superintendent who devotes his time to the advancement of the work in local meetings, assisting in making pastoral arrangements, but without authority.

Progress and Trends of the Last Half Century

The Friends General Conference, established in 1892, is a fellowship of the six "Hicksite" Yearly Meetings. The Conference meets in even years with a program of "addresses, round table discussions, and worship periods." A Young Friends Conference meets at the same time. There is a Young Friends organization in each of the six Yearly Meetings and all are members of the American Young Friends Fellowship composed of all types of Friends.

The "Conference does continuous work in four fields", each with an active committee, Religious Education, Secular Education, Social Service, and Advancement of Friends Principles. Headquarters of the Committee for Advancement of Friends Principles are at 1515 Cherry Street, Philadelphia, with a Secretary who visits Yearly Meetings, plans conferences and other activities.

"Fellowship in this group is developed by visiting ministry, by attending school together, by sharing common tasks in social service, by reading... *The Friends Intelligencer*" (published by this group) and by the biennial "conference for fellow-ship, worship and consideration of the issues that Friends are facing in a changing world."[36] This Conference is not legis-lative.

The tendency toward unity is evidenced by conferences held. In 1887 at Richmond, Indiana, occurred the first General Conference. All Yearly Meetings of the world were invited to send delegates. Dublin and London Yearly Meetings and all on the American continent responded though Philadelphia was not officially represented. The intermingling of diverse types of Friends was the chief benefit. At this conference the so-called "Richmond Declaration of Faith"[37] was prepared. "It fairly well satisfied the superficial demand of the hour," bringing closer together somewhat divergent forces. It was soundly or-thodox from the standpoint of Gurneyism—but in the opinion of many, "It missed the most essential and vital features" of Quakerism. It has been adopted and appears in the discipline of many Yearly Meetings. It does express some fundamental Friends ideas such as spirituality of life and worship without the need of sacraments.

Similar conferences were held at Indianapolis in 1892 and 1897. At the latter it was proposed that a central body be created and that a uniform discipline be prepared. This having been approved by most of the Orthodox Yearly Meetings, in 1902 "The Five Years Meeting" was established which at the present time is composed of eleven American Yearly Meetings and three outside of America, Cuba, Jamaica, and Africa Yearly Meetings.

"The Five Years Meeting is a consultative and administra-tive rather than a legislative body... The constituent Yearly Meetings remain autonomous. Its service is performed through boards and agencies which work in harmony with correspond-ing committees in the Yearly Meetings."[38] These are the boards: American Friends Board of Missions; Board on Chris-tian Education; Board on Education; Board on Peace and So-cial Concerns; Publication Board. Also there are the following Five Years Meeting Committees: on Aged Ministers and Missionaries; on Evangelism and Church Extension; on Ministerial Training; on Pensions; on Stewardship.

Other Five Years Meeting organizations are Men's Extension Movement and United Society of Friends Women which work with similar groups in some or all of the Yearly Meetings of the Five Years Meeting.

Soon after the Five Years Meeting was established a uniform discipline was prepared. Such books "containing the body of rules, regulations, principles, practices, advices, and queries" have been issued by various Yearly Meetings since the first attempt in 1738. Each Yearly Meeting has its own variation.[39]

The Central Offices of the Five Years Meeting are at 101 S. Eighth Street, Richmond, Indiana. Here are the headquarters of the various Boards and the office of the Secretary of the Executive Committee who also serves as Editor of *The American Friend,* the organ of the Five Years Meeting issued bi-weekly.

In 1917 representatives of the different groups of American Friends formed the American Friends Service Committee. At first its purpose was to care for Conscientious Objectors, to collect funds and clothing for relief in France, and to train workers for non-combatant service. In the early years the task of building houses, providing relief of food, clothing, tools, domestic animals, was done with great devotion, in all areas devastated by war. Various Quaker centers were established to help in building up morale.[40]

The work of the A.F.S.C. has been continually growing, until in 1950 it received from Friends, Mennonites and others a total of $3,970,389.83. Over half of this was spent for relief and rehabilitation. Beside this much attention has been given to the study of world problems, domestic social problems, to giving young persons opportunities to work in places of tension in work camps, to developing and strengthening spiritual life in camps, in conferences among Friends and elsewhere. The Service Committee has the "conviction that the spirit of

God moves in and through, often in spite of, all men" which "stems from the deeper confidence that God, if trusted, if addressed in the full knowledge that we have carried our share of responsibility, will bring creative answers to the greatest difficulties."[41]

The A.F.S.C. has brought an increasing feeling of unity and spiritual fellowship among Friends and with others who seek human welfare.

In 1936 the American Friends Service Committee appointed what is called American Friends Fellowship Council with offices at 20 S. Twelfth Street, Philadelphia. "It interprets the spiritual message of Friends and seeks to integrate widely scattered Friends Meetings. Isolated individual members are drawn into closer association. An estimated 30,000 Friends live beyond limits of their meetings. New and United Meetings are nurtured . . . and a program of intervisitation is directed by the Council."[42] Since 1936 the Council has assisted in organizing thirty-four Monthly Meetings. "Two . . . have been laid down, twelve have found homes in various Yearly Meetings and twenty still report to the Council." "In addition to the Monthly Meetings there are more than sixty worship groups scattered widely throughout the country."

"Another facet of the Council's work is to hold out a hand of welcome to non-Friends through the Wider Quaker Fellowship" for those who are "sympathetic to the Quaker approach to religion but who are not in a position to join Friends." Many are scattered over the United States and in various foreign countries, with a membership in 1951 of 3,825.[43]

Other recent conferences seem to show a trend toward unity without uniformity. In 1920 in London occurred an All-Friends Conference to reconsider the historic testimony of Friends, with commissions appointed to study various topics. Also a Young Friends Conference was held at Old Jordans.

In 1929 an All American Friends Conference was held under the auspices of the A.F.S.C. at Penn College, Oskaloosa, Iowa.

In 1937 again under the auspices of the A.F.S.C. a World Conference was held at Swarthmore College. For this a Handbook of the Religious Society of Friends[44] was published. A valuable result of this conference was the setting up of a Friends World Committee for Consultation which has worked for Friendly cooperation over the world. This Committee for Consultation has arranged for a World Conference of Friends to be held at Oxford, England, in the summer of 1952 with delegates from all Yearly Meetings in the world.

Young Friends Conferences promise a real unity in the future. In 1910 at Winona Lake, Indiana, occurred the first All-Young Friends Conference. Since that time various conferences, work camps, lectureships, summer schools, etc., have developed a feeling of unity in a union of worship and service.

This feeling of fellowship is further shown by the General Conference and the Orthodox Meetings working together on committees as the Associated Committee on Indian Affairs. The two groups in some localities have been worshiping together. There are seventy or more United Meetings with members from both groups. The two Philadelphia Yearly Meetings, the Orthodox (Arch Street) and the General Conference (Race Street) have an annual General Meeting together at a time different from the separate Yearly Meetings. The two Canada Yearly Meetings with the Genesee (N.Y.) Yearly Meeting meet together in the annual session. The three New England Yearly Meetings, Orthodox, Hicksite, and Conservative have formed one Yearly Meeting.

Thus we see that within the last half century a great tendency toward unity of action and a growing spiritual fellowship have been developing. It is evident that a fellowship in worship and service can be real and genuine without uniformity. Worship and service are two facets of a life led and directed by the Spirit of Jesus Christ.

Thus we have a brief picture of a small group of Christians playing a small part in the story of Christianity.

Membership in Society of Friends in America

Note that some meetings are entirely unprogrammed in worship, *i.e.,* the group sits in fellowship and in spiritual communion, the Conservative, the General Conference, some of the Five Years Meeting and some Independent Meetings. Others are pastoral meetings partially programmed. The Five Years Meetings are largely programmed. The pastoral meetings that are independent are strongly evangelistic. Indiana Yearly Meeting has one unprogrammed Meeting.[45]

I. In the Five Years Meeting

1. Pastoral with programmed meetings for worship

California	6,154
Indiana	13,886
Iowa	6,947
Nebraska (est. 1908)	1,775
North Carolina	13,147
Western (Ind. and Ill.)	12,549
Wilmington (Ohio)	5,025

2. Pastoral in general, some meetings unprogrammed

Baltimore	1,114
New England	3,303
New York	4,098
Canada	450

II. Independent Yearly Meetings

3. Pastoral and programmed

Central (est. 1926)	576
Kansas	8,284
Ohio	6,161
Oregon	4,442

4. Non-pastoral

Pacific	756
Philadelphia (Arch Street)	4,739
New and United Meetings	938

III. In Friends General Conference

5. Non-pastoral with unprogrammed meetings for worship

Baltimore	2,185
Canada (Genesee, N.Y.)	325
Illinois	552
Indiana	562
New York	3,283
Philadelphia (Race Street)	11,075

IV. Conservative Yearly Meetings

6. Non-pastoral with unprogrammed meetings for worship

Canada	107
Iowa	837
North Carolina	400
Ohio	987
Western	50

V. New and United Meetings and Members

United Members Race and Arch Streets, Philadelphia (not counted above)	776
New Monthly Meetings not affiliated with any Yearly Meeting	938
Total membership all groups	115,483

NOTES

1 *The Journal of George Fox* (Tercentenary ed.), p. 8ff.

2 R. JONES, *Original Quakerism: a Movement, Not a Sect,* p. 6.

3 *Journal,* p. 20ff. Also *see* BRAYSHAW, *The Quakers,* p. 45, note 1.

4 R. JONES, *The Faith and Practice of the Quakers,* p. 28. For discussion of the Inner Light *see* RUSSELL, *The History of Quakerism,* pp. 48-52 et al; BBQ, XXVIII, et al.

5 For origin of name *see* THOMAS, *History of Friends in America,* p. 42 n. i. RUSSELL, *op. cit.,* p. 31 and n. 7.

6 Quoted by BRAYSHAW, *op. cit.,* p. 59; *see* pp. 62-65; *cf.* BARCLAY, App. III. 5.

7 *See* RUSSELL, *op. cit.,* pp. 33-45. *Cf.* BBQ, pp. 206ff; pp. 401ff; JLPQ pp. 350-67.

8 H. H. BRINTON, *The Society of Friends* (Pendle Hill Pamphlet No. 48), p. 6ff.

9 *Journal,* p. 36.

10 Quoted from BRAYSHAW, *op. cit.,* p. 131; *cf.* pp. 42, 108n, 173n, 214ff.

THE SOCIETY OF FRIENDS IN AMERICA

11 BSPQ p. XLIV.
12 ROBERT BARCLAY, *Apology for the True Christian Divinity* (XI. 7).
13 BSPQ p. 385; *cf.* RUSSELL, *op. cit.*, p. 176ff.
14 BSPQ p. 388.
15 *Ap.* V, 15, 21.
16 *Ap.* IV, 2.
17 A good discussion of Robert Barclay by R. JONES in BSPQ, pp. XXX-XLVII.
18 JLPQ p. 34ff; *cf.* pp. 57-103 for discussion of Quaker Quietism.
19 JLPQ p. 63.
20 R. JONES in JLPQ p. 81 quotes from WOOLMAN'S *Journal*, p. 61 (Whittier, ed.).
21 GUMMERE, *The Journal of John Woolman*, p. 221.
22 *See* SIDNEY LUCAS, *The Quaker Story*, p. 119ff. Lucas says 3000 slaves were freed through efforts of Levi Coffin alone.
23 *See* RUSSELL, *op. cit.*, p. 288 for more complete statement.
24 JLPQ p. 441ff.
25 JLPQ p. 457 and p. 484.
26 *See* RUSSELL, *op. cit.*, pp. 319-328 for effects of the separation.
27 *See* RUSSELL, *op. cit.*, 339-41.
28 *Op. cit.*, p. 351ff.
29 *Op. cit.*, p. 355ff.
30 JLPQ p. 537n.
31 RUSSELL, *op. cit.*, p. 499ff.
32 *See* RUSSELL, *op. cit.*, p. 504.
33 R. JONES, *Original Quakerism: A Movement, Not a Sect*, pp. 15 and 6.
34 *See* R. JONES, *The Faith and Practice of the Quakers*, pp. 65-69.
35 From *Uniform Discipline as in Faith and Practice*, Indiana Yearly Meeting (1950), p. 72.
36 *Handbook of the Religious Society of Friends* (1941), p. 14.
37 *See* JLPQ p. 930ff. *See Faith and Practice*, discipline of Indiana Yearly Meeting of Friends, 1950.
38 *Handbook, op. cit.*, p. 13.
39 *See* JLPQ p. 142ff., 932ff.
40 RUSSELL, *op. cit.*, p. 517ff; also quoting A. RUTH FRY, *A Quaker Adventure*, p. 1ff.
41 *See* 1950 Annual Report of A.F.S.C., 20 S. Twelfth Street, Philadelphia.
42 *See Handbook* (*op. cit.*), p. 16.
43 *See* Reports of American Friends Fellowship Council (1951 and 1952).
44 *Handbook of the Religious Society of Friends* (Philadelphia, 1935).
45 Figures taken from 1952 report of Fellowship Council and corrected.

BIBLIOGRAPHY

ROBERT BARCLAY, *An Apology for the True Christian Divinity* (no place, 1678).
WILLIAM C. BRAITHWAITE, *The Beginnings of Quakerism* (London, 1912). BBQ.
———, *The Second Period of Quakerism* (London, 1919). BSPQ.
A. NEAVE BRAYSHAW, *The Quakers: Their Story and Message* (4th ed., London, 1946).
HOWARD H. BRINTON, *Creative Worship* (London, 1931).
———, *Divine-Human Society* (Pendle Hill, 1938).

THE AMERICAN CHURCH

————, "The Society of Friends" in *Religion in the Twentieth Century* (New York, 1948), edited by Vergilius Ferm.

WILLIAM WISTAR COMFORT, *Quakers in the Modern World* (New York, 1949).

AMELIA M. GUMMERE, *The Journal and Essays of John Woolman* (New York, 1922).

Handbook of the Religious Society of Friends (Philadelphia, 1935, 1941).

MARY HOXIE JONES, *Swords Into Plowshares* (New York, 1937).

RUFUS M. JONES, *The Faith and Practice of the Quakers* (5th ed., London, 1938).

————, *The Later Periods of Quakerism*, 2 vols. (London, 1921). JLPQ.

————, *Original Quakerism, a Movement, Not a Sect* (Richmond, Ind., 1945).

————, *Quakers in the American Colonies* (London, 1911).

————, *A Service of Love in Wartime* (New York, 1920).

————, *Studies in Mystical Religion* (London, 1923).

————, *Spiritual Reformers in the Sixteenth and Seventeenth Centuries* (London, 1914).

SIDNEY LUCAS, *The Quaker Story* (New York, 1949).

NORMAN PENNEY, *The Journal of George Fox*. Abridgement in Everyman's Library (Tercentenary ed., London, 1924).

ELBERT RUSSELL, *Friends at Mid-Century* (Richmond, Ind., 1950).

————, *History of Quakerism* (New York, 1942).

ALLEN C. THOMAS and RICHARD HENRY THOMAS, *History of Friends in America* (8th ed., Philadelphia, 1930).

CHARLES M. WOODMAN, *Quakers Find a Way* (Indianapolis, 1950).

PERIODICALS

The American Friend (Philadelphia, 1894-1912; Richmond, Ind., 1913-).

The Friend (Philadelphia, 1827-).

The Friends Intelligencer (Philadelphia, 1844-).

For list of Friends' periodicals *see Handbook of the Religious Society of Friends* (1941), pp. 100-102.

For more complete bibliography *see* RUSSELL, *History of Quakerism*, pp. 547-559.

XIII

THE EVANGELICAL MISSION COVENANT CHURCH AND THE FREE CHURCHES OF SWEDISH BACKGROUND

XIII

THE EVANGELICAL MISSION
COVENANT CHURCH
AND THE
FREE CHURCHES OF SWEDISH BACKGROUND

KARL A. OLSSON

THE TREND toward ecumenicity has brought the genesis of many Protestant denominations under suspicion. It is not uncommon to conclude that the multiplication of sects since the Reformation has been the result of rashness or, worse yet, of envy and vindictiveness. Nevertheless, a sober view of the nistorical process since the 16th century does not give much support to this thesis. Few centrally Christian denominations seem to have sprung from motives either shallow or base. In most instances the process of separation was slow, painful, and marked by high moral seriousness. And once the major presuppositions had been formulated, the division was more or less inevitable.

This is particularly evident where the new sect broke away, not from a sect of its own general type, but from an established church whose concept of salvation was objective and sacramental rather than subjective.[1] The two conceptions of the church are really incapable of either theoretical or practical reconciliation. This point is made because without it the origin and development of the free churches in Sweden and of their American counterparts may seem gratuitous. Actually the struggle with the National Church, out of which these Swedish American churches were born, was as inevitable as the older conflict between Lutheran and Catholic concepts of faith.

The beginning of the tension takes us back to Sweden in the year 1700. The country had then been officially Lutheran for about 100 years, having accepted the Augsburg confession as the national formula of faith in 1593. Furthermore the long and absolutistic reign of Charles XI (1660-1697) had seen the acceptance of the *Book of Concord* as the authorized explanation of the confession. Subsequent to this achievement of doctrinal purity, the church developed an organization which could safeguard and disseminate its dogmas. The introduction toward the end of the 17th century of church registers, compulsory doctrinal classes, and a system of mandatory catechising of the community gave the church rigid control over the entire process of religious indoctrination.

If dogmatic conformity extrinsically enforced had been capable of producing spiritual life, the Swedish National Church in this period would have built the New Jerusalem. Instead its absolutism bred intolerance and, what was worse, a moral indifference which provoked one of the bishops of the church[2] into exclaiming:

> I sigh and lament at heart as often as I think of it, how ill most Lutherans understand Luther's doctrines, how ill they understand what faith in our Saviour, the Lord Jesus Christ is . . . If they go to church and at certain times in the year to the Lord's Supper, and at the same time live in all sorts of sinful works of the flesh —it's no matter; 'sola fides,' strong faith, shall do the business for them. No one shall say that they are not good Lutherans and Christians, and shall not be saved without any contradiction. My God, who hast called forth and equipped Luther with Thy spirit of freedom in order that he should restore the Christian doctrine about faith, raise up another Luther, who, with like freedom and blessed effect, may again restore a Christian life![3]

Nevertheless, the importance of this dogmatic nutriment for the religious development of the nation should not be dis-

regarded. The Christian concept and vocabulary were preserved. So was the Christian community. It was, to be sure,
no more than a skeleton surgically extracted from its original
envelope of flesh, but it suggested what the body had once
been and what it might become.

Hence, it was not the church *in its official capacity* which
was to give the nation back its spiritual vitality. That achievement was reserved for dissenters: Pietists, Moravians, and a
number of awakened individuals who during the first decades
of the 18th century began to breathe new life into the dry
bones. Many of these efforts were marked by naïveté and extravagance, but the total effect was impressive. The values of
a subjective experience of sin and grace, of impassioned devotion to God and to His Word, of a positive moral goodness
which transcended the dead respectability of the community,
of lay leadership within communities of the like-minded, of
spontaneous prayer, Bible-study, and song—all these values
were rediscovered and developed by the dissenters. The movements gathered momentum during the 18th century and the
first half of the 19th. Gradually groups of the converted
formed mission societies[4] within the National Church for the
propagation of the faith, and occasionally these societies developed into sacramental unions among those who objected to
receiving communion in the indiscriminate company of the
National Church.

The Church saw the threat in these proceedings. Very early
it tried to pass effective legal measures against unofficial worship. In 1726 the notorious "Edict against Conventicles", which
forbade all gatherings for worship except under a parish priest,
became law. It was not repealed until 1858, and although it
was not applied with uniform vigor during this period, it was
frequently invoked with serious results both for the National
Church and its opposition.

It should be noted that the stir within the National Church
was not self-consciously separatistic. Many of the prominent
dissenters were priests in the National Church. Thus Henrik

Schartau (1757-1825), whose sober spirituality still retains its impress on the Lutherans of south-western Sweden, was a priest during most of his life in the cathedral at Lund; Lars Levi Laestadius (1800-1861) the eminent Swedish botanist under whose awakened ministry the northern fells bloomed, was a Lutheran priest; so was Peter Fjellstedt (1802-1879) whose preaching was so effective that "no church could accommodate the throngs . . . listening in breathless reverence to the whitebearded saint standing in the open window speaking with a clear and distinct voice, without emphasis and without gestures, his invitation to come to Christ . . ."5 Nevertheless, as the major assumptions of the dissenting movements emerged, the impossibility of consistently holding both church and sect views became apparent. Put much too simply, the church held that to be justified by faith meant to be properly baptized and confirmed, to attend worship and communion with decent regularity, and to live an orderly life within the conventions of the community. The dissenters, on the other hand, related faith to a moral choice on the part of the individual by which he entered fully into that life which was only prefigured by his baptism and confirmation.

It was, of course, possible for revivalistic state church ministers to warn their hearers of the need of awakening and to emphasize the need for personal commitment, and this they did not hesitate to do. But practically they had to treat the zealous and the indifferent as if both equally were heirs of salvation. Similarly the awakened church member was forced within the frame work of the National Church to listen with equal outward loyalty to both hireling and true shepherds and to receive communion side by side with the humble Christian and unrepentant profligate.

The break was bound to come. It was prepared for in part by the activity of non-Swedish sects like the Methodists and Baptists, of which more will be said directly, but the main impetus came from those dissenters who had remained loyal to the National Church in theology and polity and whose organizations strove for reform from within. Chief among these was the Evangelical National Foundation. The Foundation was organized in 1856 for the propagation of the faith within the framework of the National Church. It published devotional literature of a revivalist cast and supported scores of colporteurs whose function it was to distribute tracts and books in the interest of evangelism.

One of the outstanding leaders of the Foundation was Carl Olof Rosenius (1816-1868), a lay preacher who through his sermons and writings in the periodical *Pietisten* paved the way for the free church movement in Sweden. The inspirer of Rosenius was the English Methodist preacher George Scott with whom he collaborated in the Bethlehem Chapel in Stockholm. Scott had come to Sweden in 1830 as the chaplain of some English workmen, but his influence spread until it was necessary to build a chapel to hold the crowds which thronged to hear him. Scott was forced to leave Sweden in 1842 and from that time until 1868, Rosenius was the leader of nearly all free spirits within the church. Rosenius was not ordained and was frequently caustic about the National Church, but like Scott, he opposed separation.

Rosenius' successor as editor of *Pietisten* was Paul Peter Waldenström (1838-1917), an ordained minister in the National Church and professor of Greek, Hebrew and Christianity at Gävle College. A man of large intellectual dimensions and limitless moral courage, Waldenström summed up in his own personality the various tendencies of dissent although he did not, at least to begin with, give support to separation. But his career made the implicit conflict between church and sect explicit. Two things alienated him from the National Church:

1) His insistence on going directly to the Scriptures for doctrinal truth and his consequent derogation of the Augsburg confession.

2) His insistence that salvation was a matter of sub-

jective commitment to Christ and was not mediated
by the Church.

Both these concepts were inherent in the thought of Rosenius. His Biblical preaching which stressed the graciousness of
God and the necessity for conversion had close affinity with
the Wesleyan ideas of George Scott, but Rosenius was not a
trained theologian or dialectician. It took Waldenström's logical mind and ruthless directness to spell out the implications.

The first conclusion led Waldenström away from the theory
of substitutionary atonement and objective salvation. He embodied his findings in a sermon for the Twentieth Sunday after Trinity (1872) published in *Pietisten*. It is fair to say that
no sermon of the century made a more profound impression
on Swedish church life. The controversy that followed was
bitter and lasting. Basically it was a struggle between traditional theology and pure Biblicism. Waldenström declared the
individual's freedom to read the Bible for himself with only
the guidance of good linguistic exegesis. In accord with that
conviction he later published in two volumes an immensely
popular *New Testament with Explanatory Comments*. But Waldenström's commentary, with all its avowed interest in the
pure text, is largely based upon traditional Christian beliefs.
It was not an invitation to either higher or lower criticism.
When the scentific interest in Biblical study increased toward
the close of the century, Waldenström aligned himself with
the conservatives, and today the controversy which branded
him an arch heretic in the seventies and eighties seems
strangely academic, and he himself the most orthodox of think-
ers.

It would have been possible for Waldenström to remain
in the Church if his deviation had been merely theological.
His position became untenable when he violated the ordinances. It was inevitable that he should. He believed in the right
of the sacramental unions to celebrate communion privately
and when he, as an ordained priest, was asked to officiate at

such a communion, he complied. Since it was not held in a church, Waldenström was disciplined and consequently resigned from his office. This was in 1876. Two years later the Swedish Mission Covenant was formed in order to satisfy the needs of those dissenters who wanted to worship, to commune, and to give according to the dictates of their consciences. Waldenström was not at the organizational meeting, and his consent was reluctant since he was afraid of the separatistic tendency of a new organization; but it is fair to claim that more than anyone else he was responsible for the genesis of the Covenant. Since the group did not separate officially from the National Church, Waldenström was able for a period of some forty years to give leadership in both communions although he remained a layman as far as the Church was concerned until his death.

* * *

Whereas the Mission Covenant was born out of ideas and feelings within the National Church and with only few exceptions retained the Lutheran theology of that church, the Baptists and Methodists of Sweden came into being because of influences from without. In many instances the growth of these sects resulted from the contacts of Lutheran dissenters with American Baptists and Methodists.

The two dominant Swedish Baptists, Fredrik Olaus Nilsson (1809-1881) and Anders Wiberg (1820-1887), were both closely associated with Scott and Rosenius in Stockholm in the early forties. Nilsson was a sailor who had been helped to a living faith by a Baptist pastor in New York, and who after his return to Sweden became more and more influenced by the Baptist point of view. He was baptized in the Elbe River August 1, 1847, and since the affair was given considerable publicity, he returned to Sweden to find hostility on every hand. Undaunted, Nilsson launched into a vigorous campaign of preaching which brought him into difficulties with the law. His persecution and the clumsy handling of the affair by the authorities under the provision of the Edict against

Conventicles made the affair a *cause célèbre*. He was exiled in 1851 and after a brief residence in Copenhagen he proceeded with a group of other Baptists to America. He was finally pardoned by Charles XV in 1860.

Wiberg's course was less dramatic but of larger significance. He, like Nilsson, was deeply influenced by the piety of Scott and Rosenius and actually did not profess Baptist views until after he had left Sweden for America in 1852. While in America Wiberg wrote for the Swedish Press and raised a considerable sum of money for evangelistic work in Sweden. In 1855 he returned to his homeland and within a period of a few years the sect which numbered a handful in the early fifties had grown to several thousands. Much of this growth must be attributed to the generosity of American friends as well as the ability and devotion of Wiberg. The hostility of the National Church to the Baptists can be attributed largely to the unsettling influence of the doctrine of adult baptism. This came in conflict with the established ordinances of infant baptism, confirmation, and legal marriage, and until 1873 when more liberal laws were passed, the relations between the Church and the Baptist group were marked by such bitter hostility that in many instances it contributed to the rising tide of emigration.

The Swedish Methodists, like the Baptists, had their beginnings in contacts with American churches. The most celebrated Swedish Methodist pioneer is without doubt Olof Gustaf Hedstrom (1803-1877) who was pastor of the Bethel ship in New York Harbor from 1845 to 1875. Hedstrom was a sailor who had been converted to Methodism in New York and became a pastor in the Methodist Episcopal Church a few years later. After a decade's ministry, he established the mission on the Bethel ship, and there almost continuously for 30 years he ministered to the physical and spiritual needs of thousands of Scandinavian immigrants. Through his influence which spread to Sweden and through the leadership of Victor Witting who also had spent several years in America and had become imbued with American Methodism, the first Swedish Methodist church was organized in Stockholm in 1868. It is well to note that this Methodist movement was unrelated to the English Methodism represented by George Scott a quarter of a century earlier. The Methodist church which grew out of American influence was thoroughly separatistic and was the first sect in Sweden to be given independent status, whereas Scott's ministry had been within the frame of the National Church.

The Free Churches in America

The period of greatest tension between the National Church and the dissenters coincides with the period of the mass migration to America. Although there had been some emigration prior to the Civil War,[6] 1866 saw the beginnings of the flood which was to bring almost 750,000 Swedes to this country before 1900. The motives for the migration are complex, and it is difficult to assess the precise part played by religious tension. The high point on the graph comes well after the repeal of the Edict against Conventicles in 1858 and the passage of the law granting religious freedom in 1873. Furthermore, religious persecution even at its height furnished the sole motive for emigration only in isolated instances.[7] Nevertheless for thousands of dissenters who joined the stream of emigration in the sixties, seventies, and eighties, the desire for religious status was probably a very important if not a primary motive.

In the beginning the immigrants, most of them from rural Sweden, gravitated quite naturally to the cheap and fertile lands of the Middle West. In their number were many Rosenian dissenters as well as many zealous Lutherans who were loyal to the ideals of the National Church. To begin with most of the religiously interested newcomers were happy to worship in any church which used their native tongue. Consequently the Swedish Lutheran Church in America was established in strength long before the Mission Covenant broke away.[8] Meanwhile some of the Swedes did ally themselves with the Swedish Methodist and Swedish Baptist Churches, but the Lutheran cast of the majority is revealed by the fact that although both Methodists and Bapists were early in the field and aggressive in their methods, they did not succeed in winning the preponderance of the dissenting immigrants to their persuasion. Lutheran doctrine has prevailed in a pure form in the Augustana synod and in a modified form in the Mission Covenant, and these two bodies have far outnumbered the non-Lutherans throughout the history of Swedish American church life.

Nevertheless, although many of the dissenters were Lutherans and affiliated themselves with existing Lutheran churches, the central problem which had agitated the Swedish church emerged in the new setting. The burning question was the character of church membership. There were many who sincerely believed that the function of the church in the new land was to gather the immigrant community within its walls and to render it Christian through the efficacy of the gospel purely preached and the sacraments rightly administered. Others longed for a pure church in which a regenerate membership would exercise control and in which the sacrament of communion would be reserved for believers. The two positions were impossible to reconcile although many good people worked long and patiently to keep the community together. But in place after place—first in the Lutheran church in Swede Bend, Iowa, in 1867, and then in Chicago, and subsequently in villages and towns throughout the Middle West—"converted" Lutherans without real thought of separation formed societies of the like-minded to pray, sing, and listen with genuine interest to the reading of a printed sermon or to spoken testimonies. The leaders of these groups were in most instances laymen, some with previous preaching experience in Sweden, others fresh from the cobbler bench or the plow. Their messages made up in earthy vigor and conviction bred of an experience of regeneration what they may have lacked in exegetical subtlety.

One such conventicle serves both to illustrate the growing pattern and to date the unofficial origin of the Mission Covenant in America. In 1864, at the very beginning of the mass migration, a Swedish cobbler by the name of Carl August Björk came with his family to Swede Bend, Iowa. The very first Sunday he invited some people to his home for an informal meeting at which he read from *Pietisten,* sang the songs of Oscar Ahnfelt, and in general furnished his visitors with typically Rosenian fare. Otherwise he was a devout Lutheran who after a time enjoyed such high status in the church that in the absence of the pastor he was permitted to read devotional materials at the services. Good Friday 1867, when Björk was to lead the service, the sexton, who was interested in hearing him preach, hid the copy of *Pietisten* from which Björk had planned to read. As a result the latter was forced to extemporize and did this so compellingly that several of the members became convicted of their sins. This was the beginning of a serious clash with the pastor of the church which (in 1868) resulted in the formation of a mission society with Björk as the appointed leader.

The immediate cause of the final separation of the Augustana Synod and the mission societies is difficult to determine. The historical lens cannot be focused sharply and much of the detail escapes us. In any separation of this type, feelings are sure to be involved. Arrogance on the part of those in power meets the insolence of the dispossessed. But although the trigger causes have been obscured by time, the real causes have not, and something of the hopelessness and pathos of the struggle emerges sharply in two questions posed by a joint conference of Lutherans and Mission Friends in Chicago in July 1869:

1) Having among the Swedish people so many pastors and churches and the Word of God proclaimed by

word and pen, how, then can you prove the need of the Swedish Evangelical Mission Association of Chicago?

2) What is the cause of spiritual death so prevalent among our Swedish people, though we have both pastors and churches?

It need hardly be pointed out that both questions (the first obviously submitted by the church and the second by the society) assume the points at issue. The church would deny that it housed "spiritual death" and the society would seriously question that the church was meeting the "need."

In any event the debate settled nothing and the breach widened. In the period 1868-1870 most of the mission societies seceded and formed independent churches. In 1873 most of these churches, lonesome perhaps and convinced of the perils of isolation, formed the Mission Synod. It is worthy of note that the Mission Synod was theologically Lutheran being committed unreservedly to the Augsburg Confession; it differed primarily from the Augustana group in its insistence upon a converted membership.

Within the Mission Synod, however, all was not sweetness and light. Some of the pastors felt that the new synod should affiliate itself with the Synod of Northern Illinois in order to benefit from the solidarity of the larger group and in particular to receive help from the General Synod for a training school for ministers. The leader of this group was Charles Anderson, an ordained Lutheran minister, whose mastery of both English and Swedish and whose personal gifts made him a natural leader. With Anderson's encouragement a group of churches broke away from the Mission Synod in 1874 and formed the Ansgar Synod. In 1871 Anderson had begun to publish a paper, *Zions Banér,* under subsidies from the General Synod. This now became the official organ of the Ansgar Synod. The Synod also backed the training school for ministers begun at Keokuk, Iowa, in 1873 and moved to

THE MISSION COVENANT CHURCH

Knoxville, Illinois in 1875. The School, known as Ansgar College after its location at Knoxville, received help from the community and from the churches of the Ansgar Synod but the attitude of the churches in the Mission Synod was not too cooperative, and without the assistance of all the Mission Friend groups the project was doomed to failure. Ansgar College struggled on until 1884 when it closed its doors permanently.

It is not improbable that the two Synods, had they been left untouched by developments in Sweden, ultimately would have joined either the Augustana Synod or the American Lutheran Church. But in the middle seventies the rate of immigration increased, and the ferment in Swedish religious life was quickly communicated to America. These were the years of Waldenström's struggle for a Biblical view of the atonement and for the rights of dissenters, and nothing did more to redirect the Mission Friends in America than the knowledge of what was happening to their fellow believers in Sweden. In the first place, the Waldenströmian theology undermined the position historically held by the Augsburg Confession. Furthermore, the protest against the National Church, implied in the formation of the Mission Covenant in Sweden, gave support to a growing anti-denominationalism among the Mission Friends in America. Individuals and churches, formerly content with some sort of denominational body, now began to clamor for the autonomy of the local church. Leaders in this congregational movement were J. G. Princell (1845-1915), a former Lutheran pastor who had been defrocked by the Augustana Synod for Waldenströmian views and who lent his considerable ability and training to the fighting of denominations, and Fredrik Franson, a flaming apostle of the imminent and pre-millennial return of Christ. Franson's impassioned eschatology reflected itself in deliberate poverty and in scorn for what he considered the useless fabric of religious organizations. A 19th century Protestant St. Francis with a plain suit of clothes, a satchel, and a worn Bible, Franson traveled everywhere with his gospel of urgency and sacrifice and made a deep impression on the free church movement among the Swedes of America. Princell's arguments and Franson's ascetic preaching thus combined to create a sizeable bloc of Mission Friend churches who bitterly resisted union. Ironically, this very resistance to corporateness later helped to fuse the churches together into something very near a denomination.

Meanwhile an increasing number of lay preachers trained and inspired in Sweden had come to America. Among these the outstanding Mission Friend was E. August Skogsbergh who from his arrival in 1876 and throughout his long life distinguished himself as preacher, evangelist, musician, organizer, and educator. So effective was Skogsbergh's preaching that after a brief collaboration with Dwight L. Moody in the latter's large tabernacle in Chicago, he became renowned as the "Swedish Moody" and traveled widely as an evangelist through the Swedish settlements in the Middle West. Skogsbergh's activities in Chicago and later in Minneapolis fall almost exactly within the period of the greatest immigration, and there can be little doubt that the harvest of newcomers which the Mission churches gathered in was to a large extent the result of his prodigious labors.

The revival had profound effects also on the organization of the Mission Covenant. First of all the large influence of Skogsbergh was given to the project; furthermore the sense of growth tended to unify the churches psychologically and to emphasize the importance of collaboration in the work of the kingdom. Hence despite the disintegration of the two Synods, the militant independence of some churches, and the energetic propaganda of Princell and *Chicagobladet,* plans for union matured and at a historic meeting in Chicago February 18, 1885, the Swedish Evangelical Mission Covenant was formed. Sixty-two delegates represented churches from the Mission and Ansgar Synods as well as some independent groups. As their first president they elected Carl August Björk, who eighteen years before had preached the first Mission Friend sermon on American soil.

The distance already traveled from doctrinaire Lutheranism is indicated in the refusal of the organizing conference to bind the Covenant to any confession or creed. The statement in the original constitution is significant:

> The Covenant accepts the Word of God, the sacred Scriptures of the Old and New Testaments, as the only perfect rule for faith and conduct.

In theology the Covenant was still preponderantly Lutheran and most of the pioneer ministers were too deeply immersed in the tradition to entertain any other views. Hence they practiced infant baptism, conducted special Bible classes for children in confirmation age in which Luther's Catechism was a standard part of the curriculum, and resisted strongly any Calvinistic invasion. But the difference between a tradition, however loyally held, and a confession is, as any historian will agree, the difference between flesh and iron. A tradition depends upon congeniality of spirit and is powerless before the small-minded regula of credalists. Because the Covenanters were never Lutherans with a vengeance, they have been besieged from the very beginning with other doctrines which pride themselves on being more muscular. The result has been an infiltration of many points of view into the theological freedom of the denomination. So far the older tradition has prevailed, but the question which Lincoln applied to the young republic may well be posed as far as Mission Covenant theology is concerned: whether any theological position so conceived and so dedicated can long endure.

In church polity the same tradition of freedom prevailed although the Covenant has never been congregational in the ordinary meaning of the term. A great deal of autonomy was given local congregations, but the denomination acting through its annual conference reserved the right to license and ordain its ministers and by implication to administer other programs of common interest such as missions, education, and benevolence.[9]

The leadership of the Covenant has been vested in four presidents since 1885: Carl August Björk (1885-1910), Erik Gustav Hjerpe (1910-1927) and C. V. Bowman (1927-1932). The present leader of the denomination is Dr. Theodore W. Anderson who assumed office in 1933. Under his imaginative and prudent statesmanship the denomination has integrated many previously peripheral churches into its community, has achieved greater self-consciousness and unity than at any time in its history, and has greatly expanded its missions program at home and abroad.

* * *

The Covenant was organized under the standard of freedom. Theology and church polity were to be as free as the spacious air of the New Testament, and much of the enthusiasm with which the denomination was launched can no doubt be traced to this emphasis upon the spontaneous. But freedom in religious as well as political societies is absurd without responsibility. Their liberty the Mission Friends got from the time in which they lived and the land they inhabited; responsibility has been acquired through a painful process of growing up. In one sense the history of the denomination is the history of growing responsibility without loss of essential freedom in the areas of its activity.

After the collapse of Ansgar College in 1884 the Mission Friends were without any type of educational institution. Consequently when in 1885 Chicago Theological Seminary offered to open a Swedish Department and even to finance a trip to Sweden by the Covenant's president to secure a teacher, the offer was gladly accepted. It was assumed by the Congregationalists that the Covenanters were like them,[10] and it was not suspected by the younger denomination that anything could be amiss in this arrangement. In the enthusiasm of its beginnings, the Covenant felt that it could be generous about the future. Very soon, however, the threat of eventual absorption by the Congregationalists persuaded the Covenant to found its own school. This was accomplished in 1891. The school was originally located in Minneapolis, but in 1894 it was moved to Chicago where it became North Park College and Theological Seminary.

The first president of North Park College was David Nyvall (1863-1946), a young graduate of the University of Uppsala in Sweden and the son of the pioneer lay preacher C. J. Nyvall. David Nyvall's contribution to the thought and life of the Covenant was enormous. It is just to say that Nyvall originated the intellectual tradition of the denomination. Through his many books—but more than that, through his lectures over a period of fifty years—Nyvall created in the minds of his students an eagerness for inquiry which was always combined with the discipline of faith. Better than anyone else David Nyvall understood the blessing and the bane of freedom, and although he rejoiced in the liberty of doctrine and polity in which the Covenant was born, he appreciated better than anyone the necessity of earning the right to be free.

From the very beginning the Covenant school provided both academic and theological education. It used to be David Nyvall's contention that a Christian school was first of all a good *school,* and the sixty years of North Park's history has been a struggle in that direction. At the start the offerings were necessarily unimpressive, but the structure was sound and under the leadership of a handful of loyal and competent teachers the school grew in influence. Notable expansion in plant and enrollment came under the presidency of Dr. Algoth Ohlson (1924-1949.) Today under the leadership of Clarence A. Nelson the school provides Christian education of real significance for large high school, college, and seminary enrollments. North Park has a staff of 85 instructors, buildings and grounds valued at $1,200,000, and an annual operating budget of nearly $500,000.

The Covenant founders were not all theologically trained, and the memory of their devotion and effectiveness tended to retard support for theological education in the denomination. It is only recently that the denomination has insisted upon high theological standards for its ministers, and even these can be circumvented by a church which wishes to exercise its congregational right of calling an untrained minister as its pastor. This is an example of the denomination's political freedom and the problems it poses.

An example of the consequences of its theological freedom is afforded by the history of the Seminary. In the absence of a specified creed it has been virtually impossible to fashion curriculum or a teaching method which has not been open to the charge of heterodoxy by those whose credal position is crystallized. Thus, David Nyvall, Nils W. Lund, who became Dean of the Seminary in 1922, and the present Dean, Eric G. Hawkinson, who succeeded Lund in 1949, have all been forced at some time to defend historic freedom of inquiry within the framework of Biblical truth. With the thinning of the older Lutheran tradition, an even more gigantic task confronts the denomination's theologians, *viz.,* to form and communicate a dogmatic tradition which will be true to the genius of the Covenant without violating its historic freedoms.

The Northwest Conference of the Covenant supports Minnehaha Academy, a high school in Minneapolis which in some sense is a continuation of the Covenant School founded there by Skogsbergh in 1884. The first building of the Academy was finished in 1913. The school enjoyed periods of real expansion under the presidencies of Theodore W. Anderson (1914-1933) and Clarence A. Nelson (1943-1949). The present enrollment is 500 and the annual operating budget is $100,000. The school is housed in a complex of attractive buildings situated on the banks of the Mississippi River in south Minneapolis. The president is Arthur A. Anderson.

The latest Covenant school project is the Covenant Bible Institute of Canada begun in 1941. The school is located in Prince Albert, Saskatchewan, and although it has received some support from the United States in the construction of its buildings, the operating budget is met by contributions from the Canadian Conference.

* * *

The term "mission" has been closely associated with the Covenant enterprise from the beginning. Long before any official organization in Sweden or America the dissenters were eager "missioners" among the unawakened. It was consequently in character that their history in America should be a history of missions first in the frontier territories of the American west and later in areas outside the continental United States.

In 1890 the Mission Covenant had 79 churches and 4,793 members; in 1930 it had 301 churches and 27,140 members; in 1950 the total had grown to 480 churches and 51,264 members. This unspectacular but steady growth has been largely the result of an aggressive policy of expansion through home missions. Much of the work is accomplished under the direct supervision of the twelve district conferences which furnish in excess of half the cost. For the fiscal year the Covenant and its twelve districts had a total budget of $364,000 and approximately 200 small churches and mission stations were receiving support. Home missionary efforts under direct denominational supervision include the Covenant Mountain Mission in Virginia, a mission in southern Alabama, and another among the Mexicans in south Texas. Approximately seventy localities are being served through these efforts. The present Secretary of Home Missions is Joseph Danielson.

In 1888 the Mission Covenant began its foreign missions program in Alaska and in 1890 it sent Peter Matson, the man destined to become the denomination's most distinguished missionary statesman, to China. The Alaska mission has enjoyed steady growth during the past 60 years. At present 18 missionaries and 10 native workers serve in 19 stations. The China mission, despite the interruptions of rebellion and war, functioned with increasing depth and power in the province of Hupeh and in later years also in southwest China until the Chinese Communists made all further activity by foreign missionaries not only hazardous but impossible. In 1948 as a foretaste of what Western missionaries might expect at the hands of the Reds, Communist guerillas brutally murdered three Covenant missionaries: Dr. Alrik Berg, Martha Anderson and Mildred Nordlund. By September 1949 the last non-Chinese missionary had left the interior. Reports received from the mainland indicate that the indigenous church is assuming increasing responsibility for the field. In a sense the effectiveness of the native church under severe trial will indicate the measure of influence exerted by six decades of Covenant missions in China.

In 1934 missionary interest was extended to Africa and in 1937, after a period of careful preparation, a part of the field in Belgian Congo formerly held by the Evangelical Free Church was taken over by the Covenant. The African Mission now has four head stations and carries on organized work in 200 villages. The mission is staffed by 55 missionaries and some 200 native workers. There are four doctors, 11 nurses, and 40 evangelists, teachers and practical workers. In addition to a large hospital and several dispensaries, the mission also sponsors a leper colony.

A mission field in Ecuador was opened in 1947 and with the closing of missionary doors in China, aggressive activity has been initiated in Japan. At present 19 missionaries serve in Ecuador and 18 in Japan.

The annual foreign missions contribution of the denomination is close to $500,000. This serves to support approximately 135 missionaries and 23 head stations as well as hospitals, dispensaries, and schools. The administrator of this total project is the Secretary of Foreign Missions, Ralph P. Hanson.

There are probably not fewer than 100 young people in the denomination currently considering the possibility of missionary service. Many of these are enrolled in preparatory courses at North Park College, the Covenant School of Nursing, and Covenant Bible Institute of Canada.

The tradition of freedom in the Covenant has resulted in generous giving on the part of many members and churches to non-denominational missions. Chief benefactor of Covenant gifts among these non-denominational groups has been the Scandinavian Alliance Mission organized by Fredrik Franson in 1890, although other missions as well continue to attract personal gifts as well as sizeable appropriations by individual churches. Just how far such freedom can be carried without impairing the work undertaken by the denomination is a problem which the Covenanters will have to solve in terms of their own assumptions about the meaning of Christian liberty.

* * *

The history of Covenant publications deserves a separate chapter in any account of the denomination's life. However, space will only permit the barest outline of facts. Reference has already been made to *Chicagobladet,* the champion of freedom, which later became the organ of the Evangelical Free Church. It was first published in 1877 and is still in existence. *Zions Baner,* the paper of the Ansgar Synod, was later bought out by *Chicagobladet.* The strongest weekly for many years among the Mission Friends was *Missionsvännen (The Mission Friend)*, originally the organ of the Mission Synod but for unaccountable reasons sold by them to a private publishing company in 1882. Until 1915 when the Covenant finally established its own paper, *Förbundets Veckotidning (The Covenant Weekly)*, *The Mission Friend* dominated the field, and its publishing company without any denominational status profited from its semi-official character by publishing a hymnal, widely used in the churches, and a great deal of other religious material. Although this was an important service to the Covenant and although the publishing company was generous toward the denomination, the former reaped large profits which would have helped greatly in establishing the denomination if they had flowed into its own publishing company. Beginning in 1915 the tide began to turn, and today the Covenant Press, which publishes the *Covenant Weekly,* the

Covenant Quarterly, the *Covenant Home Altar,* several books annually, and the denominational Sunday School materials, is in an enviable position. In 1950 it published the new *Hymnal* of which 35,000 copies have been sold. The Editor-in-Chief of Covenant publications is G. F. Hedstrand and the Manager of the Press is Carl Philip Anderson.

* * *

The Covenant operates the Covenant Hospital and Home of Mercy in Chicago with its own School of Nursing. The hospital has a 200-bed capacity and a plant valued at $2,000,000. A large addition is now being added to accommodate convalescent patients. The denomination also operates the Covenant Palms Home in Miami, Florida, for its aged. In addition to the denominational benevolent institutions, the twelve district conferences own and operate a number of homes for the aged, orphaned children, and Scandinavian sailors.

The genius of Covenant piety has expressed itself in song. It is not at all accidental that C. A. Björk began his ministry in America with the singing of the songs of Oscar Ahnfelt, the inspired musical colleague of Rosenius. Meetings of the mission societies here and in Sweden were always characterized by spontaneous, joyful song. Even at this distance, although the music often lacks sophistication and the lyrics are embellished with poetic stereotypes, the total effect is fresh and disarming. The phenomenal sale of the new Covenant *Hymnal* (35,000 copies to a constituency of 50,000 in its first year) was due largely to the selection and translation of scores of these old favorites which are sung as enthusiastically today as 70-80 years ago.

Foremost among Covenant hymn writers were Nils Frykman (1842-1911) a school teacher and lay preacher, A. L. Skoog (1856-1934) who was for Skogsbergh what Ahnfelt had been for Rosenius, and J. A. Hultman (1861-1942), the Covenant's holy troubadour who was artist, entertainer, and evangelist rolled into one.

Freedom and responsibility, spontaneity and discipline have not always kept pace in the Mission Covenant. Nevertheless, because of its heritage of song in which the spirit is both captive and free, there have been moments of such genuine harmony that ultimate disunity seemed impossible. Perhaps this prefiguring of the song of Moses and the Lamb will suggest the way in which the denomination, although beset by all the perils of freedom, may yet find its way as one fellowship to the land of peace.

Other Free Churches

A brief survey must now be made of the development of the three other free churches which had their origin in the turmoil of religious controversy in Sweden: the Swedish Baptists, the Swedish Methodists, and the Swedish Evangelical Free Church.

It is interesting to note that the Swedish Baptist Church, which had its early impetus from American Baptists and for whom so able an historian as George Stephenson predicted early assimilation by American Baptists once Swedish had ceased to be the official language,[11] has actually moved closer to autonomy in the last fifty years. The first church was organized by Gustaf Palmquist, August 13, 1852, in Rock Island and although after fifty years the Swedish Baptists had 320 congregations and 22,000 members, they were still depending upon the American Baptists for their publications, education, and missions program. In 1909, however, they decided to start their own publishing concern and in 1911 they began publishing *Svenska Standaret,* still the official organ. Educationally the Church remained under the wing of the American Baptists until 1914 and for a long period its seminary was a part of the University of Chicago. But in 1914 it was moved to St. Paul and was affiliated with Bethel Academy. Bethel became a junior college in 1931 and a four year school in 1947. The College and Seminary have a total enrollment of 454. Its president is Henry Wingblade. In observing the 100th anniversary of the church, the school has made considerable additions to its plant.

In 1944 the Baptists took the final step toward complete independence by setting up its own foreign missions program. It now has 58 missionaries in Japan, Assam, the Philippine Islands, and Ethiopia and the annual foreign missions budget is $285,000.

The church is under the executive direction of the Rev. Carl H. Lundquist. As it prepared to observe its centennial, the denomination had 38,000 members scattered through 360 congregations. There are 323 pastors. Although theologically conservative, the Swedish Baptists are not militant fundamentalists, and their withdrawal from the struggle among American Baptists can be attributed to their moderate position and their desire to live at peace. In many ways their roots go down with those of the other free churches into the piety of Rosenius and Scott, a piety which antedates* and transcends ideological conflicts.

Meanwhile in the spirit of its founders, the church is presently sponsoring an interesting evangelistic project in which some 50 young people are sharing. The participants give a year of time without remuneration in a nationwide campaign of evangelistic house-to-house visitation. In 1951 this group, called "God's Invasion Army", made 40,000 home contacts.

* * *

The Swedish Methodist Church remained a group of independent conferences within the Methodist Church for almost 100 years, but in 1942 with the passing of the Swedish language, its right to separate existence was questioned and the various conferences were merged with their local American counterparts. Despite this merger, several of the Swedish institutions remain as reminders of their independence, and these are mostly self-sustaining. Thus the Swedish Methodist Seminary, originally founded in Galesburg in 1870 and merged in 1936 with the Norwegian Methodist Bible School in Evanston to form Evanston Collegiate Institute, is now Kendall Junior

College. Although under ultimate Methodist supervision, the College is directed by a board on which members of the now defunct conferences serve. *Sändebudet,* the official organ of the Swedish Methodist Church, founded in 1862, is still published by three former Swedish Methodists who believe in its usefulness. It has a subscription list of 1300. The Bethany Home and Hospital in Chicago, Illinois, with a hospital bed-capacity of 100 and room for 175 aged is directed by a self-perpetuating board.

Many theories have been elaborated about the modest growth of Swedish Methodism. After 75 years in America, for example, it had only 20,000 members and 200 pastors whereas the Baptists had as large a denomination in 50 years and the Mission Covenant in 30. The only adequate explanation seems to be that the Swedish Methodist Church did not have sufficient uniqueness to attract the immigrants away from their Lutheran faith or to retain its third and fourth generations. This should not be negatively interpreted. It was quite natural that the Swedish Methodists, who always remained under the supervision of American bishops, should readily orient themselves to the ways of the American Church. They did not have the fierce loyalty to a "peculiar people" which motivated the orphan groups, and consequently they were more readily assimilated into the American church life, once immigration ceased and the Swedish language lost its hold.

* * *

The Swedish Evangelical Free Church, despite its origin in revolt against denominationalism, succumbed to the need of organization and in 1908 became a church albeit with a very loose organization. By 1929 the church had grown to a membership of 6,000. In 1949 with the language barrier removed the Swedish and the Norwegian groups merged under the name of The Evangelical Free Church. E. A. Halleen is the President. This group now has a membership of 23,000 with 277 churches and 425 pastors. The two denominational schools were merged in the Trinity Seminary and Bible School in

Chicago, which gives a B. Th. degree on the basis of two years of junior college and three years of seminary. It has a faculty of 12 and a total enrollment of 176. The president is Dr. C. Raymond Ludwigson.

The denomination publishes *Chicagobladet* in Swedish, *Evangelisten* in Norwegian, and *The Evangelical Beacon* in English. It has missionaries serving in China, Japan, Belgian Congo, and South America although, like some of the other Scandinavian denominations, it also gives strong support to the Scandinavian Alliance Mission.

Theologically the Free Church is even more heterogeneous than the Covenant. Princell, as has been indicated, was a Waldenströmian on the atonement but he took a Reformed view of the Lord's Supper and had leanings toward perfectionism. Perhaps because of its size and the necessity of allying itself with American schools like Wheaton College and Moody Bible Institute, the theology of the Free Church has close affinities with that brand of conservatism which emphasizes premillennialism, adult baptism, the substitutionary view of the atonement, and the verbal inspiration of the Scriptures.

NOTES

[1] Ernst Troeltsch in his *Social Teachings of the Christian Churches* has made a significant contribution to our thinking about church and sect types. Troeltsch believes both church and sect "are a logical result of the gospel." In the life of the archaic church he finds both seminally present. Space does not permit even a listing of Troeltsch's contraries, but his thesis seems to be that the church considers itself charged with the objective salvation of the community whereas the sect addresses itself to the salvation of the individual. The church is universal and inclusive and is coextensive with the community. The sect, being a voluntary fellowship of the like-minded, is exclusive.

The implication of Troeltsch's argument seems to be that church and sect, since they have a common origin and equally significant functions, can exist side by side in the same society. The question remains whether such a relativism is possible except in the objective sociological mind. The church, if it is to retain its identity, must insist that it is the sole custodian of the "keys" of salvation; the sect must make the same claim. Both church and sect are thus committed to the task of driving the other from the field.

[2] Jesper Svedberg, Bishop of Skara (1702-1735), the father of Emanuel Swedenborg.

[3] Quoted by JOHN WORDSWORTH in *The National Church of Sweden*, p. 312.

THE MISSION COVENANT CHURCH

4 This is the origin of the name "Mission Friends" still the most common designation for Mission Covenanters in Sweden and America.

5 DAVID NYVALL, *The Swedish Covenanters,* p. 32.

6 The Swedes emigrated from Sweden to America in the following numbers, 1851-1900:

1851-1860	14,865
1861-1870	88,731
1871-1880	101,169
1881-1890	324,285
1891-1900	200,524

FLORENCE E. JANSON, *The Background of Swedish Immigration,* p. 499.

7 The Eric-Jansonists seem to be an example of those who left Sweden primarily because of religious persecution. Eric Janson (1808-1850) was the self-appointed Messiah of a group of fanatics whose extravagant behavior attracted not only public hostility but legal action under the edict against conventicles. The group left Sweden for America in 1846 and settled in Bishop Hill, Illinois. There they established a communistic experiment which lasted until 1860. Janson himself was killed in 1850 by an irate colonist who could not tolerate Janson's interference in his marriage.

8 The first Swedish Lutheran church in America was organized in 1848 and the first ordained Lutheran pastor arrived in 1849. The Augustana Synod was formed in 1860. The Swedish settlement in Delaware in 1638 had brought with it ministers from the National Church of Sweden and even after the loss of the colony, Swedish Lutheran clergymen continued to serve the old churches until the early decades of the 19th century. There was, however, no organic connection between this outpost of the National Church and the Augustana Synod. The latter has always been an independent American church.

9 The annual conference is constituted on republican principles with proportionate representation from churches and other organizations. In the interest of more efficient operation and with a view toward local support, the Covenant is divided into twelve district conferences each of which holds an annual meeting immediately preceding the denominational conference. These districts, like the churches, are autonomous and may carry on their own educational, home missionary, and benevolent activity. They are not empowered, however, to license or ordain Covenant ministers. The Covenant assists the activities of the district conferences with financial appropriations and in this indirect manner has a word in their deliberations, but the denomination is strong for "states rights" and centralization is not a popular concept.

The decisions of the annual conference are implemented through the Executive Board. The conference also delegates appropriate functions to the respective boards serving the missionary, educational, benevolent, ministerial, and publishing interests of the denomination. The president of the denomination is also chairman of the Executive Board. He does not have the episcopal powers granted the leading clergymen in the Methodist Church, but his office carries great prestige in the denomination.

10 When the Congregationalists sent M. W. Montgomery to Sweden in 1884, he carried their resolution to the Mission Covenant churches of Sweden, which expressed the conviction that "in doctrine and policy we are substantially one." M. W. MONTGOMERY, *A Wind from the Holy Spirit,* p. 4.

11 "When a Swedish Baptist congregation becomes Anglicized, there is not longer any reason for its existence." GEORGE M. STEPHENSON, *The Religious Aspects of Swedish Immigration,* p. 255.

BIBLIOGRAPHY

C. V. BOWMAN, *Missionsvännerna i Amerika* (Minneapolis, Minn., 1907), translated and published as *The Mission Friends in America* (Chicago, Ill., 1924).

Covenant Frontiers (Chicago, Ill., 1940).

Covenant Memories, 1885-1935 (Chicago, Ill., 1935).

E. J. EKMAN, *Inre Missionens historia* (Jönköping, 1921).

FLORENCE E. JANSON, *The Background of Swedish Immigration* (Chicago, Ill., 1931).

Missionsförbundets minnesskrift, 1885-1910 (Minneapolis, Minn., 1910).

M. W. MONTGOMERY, *A Wind from the Holy Spirit* (New York, 1884).

DAVID NYVALL, *Min faders testamente* (Stockholm, 1929).

———, *The Swedish Covenanters* (Chicago, Ill., 1930).

N. P. OLLÉN, *Paul Peter Waldenström, en levnadsteckning* (Stockholm, 1917).

OSCAR N. OLSON, *The Augustana Lutheran Church in America* (Rock Island, Ill., 1950).

GEORGE M. STEPHENSON, *The Religious Aspects of Swedish Immigration* (Minneapolis, Minn., 1932).

ERNST TROELTSCH, *Social Teachings of the Christian Churches* (New York, 1949).

P. P WALDENSTRÖM, *Genom Norra Amerikas Förenta Stater* (Chicago, Ill., 1890).

———, *Minnesanteckningar* (Stockholm, 1928).

JOHN WORDSWORTH, *The National Church of Sweden* (London, 1911).

XIV

THE CHURCH OF THE BRETHREN

XIV

THE CHURCH OF THE BRETHREN

Desmond W. Bittinger

The church of the Brethren is a fellowship of followers of Jesus Christ numbering a little less than 200,000. They have churches scattered across the United States from the Atlantic to the Pacific; their mission work is established in India, China, and Africa, and is being started in South America. In addition, by 1951 they had Brethren Service workers engaged in spiritual, moral and physical rehabilitation among children and adults in Germany, Italy, France, Asia Minor, Greece, Holland, Austria, India, China, South America, Africa, Puerto Rico, and the United States. Their belief concerning war and their effort to remove its causes have made them known as one of the historic peace churches, along with the Friends and the Mennonites.

I. How The Brethren Began

The organization which was to become the Church of the Brethren came into being in 1708 at Schwarzenau, Germany, in the valley of the Eder river with an initial membership of eight—three married couples and two unmarried members. Their resolve to start a new church was a part of the pietistic movement against a highly organized state church which, they believed, did not set a high enough value upon the individual and which often suppressed the rights of the individual conscience. These eight persons examined carefully the other churches growing out of the pietistic movement and found all of them falling short of bringing the individual, unhampered by restrictive creeds, into personal contact with the whole teaching of the New Testament and with Jesus Christ. They felt, therefore, that a new church should be organized. Accordingly, one of the eight baptized by trine immersion Alexander Mack (1679-1735), their recognized leader, and he in turn administered baptism to the other seven. In this manner and for this reason the Church of the Brethren was born.[1]

II. How The Brethren Grew

The early Brethren accepted the probability of persecution before they were baptized. Almost immediately thereafter the persecution began. William Penn, who also suffered persecution, saw their plight and offered refuge in Pennsylvania to the harassed group. Between 1719 and 1729 most of them emigrated to Germantown. Some moved farther inland and settled on good land in the Eastern areas of Pennsylvania. The mother church at Germantown has continued as an organization until the present time. The original church building remains; additions have not destroyed the lines of the old stone structure.

From Pennsylvania the Church of the Brethren expanded southward and westward. Most of the membership were farmers and as they pioneered in the valleys and on the plains they were able to choose and settle upon some of the best agricultural land in America. Congregations were organized and subdivided until by 1940 they numbered slightly more than one thousand.

A more recent migration has been from the rural to the urban areas. Though more than half of the Brethren church buildings are still in rural areas the city churches often have larger memberships; as a consequence even though the Church of the Brethren is still spoken of as a rural denomination about half of its membership now resides in the cities of America. There are churches in Brooklyn, Philadelphia, Washington, Johnstown, Dayton, Detroit, Chicago, Kansas City, Los Angeles, San Francisco, Seattle, Portland, and many other cities.

The Brethren did not confine their growth to America alone. In 1894 they opened mission work in India. There the work has grown to large proportions; many churches and schools have been built; hospitals have been opened. About 1946 the Indian church assumed the responsibility for the work in India with the churches of America continuing to cooperate in furnishing some leadership and some financial aid. The Church of the Brethren in China began in 1908 and likewise grew to significant proportions. The recent war retarded it but it is again pressing for expansion, perhaps in new directions. The church laid its beginnings in Africa in 1922. Here also it has grown in members and in influence. Part of its work was to bring into being a leper colony of more than 1,000 lepers. In South America mission work followed a Brethren Service project of rehabilitation. The first missionaries, as such, were sent out in 1946.

About 1941 the church began a rapid expansion of Brethren Service projects. By 1951 there remained hardly a major country in the world where Brethren personnel or Brethren relief goods had not gone. The outlook and the contribution of the church have become world-wide.[2]

III. How The Brethren Are Organized

The Church of the Brethren has undertaken to establish and maintain a democratic church organization. It is congregational in form; however a majority decision by the denominational representatives, as they meet in their regular international Annual Meeting, takes precedence over individual or congregational opinion. Thus the final authority of the church is not vested in bishops or elders but in representatives, lay or ministerial, who are elected from each individual congregation and district.

The organizational setup, briefly is as follows:

a) Each congregation, in the beginning, selected its ministers from its lay membership and appointed one of them a presiding elder. They were dependable people who have demonstrated ability in their community living and sincerity in their Christian conviction. They served the church without pay. More recently because of increasing industrialization in our American life these unpaid ministers have been replaced in many areas by a paid, professional ministry which gives full time to the work of the church.

b) Congregations which are located near to each other organized themselves together into districts to facilitate the general community work of the church. There are at present forty-nine such districts in the United States. They hold regular business and inspirational meetings at least once a year.

c) The church organization has not become static. Within the past decade the districts have associated themselves into regional organizations. There are five such regional associations in the United States. They have meetings of inspiration and discussion once a year called Regional Conferences. These will probably assume more authority as they become older in the life of the church.

d) The Annual Meeting for the entire church is held also once each year and to it are sent two groups of delegates: 1) Representatives from the districts. These become a Standing Committee. This body usually numbers about eighty; they can be brought into session during the year at the call of the Moderator. Their function is advisory rather than authoritarian. 2) Representatives from each local congregation. These are called "the delegate body"; the Standing Committee merges with this body when it is in session. All business must come before this assembly. Though the Standing Committee may make suggestions to it concerning certain items of business, it need not follow the suggestions. It speaks the final authority of the church. It will be observed that the church is lay-ruled, therefore, rather than directed by Elders and Bishops.

A General Brotherhood Board composed of twenty-five members is selected by the assembly to meet from time to time during the year to put into operation the program of the church as set forth by the Annual Meeting actions. This Board operates through five commissions: Foreign Missions, Home Missions and Ministry, Christian Education, Brethren Service, Finance. The employees of the General Brotherhood Board become the permanent staff for the church; they are nearly all located at Elgin, Illinois. The church conducts its educational work through six colleges in the United States and one theological seminary. It is developing some similar educational institutions abroad, each adapted to the country in which it is established.[3]

IV. The Body of Brethren Belief

When Alexander Mack and his followers founded the Church of the Brethren they set forth three basic principles:

a) They would have no creed other than the whole New Testament.

b) They would observe the ordinances as taught in the New Testament.

c) They would exert no force in religion; their watchwords would be brotherhood and peace.

No written amplification of these principles has ever been accepted by the church for fear that such a document might become a church creed. This fuller statement of the principles is, therefore, only an approximation of what the church in general means by a), b) and c) above.

a) The Church of the Brethren believes in the deity and the sufficiency of Jesus Christ; that he was sent by God from heaven to live, die and rise again for the redemption of mankind; that he ascended to heaven and will return; the Brethren accept the New Testament as the revelation of Christ; they accept the spirit, the words and the deeds of Christ as the revelation of God. They desire no written creed or statement of belief other than the whole New Testament; they believe that such a creed would be a confinement to the individual and a restriction of Truth. The New Testament is their creed.

b) The Church of the Brethren believes in the observance

of the ordinances as taught by Christ in the New Testament. The Brethren believe that Christ instituted the ordinances as teaching and worship techniques to enable man to grow in grace; they believe that by them man can increase his understanding of the purposes of God and can comprehend more fully the principles which undergird the kingdom of God. Among the ordinances are: believer's baptism by trine immersion, the complete Lord's Supper, anointing of the sick, consecration of Christian workers by the laying on of hands.

c) The Church of the Brethren commits itself to the way of brotherhood; this the Brethren believe implies mutual helpfulness and sharing in the realm of the spiritual, the intellectual and the material. The Brethren do not believe in violence; they renounce war and its associated evils and dedicate themselves to furthering the enterprises which will prevent war. They do not endeavor to force upon men any form of spiritual belief or intellectual understanding; rather they believe that each member should always have freedom to grow toward a fuller understanding of God and of his eternal truth.

From its inception the Church of the Brethren has given certain instructions to its applicants for baptism. These instructions might be taken as a general statement of its belief. They have varied in emphasis at different times and in different localities. Among them are the following:

The applicant is asked to state his faith in Christ, the Son of God, as his personal Savior, to renounce Satan and sin, and to pledge himself to faithfulness until death.

The applicant is asked to express his faith in the way of peace and non-violence. This means that he shall seek to have peace with God and to live in peace with his fellowmen. It means that it will be his intention not to participate in war and strife and not to follow the way of litigation in the courts.

The applicant is asked to commit himself to the simple, spiritual life. This means that he will refrain from excesses and luxuries which are for the satisfaction of the flesh rather than for the nurture of the spirit. It means that his manner of life shall be spiritual, friendly, temperate and simple.

He is asked to take the way of temperance. This means that he regards the body as the temple of the Holy Spirit and that as such he desires to keep it pure and healthful, to refrain from use of alcoholic beverages, tobacco, profanities and intemperances in any form which are injurious to his body and his social life.

He is asked to express his belief in brotherhood and in Christian service to his fellowmen. From the beginning Brethren have opposed slavery and the division of society into castes and classes. Equality in all human relations is the Brethren ideal.

He is asked to declare his intention to live the good life. This means that instead of expressing his religion in creedal statements he should seek to express it in Christian living. The good life should manifest itself in the home, in the community, in the church, and in every human relationship. The Brethren would like to live their lives in harmony with Christ and for the uplift of their fellowmen everywhere.[4]

V. Divisions and Developments

Within a sect which sets itself to be conspicuously different from the main body of Evangelical Christianity, inevitably there will develop numerous divergences of opinion. The democratic and informal pattern of the Brethren ecclesiastical organization not only permitted this but made it unavoidable.

Three such divisions will be mentioned briefly:

a. The State of Pennsylvania is now restoring the Ephrata Cloisters at Ephrata, Pennsylvania as one of the state's interesting religious monuments. Here occurred a carefully worked out monastical undertaking which operated in a communal, self-sustaining manner for nearly a century of time.

Its founder and guiding light was Conrad Beissel, a Brethren minister of the Conestoga area. His preaching gradually began to take on a peculiar emphasis: the seventh day was proper for worship instead of Sunday; the ten commandments were more binding than the Sermon on the Mount; the monastic communal order was to be preferred above all others; celibacy was especially blessed of God.

This strange ascetic monastic order began in 1728. It drew into its nunnery and monastery many Brethren. Also joining it were numerous mystically inclined Christians who were not Brethren. By 1770 the cloisters at Ephrata housed 135 members. Several monasteries founded on this manner of life sprung up at other places.

Members of the monasteries developed a manner of singing which was unique. It is being investigated by musicians and historians at the present time. They developed methods of dyeing, weaving, printing, and of agriculture which contributed to America's growing economy.

Numerous other denominations or sects received impetus from this movement such as the Seventh-day Adventists, the Rosacrucians and others. Soon after 1800 this undertaking began to decline. Only the cloisters or buildings remain now to attest to this interesting development.[5]

b. In 1881 and 1882 there occurred a major division in the main body of the Church of the Brethren. It gave rise to a sister Brethren organization which continues down to the present time. It is called the Old Order Brethren.

The division came about through differences of opinion concerning both matters of church organization or polity and matters of the personal appearance and practice of church members. Questions concerning revival meetings, Sunday Schools, prayer meeting, academies, and colleges, methods of observing feet washing, and "worldly dress" were dealt with by committees and discussed by the Annual Meetings for several years before the final division came.

In 1881 failure to agree on the above matters caused the Old Order Brethren to set up a separate church organization. About 3,000 people joined this group. They have held Annual Meetings since 1881 and continue as an active church. Their principal membership is in Pennsylvania, Ohio, Kansas, and California.[6]

c. The Progressive Brethren. During the same years that the differences of opinion concerning Sunday Schools, matters of dress, church government and other items led one group away from the Church of the Brethren because it was "too progressive" another group was being prepared for withdrawal because the main body of the church was not progressive enough.

This movement centered largely around one man, H. R. Holsinger. Actually this division centered around personalities more than it did around principles. Holsinger wanted a less authoritarian church policy, particularly a freer discussion in the church paper of varying opinions. Unable to get this he set up another paper which ran counter to the official church paper. Eventually he was disfellowshipped from the church largely because of the difficulties of dealing with him. He then began the Progressive Brethren Church. It numbered at its inception about 6,500 members. It has grown to about 20,000 members. Its headquarters are at Ashland, Ohio, where its college is likewise established. The things for which Holsinger contended have long since been accepted by the main body of the Church of the Brethren and no essential difference any longer remains between them. They are co-operating in Foreign Mission enterprises and their eventual merging is probably just a matter of time.[7]

Publications

The Church of the Brethren in its earlier years became famous throughout the colonies for its German Press located at Germantown, Pennsylvania. It was operated first by Christopher Sower, Sr. and later by his son, Christopher, Jr. These men were contemporaries of Benjamin Franklin in nearby Philadelphia. Their work in German paralleled his publications in English. The Sower Bibles are now rare collectors' items. The Sower Almanacs and other publications are almost no longer to be found.

The Sower Printing press was destroyed by the British during the Revolutionary War. Thereafter the Brethren were dispersed. The persecution, which led to their dispersal, was a result of their adherence to the principles of pacifism in the heat of war time emotions all about them. They fled to Virginia, Kentucky, Ohio, Indiana, Illinois and other states.

During the "wilderness period" following their dispersal they did not have a church paper or any longer sustained educational institutions.

One hundred years ago, or in 1851, Henry Kurtz began the publication of the *Gospel Visitor* in Poland, Ohio. Other papers sprang up throughout the years which followed. In 1883 most of these were consolidated into one church paper *The Gospel Messenger*. This has been the official organ of the church ever since. Its early editors were James Quinter, D. L. Miller, and J. H. Moore. Subsequent editors have been Edward Frantz, D. W. Bittinger, and Kenneth Morse.

The Brethren Publishing Company located at Elgin, Illinois, publishes *The Gospel Messenger* and the other publications of the church. These are for youth, children, and adults: *Journeys, Tell Me, Horizons, Brethren Monthly,* Sunday School literature, books, pamphlets, and so on.[8]

Leadership

The Church of the Brethren has produced some outstanding churchmen down through the centuries. Among those migrating with the church from Europe to America were:

Alexander Mack, Sr., founder and philanthropist

Peter Becker, pioneer, preacher and missionary

John Naas, apostle of peace

Alexander Mack, Jr., man of letters

Christopher Sower Sr. and Jr., publishers and authors.

Later leaders were:

George Wolf, itinerant missionary-preacher in the Middle West

John Kline, Christian martyr

D. L. Miller, world traveler

S. Z. Sharp, college founder

D. W. Kurtz, world lecturer

H. K. Ober, pedagogue

A. C. Wieand, E. B. Hoff, Co-seminary founders

M. R. Zigler, world churchman and peacemaker

W. B. Stover, F. H. Crumpacker, H. S. Kulp, Benton Rhodes, pioneer missionaries

Dan West, peace worker.[9]

VI. How The Brethren Serve

Service to their fellowmen has been a characteristic of good Brethrenism since the days of Alexander Mack, its founder. Alexander Mack sacrificed all of his considerable property in an effort to help his fellow-Brethren who were persecuted. After the church had migrated from Europe to Pennsylvania, a siege of yellow fever in Philadelphia tested the service interest of the early Brethren. At great danger to themselves they ministered to the citizens of Philadelphia until the epidemic was overcome. During the Revolutionary War and later during the Civil War the Brethren were persecuted because they would not take part in military enterprises. At these times they shared with each other in a brotherly way, and endeavored to render unselfish service to those who suffered on either side of the conflict.

When the Brethren began to send missionaries overseas the missionaries at once saw opportunities for very significant service. When famines raged in India and China the Brethren sent their money to be administered in relief aid to the starving peoples by the missionaries. When plagues and epidemics swept across these lands the missionaries were always in the foreground offering their services and their aid, many times at grave personal danger.

After the first World War the Brethren were outstanding givers of aid to those in Europe who were dislocated and who were starving. Aid to Armenia particularly challenged the Brethren at that time.

The ground work was well laid, therefore, for the Brethren to expand into a program of service and world-wide aid during and following the last war, which has caused their name to become known widely in Europe and Asia. In 1940 a Brethren Service Committee was organized with authorization to spearhead the service activities of the Church of the Brethren. It was also their purpose to offer services of a constructive nature as an alternative to war since non-violence is a Brethren policy.

At once this committee began to gather money, materials and personnel. One of the Brethren Service projects which attracted attention far beyond the bounds of the church was the "heifers for relief" project. Several thousand heifers were donated by churches and church groups from one end of the country to the other and these were sent to needy countries in Europe and Asia. Brethren young people and older people volunteered to work as "seagoing cowboys" to take these heifers and other livestock overseas and deliver them at the points of need. Other young people volunteered to go to Europe and Asia to help in the distribution of the relief goods which were sent. Still other young people of the church volunteered to work among the prisoners, displaced persons, orphaned children or in any enterprise where they could be of service to their fellowmen. The church designated always that this aid and these personnel services should be given to all men irrespective of their being labeled as "friendly" or as "enemy" peoples.

When the war ended, this program of service became also an educational program. Young people continued to work in the devastated countries trying to teach the people better methods of living and better philosophies of life. Thus, young men went to China, Ethiopia, Greece, and elsewhere with tractors and farm tools to teach the people how to get vast areas into production speedily.

In each place where the Brethren have gone with their program of service and missions, they have endeavored to demonstrate their belief that the Christian religion is something to be lived, not merely talked about.

VII. What Is The Brethren Purpose?

It is difficult to sum up the various enterprises of the Brethren in a single statement. The following, however, is an attempt.

The Brethren believe that Jesus came into the world to reveal the Father and to demonstrate a manner of Christlike living; that he came to save mankind and to give men an abundant life beginning here and lasting forever. They want to live as completely as possible the life which he demonstrated and taught. It is the Brethren purpose to make Christ, his way of life, and his salvation known as widely as they can throughout the world. Consequently, through evangelism, through service, through sharing, through living and through patient, kindly teaching, the Brethren purpose to work at that until he comes again.

NOTES

1 Section I Sources: M. G. BRUMBAUGH, *History of the German Baptist Brethren in Europe and America*, Chaps. 1-3. OTHO WINGER, *History and Doctrine of the Church of the Brethren*, Chap. 1.

2 Section II Sources: M. G. BRUMBAUGH, *op. cit.*, Chaps. 2-10. OTHO WINGER, *op. cit.*, Chaps. 2-3. D. L. MILLER, *Two Centuries of the Church of the Brethren*, Chaps. 1-3.

3 Section III Sources: *Annual Meeting Minutes*, 1880-1951.

4 Section IV Sources: OTHO WINGER, *op. cit.*, Chap. 13. EDWARD FRANTZ, *Basic Belief*. D. W. KURTZ, *Doctrines and Devotions*, Parts 1, 2, 3.

5 Section V Sources: *a.* M. G. BRUMBAUGH, *op. cit.*, Chap. 11. OTHO WINGER, *op. cit.*, Chap. 5. J. S. FLORY, *Flashlights from History*, Chap. 2.

6 Section V Sources: *b.* OTHO WINGER, *op. cit.*, Chap. 5. J. S. FLORY, *op. cit.*, Chap. 11. *Annual Meeting Minutes*, 1869, 1880, 1881, 1882. *Annual*

Meeting Reports, 1880, 1881, 1882. H. R. HOLSINGER, *The Tunkers and the Brethren Church,* pp. 415-469.

7 Section V Sources: *c.* OTHO WINGER, *op. cit.,* Chap. 5. J. S. FLORY, *op. cit.,* Chap. 12. *Annual Meeting Minutes,* 1881,1882. *Annual Meeting Reports,* 1881, 1882. H. R. HOLSINGER, *op. cit.,* Chap. 14.

8 Publications: D. L. MILLER, *Two Centuries of the Church of the Brethren,* Chap. 17. OTHO WINGER, *op. cit.,* Chap. 7.

9 Leadership: J. H. MOORE, *Some Brethren Pathfinders.*

BIBLIOGRAPHY

Annual Meeting Minutes, 1869, 1880, 1881, 1882 - up to 1951.

Annual Meeting Reports, 1880, 1881, 1882.

M. G. BRUMBAUGH, *History of the German Baptist in Europe and America* (Elgin, Ill., 1907).

JOHN S. FLORY, *Literary Activity of the German Baptist Brethren in the Eighteenth Century* (Elgin, Ill., 1908).

EDWARD FRANTZ, *Basic Belief* (Elgin, Ill., 1944).

JOHN LEWIS GILLIN, *The Dunkers* (New York, 1906).

H. R. HOLSINGER, *The Tunkers and the Brethren Church* (Published by author, 1901).

D. W. KURTZ, *Studies in Doctrine and Devotion* (Elgin, Ill., 1946).

D. L. MILLER, *Two Centuries of the Church of the Brethren* (Elgin, Ill., 1908).

GALEN B. ROYER, *Thirty-three Years of Missions* (Elgin, Ill., 1913).

OTHO WINGER, *History and Doctrine of the Church of the Brethren* (Elgin, Ill., 1914).

XV

THE EVANGELICAL AND REFORMED CHURCH

XV

THE EVANGELICAL AND REFORMED CHURCH

DAVID DUNN

THIS DENOMINATION was officially constituted on June 26, 1934 at Cleveland, Ohio through the merger of the Evangelical Synod of North America and the Reformed Church in the United States. These two American church bodies had their roots in the Germany and Switzerland of the Reformation. While the Reformed lineage may be traced back through Heidelberg in the Palatinate of western Germany to the work of Zwingli in Zurich and Calvin in Geneva, the Evangelicals stem from the more predominantly Lutheran regions of northern, central and eastern Germany. The Evangelical Union of 1817 in Prussia set for other German states the pattern of a merger of Lutheran and Reformed churches on the basis of a recognition that the two churches had a common evangelical heritage, and with the provision that neither Reformed or Lutheran should be required to abandon any doctrine or practises that they deemed essential.

Thus it may be held that the Evangelical and Reformed Church derives 1) from a Lutheranism, moderated at first by Melanchthon and later through the influence of Pietism, 2) from a Calvinism that had lost some of its Genevan austerity in the mellower atmosphere of the Palatinate and 3) to a Zwinglianism, considerably modified by Bullinger and other successors of the pioneer reformer of Zurich. The Heidelberg Catechism and the Palatinate Liturgy of 1563 for the Reformed, and the Revised Augsburg Confession of 1540, together with Luther's Catechisms and liturgical provisions for the Lutheran, guided and implemented the thought and the worship of the sons and daughters of these Reformation churches as they crossed the Atlantic Ocean, at different times but with largely similar purposes, to their new homeland.

These two "transplantings" took place just about a century apart.

1. *The Reformed in the 18th Century*

The first refugees from war-ravaged and impoverished western Germany, generally called Palatines because so many of them came from the Palatinate, settled in the Hudson and Mohawk Valleys in the colony of New York as early as 1709. The first unit of German Reformed worshippers, of whom there is any record, held services at Germanna Ford, Virginia in 1714.[1] Both groups were served by pastors named Haeger, thought by some to have been father and son, who had been commissioned by the Church of England's Society for the Propagation of the Gospel. Most of the New York group soon moved to the more hospitable domain of "Penn's Woods", while Palatines in far larger numbers, came into that colony by the port of Philadelphia, and settled in the valleys of the Delaware, the Schuylkill and the Susquehanna Rivers. The Reformed people among them—others were Lutherans, Mennonites and various kinds of Brethren—, as they were without ordained pastors, were ministered to at first by laymen, among them John Philip Boehm, a parochial school teacher from Worms, and Conrad Tempelmann, a tailor from Weinheim near Heidelberg. It was Boehm who organized three little congregations in what is now Montgomery County in southeastern Pennsylvania: Skippack, White Marsh and Falkner Swamp. For these and for several other congregations he prepared a constitution, based on Calvinistic church orders in use in Europe.

At Falkner Swamp, the church with the longest continuous history, the first recorded communion was celebrated on October 15, 1725, a date which is generally regarded as marking the beginning of the German Reformed Church in America on the congregational level. Boehm was ordained in 1729 by three pastors of the Dutch Reformed Church in New York. In the meantime George Michael Weiss, a young German pastor, who had accompanied most of his flock to America in 1727, had become pastor of the church in Philadelphia. He and Boehm aroused the interest of the synods of the Reformed Church of Holland in their spiritually destitute German brethren in the new land. The Dutch "fathers" in 1746 sent out Michael Schlatter, a young Swiss minister from St. Gall, to organize and supervise the scattered groups of German Reformed people in Pennsylvania and adjacent colonies. Schlatter travelled widely through eastern Pennsylvania, Maryland and northwestern Virginia, preaching and teaching, organizing and encouraging congregations. On September 29, 1747 there was organized under his leadership in Philadelphia a missionary synod, known as the coetus, consisting of 4 ministers and 27 elders representing 12 congregations. Until after the American Revolution the Holland Church continued to support the German Reformed congregations and to receive reports from them through the officers of the coetus.

Sixteen years after the Declaration of Independence (1792) the coetus became the Synod of the German Reformed Church, independent of Holland, no longer reporting to or supported by that country and able to ordain its own ministers and plan for its own educational institutions. In 1819 the Synod divided itself into eight classes. By that time missionaries had been sent to the Carolinas and across the Alleghenies to western Pennsylvania and Ohio. In 1824 the Ohio classis constituted itself a synod, independent of yet continuing fraternal relations with the mother Synod in the east.

The need for a training school for ministers was ever more pressing and a theological seminary was founded at Carlisle, Pa. in 1825, in connection with Dickinson College, then Presbyterian. Dr. Lewis Mayer was the sole professor. The seminary was moved to York, Pa. in 1829 where a classical school, soon to be known as Marshall College, was associated with it. In 1837 it was removed to Mercersburg, Pa., where it remained until its final relocation, in Lancaster, Pa. in 1871. Marshall College had preceded it to Lancaster in 1853, where it was united with Franklin College, founded in that city by the Reformed and Lutherans in 1787, to become Franklin and Marshall. The Ohio Synod started a seminary at Canton, Ohio in 1838, and again at Tiffin, Ohio in connection with Heidelberg College, founded in 1850. In 1908 this seminary was joined with the Ursinus School of Theology to form Central Seminary at Dayton, Ohio. In 1862 the Mission House was founded near Sheboygan, Wisconsin, primarily to train ministers to serve the more recent influx of Swiss and German Reformed settlers in the Northwest. Dr. H. A. Muehlmeier was the pioneer evangelist and educator in this region.

The wave of revivals that affected most of the American denominations in the early 18th century had its repercussions in the German Reformed Church. Philip William Otterbein and John Winebrenner sponsored pietistic practises then called "New Measures" and, when opposed by the majority of their fellow-churchmen, led in the founding of new denominations, respectively the United Brethren in Christ and the Church of God.

Nearer the mid-century mark the progress of the Reformed Church was enlivened, if somewhat halted for a time, by the controversy over what was known as "the Mercersburg Movement". The teachings and writings of three professors in the Seminary, then at Mercersburg, Pa., Frederick A. Rauch, John W. Nevin and Philip Schaff, opposed the subjectivism, sectarianism and revivalism of much of contemporary American Christianity. They pleaded for a "Christocentric theology", for a conception of the Church as an organism developing through history and for an altar-centered liturgy. This precipitated acrimonious arguments with the low-church or "Old Reformed" party, led by Joseph F. Berg and J.H.A. Bomberger. The controversy passed from a doctrinal through a mainly liturgical phase and, though officially concluded by the Peace Commission in 1879, left wounds and rifts that continued well into the twentieth century.

The American (Home) Missionary Society of the German Reformed Church had been organized in 1826 and published *The Missionary Magazine.* The Board of Foreign Missions dates from 1838 and during the years, 1840-1865, supported the Rev. Benjamin Schneider, a missionary of the American Board of Foreign Missions in Asiatic Turkey. Not until the fires of the controversy just described had flickered low, *i.e.,* in 1879, did the Foreign Board reorganize and send its first missionary, Ambrose D. Gring to Japan. William E. Hoy began the work in China in 1900.

In 1863, celebrating the Tercentennary of the Heidelberg Catechism, the mother synod of the east and the Ohio Synod re-united to form the General Synod. In 1869 the word "German" was dropped from the denomination's name which then became "The Reformed Church in the United States."

2. *The Evangelicals in the 19th Century*

The pioneers of the Evangelical Synod of North America came to their adopted homeland from wider and more diverse sections of Germany than did their Reformed predecessors of a century before. Political and religious persecution figured somewhat less and the quest for economic betterment somewhat more among their motives for emigration. Exaggerated reports of the riches and opportunities of America had reached and drawn them. Many landed at eastern ports and made their way inland by stagecoach and canal boat. Others in increasing numbers came up the Mississippi from New Orleans to the new frontiers in Missouri and Southern Illinois. Religiously, they represented not so much the Lutheran or Reformed churches as that "Evangelical Union" of the two which had been effected in Germany in and after 1817.

The lot of these settlers in their new and strange homeland appealed to the missionary societies of Basel and Barmen, in whom the zeal of the Pietistic revival still burned, and missionaries were sent out to meet the spiritual needs of the new settlers. Before these began to arrive, however, Herman Garlichs, an independent minister-farmer, had begun to serve as pastor of a community of Germans at Femme Osage, Missouri. In 1840 Louis Edouard Nollau, a Barmen missionary who had become pastor at Gravois Settlement, Mo., invited a number of other pastors to meet in his parsonage for mutual encouragement and discussion of common problems. Garlichs and four others came and two more expressed their interest by letter. There on October 15, 1840—one hundred and fifteen years to the day after the first Reformed communion at Falkner Swamp—the six ministers organized the German Evangelical Church Society (*Kirchenverein*) of the West and drew up 24 resolutions, reduced the following year to 16, for the guidance of their procedure as a ministerial union which congregations were eligible and invited to join. The first congregation to affiliate was St. Paul's of St. Louis in 1849. Opposed on the one hand by the stricter non-unionist (Saxon) Lutherans, the ancestors of such groups as the Missouri Synod, and on the other by the rationalists and free-thinkers among the German settlers, this litle group of comrades of the Gospel served the needs of increasing thousands of their fellow-immigrants in the spirit of unity and peace.

The people to whom these Evangelical pioneers ministered had come through experiences in the Fatherland which had made them suspicious of too much centralization of church power, and it was some time after the founding of the *Kirchenverein* before its leaders could even use the word "synod" or function as a more authoritative organization. Through the able and enlightened leadership of Adolf Baltzer this fear was gradually overcome. Two similar Evangelical groups, one in Ohio and one in the eastern states, joined the *Kirchenverein* in 1857 and 1860 respectively. Thus the way was paved for the organization of the German Evangelical Synod of the West in 1866 with Baltzer as its first president. It was divided into three districts, Eastern, Central and Northern.

After the union of this body with the Evangelical Synod of the Northwest in 1872 the name was changed (1879) to the Evangelical Synod of North America.

As early as 1850 a theological seminary was founded at Marthasville, Mo. with William Binner, a graduate of the University of Berlin, as its first professor. The school was removed to St. Louis in 1883, becoming Eden Seminary, and in 1925 to suburban Webster Groves, its present location. A school for the training of parochial school teachers, founded in Cincinnati in 1866 became in 1871 a department of the Proseminar at Evansville, Indiana, which was moved the following year to Elmhurst, Illinois to be combined with the Melanchthon Seminary of the former Synod of the Northwest to become Elmhurst College. As in the Reformed Church at an earlier period there was a struggle, though not so acute, over the transition from the German to the English language. Large numbers of young people of both groups joined English-using churches before the inevitable change was accepted.

Home Missions began in ministrations to the continuing streams of German immigrants, one of the first special projects being the Seamen's Mission at Baltimore, Md. The district conferences elected committees on Home Missions in their areas and missionaries were sent to Texas, Colorado and the Pacific Coast. A central Board for Home Missions was not organized until 1898. Until 1883 Foreign Mission activity was limited to contributions to the Basel and Barmen Missionary Societies. In that year a mission field in India was taken over from the German Evangelical Missionary Society and in 1920 the work in Honduras was begun.

The Merged Church

Coming from much the same regions of Europe, speaking originally the same mother tongue and heirs of the same tradition and culture, the Evangelical Synod of North America and the Reformed Church in the United States were well prepared for their eventual union. Their common and growing interest in federated and co-operative Protestantism was bound to bring them into contact. Though their main strength lay in different parts of the country there were some sections, like Ohio and Indiana, where their ministers and members lived and worked at close range. Both churches were charter members of the Federal Council of Churches, organized in 1908.

The first definite approaches to union were made in 1922 and Commissions on Closer Union were appointed by the supreme judicatories of both churches. A decade later a Plan of Union, prepared by these commissions, received almost unanimous approval by the Reformed Classes and the Evangelical District Conferences. On the night of June 26, 1934 in Cleveland, Ohio, the union was consummated, symbolized by the handclasp of Presidents Paul Press (Evangelical) and Henry J. Christman (Reformed) and by the observance of the Holy Communion. It was implemented the following morning by the election of temporary officers, authorized to govern the united Church under the Plan of Union, pending the preparation and adoption of a constitution which went into effect at the Synod of Lancaster in 1940. The charter was granted under the laws of the State of New York. Dr. George W. Richards (Reformed) and Dr. Louis W. Goebel (Evangelical), the chairmen of the two Commissions on Union, were the first President and Vice-President of the united Church.

At the time of the merger the Reformed Church comprised 6 synods, 58 classes, 1336 ministers, 1697 congregations and 345,912 members. The Evangelical Synod reported 21 districts, 1300 ordained ministers, 1243 congregations and 273,138 members. (The excess of ministers over congregations in the Evangelical figures was due to the fact that a number of affiliated ministers served unaffiliated congregations.) The following statistics are reported for the Evangelical and Reformed Church as of December 31, 1950: Synods: 34; Pastors: 1780; Ministers without charge: 714; Congregations: 2746; Members: 735,941; Sunday School Enrollment: 468,149; Total

Congregational Expenses: $21,085,451; Total Benevolences: $3,963,241.

The Evangelical Synod seemed to have specialized in benevolent institutions and the Reformed Church in educational ones. While Elmhurst College and Eden Seminary were the only schools of higher education in the "E" Church, the "R" Church brought into the merger a more or less direct interest in and control of three theological seminaries (Lancaster, Central—later merged with Eden—and Mission House), seven colleges (Franklin and Marshall at Lancaster, Pa., Heidelberg at Tiffin, O., Catawba at Salisbury, N. C., Ursinus at Collegeville, Pa., Mission House near Sheboygan, Wis., Cedar Crest at Allentown, Pa. and Hood at Frederick, Md.) and three academies (Mercersburg at the Pennsylvania town of that name, Franklin and Marshall—since discontinued—and Massanutten at Woodstock, Va.). On the other hand, ratios of benevolent institutions as between the "E" and "R" Churches, were as follows: Homes for the Aged: 9 to 5; Hospitals 9 to 1; Homes for Feeble-minded and Epileptic: 2 to 0; City Missions: 2 to 0; Orphanages: 5 to 5.

The Foreign Mission fields of the Evangelical and Reformed Church are in Africa (Gold Coast), Honduras, India (Central Provinces), Iraq (United Mission in Mesopotamia), Japan (Church of Christ in Japan) and South America (United Andean Mission in Ecuador). The China Mission, now closed out as far as American missionary participation is concerned, is being carried on as a part of the Church of Christ in China. Sixteen educational institutions have been established in China, Honduras, India, and Japan. The achievements of David B. Schneder in Japan and of Jacob Gass in India have been accorded special recognition in many surveys of the World Mission enterprise.

Home Mission projects include the Back Bay Mission at Biloxi, Miss., the Caroline Mission, St. Louis, Mo., the Ellis Community Center, Chicago, Ill., the Ozark Mission, Shannon County, Mo., the Winnebago Indian Mission, Black River Falls and Neillsville, Wis. and the First Church (Issei and Nisei Japanese), San Francisco, Cal. During the First World War, when the Hungarian (Magyar) churches in America were cut off from the mother church in Europe, about 80 congregations came into organic connection with the Reformed Church in the United States. There is now a Magyar Synod comprising 47 of these congregations; the remainder belong to the other synods in which they are located.

Neither denomination had to change the name of its church paper when the union was effected. Editors Paul S. Leinbach ("R") and Julius H. Horstmann ("E") served jointly in the first days of the *Messenger* of the united church. Then Dr. David D. Baker served as editor until his death in 1950 and was succeeded by Theodore C. Braun. The paper is published bi-weekly in St. Louis. *Der Friedensbote* and *Reformat Usok Lapja* are published in St. Louis, Mo. and Lancaster, Pa., respectively, for the German and Hungarian constituencies.

The Evangelical and Reformed Church is represented by congregations in 38 of the 48 states, as well as in the District of Columbia and Canada. A large proportion of the members live in five states stretching contiguously from east to midwest, *viz.,* Pennsylvania, Ohio, Indiana, Illinois and Missouri. Considerable numbers of congregations are also to be found in Maryland, North Carolina, Western New York and Wisconsin. Denominational headquarters are distributed among Philadelphia and St. Louis, the "capitals" of the former "R" and "E" churches, Chicago, where the president of the Church has his offices and Cleveland, home of the two auxiliary organizations, the Women's Guild and the Churchmen's Brotherhood, where, because of its central location, more and more of the meetings of the Boards and other agencies are being held.

Doctrine

The Constitution of the Evangelical and Reformed Church declares its doctrinal basis in the following words:

The Holy Scriptures of the Old and New Testaments are recognized as the Word of God and the ultimate rule of Christian faith and conduct.[2]

Here is the *"evangelical"* foundation, using the word in that broader and deeper sense in which all the Reformation churches share it. As over against the traditions of the "church fathers" and the decrees of later church authorities, it harks back to the evangel, the heart of which is in "the Word made flesh." The Constitution continues:

The doctrinal standards of the Evangelical and Reformed Church are the Heidelberg Catechism, Luther's Catechism and the Augsburg Confession. They are accepted as an authoritative expression of the essential truth taught in the Holy Scriptures.[2]

Thus the descendants of both the 18th and 19th century pioneers from Germany and Switzerland acknowledge their spiritual genealogy, their relation both to Luther and Melanchthon of Wittenberg and to Ursinus and Olevianus of Heidelberg, while in the following words they provide for any differences of interpretation between these confessional symbols:

Wherever these doctrinal standards differ, ministers, members and congregations, in accordance with the liberty of conscience inherent in the gospel, are allowed to adhere to the interpretation of one of these confessions. However in each case the final norm is the Word of God.[2]

Before the merger it was written of the two participating communions that "while they are confessional churches they are not heavily burdened with confessions of faith." It might be added that they have used their confessions not to compel their members to think in sixteenth century molds, but rather to maintain the historic continuity with the great liberating principles and ideals of the Reformation's return to essential Christianity. It may be due in part to this that there have been no heresy trials or doctrinal schisms in either church's history.

One might characterize the general theological complexion of the Evangelical and Reformed Church as "liberal conservative", using the two words in the sense of Philip Schaff's motto: "In essentials unity, in things doubtful liberty, in all things love." The historic-critical interpretation of the Scriptures was accepted and used by most of the leading teachers of both communions by the beginning of this century. Dr. Frederick A. Gast, professor of Hebrew and Old Testament at Lancaster was one of the pioneer American scholars in this field. The late Dr. Theodore F. Herman and Dr. Samuel D. Press, teachers of systematic theology for many years, the one at Lancaster, the other at Eden Seminary, succeeded in keeping a rather wholesome balance among the doctrinal trends of their time. As in most American churches the neo-orthodox movement of recent years has furnished considerable corrective to the more rampant liberalism of the preceding generation.

Polity

The polity of the Evangelical and Reformed Church may be described as a modified form of the presbyterial. The congregations elect as their official governing boards consistories ("R") or church councils ("E"). These in turn choose as the congregations' delegates to the Synods—of which there are 34—the pastor and one layman from each charge. The Synod has jurisdiction over its ministers and congregations, examines, licenses and ordains candidates for the ministry, elects its own officers and committees to carry on its work. Two meetings are held each year, one in the Spring for legislative business and the other in the Fall for conference together with other representatives of the congregations on the work of the Church. The General Synod is the highest judicatory of the Church and is constituted by delegates elected by the Synods on the two-fold basis of the number of congregations and the number of communicant members. It meets every three years and elects the officers of the Church: the president, the secretary, the treasurer and two vice-presidents (one a clergyman and the other a layman). The first three of these are on full time. The present officers (1951) are Dr. Louis W. Goebel, president; Dr. James E. Wagner, first vice-president; Mr. John W. Mueller, second vice-president; Dr. W. Sherman Kerschner, secretary and Mr. F. A. Keck, treasurer. The General Synod also elects eight pastors and eight laymen who compose, together with the five officers, the General Council, which directs the work of the Church and acts for it between the triennial meetings of the General Synod. The Church as an incorporated body with full-time officers and the powers assigned to its president and to the presidents of the Synods are among the features that depart from the purely Presbyterian type of polity.

Worship

There are wide variations of liturgical practice in the denomination, more among the former "R" than among the former "E" congregations. They run the whole gamut from a service as "high" as the Anglican to one as "low" as the Baptist. The Constitution allows "freedom of worship" though it commends the Book of Worship as containing the order and forms to be "followed as norms". Dr. Paul Stonesifer characterizes the Evangelical and Reformed Church in this respect as "moderately liturgical, seeking in the worship of the High God that dignity and beauty which befit the place where His Honor dwelleth."[3]

Characteristics and Contributions

Professor Carl E. Schneider of Eden Seminary, the outstanding historian of the former Evangelical Synod, has listed the following significant facts about that communion: (1) its vital strength-giving connection with the Continental Reformation, (2) its emphasis on church union, (3) its strong pietistic and missionary spirit and (4) its firm adherence to liberty of conscience as a fundamental ideal. With some little qualification of the third point, these four may be held to apply to the origins and development of the Reformed Church as well. Hence one can all the better understand the affinity of the two groups that brought them together as well as the characteristics of the merged denomination.

Among the living leaders of the Evangelical and Reformed Church who are known far beyond the bounds of the nation and denomination is Dr. George W. Richards, president-emeritus of the Lancaster Seminary, who has played a prominent part in the federation and union movements, as well as in the councils and conferences of the Ecumenical Church throughout the first half of the century. The brothers Niebuhr, Reinhold and Richard, now teaching at Union and Yale respectively, are sons of an Evangelical parsonage and continue as ministers of the E. and R. Church. Dr. Paul Tillich, also teaching in Union Seminary, has transferred his ministerial membership from the Evangelical church in Germany to the corresponding communion in his new home-land.

Both constituent denominations took an early interest in the field of Christian Education. Dr. William N. Dresel for the Evangelicals and Dr. Rufus W. Miller for the Reformed pioneered in the development of Sunday Schools and in supplying them with the ways and means of ever better instruction. Dr. Nevin C. Harner, who died in July, 1951, was widely known as a writer and a leader in this field.

Other emphases common to both "E" and "R" Churches, and continued in the united Church, are those upon the social application of the Christian gospel and upon the cause of unitive and co-operative Protestantism. Commissions on Christianity and Social Problems ("E") and on Social Service ("R"), under the leadership of men like Philip Vollmer and James M. Mullan, labored to sensitize the consciences of their fellow-churchmen on such questions as war, economic justice and racial brotherhood.

THE EVANGELICAL AND REFORMED CHURCH

In more recent years the Evangelical and Reformed Church was engaged in union negotiations with an American denomination of different background and polity, the Congregationalist-Christian Churches. The consummation of this merger was halted, temporarily at least, by an injunction obtained by a group of Congregationalist opponents in a Brooklyn court. During the discussion attending the controversy the "E and R" Church was characterized as "ready to join with anybody". The writer may have pointed, without intending to do so, to an inclination that goes back to the days and to the spirit of Melanchthon, a readiness to subordinate the differentia of doctrine and polity to the primary challenge implicit in the prayer of the Lord of all churchmen, "that they all may be one."

NOTES

[1] J. SILOR GARRISON, *History of the Reformed Church in Virginia* (Winston Salem, N. C., 1948).

[2] *Constitution of the Evangelical and Reformed Church,* 1950 edition.

[3] P. T. STONESIFER, *Know Your Church* (Philadelphia,Pa., 1948).

BIBLIOGRAPHY

D. BRUNING ET AL, *Evangelical Fundamentals* (St. Louis, 1916).

J. H. DUBBS, *History of the Reformed Church in the United States,* American Church History Series, Vol. VIII (New York, 1902).

————, *The Reformed Church in Pennsylvania* (Lancaster, Pa., 1902).

J. W. FLUCKE, *Evangelical Pioneers* (St. Louis, 1931).

J. I. GOOD, *History of the Reformed Church in the United States, 1725-1792* (Reading, Pa., 1899).

————, *History of the Reformed Church in the United States in the Nineteenth Century* (New York, 1911).

W. J. HINKE, ed., *Minutes of the Coetus of Pennsylvania* (Philadelphia, 1903).

J. H. HORSTMANN and H. H. WERNECKE, *Through Four Centuries,* Study Manual (St. Louis, 1938).

H. M. J. KLEIN, *History of the Eastern Synod of the Reformed Church in the United States* (Lancaster, Pa., 1943).

CARL E. SCHNEIDER, *The German Church on the American Frontier* (St. Louis, 1938).

PAUL T. STONESIFER, *Know Your Church* (Philadelphia, 1946).

The Constitution of the Evangelical and Reformed Church, 1950 edition.

XVI
METHODISM

XVI

METHODISM

Elmer T. Clark

The evangelical Revival of the Eighteenth Century, which was embodied in and perpetuated by the Methodist Movement, was in the main the product of the preaching and organizing genius of John Wesley, son and grandson of Anglican clergymen, who was born at Epworth in Lincolnshire on June 17, 1703, and died in London on March 2, 1791. His work thus covered almost the whole of the century. Outstanding among his collaborators were Charles Wesley (1707-1788), his brother, one of the greatest hymn writers of all time, who set the poor of England singing and thus taught them the Arminian theology and injected enthusiasm into the Movement, and George Whitefield (1714-1770), the silver-tongued preacher who electrified great crowds but who failed to organize his converts and broke with the Wesleys at the point of Calvinism.

The low state of morals, the carelessness and corruption of the clergy, and the cruelty and degradation of the social life of England in the eighteenth century are well known, and the low state of things was graphically depicted in the paintings of Hogarth. This formed a background of protest of the Evangelical Revival, and the almost total neglect of the religious needs of the poor provided its opportunity. It was among the poor miners, who were called "the beasts of men," and the other submerged elements that the Wesleyan Movement throve, and among them it produced the reforms that have caused historians to declare that the Methodists themselves were the smallest results of the Revival.

While Wesley evangelized and organized the lower elements, he worked also at the higher stages. His contacts included the outstanding personages of his century. He entered into theological controversies with the most scholarly men of the period. He wrote, edited and published three hundred or more books and pamphlets which circulated by hundreds of thousands among all classes of the people. He sponsored and encouraged every reforming movement of the day, and his influence in social reform was probably as potent as in evangelism and ecclesiastical organization; the beginnings of the British labor movement have been traced directly to the work of the Wesleys, and when the Labor Party came to power in Britain one of its leaders publicly declared that it was "not Marxist but Methodist."

Methodist Origins

John Wesley dated the rise of his "United Societies" in 1739 when he formed a group of several persons in London "who appeared to be deeply convinced of sin, and earnestly groaning for redemption." This, however, is but one of several significant dates that are significant in the beginnings of Methodism.

In 1729 Charles Wesley was instrumental in organizing the so-called Holy Club among students at Oxford for the development of personal piety and the doing of good works among prisoners and the poor. These were dubbed "Methodists" because of their systematic routine, and Wesley always referred to his followers as the "People Called Methodists."

Methodists themselves have always regarded May 24, 1738, as the most significant date in their origin, since on that evening John Wesley experienced his profound spiritual awakening when he "felt his heart strangely warmed" at the meeting of a religious society in Aldersgate Street in London. In 1735 both John and Charles Wesley went to Oglethorpe's colony in Georgia, the former to be a missionary, as he hoped, among the Indians. The mission was not successful but it brought Wesley in contact with the Moravians, by whom he was deeply influenced. Depressed by his failure, he returned to England in 1738 in a state of mind which has been characterized as "conviction of sin," from which he was led to his awakening by the tutelage of the Moravian Peter Böhler. The process involved several steps, among them being recognition that salvation is by faith alone and that it is possible by instantaneous conversion, to which was added Assurance or Witness of the Spirit and Christian Holiness or Perfect Love.

Another date of importance is April 2, 1739, when John Wesley was persuaded by George Whitefield to preach in the open air to the miners at Kingswood, near Bristol. Wesley was much averse to this step, saying he "should have thought the saving of souls almost a sin if it had not been done in a church." But he had been excluded from the parish churches when he began preaching the doctrines of Peter Böhler and field preaching became the most powerful method of early Methodist evangelism, enabling Wesley to reach the masses who were entirely untouched by any form of religious nurture.

By this time the Revival was fully launched. On May 12, 1739, Wesley laid the corner stone of the first Methodist chapel at Bristol, and later in the same year he acquired the Foundry in London and converted it into a preaching place and headquarters of the Methodist Movement. An even more significant step was taken in 1740 or early in 1741 when Wesley reluctantly consented to the preaching of Thomas Maxfield. Lay preaching then became the method so largely responsible for the evangelization of England, and it retains its place of importance in British Methodism today.

By that time the Evangelical Movement within the Church of England was assuming considerable proportions. Great crowds met the preachers everywhere; classes, bands and societies were being formed; chapels had been secured at Bristol, London and Newcastle; persecution was showing its ugly head. Some directing agency was needed, and in 1744 Wesley convened in London the first Conference, the governing body of Methodism everywhere. Present were four clergymen of the Establishment and four of Wesley's lay preachers. The body discussed "(1) what to teach, (2) how to teach, and (3) what to do." With the organization of the annual Conference the main features of Methodism had taken form.

Its Spread

The swift spread of the Methodist revival over England is one of the marvels of the country's history. Within ten years after the first Conference there were sixteen preachers and seven preaching places in London alone, one of the congregations meeting in Sadler's Wells theatre, and thirty-seven sermons were preached during the conference week in 1754. Wesley recruited lay preachers by scores and they rode into every hamlet of the land, enduring persecutions, making converts, organizing groups. Wesley himself was the most determined of all the itinerants; he rode a quarter of a million miles and averaged a sermon a day for around half a century; he went twenty times to Scotland, twenty-one times to Ireland, twenty-four times to Wales. When he died in 1791 there were nearly seventy-five thousand Methodists in Great Britain and Ireland and as many more in North America.

"The missionary character of the Methodist movement was a natural and almost inevitable outgrowth of its fundamental doctrine of universal redemption," says Barclay. It spread because of the urge that was in it. Though Wesley's most famous remark, "I look upon all the world as my parish," became and remains Methodism's honored watchword everywhere, Wesley himself made no plans or preparations for the overseas expansion of his Movement. But the Methodists themselves went abroad, and they preached wherever they landed. It was established in other lands by the converts who emigrated, and not by missionaries sent out for the purpose.

Nathaniel Gilbert and two of his slaves from Antigua heard John Wesley in England in 1758, and they established Methodism in the West Indies on their return. John Fletcher, one of Wesley's outstanding fellow workers in England, established Methodism in his native Switzerland in 1777. Laurence Couglan, an Irish emigrant, began the movement in Newfoundland in 1765 and soldiers of Wolfe's army preached in Quebec and Upper Canada. Similarly a Methodist layman in 1812 opened his home and started a class in Australia, and from there Methodism spread to New Zealand and the whole area of the South Pacific.

It was the same in what is now the United States. An Irish immigrant, Robert Strawbridge (?-1781), began preaching in Maryland around 1760 and his famous log meeting house was erected there about four years later. About the same time another immigrant from Ireland, Philip Embury (1728-1773), began preaching in his home in New York, and Captain Thomas Webb, "of the King's service, and also a soldier of the cross and a spiritual son of John Wesley," formed in Philadelphia a Society composed of converts made by James Emerson around 1767.

John Wesley sent two missionaries, Richard Boardman and Joseph Pilmoor, to America in 1769 in response to appeals from the society in New York, and two years later Francis Asbury (b. 1745) arrived to become the virtual creator and greatest figure of American Methodism.

The story of the spread of the Wesleyan Movement across the continent cannot here be described. Under the direction of Asbury the circuit riders followed the advancing frontier and blanketed the land with their message. Asbury outstripped even Wesley in his travels. He rode 270,000 miles and preached 16,000 times before he died by the side of the road in 1816. Sixty times he crossed the eastern mountains. When he came he found a dozen preachers and around twelve hundred converts, and he left a fully organized Church with nearly seven hundred ordained preachers and a membership considerably above two hundred thousand souls.

The Methodists reached these shores a century and a half later than the pioneers of the other denominations. In twenty-five years they increased 153% while the population grew only 36%. In 1810 one person in 39 was a Methodist, but thirty years later the ratio was one in 19, and by 1860 one-third of all the Protestants in America were Methodists.

Methodism Becomes A Church

It was in the United States that the Methodist Movement first became a Church, nearly a quarter of a century after Strawbridge and Embury began preaching. Separation from the Church of England had not entered into Wesley's thinking, though in his later years he took the steps that made it inevitable by ordaining preachers and drawing up his Deed of Declaration (1784) which gave legal form and government to Methodism. In both England and America the preachers were forbidden to administer the sacraments or to exercise the functions of a regularly ordained ministry.

But separation from the Church of England was brought about by a combination of circumstances which Wesley himself could not have resisted. The demand on the part of the Methodists in both England and America to receive the sacraments from the hands of their own preachers was insistent; in America Strawbridge administered the sacraments in defiance of both Wesley and Asbury and there was a schism in Virginia on the subject. The fact that the United States had become independent of Great Britain added strength to the demand. At the same time the Bishop of London steadfastly refused Wesley's request that some of the Methodists be ordained.

In 1784 Wesley made the decision which took Methodism forever out of the so-called "apostolic succession". Under the pressure of the demands upon him he restudied the theory of the Church, and a reading of King's *Enquiry into the Constitution, Discipline, Unity and Worship of the Primitive Church* convinced him that presbyters and bishops were of one and the same order. It followed that he, as a presbyter, had the right to ordain. In September, 1784, therefore, he ordained or "set apart by the imposition of my hands and prayer," three ministers, Richard Whatcoat, Thomas Vasey, and Dr. Thomas Coke (1747-1814). In the service, which was at Bristol, he was assisted by James Creighton, a presbyter of the Church of England. Whatcoat and Vasey he ordained as presbyters or "elders" and Dr. Coke, who was already a presbyter, he "set apart as a Superintendent." Other ordinations followed from time to time until Wesley had laid hands upon nearly two dozen persons.

Wesley at once sent Coke, Whatcoat and Vasey to the new world under instructions to ordain or set aside Francis Asbury as Superintendent for America. At a famous meeting at Barratt's Chapel, near Dover, Delaware, on November 14, 1784, Asbury declined to accept the office unless unanimously elected by the preachers, whereupon the famous Christmas Conference convened at Baltimore and the Methodist Episcopal Church was formally organized. Both Coke and Asbury were unanimously elected as Superintendents, and on three successive days Asbury was "set apart" as deacon, elder and superintendent. Twelve others were also elected and ordained as elders.

This is not the place to raise again the long-debated subjects of the validity of Methodist orders and the position and place of Methodism in the whole Body of Christ. Methodist scholarship in America tends to the opinion that Wesley did not intend to found an independent Church in America, but that he expected the American Methodists to remain under his jurisdiction and to retain some kind of a relation to the Church of England. Nowhere is the word "bishop" used in connection with Coke or Asbury. "Wesley never considered Coke and Asbury bishops in the Anglican sense," writes Dr. William Warren Sweet, the Methodist historian, and Coke later admitted that he probably "went farther in the separation of our church in America, than Mr. Wesley, from whom I received my commission, did intend. He did indeed solemnly invest me, as far as he had a right to do, with Episcopal authority, but did not intend, I think that an entire separation should take place."

But Wesley said nothing about "Episcopal authority." Coke

and Asbury assumed the title of "bishop" on their own authority and were sharply reprimanded by Wesley himself for doing so. American Methodism has retained the title but does not use the word "ordain" in connection therewith; when the word crept into the *Discipline* it was ordered expunged by the General Conference. Methodist deacons and elders are ordained, but Methodist bishops, as well as deaconesses, are "consecrated." Methodist episcopacy is an office, and not an order, and its functions, even to the extent of consecrating bishops themselves, may be and have been exercised by elders in the absence of a bishop. Methodism everywhere shares the conviction of John Wesley that elders and bishops are of one and the same order.

Aside from this point there has not been great theological divergence between Methodism and the Church of England. The American Methodists adopted the Sunday Service which Wesley abridged from the Prayer Book and the Methodist Twenty-five Articles of Religion were taken from the Articles of the Anglican Church. Certain differences in the rituals of the two communions have grown up through the years but these have not been great.

Methodist Doctrines

In discussing the doctrines of Methodism one is as likely to be led into dissertations as lengthy and as theoretical as those which tempt one who considers its theory of the Church. For on the one hand Methodists have always declared that they had little or no theology, and on the other hand they have contended mightily and against all comers for certain tenets, particularly for universal redemption or Arminianism and against predestination or Calvinism.

John Wesley specifically declared that "the distinguishing marks of a Methodist are not his opinions of any sort." That was in 1742. In 1788 he further declared, "There is no other religious Society under Heaven which requires nothing of men in order to their admission into it but a desire to save their souls. . . . The Methodists alone do not insist on your holding this or that opinion; but they think and let think. Neither do they impose any particular mode of worship; but you may continue to worship in your former manner, be what it may. Now I do not know any other religious society, either ancient or modern, wherein such liberty of conscience is now allowed, since the age of the Apostles."

So "Methodism has long been regarded," says Dr. Umphrey Lee, "as a religious movement—later a church—which does not have creedal obligations for its members, and has consequently been admired or despised according to the predispositions of the onlooker. It cannot be denied that Wesley thought that orthodoxy, in some sense, was not a necessary part of Christianity and that he organized his religious societies with this deliberate provision."

Wesley laid down only one condition for membership in the Methodist societies, namely, "a desire to flee from the wrath to come, and to be saved from their sins." This desire "will be shown by its fruits," and it is "expected of all who continue therein that they shall continue to evidence their desire of salvation, First by doing no harm, by avoiding evil of every kind. . . . Second, by doing good . . . . Third, by attending upon all the ordinances of God." These provisions appear in what are known as the General Rules but church members are not asked to subscribe to them.

At baptism in The Methodist Church the candidates are expected to give affirmative replies publicly to three questions: "Do you truly repent of your sins and accept and confess Jesus Christ as your Saviour and Lord?" "Will you earnestly endeavor to keep God's holy will and commandments?" "Do you desire to be baptized in this faith?" On being received into full membership in the church the following questions are asked: "Do you confess Jesus Christ as your Saviour and Lord and pledge your allegiance to His Kingdom?" "Do you receive and profess the Christian faith as contained in the New Testament of our Lord Jesus Christ?" "Will you be loyal to

The Methodist Church, and uphold it by your prayers, your presence, your gifts, and your service?" The total absence of any doctrinal requirements for membership has been referred to as an "amazing omission," of which Dr. Umphrey Lee says "it has sometimes been hard for Methodists to believe that Wesley meant this, or that the qualification survived in the Methodist Church."

The above refers to membership. The case is somewhat different with regard to the ministry, although even here the doctrinal requirements have "amazing omissions." In the licensing of local or lay preachers several questions are asked concerning spiritual experience and holiness of life and candidates are required to pass examinations on certain studies and "be examined on the subject of doctrine and discipline." On being admitted *on trial* to the Conference there are no further intellectual or doctrinal tests. When a preacher is admitted into *full connection* in the Conference there are further questions concerning spiritual experience and church work and the candidate is asked whether he knows and will keep the General Rules, believes the Methodist doctrines are in harmony with the Holy Scriptures and will be preached and maintained, approves and will support and maintain the church government and polity. On ordination the minister must declare his belief in the Holy Scriptures and that they contain all things necessary to salvation.

While this represents considerable freedom from theological rigidity it must not be assumed that "Methodism has no creed," or that one so well versed in theology as was John Wesley set up a creedless system. On the contrary, he expounded his doctrines in several volumes and insisted that his preachers give assent to and preach them. The first question in the first conference ever held was "what to teach." Wesley's doctrines were contained in his four volumes of *Sermons* and his *Notes Upon the Old Testaments* and *Notes Upon the New Testaments*. These writings constitute what Methodists refer to as the "Standards," and while assent to their contents is not required many Methodist theologians regard them as parts of Methodist doctrine, along with the Articles of Religion (1784). Wesley himself seems to have held that opinion, for when he drew up the form of deed for his chapels in 1763 it was specifically provided that preachers could use the buildings only if "the said persons preached no other doctrines than is contained in Mr. Wesley's *Notes Upon the New Testaments,* and four volumes of sermons." Even Anglican clergymen should not expound contrary doctrines when invited to preach in these chapels.

Wesley sought to resolve the seeming conflict between the liberality which did "not insist on your holding this or that opinion" and the insistence on strict adherence to the doctrines in his *Notes* and sermons by distinguishing between "essential doctrines" and "opinions." In this he was not very successful and not always clear. Certainly he adhered strongly to the basic doctrines of the Protestant faith, and expected his preachers to do so, but he declared that ten thousand mistakes in opinion might still be consistent with real religion. He thought, for example, that it was not possible to have vital religion without accepting the doctrine of the Trinity, but theories about the Trinity or attempts to explain it were regarded as falling in the category of "opinions."

Without following the intricacies and changes in Wesley's thinking, it may be said that neither he nor any other Methodist claimed any *distinctive* doctrines. Great, and sometimes extreme, latitude in matters of belief has always been allowed, but it has been understood that this latitude must be exercised within the framework of the universals of evangelical Protestant Christianity. Methodists repeat the Apostles' Creed in their services, although they are not required to give assent to it as a condition of membership. The General Conference, supreme legislative body of The Methodist Church, which contains a large majority of all the Methodists on earth, has no power to alter the Articles of Religion, which are guarded by such an intricate process that any important change is virtually impossible. The preachers are pledged to maintain and defend these Articles. They are regarded as a part of the grand deposit of Christian doctrine, and nothing is required among Methodists that is not accepted by numerous other groups.

Methodists are neutral on many matters on which others hold decided convictions. They accept any form or mode of baptism and recognize the rite when performed by any other church. They commune with all Christians and invite all to their own table. They raise no question about the validity of the ministry of any church, and their conferences by simple vote may and do recognize ministerial orders conferred by other denominations. In these and similar matters it remains true that "the distinguishing marks of a Methodist are not his opinions of any sort." The Methodist emphasis is placed on life. Accepting as a truism the authority of the grand deposit of the Protestant creed, there has always been more interest in what men are than in what men think. Methodists have stressed experience, and have argued with other groups only on experiential matters.

In the first place, Methodism espouses Arminianism; it has everywhere insisted on the freedom of man's will, universal atonement, and salvation by faith alone, and it has combatted the limited theory of atonement and the predestinarian features of Calvinism.

In the second place, it has upheld the principle of Christian Perfection or Perfect Love, though difficulty has been experienced in defining it and opinion has varied on the subject. Wesley and other Methodist leaders preached it without claiming to have attained it; indeed it has been said that there has always been "the maximum of aspiration with the minimum of profession." Nevertheless perfectionism has, at least until recent times, been an outstanding Methodist principle. To this day Methodist preachers must give affirmative answers to the questions, "Are you going on to perfection? Do you expect to be made perfect in love in this life? Are you earnestly striving after it?" It must be admitted that holiness as a vital principle has declined in the greater Methodist bodies, but it remains imbedded in their history and tradition and has been the direct or indirect cause of numerous schisms in American Methodism.

In the third place, Methodism has insisted on the direct and immediate experience of God on the part of Christians. It preached the Witness of the Spirit. This is bound up with human freedom, universal atonement, conversion, perfection and other ideas that have experiential connotations. It was one of the strongest factors in the spiritual awakening of John Wesley at Aldersgate. In describing the momentous experience Wesley declared, "I *felt* my heart strangely warmed. I *felt* I did trust in Christ, Christ alone for salvation: and an *assurance* was given me that he had taken away my sins. . . . I then testified openly to all there what I now first *felt* in my heart." Assurance was held out as the privilege of all Christians and a goal of striving. In it the feeling element was strong. "I know, because I feel," Wesley once declared, and he said that he wanted "a faith which none could have without knowing that he hath it."

Volumes could be, and have been, written about these principles. In spite of lack of clearness and agreement on details, they have always loomed large in Methodist theology. But neither Wesley nor any other Methodist ever regarded them as distinctive; they were revived and rescued by Wesley but they were not discovered or created by him. He did not think they constituted any departure from the thesis that "Methodists do not insist on your holding this or that opinion."

Methodist Divisions

The theological latitude on the one hand, and the ardent attachment to such tenets as universal atonement and holiness on the other, combined to produce several splits in the Methodist body. Wesley's autocratic control, his hesitancy to break with the Anglican Church, and the episcopal system set up by Coke and Asbury in America were factors in the schisms.

There have been around fifty Methodist divisions and most of them resulted from what the dissidents regarded as departures from the early perfectionism or the exercise of autocratic power.

Wesley himself broke with the Moravians over the latter's principle of "stillness," which Wesley felt carried immediacy to extremes and despised the customary means of grace. There was a more serious split, which prevails to this day, between the Wesleys and the Calvinistic or predestinarian advocates under the leadership of the Countess of Huntington and George Whitefield. Within a few years after the death of Wesley British Methodism broke into half a dozen separate bodies in disputes over democratic procedure, the admission of laymen to the conference, the administration of the sacraments by the preachers, methods of evangelism and similar issues.

In America dissatisfaction with episcopacy and insistence on greater lay participation in church affairs caused the defection of half a dozen bodies. The holiness disputes caused numerous others. The controversy over slavery split the church into its great northern and southern branches and questions of race and language gave rise to the Negro churches and to several German-speaking groups closely related to the Methodist movement.

There are twenty-two independent Methodist churches in the United States, having a total membership of more than eleven million persons, with a constituency several times as large; nine of these are all-Negro bodies with around two million members. They are as follows, the last nine being the Negro churches:

Church	*Approximate Membership 1952*
The Methodist Church	9,066,000
Apostolic Methodist Church	100
Congregational Methodist Church	11,000
Congregational Methodist Church of U.S.A., Inc.	6,000

Evangelical Methodist Church	5,000
Free Methodist Church	50,000
Holiness Methodist Church	1,000
New Congregational Methodist Church	1,500
Primitive Methodist Church	12,000
Reformed Methodist Church	500
Reformed New Congregational Methodist Church	500
Wesleyan Methodist Church of America	33,000
Southern Methodist Church	6,000
African Methodist Episcopal Church	1,066,000
African Methodist Episcopal Zion Church	525,000
African Union First Coloured Methodist Protestant Church	2,500
Coloured Methodist Episcopal Church	385,000
Coloured Methodist Protestant Church	200
Independent African Methodist Episcopal Church	1,500
Reformed Zion Union Apostolic Church	20,000
Reformed Methodist Union Episcopal Church	1,500
Union American Methodist Episcopal Church	10,000
Totals	11,204,300

Ecumenical Spirit

If the theological latitude allowable in the Methodist fold has been operative in some degree in the splits that have occurred, it has also had an opposite effect in that the social conscience has had rather free range and enabled the large Methodist bodies to take a forward position in all social movements, following the example of John Wesley himself. At the same time ecumenicity has been easy for a people who set no great store on niceties of dogma and disputed with nobody over the validity of orders. The Methodists, therefore, are among the foremost supporters of all union movements and interdenominational cooperation.

Several independent churches have been formed from the members of the parent bodies in foreign mission fields; among these are the Methodist Churches of Mexico, Brazil, and Korea. There have been mergers among various branches of the Wesleyan family. The first important union was in Canada in 1884. Forty-eight years later, in 1932, unification in England brought into being the British Methodist Church, embracing all the separate bodies except the small Wesleyan Reform Union, the Irish Conference and some independent churches. In 1939 three large Methodist bodies in the United States, the Methodist Episcopal Church, Methodist Episcopal Church, South, and Methodist Protestant Church, united to form The Methodist Church, the largest Protestant body in America.

The Methodists have not only led in union among themselves but they have been involved in all the wider ecumenical mergers, and have nearly always furnished most of the members. They contributed two-thirds of the total membership to the United Church of Canada in 1925, one-third to the Church of Christ in Japan in 1940, and more than one-half to the Church of South India in 1947.

The Status of Methodism

World Methodism consists of forty different denominations in seventy-five countries or political divisions, with over fourteen million members and a much larger constituency. The various bodies are federated in the World Methodist Council. There are no important theological differences among them. Only the larger groups in the United States and the churches of the mission fields under American sponsorship are episcopal in character, and, as already mentioned, among these episcopacy is an office and not an order.

The total strength of Methodism throughout the world, including a proportionate number of the now united churches in Canada, Japan and South India, which are represented in the World Methodist Council, is as follows (1952):

EUROPE
British Isles 796,200
Continental Europe 132,200
AMERICA
United States of America 11,204,300
Canada 528,000
Mexico 16,300
Central and South America 188,400
West Indies 66,800
AFRICA 589,250
ASIA 568,500
AUSTRALASIA 310,300
Grand Total 14,400,250

By far the largest Methodist body in the world is the Methodist Church, which has more than 9,000,000 members, 40,000 churches, and 24,000 ministers in the United States and around 1,250,000 members and 5,000 churches in its overseas conferences. In the United States the denomination has 150 institutions of learning, including nine universities and ten theological seminaries; these enroll more than 220,000 students and have properties and endowments worth $420,000,000. It operates 74 hospitals and 178 homes for children and the aged in this country, and these have assets of $185,000,000. When the value of the houses of worship ($1,100,000,000) and parsonages ($155,000,000) is added, the total value of the property and endowments owned by The Methodist Church in the United States is above $1,760,000,000.

The governing bodies in American Methodism, as elsewhere, are the Conferences. The quadrennial General Conference is the supreme legislative body, but final authority rests with the Annual Conferences, of which there are 119 in the United States; these own and control practically all the institutions and admit the preachers and assign them to their charges. Between the General and Annual Conferences are six Jurisdictional Conferences, which are not found in other branches of Methodism; five of these (Southeastern, North Central, Northeastern, South Central and Western) are geographical in nature and the Central Jurisdiction embraces the 340,000 Negro members. The Jurisdictional Conferences elect the bishops, who administer within the Jurisdictions which elect them, determine the boundaries of their Annual Conferences, elect their representatives on the general boards of the church, and "provide for the interests and institutions within their boundaries." The Southeastern, which is the largest, and the North Central Jurisdictions contain half of the total membership of The Methodist Church in the United States.

BIBLIOGRAPHY

The basic documents of Methodism are the *Sermons* of JOHN WESLEY, his *Notes* on the Old and New Testaments, *The Journal of John Wesley* (1909-16), edited by N. Curnock (8 vols.), and *The Letters of John Wesley* (1931), edited by J. Telford. Important early works are *The Poetical Works of John and Charles Wesley* (13 vols.), *The Lives of Early Methodist Preachers, Chiefly Written By Themselves,* edited by Thomas Jackson (6 vols.), and the works listed in the bibliographies of Richard Green, *The Works of John and Charles Wesley* and *Anti-Methodist Publications.* See the *Proceedings of the Wesley Historical Society,* published annually since 1898.

The first biography of John Wesley was *Memoirs of the Late Rev. John Wesley, A.M.,* by JOHN HAMPSON (1791), quickly followed by *The Life of the Rev. John Wesley* by COKE and MOORE (1792) and another by WHITEHEAD. The most authoritative and exhaustive of the numerous biographies of Wesley is TYERMAN'S *The Life and Times of the Rev. John Wesley* (3 vols., 1872).

Among histories of Methodism, *see* J. S. SIMON'S *Five Studies of John Wesley* (5 vols.), *A New History of Methodism* (1909), 2 vols., by W. J. TOWNSEND, H. B. WORKMAN and G. EAYRES, and *Wesleyan Methodist Missionary Society* (5 vols.), by FINDLAY and HOLDSWORTH. From the American angle *see* the *Histories of Methodism* by ABEL STEVENS (3 vols.), BUCKLEY (2 vols.), HURST (7 vols.), and W. W. SWEET. The classic of American Methodism is *The Journal of Francis Asbury* (1821), condensed in *The Heart of Asbury's Journal,* by TIPPLE. The earliest American Methodist history was that of JESSE LEE (1810).

On Methodist theology see H. B. WORKMAN, *The Place of Methodism in the Christian Church,* U. LEE, *John Wesley and Modern Religion* (1936), CANNON, *The Theology of John Wesley,* CARTER, *The Methodist Heritage,* R. N. FLEW, *The Idea of Perfection* (1934), W. E. SANGSTER, *The Path to Perfection* (1943), PIETTE, *La Réaction Wesleyenne dans l'Evolution Protestante.*

XVII
THE UNIVERSALIST CHURCH OF AMERICA

XVII

THE UNIVERSALIST CHURCH OF AMERICA

Robert Cummins

WHAT IS IT that we who call ourselves Universalists[1] have in view? What called us into being, and what purposes do we now serve? What is there about us that is distinctive?

We believe those persons are wrong who tell us man is inevitably selfish, that cut-throat competition is the law of life, that war is the means by which the strong will ever overcome the weak. We hold that such doctrine is atheism of the worst kind—an utter denial of the best in religion. We insist God created man in His own image, that is, God gave to man a mind to understand the right, a will to choose the right, and the capacity to attain such relationship with the Creator as will enable him to live righteously. As a child of God, this is man's spiritual heritage; and the responsibility is his of developing it by putting it to use.

Almost certainly there are some erroneous impressions which call for correction. It may be helpful, therefore, to suggest some of the things we are *not*.

We are not merely a company of men and women seeking to build another denomination. Most churches attempt to justify their separate existence by identifying their own organization or their particular faith with that of the "primitive church"—the church as it was during the early centuries of the Christian era; but such basis for separateness is scarcely tenable. The scholarly research of so eminent and unbiased a student as the late Canon B. H. Streeter[2] of Queens College, Oxford, proves beyond doubt that the early church possessed no single, distinct form, that its forms were many and varied, and that, while any one of today's churches might rightly claim to be patterned after one or another of the early churches (for there were several, not just one), so also might every other. In any event, what virtue would there be in such a claim, even were it true? Five of the seven schools extant in those early days were Universalist in their sympathies. Therefore, theologically, we may be said to have been in the majority and holding the "orthodox" viewpoint; but it would not occur to us to claim our right to separate existence today by reason of the situation which then prevailed.

Nor are our dominant characteristics a more elastic theology and a more humane doctrinal outlook. If these—and only these —were our dominant characteristics, our mission would cease to exist, for other churches are tending swiftly in the same direction. There are those who look upon us as a creedless church in which dwells the spirit of freedom, and, while this is true, it could scarcely be judged sufficient to warrant our being. Our intent is to be plain-spoken yet humble. Instead of regarding ourselves as a company of people who have already "arrived" theologically (religiously), we prefer to conceive of ourselves as *learners,* keeping our minds open, consulting unprejudiced scholarship, respecting human experience, refusing to conceive God's revelation as confined to so many properly dotted *i's* and crossed *t's,* or enclosed within the covers of a single Book.

Nor is it true that we are a people who merely "don't believe." The technique just referred to leads inevitably to the conclusion that there are some things we do not believe. Such matters as those over which, down across the years, the Christian church has fought, bled, and all but died—belief in the Trinity, the Virgin Birth, the Immaculate Conception, miracle-working power of the Sacraments, literal interpretation of all portions of the Old and New Testaments—any and all of these, most Universalists do not accept; but we do not make the grave mistake of *prescribing* that our people shall not accept them. They may or they may not, as *they* choose; and, therefore (significantly), they do not. We hold a man's relationship with God is too sacred a thing to be tampered with from without. After all, who are we—who is anyone else—to dictate the terms of such relationship? As a matter of fact, such beliefs make no real difference anyway,—no difference, that is, *morally* and *ethically*. They are matters of opinion only and have nothing to do with richness of character, personal or social, which should constitute the primary concern of the church.

Universalism did begin as a protest, and properly so; but it was a moral protest, theological in form. There were in those early days a few souls who had the courage to rise up in protest against what they conceived to be a cruel, Moloch-worshiping Calvinism, and to call the Christian world back to Jesus' conception of God as Father of all His Creation. Universalists were the protestants of the Protestants, branded as heretics and rebels; but they proved to be in the vanguard of theological thought, pioneers in social reform, gadflies to themselves and others, one of the most humanitarian movements in the history of the Christian church.[3] Yet *all this is only a lesser aspect of the thing we are banded together to do.*

It is our judgment we *are* different; but we are not so simply because we wish to be. We are different because the very logic of the situation makes it inevitable. Universalism, by the very nature of the case, is an inclusive gospel. Universalist Fellowship is inclusive in character, that is, any exclusion is *self*-exclusion. We attempt to stand not only for a more liberal kind of religion, but for a point of view so radically at variance with most of the existing faiths as to make ours a different religion. The conception we have of the Church itself is fundamentally unlike that held by most of the established institutions of religion.

Orthodoxy (by this we mean that phase of religious life which includes both Catholic and Protestant friends) conceives of religion as constituting a body of truth to be *believed*. There may be differences of opinion as to what the truth is, and there may be an endless variety of interpretation of the same truth; but, beneath all opinions and interpretations, there is common agreement that religion is inevitably associated with a body of truth.

The second major proposition of orthodoxy is that the acceptance of this body of truth is essential to salvation. In other words, faith is belief in the truth which saves—and to be outside belief in such truth is to be both in error and in danger. The "elect" are on the inside, that is, on the inside of the right church or denomination. The "Church" is distinct from the world. It is a separate society whose primary functions are to provide fellowship for believers and to win them in ever increasing numbers. Thus, as viewed by the Universalist, there goes on and on this process of divisiveness, separating believers from non-believers, the saved from the unsaved, saints from sinners, the evangelical from the unevangelical; but, in all this (and frequently escaping notice), is the fact that, underlying the orthodox conception, there is the conviction that religion is something one obtains from outside oneself, something one "catches" (as one catches measles), something one "puts on" (as one puts on one's hat and coat). Man is not by nature a child of grace. Religion is not his natural environment, his native endowment. Rather, it is a relationship he enters through *faith*—an act of volition; or, it is an experience which enters him. In any event, we become truly religious only through faith.

Here is the Universalist's real point of departure. He starts with the assumption that religion *is* man's natural environment, is native to him, not foreign. A man may have a special kind of religious experience, or he may go through life without it; but religion, as such, is a permanent attribute of his nature. There is no distinction as among us between believers and unbelievers, redeemed and lost. To us, that sort of thing is not an act of faith, or a particular relationship into which one enters of his own volition. We build on the assumption man *is* religious, in much the same sense he is gregarious, needs shelter, clothing, food, falls in love, marries, and begets children, or enters into any other of the thousand and one perfectly natural and normal relationships of life. And it would seem the social sciences substantiate this assumption.

Universalists part company with most churchmen by reason of this,—their conception of human nature. We emphatically repudiate the idea of original sin resulting from the fall of man. There never was "a fall" of man. If there is truth to be gleaned from modern knowledge, it is that man has come up from primitive origins. Our first ancestors were not an innocent pair in a garden, eating its fruits in peace. They were primitive creatures in a forest, fighting wild beasts, living upon roots and nuts and captured prey. Just how self-consciousness arose, or how the first personality developed, we do not know; and we find ourselves under no necessity to settle these problems of human origins, except to recognize that there never could have been an innocent, free being meeting a single fateful test which was to determine the moral nature of his descendants for all time.

We regard the doctrine of man's degradation, with its penal consequences, as one of the most ghastly ideas ever to misdirect the thoughts of men,—a concept altogether unworthy of an intelligent human being or a good God. We hold, rather, to confidence in the moral potentialities of man, and in salvation as a matter of human cooperation with God in organizing life so that the rude instincts which are our biological inheritance may become habits of a cooperative society animated by love.

For us, then, religion need not be associated with a prescribed set of beliefs, although it may result in beliefs. We have beliefs, and those we have are great indeed. Our present Great Avowal, for example, reads:

The Bond of Fellowship in The Universalist Church shall be a common purpose to do the will of God as

Jesus revealed it and to cooperate in establishing the Kingdom for which he lived and died.

To that end, we avow our faith in God as Eternal and All-Conquering Love, in the spiritual leadership of Jesus, in the supreme worth of every human personality, in the authority of truth known or to be known, and in the power of men of good will and sacrificial spirit to overcome all evil and progressively establish the kingdom of God.[4]

But the agreement between us is comparable to the agreement between scientists. Beliefs held by scientists are not prescribed. Scientific truth issues from use of the scientific method: laboratory testing and experimentation; unhampered and unbiased research. All we insist upon is that our beliefs do not result from revelation; nor are they essential either to our personal salvation or to the life of our Church. They are inferences, fruit of the scientific method as applied to religion. They are —as they should be—*working hypotheses,* used as hypotheses are used in every other department of living, as *tools* by use of which we are aided in our growth toward the state of all-round maturity for which the privilege of life was given us and for which we are intended.

Thus do Universalists have faith, but in a very different sense. Our faith is not in doctrines and creeds, but in *purposes* and *goals.* Our faith would liberate man from speculative dogmas which, in any case, cannot be verified, and set him free to harness his spiritual energies to the realization of ideals and values in his personal and social life. This is the very thing which Jesus himself called faith, and the selfsame manner in which he used it: the free, creative spirit of man at work on the stuff of life, saying to the future, "It shall be thus and so, because—*we will it* to be!"

In other words, Universalists conceive of themselves as striving to be a voluntary association of men and women, children and youths, seeking to apply both intelligence and heart to the social organization of man's religious endowment, in order to achieve desirable goals in individual and social living. The supreme aim of The Universalist Church is not to glorify God (although it may result in God's glory), or to win men to Christ (although it may prove a most effective means of demonstrating the spirit exemplified by Jesus of Nazareth). No; The Universalist Church is a very human institution, created solely for the purpose of enriching, enlarging, and fulfilling the life which is man's.

There are approximately eighty thousand persons known to be associated with the four hundred forty-eight Universalist churches in the United States. Doubtless, there are an even greater number (uncounted, but avowed Universalists) residing in communities where there are no Universalist churches. Together they constitute an earnest fellowship, utilizing much the same form of organization as is used by the several other denominations practicing congregational polity. Here is a fellowship led by a well-trained and able ministry; sponsoring its own publishing house; utilizing as a matter of course the most up-to-date methods and scholarly materials in the field of religious education; responsible for the founding of several colleges, universities, and theological schools;[5] carrying on, through its women, perhaps the most outstanding work being done for diabetic children, under the leadership of America's famed specialists in diabetes;[6] maintaining for Negroes a kindergarten, health clinic, and social betterment unit;[7] administering relief in both Europe and Asia to the sufferers of war; working hand in hand with several commissions of the National Council of Churches (although deprived of membership in that body); striving to care for its aged and infirm;[8] encouraging sex education and birth control, opposition to war, rights of labor to organize; and advocating one of the most advanced of the "social creeds." Here is a fellowship bringing to men the vision of religion as a liberating force, setting minds free, and, in that process, begetting spiritual liberty also, removing hidden phobias and directing the gaze to horizons unclouded by dogmas, inviting men to venture uncharted seas, and gripping the heart with the dynamic of a creative faith to which all things are possible.

Universalism brings to its people a message of assurance. Based squarely upon the firm conviction that man is naturally religious, it brings to many who have felt themselves outside the pale an appreciation of their own religious impulses, and encourages the spiritual longings and aspirations which are theirs to become more articulate. Fellowship in the Universalist Church is a perfectly natural and rational thing. While we guard zealously against the practice of proselytizing, we endeavor to welcome into full fellowship former members of any and all churches, or of none. Generally speaking, Universalist churches are not made up of residents of the neighborhood only. Constituents are widely scattered and often travel many miles to services. Their association issues from conviction. Over fifty per cent of the ministers have come from non-Universalist background. This influx of laity and clergy alike is due, in part at least, not to the mood of mere tolerance on the part of Universalists, but to a growing respect for their assumption that the inclusion of differing viewpoints is both democratic and educationally acceptable. Ours is an *inclusive* fellowship. Any exclusion becomes *self*-exclusion. Here, in embryo, is the kind of fellowship which, if the world is to survive, the world must have.

Universalism has produced persons who have dared to live courageous lives, to think new thoughts, to perform pioneering deeds.

In 1790 in Philadelphia (years before Lincoln was born), Universalists—the first body of religionists so to do—went on record as opposing human slavery in any form. One of the twelve charter members of the first Universalist church to be organized on American soil was "Gloster Dalton, An African."

Hosea Ballou's (1771-1852) *A Treatise on Atonement*, in 1805, was the first book published in America advocating the strict unity of God. This was ten years prior to the famous Unitarian controversy in 1815 between William Ellery Channing and Samuel Worcester.

Lombard (a Universalist college) and Oberlin were the first of all American colleges and universities to adopt co-education. Universalists were among the first to champion public schools free from ecclesiastical control.

Adin Ballou, a Universalist at Hopedale, Mass., was instrumental in founding the Hopedale Fraternal Community, 1842, one of the early cooperative communities which endeavored to apply to social and economic life the ideals of religion.[9]

The Universalist Church was the first to sponsor women for its ministry, not because they were women but because they were *persons*. The very first body of women in America to organize on a national scale was a body of Universalist women. The first journal[10] devoted to the welfare of working women was edited by a Universalist minister.

The first official State Labor Conciliator was the Rev. LeGrand Powers, a Universalist minister appointed to that post by the Governor of Minnesota in 1887.

Universalists were first to sponsor prison reforms. The Rev. Charles Spear edited *The Prisoners' Friend,* the first prison paper. Spear paved the way for successful prison reform movements in which some of his Universalist descendants, such as Orlando F. Lewis and Thomas Mott Osborne, were active. Universalists were first to propose parôle; first to oppose capital punishment.

Benjamin Rush, Universalist layman (Philadelphia physician) and signer of the Declaration of Independence, was a pioneer in the field of temperance education; he helped organize the first anti-slavery society. In 1791, he founded the First Day Sunday School Society, which met January 5, and, three months later, established the first non-sectarian Sunday School in America.

The Rev. Charles H. Leonard, then minister in Chelsea, Mass., and later to become the beloved Dean of the School of

Religion at Tufts College, founded Children's Day.

William E. Barton's *Lincoln's Religion* contains the following:

> The religious spirit of Abraham Lincoln was in harmony with Universalism. He censured his friend, Peter Cartright, the evangelist, for the latter's attack upon Universalism. 'Pastor,' said he, 'I used to think it took the smartest kind of man to defend and uphold Universalism. But now I think differently. They have the whole Scripture on their side and so many witnesses it would be impossible to lose.'

It is an accepted fact that the influence of Thomas Starr King, a Universalist minister, kept the state of California in the Union during the Civil War.

Clara Barton, founder of the American Red Cross, was a Universalist.

The first Universalist church, organized in Gloucester, Mass., in 1779, was destined to "make history." A man named Gregory visited the town in 1769, bringing with him the writings of the London preacher, James Relly (1722?-1778). This book, *Union,* caused great interest. Universalism, *per se,* was then unknown; but Relly taught "universal salvation" and Gloucester followers became known as "Relly-ites." The Universalist Church in America dates from the advent from England in 1770 of the Rev. John Murray (1741-1815)[11], (denominational organization was achieved in 1790). Murray was a Relly convert from English Wesleyanism; and the small group of "Relly-ites" in Gloucester called him to serve as their leader. The book, *Union,* only needed public proclamation by Murray to unite these people organizationally, and to crystalize the opposition. An attack was made upon Murray after his second appearance in Boston in 1774. He and his followers were forced to continue their meetings in private homes, chief of which was the home of Winthrop Sargent. In January of 1779, they achieved formal organization as a church, and on

Christmas Day the following year their new meeting house was dedicated.

Opposition again asserted itself, this time on the question of taxation. Assessors of the First Parish held that the persons who had withdrawn to follow Murray were still liable to taxation for the support of the First Parish. Universalists countered by insisting that the Bill of Rights[12] attached to the Constitution of the Commonwealth of Massachusetts provided for the support by each and every individual of the religion of his choice. First Parish then claimed that Murray's congregation was not religious in character, nor was it incorporated, and that Murray himself was not properly ordained.

Property of Universalist people was seized for non-payment of taxes and sold at public auction; whereupon, Universalists brought suit to recover. The case came to trial in 1783 and continued in litigation on appeal and review until 1786, at which time the Universalists obtained a favorable verdict. This verdict (by Judge Dana) freed Universalists of Gloucester from the necessity of supporting a church in which they could not believe. This was the first test case of its kind, and is a landmark in the history of free religion. Gloucester Universalists and their leader, Murray, were fighting the battle of freedom for other religious groups as well as for themselves.

While Universalist ideas reach back twenty-five hundred years to the obscure author of the *Book of Malachi* ("Have we not all one Father? Hath not one God created us?"), Universalism finds itself peculiarly at home in free-born, democratic America. In fact, it is one of the few religious denominations of purely American origin.

Its genius is its liberty. Its fathers dared challenge tyrannies of ecclesiastical authority, interpreting life in larger, more triumphant terms. Its beginnings were linked with stormy days of political and industrial revolution. Its prophets were stoned and ostracized.

One of its most admirable characteristics is its determination to uphold the right of every person to interpret the fundamentals of religion according to his conscience. Absolute freedom of utterance and latitude for adventure are secured for laity and clergy alike. It has pledged itself to struggle for complete emancipation.

The Universalist Church offers a moral and spiritual fellowship of persons whose ideal is the drawing together in the spirit of fraternity all men, learning and teaching the values of basic religion, and devoting themselves to such obviously essential tasks as the relief of suffering, the rebuilding of that which war has destroyed, and the establishment of moral principles of world government.

Universalist churches adhere strictly to congregational polity, calling or dismissing their ministers, and, in other ways, determining their own destiny. Churches within an area are sometimes gathered, for purposes of fraternity and teamplay, as "associations"; but the major unit of organization between the parish-church and the denomination whole is the state convention (composed of churches within the state). Delegates of these local churches and state conventions, together with ordained clergymen, meet biennially in General Assembly (constituting the governing body of the Church). The Assembly elects a president (who serves as moderator of the Assembly and may serve as chairman of the denominational Board of Trustees) and a Board of Trustees. The Trustees, in turn, elect a General Superintendent, a Treasurer, and a Secretary,— the Superintendent serving as ecclesiastical head and chief executive officer of the denomination.

The denomination is organized so as to function by departments: Depts. of the Ministry, Church Extension, Service Projects, Education (with Divisions: Children, Youth, Adults), Public Relations, Publications, Business Administration, and Survey & Evaluation. Each department has its executive director, a member of the denominational staff. Each department operates through its department board (members are chosen by the Trustees), the chairman of which is a Trustee. Denominational auxiliary groups are: the Association of Universalist Women; the National Association of Universalist Men; the Universalist Youth Fellowship; and the Universalist Publishing House. The denominational journal is *The Christian Leader*. Executive offices are at denominational headquarters: #16 Beacon Street, Boston 8, Mass.

The program of relief and rehabilitation in Hungary, the Netherlands, and Germany, sponsored by The Universalist Church, has been cited as most outstanding by the International Relief Organization of the United Nations. Modern missions are established in Japan; and groups akin to and affiliated with American Universalists may be found both in England and Holland (London and Amsterdam).

Now, in conclusion, it must be understood that, with respect to theological views, not all my fellow Universalists would accept these statements of mine. We have no accredited theology. The truth makes men free, and when they are free they are free to differ. Universalists are united by no hierarchy, by no set of mandates agreed upon, but by a common spirit, a mutual purpose, and a freedom for all. Frankly, we do not know what we shall believe eventually, for our faith is not set in authorities and infallibilities. It is meant, rather, to be a growing, developing, broadening, deepening thing—now from some new insight of philosophy or science, now from some fresh revelation of human goodness, now from some mystic experience of God which surpasses the power of lips to utter, now from some simple fellowship of those who join hands to make this a better world, a happier nobler place for the children of God. The Universalist believes all each day's experience enables him to believe.

NOTES

1 What Universalism is:

Universe; universal; universalism: all-pervading; embracing or comprehending the whole; general. The doctrine that all men will ultimately be saved.
—*Webster's New Standard Dictionary*.

"We have all one Father who will succeed in his purpose of love. The entire family of mankind will finally attain to the spirit that is in Jesus . . . Good will triumph over evil, and God will be all in all."
—*Scriptural cornerstone of Universalism*.

Universalism's message is based squarely upon: (1) the primacy of man; (2) the unity of the human family; and (3) the universality of truth. And this is God's own message, its truth inscribed on every page of man's recorded rise.

Universalism is the philosophy and religion of the all-inclusive. The whole is greater than its parts. It interprets life in terms of universals and unities, levels barriers, abjures prejudice, renounces all that sets man against his fellow man, endeavors to integrate humanity into one harmonious co-operating society. Universalism is found wherever men work together for a better world, embraces all religions, works with science to create a finer, happier world.

Universalism is being re-born. It is a "one world" faith in the making. It must come because without it the world cannot continue, except on the present path which leads toward suicide. Universalism is a reconciling, unifying faith; more than a negative protest against errors of the past, more than a mere social credo. It is a faith broad enough and deep enough to command the loyalty of all men.

2 *The Primitive Church* (New York, 1929).

3 "As for the Universalists, the record of their fidelity as a body to the various interests of social morality is not surpassed by that of any other people." (From BACON'S *History of American Christianity*.)

4 This "Great Avowal" of Universalists (adopted in 1933 at Worcester, Massachusetts, and ratified in 1935 at Washington), represents the latest affirmation of faith made officially by The Universalist Church of America.

The earliest "Profession of Belief" was adopted in 1803 at Winchester, New Hampshire:

"We believe that the Holy Scriptures of the Old and New Testament contain a revelation of the character of God and of the duty, interest and final destination of mankind.

"We believe that there is one God, whose nature is Love, revealed in one Lord Jesus Christ, by one Holy Spirit of Grace, who will finally restore the whole family of mankind to holiness and happiness.

"We believe that holiness and true happiness are inseparably connected, and that believers ought to be careful to maintain order and practice good works; for these things are good and profitable unto men."

And this was followed (1899, at Boston) by the "Five Principles":

"The Universal Fatherhood of God. The Spiritual Authority and leadership of His Son, Jesus Christ. The trustworthiness of the Bible as containing a revelation from God. The certainty of just retribution for sin. The final harmony of all souls with God."

5 Tufts College and Tufts College School of Religion; St. Lawrence University and Canton Theological School; Lombard College; Akron University (Buchtel); Goddard College; Clinton Liberal Institute; Westbrook Junior College; Dean Academy.

6 Dr. Elliot P. Joslin and his medical staff.

7 Jordan Neighborhood House, Suffolk, Va.

8 Foxboro, Mass.; Jamaica, Long Island, N. Y.; Philadelphia, Pa.

9 It was to BALLOU'S book, *Christian Socialism*, that both Tolstoi and Gandhi attributed the source of their philosophies.

10 *The Star of Bethlehem*, edited by A. C. Thomas and T. B. Thayer, Lowell, Mass.

THE UNIVERSALIST CHURCH OF AMERICA

11 Perhaps the earliest preacher of Universalism in America was Dr. George de Benneville (1741, a physician, in Pennsylvania).

The place of Elhanan Winchester in the early history of the Universalist Church has never been adequately appreciated. He was an eloquent and popular Baptist preacher, a man of wider learning and profounder Biblical scholarship than Murray, who had been converted to Universalism largely by the influence of George de Benneville. He was one of the pre-Murray Universalists in this country whose earlier seed-sowing helped prepare the ground for Murray's work. When Winchester became convinced of the truth of Universalism, he left his great Baptist church in Philadelphia, led in the formation of a Universalist church in that city, and cast his lot with the (then) despised heretics.

Dr. Charles Chauncy, who graduated from Harvard in 1721, and was ordained pastor of the First Church (Congregational) in Boston in 1727, was distinguished for his learning and patriotism. He became a Universalist some years before making a public avowal of his convictions, though he expressed himself freely to his friends, and submitted to them his writings on the subject.

About the year 1750 he undertook a close and critical study of the Scriptures, particularly of the epistles of Paul, in which he occupied seven of the best years of his life. As a result, he came into the belief of Universalism.

12 "Congress shall make no law respecting the establishment of religion or prohibiting the free exercise thereof." (From the First Amendment of the Constitution of the United States of America.)

BIBLIOGRAPHY

CHURCH ORGANIZATION, ADMINISTRATION, PROGRAM

Charter, Constitution & By-Laws of The Universalist Church of America.
ROBERT CUMMINS, *Parish Practice in Universalist Churches* (UPH,* 1946).
Laws of Fellowship, Government & Discipline.
Year Book & Directory.
One Humanity—Dept. of Service Projects.
Education—Dept. of Education.
Teamwork—Universalist Ministerial Association.
The Bulletin—Association of Universalist Women.
Youth Leader—Universalist Youth Fellowship.
The Christian Leader—(UPH).
 * UPH—Universalist Publishing House.

HISTORY OF UNIVERSALIST THOUGHT

J. W. HANSON, *Universalism in the First Five Hundred Years of the Christian Church* (UPH, 1899).
ADIN BALLOU, *Primitive Christianity and its Corruptions* (UPH, 1870).
JOHN COLEMAN ADAMS, *Short Studies in the Larger Faith* (UPH, 1918).
FREDERICK W. BISBEE, *From Good Luck to Gloucester* (UPH, 1920).
ROGER SHERMAN GALER, *A Layman's Religion* (UPH, 1921).
BRUCE W. BROTHERSTON, *A Philosophy of Liberalism* (Boston, 1934).
CLARENCE R. SKINNER, *The Social Implications of Universalism* (UPH, 1915).
——, *Liberalism Faces the Future* (New York, 1937).
——, *A Religion for Greatness* (Murray Press, 1945).

[347]

————, *Human Nature and the Nature of Evil* (UPH, 1939).
A Symposium, *Tufts Papers on Religion* (UPH, 1939).
RICHARD EDDY, *History of Universalism in America*, 2 vols. (UPH, 1886).
————, *Universalism in Gloucester* (Proctor Bros., 1892).
A. GERTRUDE EARLE, *Beginnings of Universalism* (UPH, 1940).
ROBERT CUMMINS, *An Authoritarian or a Free Church?* (UPH).
————, *Religious Implications of the Democratic Process* (UPH).
JOHN M. RATCLIFF, *Lifting Life to a Religious Level* (UPH).
IDA M. FOLSOM, *The Christian Citizen at Work in the World* (UPH).
E. G. BROOKS, *Our New Departure* (UPH, 1874).
EDGAR R. WALKER, *The Life and the Way* (Teachings of Jesus) (UPH).
FREDERICK WILLIAMS PERKINS, *Beliefs Commonly Held Among Us* (UPH).
HOSEA BALLOU II, *Ancient History of Universalism* (Marsh & Capen, 1829).
A Symposium, *Life's Inevitables* (UPH).
A Symposium, *Universalism—The Bond of Fellowship* (UPH).
MAX A. KAPP, *These Universalists* (UPH).
JOHN E. WOOD, *Charter of Our Faith* (UPH).
CLARENCE R. SKINNER and ALFRED S. COLE, *Hell's Ramparts Fell* (UPH).
CLINTON LEE SCOTT, *Your Church and You* (UPH).
————, *Universalism, A Philosophy for Living* (UPH).
E. H. LALONE, *And Thy Neighbor As Thyself* (UPH).
————, *Pioneer Personalities* (UPH).
————, *Universalism Speaks to the Economic Problems of Our Time* (UPH).
ALBERT F. ZIEGLER, *Universalism Speaks to the Atomic Age* (UPH).
JOSEPH W. BEACH, *Universalism Speaks to You and Me* (UPH).
C. H. MONBLEAU, *Universalism Speaks a Reasonable Philosophy for a New Age* (UPH).
ALFRED S. COLE, *Our Liberal Heritage* (Boston, 1951).
FRED GLADSTONE BRATTON, *Legacy of the Liberal Spirit—Men and Movements in the Making of Modern Thought* (New York, 1943).

THEOLOGY

J. S. CANTWELL, ed., *Manuals of Faith and Duty* (UPH).
  I JOHN COLEMAN ADAMS, *The Fatherhood of God* (1890).
  II STEPHEN CRANE, *Jesus the Christ* (1890).
  III ISAAC M. ATWOOD, *Revelation* (1891).
  IV W. S. WOODBRIDGE, *Christ in the Life* (1890).
  V O. CONE, *Salvation* (1893).
  VI CHARLES FOLLEN LEE, *The Birth From Above* (1891).
  VII CHARLES ELLWOOD NASH, *The Saviour of the World* (1895).
  VIII HENRY W. RUGG, *The Church* (1891).
  IX CHARLES SUMNER WEAVER, *Heaven* (1892).
  X WILLIAM TUCKER, *Atonement* (1893).
  XI GEORGE HENRY DEERE, *Prayer* (1893).
ABEL TOMPKINS, *Treatise on Atonement* (1852); HOSEA BALLOU (UPH, 1902).
E. E. GUILD, *Universalist's Book of Reference* (UPH, 1901).
J. W. HANSON, *A Pocket Cyclopedia* (UPH, 1895).
————, *Bible Proofs of Universal Salvation* (UPH, 1888).
J. D. WILLIAMSON, *An Examination of the Doctrine of Endless Punishment* (UPH, 1890).
JOSEPH SMITH DODGE, *The Purpose of God* (UPH, 1894).

THE UNIVERSALIST CHURCH OF AMERICA

BIOGRAPHY

OSCAR F. SAFFORD, *Hosea Ballou* (UPH, 1889).

W. H. McGLAUFLIN, *Faith With Power, A Life Story of Quillen H. Shinn* (UPH, 1912).

SUMNER ELLIS, *Life of Edwin H. Chapin* (UPH, 1882).

MARION D. SHUTTER, *James Harvey Tuttle* (UPH, 1905).

DEVOTIONAL

Antiphonal Readings for Free Worship (UPH, 1933), arranged by L. Griswold Williams.

Hymns of the Spirit (UPH and Beacon Press, 1937), prepared jointly by Unitarian and Universalist commissions.

Beacon Song and Service Book (UPH and Beacon Press, 1935), prepared jointly by Unitarian and Universalist commissions.

Advent and Lenten Manuals (UPH), published annually.

XVIII

THE EVANGELICAL UNITED BRETHREN CHURCH

XVIII

THE EVANGELICAL UNITED BRETHREN CHURCH

PAUL H. ELLER

THE EVANGELICAL United Brethren Church is among the newest of the American denominations, for as such it was born November 16, 1946, at Johnstown, Pennsylvania where amid suitable ceremonies the Evangelical Church and the Church of the United Brethren in Christ joined and became the Evangelical United Brethren Church.

Backgrounds

The Evangelical and United Brethren Churches were American-born churches and like a number of other ecclesiastical bodies, owe their origin to a set of unique circumstances which obtained in the new American nation immediately after the Revolutionary War. On the one hand, there was a general decline in the practice of religion of such proportions that it was held that in two generations, Christianity would altogether disappear.[1] Popular secular philosophies from England, but more especially from France, were proclaimed by popular revolutionary leaders and skepticism and indifference spread upon the great body of the American people.[2] Tom Paine made sport of the "fable of Jesus Christ". Unitarianism rose to challenge traditional orthodoxy. Perhaps as low as six per cent of the American people were affiliated with organized religion in 1790[3]—not unrelated to this is the judgment that at this time "religious and moral conditions of the country as a whole reached the lowest ebb tide in the entire history of the American people."[4]

Nevertheless, evidences of ecclesiastical activity were not wanting. Churches were built; clergy were ordained; and the sacraments were distributed for the faithful. However, religion came to be identified with ecclesiastical conventionalities—routines to be borne rather than an abiding experience of the grace of God which brought lift and life to the overborne.

Happily there were promises of hope in the generally discouraging picture. Pietism had found a small but fruitful place in parts of the Lutheran and Reformed churches.[5] Methodism under the apostolic zeal of Francis Asbury (1745-1816) challenged the formalism of churchmanship. Then as the century came to its close, the Great Revival broke out in the frontier country of Tennessee and Kentucky and slowly made its way to the urban and cultural communities of the seaboard. In the West this religious expression was enthusiastic, sincere and unsophisticated;[6] in the East the more elemental expressions were chastened and disciplined. This movement above all else broke the spell which indifference and skepticism exercised upon American Christianity.

Evangelistic Preachers

Some preachers of this rediscovered gospel of salvation are to be found in each of the denominations, while some proclaimers of this newly-found treasure were not ordained ministers at all. The years after the Revolution found the Reverend Philip W. Otterbein (1726-1813) preaching in Baltimore. He was born in Germany, the son of a German Reformed clergyman. After graduate theological study at Herborn he was in his first pastorate when he responded to the appeal of Michael Schlatter for missionaries for Pennsylvania. In 1752 he began his pastoral service in Lancaster. Thereafter he served German Reformed congregations in Tulpehocken, Frederick (Maryland), and York before accepting the call to the Baltimore congregation. During his stay at York his path first crossed that of Martin Boehm (1725-1812), a Pennsylvanian born Mennonite, who in the pursuit of his pastoral duties in a religious experience had come to know the power of the gospel. In a "pentecostal meeting" in Long's Barn, perhaps in 1767,[7] it is held these two men met. Here Otterbein greeted Boehm with the memorable phrase: "We are brethren". The third figure is that of Jacob Albright (1759-1808), a Pennsylvania born German, who early in life had been under Lutheran religious influence. These influences had all but disappeared when in 1791 he came to a religious experience which brought him new goals and new motivations. Then in 1796 Jacob Albright went preaching without benefit of any ecclesiastical credentials.[8]

Though of diverse backgrounds, talents and education these three men had in common the conviction that salvation was the first and foremost of the articles of faith. They agreed that God spoke to men particularly, and that each man had to hear this word for himself, by faith, in his own heart. Their exhortations were simple invitations to self-respecting, self-reliant men to humble themselves, confess their need of the forgiveness and grace of God and to accept the salvation offered them. To do so was a personal act which brought cleansing and strength.

There were people who heard these preachers who detected in their spoken words the voice of God. Vital religion always creates a fellowship: something of a following or movement evolved around each of these three men. The groups were small but enthusiastic; they were characterized by their simplicity and freedom. They were the source of the organizations which subsequently evolved. Two factors in the American scene go far in explaining the rise of these and kindred ecclesiastical organizations. On the one hand, the Great Revival emphasized dynamic, individual religion and called upon the individual to challenge his cultural, social and ecclesiastical environment. On the other hand, the newly adopted Constitution and the Bill of Rights proclaimed religious liberty. This signified that every man might choose any or no faith; that in the eyes of the law, all churches were equal; that each church must make its way on the contributions of its members; and that persons dissatisfied with existing churches were at liberty to form others. Thus the legal privileges of religious liberty and the deep drives of revivalism providing motivation conspired to engender new church organizations.[9]

Organization

In these circumstances, evidences of Otterbein-Boehm organization appear in 1789, and again in 1791: but on September 25, 1800, the first of their regular, annual meetings was held. The unecclesiastical tone of the group is attested by the name, "the unsectarian preachers" which appears in the first minutes.[10] Slowly a decisive organization emerged, but it was won over an opposition that resisted sturdily. On October 2, 1813, in his parsonage home in Baltimore, Otterbein ordained three men for the Christian ministry in an act as difficult to explain as the ordinations administered by John Wesley in 1784.

In the Albright circle, while evidences of organization are noted by 1800,[11] the first of the regular, annual meetings was held November 13, 1807. Church names were successively chosen: The Newly Formed Methodist Conference (1807); The SoCalled Albright People (1809); and The Evangelical Association (1816). However, when Albright died in 1809, the group had no official creed, no official rule book, nor was there an officially ordained ministry.

Much of the responsibility for the actual organization of these churches must be attributed to others than those who inspired the evangelistic movements. Among the Otterbein-Boehm group, Christian Newcomer (1749-1830) was the champion of organization. This man of Mennonite background discovered that Otterbein "preached the same gospel which I had experienced"[12] so he was attracted to the Baltimore preacher. As age and ill health prevented Otterbein and Boehm from attending the annual meetings, the reins of leadership fell into Newcomer's able hands. He organized the first classes. He urged the case for a Confession and a Discipline[13] and the first general conference met in 1815 was convened in part

[356]

to confront these proposals: the second general conference, in 1817, provided formal sanction for them both. Though he had been itinerating for many years, he did not receive ordination until 1813, and in the same year he was elected bishop for one year. Thus around the person and work of Christian Newcomer a definitive ecclesiastical organization appeared among the United Brethren.

Several months after the death of Jacob Albright, George Miller (1774-1816), one of his helpers, took to compiling a Confession and a Discipline. These he presented to the annual meeting in 1809,[14] and they were adopted. Later that same year, formal ordinations occurred. In 1816 the first general conference of the group was held. Thus around the person and work of George Miller a definitive ecclesiastical organization appeared for the Evangelicals. The episcopal office in this communion was continuous after the election of John Seybert in 1839.

These two emerging churches had much in common. They ministered chiefly to German-speaking peoples in the German language. They were emphatically and distinctively evangelistic. Theologically, both were Arminian and pressed the needfulness of an experience of salvation. Both were indelibly impressed with Methodist patterns of church polity. Nevertheless, each went its way independently of the other.

Westward Expansion

The ever expanding frontier was a challenge to both of these churches. This was due in part to the fact that some of their own number had removed to the frontier, taking in addition to the broad-axe and the hunting rifle, the Bible and a concern for the spiritual quality of life. In part this was due to the desperate needs of the frontier:

> The East was shocked at the balls, drinking, fighting and the utter disregard paid to the Sabbath. Pious men were terrified at the drunkenness, the vice, the gam-

bling, the brutal fights, the gouging, the needless duals they beheld on every hand.[15]

In 1847 Horace Bushnell made his declaration "Barbarism—the First Danger" which affirmed that either Christendom must evangelize the frontier, or the frontier would paganize the established settlements of the nation.

Thus doubly motivated—by a concern for the erring and a love for those of their own number who had removed to the frontier, Evangelicals and United Brethren joined in the Christian conquest of the continent. By 1853 J. G. Conner was founding United Brethren work in Oregon: by 1858 Israel Sloan was serving the same church in California. In 1864 the first Evangelical missionaries began their work in the Pacific states.

Much of the credit for this march across the continent must be attributed to the innumerable pioneer preachers among whom Christian Newcomer (United Brethren) and John Seybert (Evangelical) stand as samples and symbols. These were simple men committed to one thing only—to proclaim the light of the gospel. In a natural and unembarrassed way they made their witness to the living Christ. There was much they did not know, but they knew their Lord and His power to transform lives, and this they declared persuasively in a language the people could understand.

Challenges and Achievements

While these churches were expanding numerically and geographically in the nineteenth century, similar issues confronted both groups. Both had been German-speaking in their beginning; however, in 1813 the United Brethren licensed their "first English Preacher"[16] and the transition to English was begun. The first denominational periodical was an English periodical and by 1830 English was definitely on the ascendency and the language question was on its way to solution. In contrast, Evangelicals clung tenaciously to the German language. The nonconformity of the first English preacher in

the denomination led the general conference in 1830 to admonish that preachers "confine their labors to the German
portion of the population."[17] The first denominational periodical was a German language paper. The use of the German
language continued in significant strength until World War
I: today the German language has all but disappeared in the
congregations of this denomination.

The demands of meeting the challenge of the frontier and
maintaining unity in the rapidly growing denominations
evoked various responses. The absence of official leadership
was rectified by Evangelicals in general conference in 1839
when John Seybert was elected to the episcopacy. To guard
against disaffection and divergence in an age of sectionalism
and sectarianism the United Brethren general conference, May
14, 1933, declared their Confession of Faith could never be
altered.[18] Motivated by the same circumstances, the Evangelicals in 1839 forbade any alteration of the approved nineteen
Articles of Faith.[19]

The desire for a "voice of the church" which would make
for unity within and expansion without the fellowship led to
the founding of publishing interests. Following several ventures elsewhere, in 1834 the pastor and several laymen in Circleville, Ohio, took the initiative and purchased a press, and on
December 31, 1834, *The Religious Telescope,* edited by W. R.
Rhinehart appeared. This venture of the Scioto Conference
became denominational in character, and in 1853 the press
was transferred to Dayton, Ohio, where it continues to operate
as The Otterbein Press. Evangelicals had entered the publishing business in 1816 but inexperience and "hard times" led
the church to dispose of its equipment in 1828. Within a few
years there was a new demand for a church periodical, and on
January 1, 1836, *Der Christlicke Botschafter* appeared, edited
by Adam Ettinger. The printery prospered, but circumstances
prompted its removal to Cleveland, Ohio, in 1854. With the
schism in the Evangelical household after the general conference of 1887, a publishing enterprise was established at Har-

risburg, Pennsylvania. At the union of Evangelicals in 1922 both houses were continued, but in 1934 it was decided that the publishing interests of the Evangelical Church should be united at Harrisburg. The Otterbein Press, Dayton, and the Evangelical Press, Harrisburg, are the two printing houses of the Evangelical United Brethren Church today.

While the Otterbein-Boehm and Albright movements had been missionary in their inception, there came a time when the urge to unity and expansion called for the creation of missionary organizations. Inspired by the reading of the *Baseler Missions Magazin,* W. W. Orwig in 1838 persuaded his conference to organize a missionary society. The next year a committee which included Orwig petitioned the Evangelical general conference and "The Missionary Society of the Evangelical Association of North America" was organized.[20] In the wake of four conference missionary societies, in 1841 general conference organized "The Parent Missionary Society of the United Brethren in Christ." This organization was not well organized or supported and general conference in 1853 created a new missionary organization, "The Home, Frontier and Foreign Missionary Society." In a drastic organizational revision in 1905 the home and overseas missionary administrations were separated.

Still another measure making for unity in these churches was the framing of constitutions. Evangelicals in 1839 adopted one, but its broad character saved it from controversy. A constitution was proposed to the United Brethren general conference in 1837 and approved, but inasmuch as the matter had come before the conference somewhat irregularly, it was proposed that the following general conference should act officially on the matter. At the latter meeting there was a spirited debate on the matter of a constitution, but by a 15 to 7 vote, it was determined that a constitution should be composed. A committee of nine was appointed to draft the document which sought to "guard against apostacy, to sustain a balance of power between clergy and laity . . . and establish points of polity which should stand unalterable."[21] This instrument forbade slavery, prohibited membership in secret societies, and precluded any change "except by the request of two-thirds of the whole society."[22]

Separations

Evangelicals, with only a few congregations south of the Mason and Dixon line were ardently abolitionist during Civil War days. With more congregations in the South, the slavery issue posed a knotty problem for the United Brethren. In 1821 slavery had been prohibited,[23] but in 1837 church rules were made subject to the laws of the individual states. To combat the abolitionism of *The Religious Telescope*, W. M. K. Cain began to publish *The Virginia Telescope*. In the Auglaize Conference there was a small circle of clergy who were opposed to slavery and also opposed to the passions of abolitionism. Led by A. Schindeldecker these withdrew to form the "Reformed United Brethren Church." In 1864 these seceders joined with seceders from the Methodist Protestant, Methodist Episcopal and Presbyterian churches to form "The Christian Union."[24]

Controversies, particularly about membership in secret societies, continued to plague the United Brethren. The Evangelicals in 1847 narrowly avoided authorizing a rule forbidding participation in secret societies to members of the church. The Constitution of the United Brethren, 1841, expressly forbade such membership. But as there appeared a disposition to relax this prohibitory law, the controversy left the peripheral matter of membership in secret societies to confront the constitution. Was the constitution alterable? If so, how? Passions rose, inspired by inflammatory literature and oratory. Despite opposition in 1885 general conference directed a Church Commission to prepare amended forms of the Confession of Faith and Constitution and to submit these to the membership of the denomination in a referendum. When the general conference in 1889 confronted the vote which overwhelmingly approved the changes, it adopted the altered Confession and Constitution. Thereupon the minority, which is known as "The Church of the United Brethren in Christ (Old Constitution)" effected its independent organization.[25]

Simultaneously, strife had entered the Evangelical ranks. It broke into the open at the general conference of 1887 and for the ensuing four years there was a slow disintegration of the ecclesiastical organization. In 1891 separate general conferences were held and in 1894 the minority organized as "The United Evangelical Church."

Union

Within ten years of the division, the first unofficial gestures looking toward the reunion of the "sons of Albright" were apparent. In 1911 the officially appointed commissioners of both Evangelical churches began their arduous work on a basis of union. On October 14, 1922 the union of the two Evangelical churches was consummated and "The Evangelical Church" came into being. To the regret of the united church, a group of the former United Evangelical Church determined not to join in the union. This minority continues its independent existence as "The Evangelical Congregational Church."[26]

The overseas outreach of the Evangelical United Brethren Church is primarily the fruit of endeavors by United Brethren of Evangelicals before the union. The story of missionary efforts begins with the Evangelical missionary foundation in Germany in 1850. Following this one which has spread into Switzerland and France came the United Brethren foundation in Sierra Leone. Missionaries of both churches went to Japan and China; the United Brethren went to Puerto Rico and the Philippines; the Evangelicals to Nigeria; the United Brethren joined others in Equador in an Indian mission. A new venture in central Brazil has been undertaken since the union.[27]

Evangelicals and United Brethren in their prejudice against formal education were faithful to the frontier environment which enveloped them.[28] The appearance of the Sunday School

—among the United Brethren in 1820 and among the Evangelicals in 1832—did much to prepare both groups for the acceptance and support of educational institutions. In 1845 general conference opened the way, and two years later, Otterbein College, the first of the United Brethren schools was launched. In addition to the college named, the Evangelical United Brethren Church supports Shenandoah College, Dayton, Virginia; Albright and Lebanon Valley colleges, in Reading and Annville, Pennsylvania, respectively; Indiana Central College, Indianapolis, Indiana; North Central College, Naperville, Illinois; Westmar College, LeMars, Iowa; and York College, York, Nebraska. The prejudice against theological training was formidable, but it too was overcome and the Evangelical United Brethren Church supports three accredited theological schools in the United States: Bonebrake Theological Seminary, Dayton, Ohio; Evangelical Theological Seminary, Naperville, Illinois; and Evangelical School of Theology, Reading, Pennsylvania.

Both churches established and maintained benevolent institutions. The first of such was the Flat Rock Orphans Home which Evangelicals established soon after the Civil War. Homes for children and/or the aged are currently maintained at Philadelphia, Lewisburg and Quincy, Pennsylvania; Lebanon, Ohio; New Carlisle, Indiana; Cedar Falls, Iowa; and not far from Los Angeles there are two homes.

Evangelical United Brethren

The executive offices of the denomination are located in Dayton, Ohio. Bishops are elected for the whole church, but each is assigned to one of the seven episcopal areas. Apart from the Sunday School literature, denominational programs are publicized in two publications, *The Religious-Telescope* and *Builders,* the latter a weekly for youth. At the time of the union in 1946 there were fifty-one annual conferences in North America. Consolidations of conferences, however, have reduced the number of North American conferences to thirty-nine and these report 3,526 ordained elders; 4,443 organized congregations; 730,123 members; who last year contributed $4,649,828 for missionary and benevolent purposes, and a grand total of $25,905,701 for all purposes.

Polity

There is one order of ministry in this communion. Advancement to the order of elder comes after the prospective minister has been recommended by a Local Conference, licensed by an Annual Conference and has successfully passed the stated requirements in professional training.[29] The ordinand must be voted advancement to the Order of Elder by the Annual Conference and take the vows prescribed in the Discipline. Inasmuch as the ministerial calling be the work of God, not of ecclesiastical making, this church in its ordination simply recognizes and publishes what God has done. The ministry is not made by the rite of ordination: ordination simply proclaims what God has already declared in the heart of the ordained.

There are bishops in the Evangelical United Brethren Church, but the episcopacy has been so modified that really the government of the church is more presbyterian than episcopal. Bishops are simply elders of the church who have been elected by general conference for a term of four years to supervise and administer the church. They are agents of supervision, entrusted with administrative power, not priestly, and only for a given period of time. They act for and by the authority of general conference implementing the program which has been determined by that body.[30]

The church is governed by its *people in council;* that is, representatives or the membership of the church govern the church. This is done through three kinds of conferences. In each station or circuit there is a Local Conference (formerly Quarterly Conference)[31] composed of elected officers of the congregation and its auxiliaries, together with the preacher and the Conference Superintendent. Among the duties of this

Conference is the election of a lay delegate to the Annual Conference.

The Annual Conference[32] consists of all ordained and licensed ministers belonging to the Conference and one lay delegate from each charge of the conference. A bishop presides at this conference: the remaining officers are elected by the ballot of the conference. Laymen and ministers sit side by side during the annual conference with equal rights and privileges except in the election of the ministry where the laity is not entitled to vote. The bishop and superintendent or superintendents constitute the Stationing Committee which appoints the preachers of the conference annually to their congregations.

The highest tribunal in the church is the General Conference[33] which meets quadrennially. This body, too, is composed of an equal number of preachers and laymen, chosen by their respective conferences on a proportionate basis. At this meeting the bishops and general officers of the denomination are elected for a term of four years.

To meet emergency situations and other circumstances, Councils of Administration,[34] have been provided on the congregational, conference and denominational levels. The promotional functions of the Councils, especially on the conference and denominational levels, are very important.

Theological Positions

Though the Evangelical and United Brethren churches arose in a day when there was little sense of Church among Protestant Christians, these two groups in the nineteenth century gave evidence of the ecumenical spirit. Both repeatedly considered the wisdom of church unions. Moreover, both were charter members of all the major cooperative enterprises, particularly those in the areas of missions and church federation.

The formal statement of faith of the Evangelical United Brethren Church consists of the two distinct affirmations which each fellowship brought into the union in 1946. The

XIII Articles of Section I[35] were those adopted by the United Brethren general conference in 1889, which in turn are an alteration in form but not in substance of the first published Confession, presumably drafted by Newcomer and Grosh.[36] The kinship of this to the Heidelberg Catechism has been noted. On the other hand, the XIX Articles[37] of Section II are of Evangelical background. These were the Articles which the general conference in 1839 declared must not be changed. Before that conference there had been more Articles; in fact, the first Discipline (1809) contained twenty-six. Of these twenty-five were intimately related to the Methodist Articles of Faith, and one, On the Last Judgment, was reminiscent of the Augsburg Confession. Of course, Methodism's Articles stem from the Anglican XXXIX Articles and they in turn are dependent upon the XLII Articles drafted in the days of King Edward VI by Englishmen and Continentals. The Evangelical United Brethren Church proclaims no theological novelties. The Evangelical United Brethren Church is a thoroughly Protestant Church with a faith that is rooted in Christ and His message which was newly discovered in the sixteenth century by the Reformers.

The Evangelical United Brethren Church is a part of the broad body of Evangelical Protestantism, affirming the supreme authority of Scripture, the power of the Spirit to lead any man to an understanding of God's Word, the sanctity of all of life and salvation by faith in Jesus Christ. While men of diverse theological traditions were instrumental in molding these churches—men of Reformed, Mennonite and Lutheran extraction—the dominant influence of Methodism is attested by the Arminian tone of its theology.

It would be misleading to even imply that the Evangelical United Brethren Church in her past or today is extraordinarily theologically minded. With the exception of some controversy over human depravity and sanctification in the nineteenth century, there has been no theological strife. The schisms which both groups suffered involved no decisive theological issues.

Consistently the emphasis has been upon religious experience and practical rather than speculative religion. Men are implored to make the discovery that the Lord was not only their Maker, but what is more important, their Savior. Every man is invited in a wholly new and unrepeatable way for himself to return his own answer to the divine Word and Son. Any man through Christ can know health, wholeness, holiness— (these words have a common source)—as he comes into right relationships with God, with men, and with God's order of things.

NOTES

[1] D. DORCHESTER, *Christianity in the United States* (Cincinnati, 1888), p. 324.

[2] A. L. DRUMMOND, *Story of American Protestantism* (Boston, 1950), pp. 161ff. W. W. SWEET, *Story of Religions in America* (New York, 1930), pp. 322ff.

[3] D. DORCHESTER, *op. cit.*, p. 750.

[4] W. W. SWEET, *Revivalism in America* (New York, 1945), p. 117.

[5] C. H. MAXON, *Great Awakening in the Middle Colonies* (Chicago, 1920), pp. 11ff.

[6] C. CLEVELAND, *The Great Revival in the West* (Chicago, 1910), p. 87.

[7] A. W. DRURY, *Life of Philip W. Otterbein* (Dayton, Ohio, 1884), p. 138.

[8] R. W. ALBRIGHT, *History of the Evangelical Church* (Harrisburg, Pa., 1942),p. 43.

[9] J. WACH, *Sociology of Religion* (Chicago, 1945), p. 27ff.

[10] A. W. DRURY, *Minutes of the Annual and General Conferences, 1800-1812* (Dayton, 1897).

[11] R. YEAKEL, *History of the Evangelical Association* (Cleveland, Ohio, 1894), p. 52.

[12] Quoted by H. A. THOMPSON, *Our Bishops* (Chicago, 1899), p. 132.

[13] A. W. DRURY, *History of the Church of the United Brethren in Christ* (Dayton, Ohio, 1924), pp. 281, 315.

[14] W. W. ORWIG, *History of the Evangelical Association* (Cleveland, 1858), p. 58.

[15] J. B. McMASTER, *History of the People of the U. S.* (New York, 1917), Vol. II, pp. 152, 577, 578.

[16] A. W. DRURY (*History*), *op. cit.*, p. 373.

[17] W. W. ORWIG, *op. cit.*, p. 153.

[18] H. G. SPAYTH, *A History of the Church of the United Brethren in Christ* (Circleville, Ohio, 1951), p. 182.

[19] W. W. ORWIG, *op. cit.*, p. 153.

[20] P. H. ELLER, *History of Evangelical Missions* (Harrisburg, Pa., 1942), p. 15ff.

[21] Quoted by DRURY (*History*), *op. cit.*, p. 411.

[22] *Ibid.*, p. 411.

[23] *Ibid.*, p. 337.

[24] *Religious Bodies:* 1936, Vol. II, Part I (Washington, 1941), p. 366.

25 *Ibid.,* Vol. II, Part ii, p. 1635.
26 *Ibid.,* Vol. II, Part i, p. 630.
27 P. H. ELLER, *These Evangelical United Brethren* (Dayton, Ohio, 1950), p. 77.
28 *Ibid.,* p. 92ff.
29 *The Discipline of the Evangelical United Brethren Church* (1947 edition), pp. 331-361, pp. 114-120.
30 *Ibid.,* pp. 426-442, pp. 132-137.
31 *Ibid.,* pp. 92-111, pp. 65-70.
32 *Ibid.,* pp. 120-179, pp. 70-83.
33 *Ibid.,* pp. 201-236, pp. 83-91.
34 *Ibid.,* p. 656.
35 *Ibid.,* p. 41.
36 A. W. DRURY (*History*), *op. cit.,* p. 282.
37 *Discipline,* etc., p. 44.

BIBLIOGRAPHY

R. M. ALBRIGHT, *History of the Evangelical Church* (Harrisburg, 1942).
D. BERGER, *History of the Church of the United Brethren in Christ* (Dayton, 1897).
S. C. BREYFOGEL, *Landmarks of the Evangelical Association* (Reading, 1888).
A. W. DRURY, *The Life of Philip William Otterbein* (Dayton, 1895).
————, *Disciplines of the Church of the United Brethren in Christ* (Dayton, 1895).
————, *History of the Church of the United Brethren in Christ* (Dayton, 1924, revised, 1931).
P. H. ELLER, *History of the Evangelical Missions* (Harrisburg, 1942).
————, *These Evangelical United Brethren* (Dayton, 1950).
P. KOONTZ and W. ROUSH, *The Bishops. Church of the United Brethren in Christ,* Volumes I and II (Dayton, 1950).
J. LAWRENCE, *The History of the Church of the United Brethren in Christ* (Dayton, 1860).
C. NEWCOMER, *The Life and Journal* (Hagerstown, 1834).
W. W. ORWIG, *History of the Evangelical Association* (Cleveland, 1858).
H. G. SPAYTH, *History of the Church of United Brethren in Christ* (Circleville, 1851).
E. H. SPONSELLOR, *Crusade for Education* (Frederick, Maryland, 1950).
S. P. SPRENG, *Seybert* (Cleveland, 1888).
A. STAPLETON, *Evangelical Annals* (Harrisburg, 1900).
H. A. THOMPSON, *Our Bishops* (Chicago, 1889).
R. YEAKEL, *History of the Evangelical Association,* Volumes I and II (Cleveland, 1894).
————, *Albright and His Co-Laborers* (Cleveland, 1883).
Discipline of the Evangelical United Brethren Church (1947 edition).

XIX

SEVENTH-DAY ADVENTISTS

XIX

SEVENTH-DAY ADVENTISTS

LeRoy Edwin Froom

I. Historical and Modern Beginnings

THE ADVENT hope has been the cherished possession of the
Christian church throughout the centuries. But during the early
decades of the nineteenth century a profound conviction of its
imminence developed simultaneously and spontaneously among
pious scholars in practically all religious bodies in the different
countries of Christendom. Hundreds, in both Old World and
New, gave voice to the belief that, according to the prophetic
portions of the Bible, mankind had entered the closing period
of earth's history. That time they designated as the "last days,"
the "time of the end," or "end of the age," according to Scripture phrasings. The second coming of Christ was widely believed to be drawing near, and the long anticipated millennial
age approaching. The development of numerous Bible societies, foreign and home missionary societies, tract societies and
Sunday school unions, temperance and other reform movements, all tended to substantiate that belief.[1]

In Great Britain some 300 clergymen of the established
Church of England, were heralding this belief in the 1820's
and '30's, and more than twice that number of non-conformist
ministers were teaching the same concept. On the European
continent it permeated the various Protestant bodies, and was
especially marked among the Pietists. In the Old World the
development was well called the Great Second Advent Awakening of the nineteenth century. It was principally an intra-
denominational emphasis, fostered by individuals, but not assuming the form of an integrated movement.[2]

In America, however, in the early 1840's, this same emphasis appeared in more pronounced form, and developed into an extensive Second Advent Movement. Likewise manifesting itself at first as an inter-church, or more accurately an interchurch development, and stressed by scores of leading clergymen of the various Protestant faiths—Presbyterian, Congregationalist, Baptist, Lutheran, Reformed, Episcopalian, Christian, and Disciple—over here it took on, in time, the dimensions of a distinctive movement, just as the Wesleyan and Disciples groups finally emerged into distinct denominations.

William Miller, licensed Baptist minister of Low Hampton, New York, was the recognized leader of this American movement, some 200 clergymen and 500 public lecturers joining him, and between 50,000 and 100,000 identifing themselves as Second Adventists around 1843-44. Some contemporaries, such as the Hartford *Universalist,* alluded to 1,000,000 adherents.[3] So conspicuous was the evangelizing vigor of this movement that the terms "Millerite," and "Millerism" became household words, with the movement under constant discussion in the public press.[4] Miller believed that the second advent would occur "about the year 1843," or more specifically, between "March 21, 1843 and March 21, 1844." After the passing of this time, the date was revised by Miller's associates to October 22, 1844.

This time aspect, in both Old World and New, rested primarily on a widely supported interpretation of the 2300 year-days of Daniel 8:13, 14, which predicts the cleansing of the "sanctuary," at the close of this long period. This was at first understood by Miller to involve the cleansing of the earth by fire, just as the antediluvian world was cleansed by water— and this cleansing by fire constituting the "end of the world."

Miller contended that the basic rules of prophetic interpretation which he followed were in full agreement with the exposition of hundreds of learned divines of various faiths in preceding centuries, as well as of contemporary times. And scores of scholars, prior to Miller's first book in 1836, had pointed to 1843, 1844, or 1847, as a crucial date.[5] Even Miller's most determined theological opponents generally conceded this, many agreeing that Bible prophecy had marked out the 1840's for some important prophetic event, or fulfillment, but insisting that it was a moral regeneration or reformation, involving world conversion instead of physical conflagration and cataclysm, that was destined to take place.

Times were tense, and distortion was common. And most of the fanciful stories circulated at that time regarding alleged donning of "ascension robes" by the Millerites, and concerning widespread insanity, suicide, and murder resulting from their perfervid preaching, have become a persistent part of American folklore—but without factual foundation.[6]

II. *Formation of the Church and Its Polity*

When the Lord did not descend from heaven to raise the righteous dead and translate the righteous living on October 22, 1844, the loose-knit movement broke up after the great disappointment. Some repudiated their former positions entirely, and returned to the churches from which tens of thousands had withdrawn before the time of expectation. A rather large group banded themselves together, however, at Albany, New York, in May, 1845, to continue the general heralding of the Advent teaching. Some of this group set the time of the advent in terms of definite future dates; others lapsed into indefinite waiting, holding that no Bible prophecy had actually been fulfilled on October 22, 1844.

Another though very much smaller group, largely in New England, held that the historical and prophetic evidence which led them to fix upon October 22, 1844, as the date of the precise ending of the 2300-year prophetic period of Daniel 8:14, was unimpeachable. They believed that the mistake lay in misunderstanding the event that was to take place,[7] and held that the inspired prediction really indicated a work of final investigative judgment in the sanctuary in heaven, to begin shortly before the second advent. Prominent in this latter group, sponsoring this interpretation, were Hiram Edson, Joseph Bates, James White, Ellen Harmon (soon becoming Mrs. James White, on August 30, 1846), Frederick Wheeler, and S. W. Rhodes. And, along with the acceptance of this position, they and others soon began the observance of the seventh day as the Sabbath, which they had in turn received from the Seventh Day Baptists. Captain Bates, who had been prominent among the Millerites, took the lead in promulgating this view through a tract he wrote in 1846.[8]

Shortly after the Disappointment, Hiram Edson and O. R. L. Crosier, of Port Gibson and Canandaigua, New York, introduced the position that, according to the Old Testament sanctuary service type, there were two phases to the earthly high priest's ministry, and that there are similarly two phases to Christ's antitypical High Priestly ministry in heaven. They held that Christ had entered upon the first phase of His ministry at His ascension, and in line with the long prophecy of Daniel 8:14, that He had entered upon the second and final phase on October 22, 1844. At the close of this final ministry for mankind, man's probation would end and Christ would soon return to resurrect the righteous dead and translate the righteous living. This view came to be generally accepted by the Sabbatarian group.[9]

Added to the distinctive teachings on the Sabbath and the sanctuary, was a third, a belief that the gift of the Spirit of prophecy was manifest in the person and writings of Ellen G. White. But they maintained that these writings do not in any way supersede or add to the canon of Scripture, which the Adventist considered complete and closed. Ellen White always and only called herself a "messenger," commissioned to convey messages of comfort, guidance, and reproof, her mission being to confirm positions of truth and to expose error, and ever to draw men back to the Bible as the sole rule of faith and practice.

A nucleus had begun the observance of the seventh day Sabbath at Washington, New Hampshire; the sanctuary position was being promulgated from Canandaigua, New York; and spiritual gifts, with emphasis upon the Spirit of prophecy, were being stressed from Portland, Maine. Soon all three features were blended in a slowly emerging church movement. In 1848 and 1849 a series of Sabbath conferences was held that reaffirmed the distinctive doctrines that were beginning to set them apart as a separate religious group. Here they crystalized their views into a harmonious body of teaching. At the outset the growth of this group was inevitably slow, first, because of the general derision in which all Adventists were held, as a result of the mistake concerning the prophetic event to take place in 1844, and because of the fictitious and malicious stories of fanaticism circulated concerning them; and, second, because of the economic and social handicap inherent in the observance of the seventh day as the Sabbath. But, though slow, their growth was sure.

In 1849 they began publication of their first paper, which was succeeded in 1850, by *The Advent Review and Sabbath Herald,* which ever since has continued to be their official church paper. Other periodicals followed. In 1855 a headquarters was established in Battle Creek, Michigan, which marked their expansion beyond the borders of New England. Their publishing house at Battle Creek, became, for nearly half a century, the center of their activities. Meantime, at a conference in Battle Creek in September, 1860, the name "Seventh-day Adventist" was officially adopted, and in May, 1863, a formal denominational organization was established, with a constituency of 125 churches and 3,500 members. In 1874 their first missionary, John N. Andrews, was sent abroad.

From 1855 to 1901 there was gradual but steady growth in membership, institutions, and foreign missions. Then a turning point was reached. At the General Conference session of 1901, steps were taken to co-ordinate the various phases of church work and to set up a well integrated organization throughout the world. Strong departments were established to foster the various phases of church activities and interests. A new impetus was also given to foreign mission endeavor, which began to expand rapidly into every section of the globe. Then, in 1903, the general headquarters was moved to Washington, D. C., and further expansion followed.

In their world mission work, all missionary appointees are selected, sent out, and sustained by the General Conference, not by local churches or local mission boards. Admission to church membership is through baptism by immersion; hence no infants or small children are included in their membership figures at home or abroad. The standards for membership are high, as to manner of life, including complete abstinence from liquor and tobacco.

Their membership in North America, in 1951, was 250,939, and in other lands, 505,205, or a total of 756,712 baptised members.[10] The organization embraces 10,237 local churches (and 16,694 Sabbath Schools with 952,229 pupils) grouped in 370 local conferences—these forming 80 union conferences, operating under 11 divisional organizations and these in turn making up the general or world conference, with its headquarters at Takoma Park, Washington, D. C.

Seventh-day Adventists do not regard themselves as simply one more church body in the world, but as a prophetic movement having the everlasting gospel to proclaim in what they believe to be the setting of "the hour of God's judgment." They conceive their mission to be to help to prepare men for the second advent of Christ. This explains their evangelistic zeal, displayed in both Christian and heathen lands, and the large per capita contributions by their members for the support of this world program. They are now operating in 193 countries out of the 230 listed in the *World Almanac* and *Statesman's Yearbook,* employing 197 printed languages and working orally in 517 additional languages and dialects—or a total of 714—with a force of 17,959 evangelistic workers, and 38,927 workers in all categories.[11] As a body they practice tithing, in addition to freewill offerings, for the support of the church. In 1950 these totalled $45,908,057 ($27,728,250 in tithe, and

$18,179,807 in offerings) for the work of the church—$150.87 per capita in North America for 1950.[12]

In church polity they follow a highly representative form of church government. Sessions of their General Conference, constituted of delegates chosen on a membership basis from the various component parts of the organization throughout the world are held quadrennially. Responsibility for all interim business is vested in a large Executive Committee. The active administration of affairs in the different Division organizations is conducted by the divisional committees, acting under the General Conference. The divisions, in turn, are comprised of union conferences. And these, again, are made up of local conferences—the smallest executive units in the system.

Each administrative unit has officers and an executive committee, and each exercises a large degree of autonomy in its operation. The local congregations select their own lay elders, deacons, and various other officers to perform the functions usually assigned to such officers in Protestant churches. But all regular pastoral supervision of churches and districts is provided from the local conference headquarters, which pays all ministers and other gospel workers from a central fund.[13]

III. Epitome of Beliefs and Practices

Seventh-day Adventists have no formally adopted creed. The simple Statement of Faith, appearing annually in their *Yearbook*,[14] is based, they believe, wholly on the Bible. As noted, they believe that mankind is now living in the predicted hour of God's judgment, and that full preparation for Christ's return is the supreme message due mankind today. They feel they have been raised up to help to give that special message to the world, at this time. As their name implies, two distinctive points of their faith are: 1) Belief in the imminent, personal, visible, and pre-millennial return of Jesus Christ to redeem His followers; and 2) the observance of the seventh day as the Sabbath in obedience to the changeless obligation of the moral law and the express example of Christ. But in and through their entire system of belief, Christ is ever exalted as the Center and Circumference of man's faith, hope, and salvation.

Seventh-day Adventists belong to the conservative evangelical wing of Protestantism. In fact, they are usually regarded as ultra-conservative, both in doctrine and standards of living. They take the Bible, both Old and New Testaments, as their sole rule of faith and practice. They believe in one God, revealed as Father, Son, and Holy Spirit, each equally and uniquely divine, personal, and eternal. They hold to a fiat creation, and reject the evolutionary theory of the development of the earth or man. They believe in the fall of man, and his redemption solely by grace through Christ.

They believe in Jesus Christ's virgin birth and sinless life, His vicarious atoning death, His literal resurrection and ascension, and thenceforth His heavenly ministry as Great High Priest in heaven above—with His second advent as near at hand, but at a time not disclosed. They believe that personal salvation includes regeneration, justification, sanctification, and final glorification. And they believe that works follow as the natural and inevitable result of salvation.

In harmony with the classical positions set forth in the great historic creeds of Protestantism, they regard the ten commandments as the moral standard for all men in all ages. They understand the "seventh day" of the fourth commandment to require keeping holy the seventh day of the week. They believe in the payment of tithe, or a tenth of their "increase," for the support of the ministry. They believe in the gift of prophecy in the church, along with other gifts of the Spirit. They believe in the mortality of man, and his unconscious state in death; and in the resurrection of the body at the last day, with immortality bestowed then on the righteous, with ultimate destruction by fire for the wicked.

They believe in religious liberty and the complete separation of church and state. They take most literally the Biblical declaration that the body is the "temple of the Holy Ghost," and believe this requires abstinence from intoxicating drinks, tobacco, and other injurious foods and substances. They believe the great prophetic outlines are nearing their consummation, with a cataclysmic end of the age impending. They are pre-millennialists, believing the millennium will follow the return of Christ and the resurrection of the righteous, with the resurrection and destruction of the wicked at its close. They believe that the saints will be with Christ in heaven during the thousand years, with Satan and his legions confined to this desolated earth during that period. They believe that a new earth, created from the ruins of the old, will be the eternal abode of the redeemed, with all traces of sin removed forever.

They practice the ordinance of feet washing as preparatory to the Lord's supper. They practice simplicity of life and stress modesty of dress and deportment. They are patriotic non-combatants, or "conscientious co-operators," and conduct strong medical cadet training in their colleges, training for life-saving service for their country, having had 12,000 medical cadet corpsmen in World War II.

IV. Bible Prophecy Given Unique Place

Seventh-day Adventists hold that the second coming of Christ has ever been the hope of the Christian church in the days of its greatest purity—in the early church before the great Latin departure, and in the evangelical church of Reformation and post-Reformation times. It brings the gleam of hope, not the gloom of despair. It has ever inspired and nerved the church for its conflicts and its triumphs. The Adventists contend that they are not pessimists, as some assert, but are genuine optimists. They hold forth the second Advent as the sole hope of a distraught world. In a time when mankind has become fearful of its very survival because of atomic developments, they have a calm and sustaining belief in coming deliverance.

And Bible prophecy, they hold, has always been tied in with the second Advent hope. Where one is found the other is bound to be, as they are inseparable. They hold that these prophecies reveal God's plan of the ages and disclose where we are in God's great timetable of the centuries. They hold that the primary purpose of prophecy is to set forth the great redemptive acts of God, and to disclose the provisions of full redemption through the two advents of Christ. The first advent came through the incarnation, with Christ born as a babe in Bethlehem, growing to manhood without sin, and dying as a vicarious, atoning Sacrifice on the cross to provide an all-sufficient atonement for man's sin. Then, after His resurrection and ascension, and ministering His redemptive blood for us before the Father in heaven, He will at last come back to earth the second time, in power and glory, "without sin unto salvation." That, they believe, to be the goal of the ages and the glorious climax of the plan of redemption.

Between these two advents, the conflicts of the church, involving assaults from without and within, are the major subjects of Bible prophecy. The vicissitudes of the church are, in prophecy, given in the setting of the course of empire and the march of nations, as well as the upsurge of the great Roman apostasy in the church and the Mohammedan scourge that plagued Europe through the medieval centuries. Then comes the final revival and triumph of truth at the climax of earth's history.

Seventh-day Adventists hold that this is all disclosed in the prophecies of Daniel in the Old Testament, and in the complementing Revelation of the Apostle John in the New Testament. They refuse to consider themselves just another sect or cult, or simply another in the maze of denominations, but rather are in the line of those dissentients of the centuries who have ever upheld apostolic truth in contradistinction to apostasy and error. They hold that they are the continuation of the line of the Waldenses, Wycliffites, Hussites, Reformers, Baptists, and Wesleyans, who have been raised up at various times to revive neglected and forsaken truths, and to enunciate special truth whose time for emphasis had come.

They hold that the arrested Reformation is to be completed before the second advent of Christ, to prepare a people to meet their returning Lord. This, they believe, calls for a repudiation of all innovations and departures introduced through apostasy during the centuries, particularly those brought in by the great Latin departure, and for a revival and restoration of apostolic faith and practice. They maintain that the principles and applications of prophetic interpretation which they stress are not some new discovery, belatedly made by Adventists, but are instead a recovery of what was held in the full vigor and purity of the early church and in Protestant Reformation times —not an invention, but a retention of what others had let slip; not an innovation, but rather a continuation.

They consequently belong to the historical school of prophetic interpretation, believing that the great prophetic outlines are nearing their climax, with the second advent and the cataclysmic end of the age impending. They stand apart from most Protestants in this belief, contending that Modernists have now generally accepted the Preterist theories of Alcazar, Spanish Jesuit of 1600, who thrust the fulfillment of prophecy largely back into the early centuries. On the other hand, Fundamentalists now largely follow the Futurist thesis of Ribera, another Spanish Jesuit of appproximately the same date. The projection of these two counter-interpretations of the counter-Reformation, they maintain, has unwittingly led Protestantism to abandon its historic platform on prophecy. Consequently, they consider that they have simply recovered and retained what all early Protestantism once held. Their Advent Source Collection, on the exposition of prophecy is the largest extant.[15]

V. Multiple Interests and Activities

Seventh-day Adventists are an intensely missionary people, with 1,522 foreign missionaries in 1950, now operating overseas in 193 foreign countries. Their mission budget for 1951 was $17,060,650. They carry their work forward through efficiently organized departments—Sabbath School, Young People's, Educational, Ministerial, Medical, Home Missionary, Religious Liberty, Temperance, and Radio, and by numerous commissions and bureaus, such as the Bureau of Press Relations, and the War Service Commission.[16]

They believe in Christian education to the extent of operating a separate denominational school system, with 4,155 church schools and 283 academies and colleges. These utilize the services of 8,273 teachers and care for 202,677 students.[17] They also conduct two accredited graduate schools—the Seventh-day Adventist Theological Seminary, in Washington, D.C., and their medical school, the College of Medical Evangelists in California. They also have a Home Study Institute for correspondence home study.

Seventh-day Adventists stress healthful living, holding that the physical definitely affects the spiritual, and that the laws of nature are likewise the laws of God. This has resulted in a well-defined position regarding the healthful care of the body, based upon sound medical and scientific foundations. This tenet of their faith is promoted through health publications, such as the nationally known *Life and Health* magazine, and by the chain of sanitariums, hospitals, and clinics found in all the principal countries of the world.

These sanitariums seek to educate in sound principles of healthful living, and stress rational therapeutics—physiotherapy, physical medicine, and nutritional therapy. Their first medical institution was the famous Battle Creek Sanitarium founded in 1866. In 1950 they operated 106 sanitariums and hospitals, with a total bed capacity of 10,725, in addition to 57 dispensaries and clinics—with 8,206 medical workers, including student nurses. These are comprised of 376 doctors, 2,381 nurses, and 6,974 others. These groups treat nearly 2,000,000 in-patients and out-patients annually, and through charity help a half-million more.[18] They conduct 26 nurses' training schools.

Adventists stress practical religion. Their welfare organization distributed 1,481 tons of clothing and 1,732 tons of food for post-war Europe and Asia in 1946-49.

In their extensive publishing work—including doctrinal, devotional, expositional, health, home, educational, youth, and related books, together with the issuance of 317 periodicals —they operate 33 publishing houses with printing facilities, which are located in the principal countries of the world, with six in North America, including the Christian Record, of Nebraska, which issues books and periodicals in Braille for the blind. The total retail value of books and periodicals published and sold in North America, in 1950, was $8,374,147, with the total world sales for the same period, in practically 200 languages, coming to $12,602,589.[19] They have over 4,500 colporteurs devoting their lives to the distribution of gospel and health literature.

The Adventist radio work is world-encircling, with 862 broadcasts each week, utilizing some 665 stations in North America, and 196 more in foreign countries. Their internationally known world radio program (The Voice of Prophecy) is now going out over 696 stations, in 11 languages and 18 countries, with television programs from New York and California outlets. Their Bible Correspondence schools have approximately one and a half million enrollments in 45 languages. This all calls for an annual budget of almost $2,000,000.

Such are the multiple activities and interests of the Seventh-day Adventist church, with their world headquarters in America, at the nation's capital.

VI. Five Lesser Advent Bodies

Disappointment and confusion reigned, in Adventist circles, when the second advent failed to materialize in 1844. As noted, several groups eventuated. In addition to the Seventh-day Adventist Church, just surveyed, and which is now by far the largest, there were five other lesser groups that emerged. These were:

1. *The Advent Christian Church,* a branch of the original body led by Jonathan Cummings in New England and first known as the American Millennial Association, which held to the main teachings of Miller but challenged the concept of the heavenly sanctuary, the state of the dead, and the date of the advent—holding that an error of ten years had been made, and setting 1853-54 as the time. By 1860 the Advent Christian Church was organized, believing in the imminence of the advent, the unconscious state of the dead, and baptism by immersion. It is congregational in government, each church being completely independent. In 1950 there were 33,063 members in 423 churches.[20]

2. *The Church of God* (Oregon, Illinois), grew out of a merger of six small independent Adventist groups, joining in 1888. Holding to much of the Advent faith, and observing the first day as the Sabbath, they hold that Christ will set up His Messianic Kingdom at Jerusalem and from there rule over all peoples. The ancient favor of God will be restored to the Jews, and the saints be given special positions of honor, while the wicked suffer the second death. Their churches are independent units, but grouped into congresses. There is no formal ordination of ministers. They have a training school and a publishing house, with 5,295 members in 79 churches. Their General Conference was not organized until 1921.[21]

3. *The Church of God* (Abrahamic Faith), lays much stress on their name, and believe in the nearness of the second advent, and the establishment of Christ's kingdom on earth. They teach that man is mortal and sleeps in death until the resurrection and judgment, that the wicked will be destroyed, and the righteous raised to live forever on the earth. They have about 4,000 affiliated members in 78 churches.

4. *Life and Advent Union,* organized by John T. Walsh, who, in 1848, maintained there would be no resurrection of the wicked. A group of those sharing his views was organized in Massachusetts under this name in 1863. Adventist in some beliefs, they observe the first day as the Sabbath and deny there

will be a millennium, holding that the only thousand years of Revelation 20:2 is in the past. Peace and happiness await the second advent, when the righteous will live forever, on a purified earth, and the wicked will sleep on forever, having no resurrection. There are only 313 members in four churches.

5. *Primitive Advent Christian Church,* a recent development from the Advent Christian Church, which lists 593 members in 14 churches, living mostly in rural West Virginia.

NOTES

1 LeRoy E. Froom, *The Prophetic Faith of Our Fathers,* Vol. III, Part II, and Vol. IV, Part I, where full documentation and the source readings are found.

2 *Ibid.,* Vol. III, Part II.

3 *The Universalist,* August 22, 1842 (Vol. 3, No. 52), p. 416; *The Proceedings of the American Antiquarian Society* (1872), p. 45, puts it at 200,-000; John Bach McMasters, *A History of the People of the United States,* Vol. 7, p. 136, also gives 1,000,000 as the claimed number of adherents.

4 Froom, *op. cit.,* Vol. IV, Parts I and II.

5 Froom, *op. cit.,* Vol. IV, Part I, where the documented sources are given.

6 Francis D. Nichol, *The Midnight Cry,* chapters 25-27—a comprehensive and fully documented investigation; Joshua V. Himes, *The Outlook,* Nov. 24, 1894, p. 875; Jane Marsh Parker, "A Little Millerite," *Century* Magazine, Dec., 1886, p. 316.

7 Froom, *op. cit.,* Vol. IV, Part II; Arthur W. Spalding, *Captains of the Host,* chapters 6-8; Everett N. Dick, *Dictionary of American Biography,* Vol. XII, art. "Miller, William."

8 Joseph Bates, *The Seventh Day a Perpetual Sign* (1846).

9 Froom, *op. cit.,* Vol. IV, Part III; Joseph Bates, *Way Marks and High Heaps* (1847).

10 E. J. Johanson, *Eighty-eighth Annual Statistical Report of Seventh-day Adventists* (1950), pp. 2, 18, 19, 32.

11 *Ibid.,* pp. 18, 19.

12 *Ibid.,* p. 2.

13 *See Constitution, By-Laws, and Working Policy* (1949); *Yearbook* (1951), pp. 7-13.

14 *Yearbook of the Seventh-day Adventist Denomination* (1950), pp. 5-7; *Church Manual* (1951), pp. 29-36.

15 Housed in Seventh-day Adventist Theological Seminary, Washington, D. C.

16 Complete portrayal provided in current Seventh-day Adventist *Yearbook.*

17 *Eighty-eighth Annual Statistical Report,* pp. 19, 23, 26.

18 *Ibid.,* pp. 24, 25.

19 *Ibid.,* p. 26. All 197 languages listed in the 1950 *Eighty-eighth Annual Statistical Report.*

20 George F. Ketcham, *Yearbook of the Churches* (1951 ed.), pp. 21ff.

21 On these five Adventist bodies, in addition to the *Yearbook of the Churches* (1951), *see* also Frank S. Mead, *Handbook of Denominations in the States* (1951), pp. 17-19.

BIBLIOGRAPHY

JOSEPH BATES, *The Sabbath a Perpetual Sign* (New Bedford, 1846).

———, *Second Advent Way Marks and High Heaps* (New Bedford, 1847).

SYLVESTER BLISS, *Memoirs of William Miller* (Boston, 1853).

Constitution, By-Laws, and Working Policy of the General Conference of Seventh-day Adventists (1949).

Church Manual [Seventh-day Adventist], (Washington, 1942).

EVERETT N. DICK, *Founders of the Message* (Washington, 1938).

———, "William Miller", article in the *Dictionary of National Biography*, Vol. XII.

Eighty-eighth Annual Statistical Report of Seventh-day Adventists (Washington, 1951).

First Report of the General Conference of Christians Expecting the Advent (Boston, 1840).

LEROY EDWIN FROOM, *The Prophetic Faith of Our Fathers*, 4 vols. (Washington, 1946-1952).

ALBERT E. JOHNSON, *Advent Christian History* (Boston, 1918).

JOHN N. LOUGHBOROUGH, *The Great Second Advent Movement* (Washington, 1905).

JOHN BACH MCMASTERS, *A History of the People of the United States*, Vol. 7 (New York, 1910).

FRANK S. MEAD, *Handbook of Denominations in the United States* (Nashville, 1951).

WILLIAM MILLER, *Evidence From Scripture and History of the Second Coming of Christ, About the Year 1843* (Troy, 1836).

———, *Apology and Defence* (Boston, 1845).

OLIVER MONTGOMERY, *Principles of Church Organization and Administration* (Washington, 1842).

FRANCIS D. NICHOL, *The Midnight Cry* (Washington, 1945).

———, *Mrs. E. G. White and Her Critics* (Washington, 1951).

M. ELLSWORTH OLSON, *A History of the Origin and Progress of Seventh-day Adventists* (Washington, 1925).

Second Advent Library, 8 vols. (Boston, 1842-1844).

ARTHUR W. SPALDING, *Footprints of the Pioneers* (Washington, 1947).

———, *Captains of the Host* (Washington, 1949).

———, *The Last Legion* (Washington, 1949).

United States Bureau of the Census, 2 vols. (Washington, 1941).

ISAAC C. WELLCOME, *History of the Second Advent Message and Mission* (Yarmouth, 1874).

JAMES WHITE, *Life Incidents* (Battle Creek, 1868).

———, *Sketches of the Christian Life and Public Labors of William Miller* (Battle Creek, 1875).

Year Book of American Churches (Lebanon, 1951).

Year Book of the Seventh-day Adventist Denomination (Washington, 1951).

PERIODICALS

The Advent Shield and Review, Vol. I (Boston, 1844-1845).

Century Magazine (New York, 1886).

The Midnight Cry, Vols. 1-7 (New York, 1842-1844).

The Outlook (New York, 1894).

The Signs of the Times and Advent Herald, Vols. 1-8 (Boston, 1840-1849).

The Universalist, Vol. 3 (Hartford, 1842).

XX

DISCIPLES OF CHRIST

XX

DISCIPLES OF CHRIST

Ronald E. Osborn

THE DISCIPLES of Christ are a predominantly American communion, non-creedal[1] but biblical in doctrine, congregational in polity, historically committed to the dual goals of Christian unity and the restoration of the simple Christianity of the New Testament.[2] Because of their devotion to these goals, and because in their life as a people they have sought to fulfill the conditions for attaining them, Disciples have not liked to think of themselves as a denomination, nor yet as a church. They prefer to speak of "the brotherhood," or "our communion," or, less frequently, "our movement."

Locally their congregations are known as Christian Churches or Churches of Christ, generally being designated numerically (First, Second, Third) or geographically (Central, Main Street, University Place). Officers chosen within a church are elders and deacons (sometimes deaconesses also), who manage the affairs, subject to the approval of the congregation itself on important matters.[3] The minister, according to a common tradition, is regarded as one of the elders, though in some areas there has been recognition of his special office as minister, or pastor, in biblical terms. In current practice he is the spiritual and administrative leader of the church, yet in theory he is but a member of the congregation with no sacramental powers. Worship is free, centering in the "ordinance" of communion, which is observed every first day of the week, with elders presiding at the Lord's table. Also observed as an ordinance is believer's baptism by immersion.

Disciples cherish a historic bias against "theology," their attitude being set forth in three familiar slogans: 1) "Where the Scriptures speak, we speak; where the scriptures are silent, we are silent;" 2) "In faith unity, in opinions liberty,[4] in all things charity;" 3) "No creed but Christ, no book but the Bible, no law but love, no name but the divine." Profession of faith is in terms of Peter's confession in Matthew 16:16, and is regarded as a rational act, of which the natural man is capable in response to the preaching of the Gospel; yet faith is no merely intellective process, but a volitional act as well, the personal commitment of the convert's life in love to the Person of Christ as Saviour and Lord. Empowering this free movement has been a sense of mission—the plea for the reunion of the divided church upon a "simple New Testament basis."

World membership of the Disciples totals 1,913,192, of whom 1,776,490 are in the United States.[5] Their strength in this country is most heavily concentrated in the states of Indiana, Missouri, Illinois, Ohio, Kentucky, and Texas. There are 7,844 congregations in the United States and Canada. The largest number of baptisms in any one year of the past decade was 59,350 in 1947.

Strictly speaking, the European backgrounds are backgrounds only.[6] Similar restoration efforts, with variations in detail, are to be seen in the labors of John Wycliffe, of the Anabaptists, of Ulrich Zwingli, of English Independents and Baptists, and especially of various small British groups in the late eighteenth century. Most important in direct contribution of ideas or personalities to the Disciples were the small movement led by John Glas and his son-in-law Robert Sandeman in Scotland, the revivalism of the Haldane brothers (Robert and James Alexander), and the work of the Scotch Baptists. These groups, especially the latter three, gave little thought to the problem of Christian union; their concern was apostolic purity, conceived in literal and legalistic terms.

Some voices in Europe had, of course, spoken out for toleration among Christians and for the reunion of the churches. Notable among these were Rupertus Meldenius (who coined the slogan about essentials and non-essentials, or opinions, which later proved so popular with the Disciples), Hugo Grotius, Edward Stillingfleet, and John Locke (to whom Alexander Campbell, like Thomas Jefferson, was considerably indebted).[7] But none of these had launched a religious movement.

In the new nation of the United States two groups arose which were to touch the life of the Disciples and then go a different way. One of these was the "O'Kelly secession" from the Methodist Church in 1792, which protested the new and autocratic episcopal polity inaugurated by Francis Asbury. The associates of James O'Kelly in Virginia and North Carolina first called themselves Republican Methodists, but in 1794 they adopted the scriptural name of Christians.[8] Just after the turn of the century two New England Baptists, Elias Smith and Abner Jones, rebelled against the Calvinist theology and began to organize "Christian" churches, having as yet no connection with the O'Kelly Christians. In 1808 Smith established the *Herald of Gospel Liberty,* one of the first religious journals in America.[9]

A third "Christian" movement, arising in Kentucky and associated with Barton W. Stone, was to unite with the Disciples in 1832.[10] Stone was the Presbyterian minister at Cane Ridge, in Bourbon County, where the largest and most spectacular meeting in the Great Western Revival took place in 1801. Baptists, Methodists, and Presbyterians joined together in the preaching, and the fervor of the converted expressed itself in such so-called "exercises" as the "barks" and the "jerks." Charges of heresy against two of the "revival men" brought about their withdrawal from the synod of Kentucky. Along with them went three of their associates, including Stone, to establish the Springfield Presbytery. But in June, 1804, they determined to drop their denominational name and be known as Christians, writing in the whimsical *Last Will and Testament of the Springfield Presbytery,* "We *will,* that this body die, be dissolved, and sink into union with the Body of Christ at large."[11]

The Kentucky Christians multiplied rapidly in the West, a democratic and non-creedal people, anti-Calvinist in doctrine, congregational in polity, fervently evangelistic, taking "the Bible as the only sure guide," and holding to the "principle of love to Christians of every name." In course of time they came to the practice of baptism by immersion, though it was not made a requirement in the case of persons previously baptized by another mode. Contacts were established with the Christians in Virginia and North Carolina, and with those in New England, and there gradually developed among the three groups a sense of belonging to a common movement. In 1826 Stone began to publish the monthly *Christian Messenger.*

Meanwhile Thomas Campbell, an Old Light Anti-Burgher Seceder Presbyterian minister had come from Ireland to western Pennsylvania in 1807.[12] In the Old Country he had tried unsuccessfully to unite the various parties among the Seceders. Now in America he refused to "fence the table" at a "sacramental celebration," (he disregarded the particular creedal requirements of his denomination at a communion service) conducted in a frontier community. His orthodoxy was immediately suspected, and charges were brought against him in his presbytery. The most damaging (and most accurate) of these accused him of denying the necessity of a mystical or emotional assurance of salvation, of saying that there is no divine warrant for holding creeds as terms of communion, and of encouraging his parishioners to hear preachers of other denominations.

Campbell withdrew from the presbytery, but continued to preach on his own. About him he gathered a company of persons from various denominations who constituted the Christian Association of Washington (Pennsylvania). For this association he drew up in 1809 his famous *Declaration and Address,* affirming,

THAT the church of Christ upon earth is essentially, intentionally, and constitutionally one; consisting of all those in every place that profess their faith in Christ and obedience to him in all things according to the scriptures, and that manifest the same by their tempers and conduct.

The *Address* further held that
nothing ought to be inculcated upon Christians as articles of faith; nor required of them as terms of communion; but what is expressly taught and enjoined upon them, in the word of God.

The slogan, "Where the Scriptures speak . . ." was thus early taken seriously as a principle.

In the same year Campbell's twenty-one-year-old son Alexander came to America.[13] While studying at Glasgow, the young man had, under Haldanean influences, thought his way out of Seceder Presbyterianism. His concern had become the reformation of the church in accordance with the primitive pattern. Thus his position was similar to that of his father, though with no explicit concern yet for Christian unity. He soon began to preach and before long took over the leadership of the movement. In 1811 the adherents of the Campbells organized the Brush Run Church (in Washington County, Pennsylvania), and in the following year, as a result of their biblical studies, they were immersed. In 1813 the congregation was admitted to the Redstone Baptist Association without subscribing to the Philadelphia Confession of Faith.

Young Alexander Campbell now had a larger field in which to work. As a preacher he soon won a wide reputation, though the sharp distinction he drew between the covenants in his famous Sermon on the Law (1816) caused orthodox Baptists to regard him with suspicion.[14] As a debater he won greater acclaim among his new brethren, defending immersion against the Presbyterians, John Walker (1820) and W. L. Maccalla (1823), and Christian theism against the celebrated infidel,

Robert Owen (1829).[15] As an editor he circulated his views through the monthly *Christian Baptist,* which he began to publish in 1823. It gave him his best opportunity to promote this "new reformation," and he wrote vigorously against creeds, clergy, and modern church organizations (missionary societies, Sunday schools, and the like) as unscriptural. He found it advisable in time to transfer to the Mahoning Baptist Association in Ohio, where his outlook was more acceptable.

In 1827 the Mahoning Association employed Campbell's friend Walter Scott as evangelist.[16] Searching out the normal process of conversion in the New Testament, Scott reduced it to five "steps"—faith (rational acceptance of testimony), repentance, baptism, remission of sins, and gift of the Holy Spirit. These constituted his famous "five-finger exercise," preached with eloquence, logic, proof-texts, a great concern for the lost, and a genuine belief that the "ancient Gospel," lost for centuries, had now at last been restored. In a matter of months Scott won literally thousands of converts and swamped the association with new Reformers.

In August, 1830, at the annual meeting it was unanimously voted "that the Mahoning Association, as an advisory council, or an ecclesiastical tribunal, should cease to exist."[17] This date is generally taken for convenience as marking the beginnings of the Disciples as a distinct people. Actually, a process of separation by withdrawal, expulsion, or dissolution of Baptist associations had already begun, and it continued for some time. The followers of Campbell and Scott were variously known as Reformers, Reforming Baptists, New Testament Baptists, and Disciples of Christ, with the latter name predominating. Their congregations called themselves by biblical names, generally Churches of Christ.

Meanwhile in Kentucky the Christians associated with Barton W. Stone had come to know Campbell and his adherents and to feel a strong sense of common purpose with them. Stone advocated union between the two movements, but Campbell was not enthusiastic. Nevertheless, on January 1, 1832, a large company made up of both groups met in Lexington, Kentucky. The Christians and the Disciples present gave each other the right hand of fellowship, partook of communion together on the next Lord's Day, and sent out a minister from each of the former connections to commend the union to the churches. Within the next few years, by congregational action, the merger was cemented. While nearly all of the western Christians thus joined forces with the Disciples, the two eastern bodies by the former name did not do so. They retained a separate denominational existence until their merger with the Congregationalists in 1930.

The Christians came into the union approximately 10,000 strong; while the Reformers contributed from 12,000 to 20,000 erstwhile Baptists. Throughout the nineteenth century with its phenomenal westward migration the Disciples grew apace. Though they failed to make any appreciable impact upon New England or the cities of the Atlantic seaboard, they regarded their amazing growth upon the frontier as a divine demonstration of the validity of their plea. By 1860 their membership stood at almost 200,000; by 1900 it had reached 1,120,000.[18]

Walter Scott's "five-finger exercise" proved an evangelistic technique as successful as it was simple. Hundreds of zealous preachers who farmed, taught school, or engaged in business during the week and made known "the whole counsel of God" on the Lord's Day won thousands of converts by this formula. It was an age of revivalism, and the frontiersman who distrusted anything complicated or esoteric warmed to the Disciples' denunciation of theology, their attack upon creeds, and their exaltation of the simple doctrines of the New Testament. The assumptions of Jacksonian democracy, self-evident to the westerner, unconsciously found religious expression in the congregational life and the teachings of this American religious movement.

Alexander Campbell exercised a powerful leadership in the movement for a generation after the merger with the Christians. Among this free and congregational people he held no post of authority, either ecclesiastic or dogmatic. Their only authority was the New Testament. And if they read it through Campbell's eyes, they steadfastly refused to be dubbed Campbellites. They would wear only a biblical name and would be called after no man. Yet he was the symbol of the movement and formulated the classic expressions of its position.[19]

In 1830 Campbell had ceased publication of the *Christian Baptist* in favor of his new monthly, the *Millennial Harbinger*.[20] Decidedly not a premillennialist, he hopefully looked forward to a messianic age, a new social order of peace and blessedness, which would come after a purified and united church had proclaimed the ancient Gospel to the whole world. Hence the name of his journal and his concept of his mission. His approach in the *Harbinger* became more constructive than it had been in the earlier paper. His task now was to give guidance to an independent movement. He reversed some former opinions and joined other Disciples in advocating cooperative organization for missionary purposes. When the American Christian Missionary Society was established in 1849 he accepted its presidency, in which position he actively served till his death in 1866. He encouraged the formation of state missionary societies to evangelize, plant new churches, and provide guidance and aid to churches already in existence. He gave active leadership to the work of these societies.

Campbell was tireless as a preacher, publisher, and educator. He debated Bishop Purcell on Roman Catholicism in 1837 and N. L. Rice on baptism in 1843.[21] He published *The Christian System* in 1836, not as a creed, but as a methodical presentation of the principles advocated by his movement. He founded Bethany College in 1840 and served as president for more than 20 years. Although he released his own slaves, he held that slavery was not forbidden by the letter of the New Testament and thus averted a schism among Disciples in the days of sectional controversy. In the *Harbinger* he answered countless questions on all sorts of issues to the general satisfaction of the brotherhood. He published a new and scholarly translation of the New Testament in the common speech.[22]

The failing health and death of Campbell ushered the Disciples into a crucial period. The Civil War, the assassination of Lincoln, and the bitterness of reconstruction had created an atmosphere of dissension and frustration. Tensions had arisen within the movement: its uncritical assumptions about restoring the ancient order lent themselves to conflicting interpretations, and Campbell's own about-face on the matter of missionary organization and his general change in attitude had confused the picture. His son-in-law and chosen successor as editor of the *Harbinger* and president of Bethany College, W. K. Pendleton, was a man of character and ability, but he never exercised Campbell's leadership.[23]

The controversies of this era arose from basic differences in conceptions of the movement. On the one hand stood those who held that its foremost mission was the restoration of the ancient order, that in its early days it had actually achieved such a restoration, that recent "innovations" were unscriptural and consequently sinful.[24] With great ardor various persons of this persuasion opposed some or all of the new developments, such as missionary societies, the use of musical instruments or of choirs in worship, the setting up of Sunday schools, the admission of unimmersed persons (members of paedobaptist denominations) to the communion table, the employment of fulltime resident pastors, the acquiescence of some ministers in being designated as "Reverend." To these brethren the silence of the Scriptures on any matter meant its prohibition. On the other hand stood leaders (including Pendleton) who held such a view of restoration to be narrow and legalistic, who regarded the silence of the Scriptures as leaving a matter open to the wisdom of the churches, who spoke of the innovations as legitimate "expedients." Generally, this latter group had a keener sensitivity to developments in the religious world outside the brotherhood. But the cultural isolation of the movement during the latter half of the nineteenth century accentu-

ated the controversies. The two Campbells had studied at
the University of Glasgow, Scott at the University of Edinburgh, and Stone at David Caldwell's Academy in North Carolina. To the extent that the leaders in the generation after
the Civil War enjoyed a formal education, it had been received exclusively in most cases in the schools of the Disciples.

The disaffection over innovations increased until lines began
to be drawn. Those who opposed musical instruments and
societies as unscriptural could not conscientiously offer fellowship to persons who used them. Decisions on these matters
were taken by congregations, and by 1906 (at the request of
the "conservatives") the Federal religious census recognized
the existence of two distinct groups—Churches of Christ (con-
struing the New Testament strictly) and Disciples of Christ.
The separation has continued to the present, with the two
groups drawing farther apart as each has followed out the
logic of its position.[25]

Meanwhile those developments went on which have come
to characterize the Disciples as they are today. After disap-
pointments in the three fields which the American Christian
Missionary Society had entered (Palestine,[26] Jamaica, Liberia)
and after much controversy and experiment, an effective program of missionary organization was worked out.[27] In 1874
the Christian Woman's Board of Missions was organized and
soon had hundreds of auxiliaries within local congregations,
and the following year the Foreign Christian Missionary Society was formed. Within a relatively short time these boards
entered Jamaica, India, Japan, China, Mexico, Belgian Congo,
Puerto Rico, the Philippines, Tibet, Argentina, and Paraguay,
while the A.C.M.S. and the C.W.B.M. carried on aggressive
evangelism in the American West. The foremost statesman of
the missionary advance was Archibald McLean, who began to
serve the Foreign Society in 1882 and continued till the time
of his death in 1920. He helped establish the legitimacy of
societies in the mind of the Disciples. But more important, he
became their apostle of missions and did much to win them

from a midwestern provincialism to world-mindedness. He personally took part in the selection and sending of the scores of missionaries who went out under the Foreign Society. Though an administrator he was a favorite convention preacher, a biblical expositor, and a leading author, who helped to form the mind of the Disciples.[28]

In 1920 the three boards mentioned merged their interests and functions with certain other organizations to become the United Christian Missionary Society. Its tasks include home and foreign missions, Christian education, social action, church development, and evangelism. Among other national agencies are the Board of Church Extension, the Board of Higher Education, the Pension Fund, the National (Negro) Christian Missionary Convention,[29] the Association for the Promotion of Christian Unity (all, like the U.C.M.S., in Indianapolis), the National Benevolent Association and the Christian Board of Publication (both in St. Louis), the Disciples of Christ Historical Society (in Nashville), as well as others.[30] These boards all report to the International (United States and Canada) Convention of Disciples of Christ, a constitutional mass meeting with a delegated Committee on Recommendations, a continuing Board of Directors, and an administrative staff with offices in Indianapolis. The convention meets annually and acts in an advisory capacity to the churches and the reporting agencies. Throughout the nation there are state (or regional) missionary societies and state (or regional) conventions, which are also service agencies.

A World Convention of Churches of Christ (Disciples) has met in 1930 (Washington, D. C.), 1935 (Leicester, England), 1947 (Buffalo, N. Y.), and is scheduled for 1952 (Melbourne, Australia). Churches are reported in 41 nations outside the United States. Major strength is in the Belgian Congo (75,973), Australia (30,011), Great Britain (9,811), Canada (8,196), Philippine Islands (6,810), Puerto Rico (5,461), and New Zealand (4,345).

In the United States itself, as has already been suggested,

the strength of the Disciples is in the midwest. Their major boards are in Indianapolis and St. Louis. Their most influential journals have been published in Cincinnati, St. Louis, Nashville, and Chicago. All of their seminaries are in the Mississippi valley. Their lone president of the United States was James A. Garfield, once a preacher and educator in Ohio. Their best poets were men of Illinois (Vachel Lindsay and Thomas Curtis Clark) and of the far West (Edwin Markham[31]). Their most popular novelist, Harold Bell Wright, was a midwesterner. Their greatest preachers[32] have graced inland pulpits—Alexander Procter, George Hamilton Combs, Raphael H. Miller, and Burris Jenkins (all in Kansas City), C. M. Chilton (St. Joseph, Missouri), A. W. Fortune (Lexington, Kentucky), E. L. Powell (Louisville), Z. T. Sweeney (Columbus, Indiana), Roger T. Nooe (Nashville), Hugh McLellan (San Antonio), and Edgar DeWitt Jones (Detroit); the outstanding exceptions are Peter Ainslie (Baltimore), Finis Idleman (New York), and Frederick W. Burnham (Richmond, Virginia). Charles Reign Scoville held his largest evangelistic meetings in the west, and Kirby Page wrote of pacifism and of prayer from the Pacific coast. Their most brilliant galaxy of scholars was in Chicago—Herbert L. Willett, Edward Scribner Ames, Winfred Ernest Garrison, Charles Clayton Morrison, William Clayton Bower.

With their peculiar looseness of organization, Disciples have developed a sense of cohesion largely through their journals. Literally hundreds of editors have sent forth their papers, of which more than a dozen have been genuinely influential. Campbell set the pattern with his *Christian Baptist* and *Millennial Harbinger* and Scott with his *Evangelist* and *Protestant Unionist*. In the controversial period after the death of Campbell two new weekly publications guided the majority of the brotherhood in the direction it has since followed. First in importance was the *Christian Standard,* founded in 1866 with Isaac Errett as editor.[33] He was a man of broad sympathies, progressive outlook, and cultured mind, who justified the "expedients," was a foremost leader in the Foreign Christian Missionary Society, and steered his generation of Disciples away from the path of legalism taken by the Churches of Christ. The other was *The Christian-Evangelist,* edited by J. H. Garrison, who likewise championed missionary societies and instrumental music. His long editorial career extended well into the twentieth century, when new issues arose. Garrison advocated federation (councils of churches) and opened his columns to leaders in the new biblical scholarship, notably to Herbert L. Willett. In 1909 Garrison's publishing interests were bought out, and the Christian Board of Publication was set up as a "brotherhood publishing house." Under these new auspices *The Christian-Evangelist* continued its established policies and speaks in behalf of the cooperative agencies of the Disciples. This development accentuated a tendency already apparent on the part of the *Christian Standard* after the death of Isaac Errett to assume more and more the role of critic. It is still published by private interests in Cincinnati.

The most influential journalistic advocates of those views which prevailed among the Churches of Christ were the *Gospel Advocate* edited by David Lipscomb and Tolbert Fanning, the *American Christian Review* published by Benjamin Franklin, and the *Christian Leader* issued by John F. Rowe. The first two of these still circulate among members of the Churches of Christ. Of these editors, David Lipscomb was by all odds the most influential upon his own and subsequent generations. He was an earnest farmer-editor who sought to put the law of God as he read it in the New Testament above the opinions and inventions of men and who wrote with persuasive power.

One journal edited by Disciples has become a leading voice in American Christianity, with about one-fourth of the Protestant ministers of the nation on its list of subscribers. Begun in 1884 as the *Christian Oracle,* it was later named the *Christian Century.* Espousing liberal views on all brotherhood issues, it entered its most aggressive period after Charles Clayton Morrison assumed control in 1908, and about ten years later began to designate itself "An Undenominational Journal of Religion." Since that time noted journalists who were not Disciples have been added to its staff, and its only peculiar connection with the communion of its origin has been through its long-time editor and his associates, Herbert L. Willett, O. F. Jordan, W. E. Garrison, Thomas Curtis Clark, and Harold E. Fey. The present editor is a Methodist.

Almost a year before the United Christian Missionary Society was created, the interests of the magazines previously issued by the uniting boards and by other general agencies were merged in a new monthly publication, *World Call*.[34] With a vigorous promotional program carried on through local missionary organizations and with a succession of able editors, this magazine has gained a circulation of more than 60,000 and become an influence for world-mindedness and the ecumenical point of view.

Next to their journalists, their educators have probably done most to shape the opinions of the Disciples. Their first school, Bacon College, named in honor of Francis Bacon, opened at Georgetown, Kentucky, in 1836, with Walter Scott as president, and by a devious line of succession continues as Transylvania College in Lexington. By far the most influential center in the nineteenth century was Bethany College, founded in 1840 by Campbell himself, which produced a host of leaders for pulpit and pew and which educated nearly all the teachers in the later schools of the brotherhood until those schools were old enough to begin adding their own graduates to their faculties. One weakness of higher education among the Disciples, particularly in the training of ministers, has been this tendency to academic inbreeding. Various liberal arts colleges served their immediate area and the brotherhood at large through educating preachers and leaders.

Graduate study for ministers was uncommon before 1890, and even today most of the fulltime preachers are men without a Bachelor of Divinity degree. But young men have been going to the seminaries in increasing numbers for a generation.

The oldest of them is the College of the Bible in Lexington, Kentucky, with a lineage running back to 1865, though it did not become an institution of graduate rank until 1914. Its best-known professor in its first half-century was John W. McGarvey, teacher and, after a time, president from its founding until his death in 1911.[35] A diligent student of the English Bible, McGarvey presented his understanding of biblical doctrines with dogmatic clarity, compelling logic, and mechanical precision. His *New Commentary on Acts* remains a basic textbook among conservative Disciples to the present day. He was best known to the brotherhood through his column on "Biblical Criticism" in the *Christian Standard,* which stoutly defended the traditional assumptions. A. W. Fortune, W. C. Bower, and E. E. Snoddy,[36] who came to the faculty shortly after McGarvey's death, represented a new generation of scholars who had received advanced degrees in universities outside the brotherhood.

Four other seminaries are operated under auspices of the Disciples: the School of Religion of Butler University, the College of the Bible of Drake University, the Graduate Seminary of the College of the Bible of Phillips University, and Brite College of the Bible of Texas Christian University. All of these are approved by the American Association of Theological Schools, and members of their faculties hold degrees from various universities in America and Europe. In addition, the Disciples Divinity House at the University of Chicago and the Disciples Divinity House at Vanderbilt University offer work in connection with larger seminary faculties. No seminary of the Disciples offers a doctor's degree in course. More and more ministers have been doing work toward B. D., Ph. D., or Th. D. degrees in such schools as Yale, Chicago, Union, Harvard, Hartford, Duke, and Pacific School of Religion.

Thus in the twentieth century the Disciples have emerged from that cultural isolation which surrounded them in the nineteenth century and which was in large measure a product of the sectarianism which they had arisen to protest. They have felt and been a part of the major religious movements of the times.

Their historic interest in Christian unity has been to many Disciples an incentive to participate actively in the ecumenical movement. They were in the Federal Council of Churches from the beginning and provided one president of that body, Edgar DeWitt Jones. Peter Ainslie of Baltimore was one of the pioneer spirits in the early conferences on Faith and Order;[37] in 1911 he founded the *Christian Union Quarterly,* which Charles Clayton Morrison continued as *Christendom* after 1935. In 1948 it yielded to the new *Ecumenical Review* under the auspices of the World Council of Churches. Disciples have shared in the various activities of the World Council, in which their International Convention is a participating member.[38] They have contributed in a large way to the staffs of various national, state, and local councils.[39] Their Association for the Promotion of Christian Unity has given active support to all such movements and has inaugurated the annual Peter Ainslie Memorial Lecture on Christian Unity at Rhodes University in South Africa. A bequest from one of their businessmen maintains the annual William Henry Hoover Memorial Lectureship on Christian Unity under the direction of the Disciples Divinity House at the University of Chicago. Twice since World War I the International Convention of Disciples of Christ has entered into negotiations with the Northern (now American) Baptist Convention, looking toward a merger. The International Convention was instrumental in the establishment of the Conference on Church Union and has been active in its deliberations seeking a way toward the uniting of eight or more denominations into a United Church of Christ.

With the passing of the era of personal journalism, with the development of numerous seminaries having sizeable and diverse faculties, with nearly a century and a half of experience, and with a world membership approaching two million, the day of dominant individual leaders would seem to be gone. Apparently there is no one today who is affecting the life of the whole brotherhood as profoundly as Errett, McLean, Lipscomb, McGarvey, or Ainslie, to say nothing of the "founding fathers." The emerging instrument of brotherhood policy is the International Convention in which the cooperative life of the Disciples centers. With a fulltime staff since 1946, the convention has been proving itself increasingly effective as an organ of opinion and action.

Various developments here mentioned, as well as others, have combined to produce a forceful reaction on the part of those who conceive of the brotherhood primarily as the "Restoration Movement" and cling to traditional patterns of life and thought. According to their point of view, the brotherhood is not a denomination, but is one with the Church which was founded on the day of Pentecost and is set forth in the New Testament. Consequently, to participate in councils of churches is out of the question, for to do so Disciples must accept denominational status and recognize the legitimacy of "other" denominations. Likewise merger is unthinkable except on the restoration basis, for the Disciples would be "leaving ultimate ground" to become a sect. (Such views, obviously, are similar to the general outlook of the Churches of Christ.) The restorationists[40] have been troubled by such policies of the United Christian Missionary Society as the adoption of comity agreements and participation in union theological seminaries on foreign fields. They have also been disturbed by "destructive criticism" and "liberalism" in the historic colleges and seminaries. The greatest objection of all is to the practice by many liberal churches of "open membership" (receiving by transfer and without the requirement of immersion persons who have been baptized by sprinkling or pouring in other communions). Ministers of open membership churches have been elected to the presidency of the International Convention.

In 1927 the restorationists organized the North American

Christian Convention as a platform for proclaiming the "old Jerusalem Gospel." Since this annual gathering is a preaching convention only and transacts no business, it has not become a means of schism except as it separates fellowship by providing a different focus. Many regional preaching rallies on the same order have been held. The restorationists have sent out many "independent" or "direct support" missionaries[41] and have been vigorous in recruiting large numbers for the ministry, especially through Christian Service Camps which they promote in lieu of, if not in competition with, the young people's conferences of the United Christian Missionary Society. They have shown equal energy in establishing Bible Colleges —33 by a recent count. Most of these are small, non-accredited, four-year schools concentrating on courses in Bible and pastoral methods, with a minimum of work in the liberal arts and sciences. The stated policy of most of them is to oppose the work of the agencies reporting to the International Convention and to deny that they themselves belong to the "Disciples of Christ denomination;" they belong to no sect, but only to Christ's Church. Except at the point of conversion, where they hold to the conceptions of Walter Scott, they are essentially fundamentalist in general religious outlook, and a few have set forth systematic statements of doctrine to which faculty members and trustees are required to subscribe. By and large, in the present century the *Christian Standard* has reflected the restorationist outlook and in recent years it has promoted the "loyal" colleges rather than the schools which belong to the Board of Higher Education. A policy of intense opposition to the agencies and their program is pursued by the *Restoration Herald*.[42]

An aversion to organization, a scattering of leadership among the "independents," and a general reluctance to force a division, have kept an overt schism from developing. In some of the colleges and seminaries persons of both viewpoints maintain an uneasy fellowship, and the situation is perhaps no more explosive, although perhaps no more hopeful, than it was twenty-five years ago. Increasingly, however, as each group goes its separate way and maintains its own institutions it has less and less fellowship with the other.

In 1934 the International Convention set up a Commission on Restudy of the Disciples of Christ. Made up of representative leaders of various shades of thought it was charged "to restudy the origin, history, slogans, methods, successes and failures of the movement . . . with the purpose of a more effective and more united program and a closer Christian fellowship among us." In 1946, after more than a score of meetings, the Commission presented the first of three annual reports. It analyzed the differences which have been "the chief causes of unrest in our brotherhood." The third report voiced a plea to "sink into oblivion the particularisms which divide us." The second report set forth a series of basic principles to which, it is agreed, "the great body of Disciples" hold:

1. The acknowledgment of Jesus Christ as Lord and Saviour is the sole affirmation of faith necessary to the fellowship of Christians.

2. The New Testament is the primary source of our knowledge concerning the will of God and the revelation of God in Christ, and is the authoritative Scripture by which the will of God is conveyed to men.

3. Each local church is, under Christ, a self-governing unit; . . . organizations and agencies are in no sense governing bodies but may be useful instruments in carrying on Christian work and in fostering and expressing fellowship. . . .

4. In the proclamation of the Gospel of Christ as the message of salvation to the affection and intelligence of men, we have found our largest unity. . . .

5. The unity of Christians according to the program and prayer of our Lord, with Christ himself the center of that unity, by the restoration of New Testament

Christianity, is necessary to the realization of God's program for human redemption.

6. Their historical position has given them practical insight into the New Testament fellowship which they desire to share with the whole divided body of Christ.[43]

A new commission which is now being constituted for the purpose of cultivating throughout the whole brotherhood a spirit of mutual respect and understanding is thus assured of a large ground of agreement as the basis for its work.

NOTES

[1] "Non-creedal" is here used in the sense of "having no formal statement of dogma." Disciples have contested for "freedom of opinion," and theology is regarded as opinion. Yet the slogan, "No creed but Christ," reveals both the nature and the object of faith. See note 4.

[2] Historically these dual goals have been intertwined in the thinking of the Disciples, sometimes so intimately related that some Disciples deny the existence of two goals. Yet the relationship between the two concepts has by no means been fixed in the thought of the movement. Some have seen restoration as the purpose, with unity as an incidental result. Others have seen unity as the goal with restoration as the means. Some have held that unity is the goal, that restoration has failed as a means, and that new means must be explored.

The doctrinal positions traditionally held by Disciples are systematically (but not authoritatively) set forth in ALEXANDER CAMPBELL, *The Christian System* (St. Louis, n. d.) and in ROBERT MILLIGAN, *The Scheme of Redemption* (St. Louis, 1888). A popular treatment by a layman is given in T. W. PHILLIPS, *The Church of Christ* (Cincinnati, 1915). Two series of lectures on New Testament doctrines of the church by contemporary scholars are STEPHEN J. ENGLAND, *The Apostolic Church* (Eugene, Oregon, 1947) and WILLIAM ROBINSON, *The Biblical Doctrine of the Church* (St. Louis, 1948). Two traditional discussions of the Disciples are B. A. ABBOTT, *The Disciples: An Interpretation* (St. Louis, 1924) and P. H. WELSHIMER, *Concerning the Disciples* (Cincinnati, 1935). Eight interpretations in the light of recent movements in the world church are PETER AINSLIE, *The Message of the Disciples for the Union of the Churches* (New York, 1913), WILLIAM ROBINSON, *What Churches of Christ Stand For* (Birmingham, England, 1926), DEAN E. WALKER, *Adventuring for Christian Unity* (Birmingham, England, 1935), EDWARD SCRIBNER AMES, *The Disciples of Christ* (Chicago, 1936), A. W. FORTUNE, *Adventuring with Disciple Pioneers* (St. Louis, 1942), STEPHEN J. ENGLAND, *We Disciples* (St. Louis, 1946), ROY C. SNODGRASS, *Trustees of Our Heritage* (Eugene, Oregon, 1948), and HOWARD E. SHORT, *Doctrine and Thought of the Disciples of Christ* (St. Louis, 1951).

[3] The older conception of the duties of church officers is set forth in M. M. DAVIS, *The Eldership* (Cincinnati, 1912). A recent study of church administration, presenting both principle and method, is O. L. SHELTON, *The Church Functioning Effectively* (St. Louis, 1946).

[4] The first two phrases of this slogan of Meldenius often appear with the

words, "essentials" and "non-essentials," but Disciples like to quote it as it is given here. To them, the events recorded in the New Testament about Christ and his saving acts are the facts on which faith rests; theological interpretations, even by church councils, are opinions. The facts are essentials; the opinions are non-essentials.

5 *Disciples of Christ, 1950 Year Book of International Convention* (Indianapolis, 1950), p. 753.

6 The most thorough history, with a good discussion of background, is W. E. GARRISON and A. T. DEGROOT, *The Disciples of Christ: A History* (St. Louis, 1948). An excellent account in brief compass is W. E. GARRISON, *An American Religious Movement: A Brief History of the Disciples of Christ* (St. Louis, 1945). For English and Scottish phases, *see* A. C. WATTERS, *A History of British Churches of Christ* (Indianapolis, 1948).

7 The earliest extensive discussion of the Lockian influence upon Campbell's thought was WINFRED ERNEST GARRISON, *The Theology of Alexander Campbell* (St. Louis, 1900). Some scholars (notably F. D. Kershner and Arthur Holmes) hold that Campbell was influenced by the Scottish "Common Sense" school of philosophy more significantly than by Locke.

8 The only biography of O'Kelly is W. B. MACCLENNY, *The Life of Rev. James O'Kelly and Early History of the Christian Church in the South* (Indianapolis: Religious Book Service, 1950).

9 *See* J. BARRETT, *The Centennial of Religious Journalism in America* (Dayton, 1908).

10 In his old age STONE wrote his memoirs, *The Biography of Elder Barton Warren Stone, Written by Himself* (Cincinnati, 1847). A recent biography is CHARLES C. WARE, *Barton Warren Stone, Pathfinder of Christian Union* (St. Louis, 1932). A good discussion of the Stone movement and of other important developments is in A. W. FORTUNE, *The Disciples in Kentucky* (Lexington: The Christian Churches in Kentucky, 1932).

11 The *Last Will and Testament* and the *Witnesses' Address* may be found in CHARLES ALEXANDER YOUNG, *Historical Documents Advocating Christian Union* (Chicago, 1904).

12 A useful biography of Campbell, giving careful attention to the minutes of the Presbyterian courts, is W. H. HANNA, *Thomas Campbell, Seceder and Christian Union Advocate* (Cincinnati, 1935). For the *Declaration and Address, see* YOUNG, *Historical Documents (op. cit.).*

13 The fundamental biography of Alexander Campbell, upon which all subsequent studies have perforce drawn, is the massive work by his admirer and co-laborer, ROBERT RICHARDSON, *Memoirs of Alexander Campbell,* 2 vols. (Philadelphia, 1868. Reprint, Cincinnati, 1947). A definitive biography of Campbell is forthcoming, the work of Miss Eva Jean Wrather of Nashville, Tennessee, after research and travel for more than a decade.

14 The Sermon on the Law may be found in YOUNG, *Historical Documents (op. cit.).*

15 *See* CAMPBELL-WALKER, *Infant Sprinkling, . . . the Substance of a Debate on Christian Baptism* (Steubenville, Ohio, 1820). CAMPBELL-MACCALLA, *A Public Debate on Christian Baptism* (London, 1842. Reprint, Kansas City, 1948). CAMPBELL-OWEN, *Debate on the Evidences of Christianity* (Bethany, Va.: A. Campbell, 1829. Reprint, Cincinnati, n. d. Reprint, St. Louis, 1906). For Campbell's later debates, *cf.* note 21. *See also* JESSE JAMES HALEY, *Debates That Made History* (St. Louis, 1920).

16 An older and uncritical biography of Scott by an associate and devoted

admirer is WILLIAM BAXTER, *The Life of Elder Walter Scott* (St. Louis, 1826). Briefer, but more nearly definitive and drawing upon sources not used by Baxter, is DWIGHT E. STEVENSON, *Walter Scott: Voice of the Golden Oracle* (St. Louis, 1946). For the evangelist's own views *see* WALTER SCOTT, *The Gospel Restored* (Kansas City, 1949).

17 The resolution is thus quoted by GARRISON and DEGROOT, *op. cit.*, p. 192; the source is not cited.

18 GARRISON and DEGROOT, *op. cit.*, pp. 329, 410.

19 The mind of Alexander Campbell and the influences contributing to his thought were first explored by W. E. GARRISON, *The Theology of Alexander Campbell* (*op. cit.*). A more recent study is ROBERT FREDERICK WEST, *Alexander Campbell and Natural Religion* (New Haven, 1948).

20 The entire series of the *Millennial Harbinger* is now being re-issued in annual volumes by the Harbinger Book Club, Nashville, Tennessee.

21 *See* CAMPBELL-PURCELL, *Debate on the Roman Catholic Religion* (Cincinnati, 1837. Reprint, St. Louis, n. d.). CAMPBELL-RICE, *Debate on the Action, Subject, Design and Administrator of Christian Baptism* (Lexington, 1844. Facsimile edition, Cincinnati, 1917). The latter debate, while centering on baptism, actually involved a defense of the whole movement.

22 *The Sacred Writings of the Apostles and Evangelists of Jesus Christ, Commonly Styled the New Testament* (Buffalo, Brooke County, Virginia: Alexander Campbell, 1826. Reprint, Nashville, 1951). The work is familiarly known by the binder's title as *The Living Oracles*. For a discussion of this translation, *see* P. MARION SIMMS, *The Bible in America* (New York, 1936). *See* also EDGAR J. GOODSPEED, *Problems of New Testament Translation* (Chicago,1945).

23 *See* F. D. POWER, *The Life of William Kimbrough Pendleton* (St. Louis, 1903).

24 For a discussion from the standpoint of the "Churches of Christ" which draws heavily upon sources only slightly treated by most historians of the Disciples, *see* EARL WEST, *The Search for the Ancient Order*, 2 vols. (Nashville: Gospel Advocate Company, 1949). *See* also West's article on the Churches of Christ appearing elsewhere in this volume. For a historical analysis of the factors in the separation, *see* ALFRED THOMAS DEGROOT, *The Grounds of Division among Disciples of Christ* (Chicago: privately printed, 1940).

25 No historian of the movement has adequately examined the role of sectionalism in this schism. To begin with, the vast preponderance of churches opposing the innovations was in the defeated South; while several of the most prominent leaders of the "progressives" had served in the Union army. Can the root of some of the bitterness be found here? Lipscomb was a pacifist and believed that Garfield had lowered himself when he gave up preaching for politics and for a commission in the Union army. Again, the way in which the leaders of the Churches of Christ interpreted the New Testament is strikingly similar to the manner in which John C. Calhoun and other southern leaders strictly construed the Constitution of the United States. Perhaps a parallel may be seen between the separatist stand taken by groups or congregations opposing the innovations, and the doctrine of nullification. To the extent that these suggestions may be proved valid, the Disciples, like other major American communions of the time, suffered a sectional division.

26 DAVID STAATS BURNET (comp.), *The Jerusalem Mission* (Cincinnati, 1853. Reprint on microcards, Canton, Missouri: Disciples of Christ Historical Society, 1951).

27 For this period a useful account is given in W. T. MOORE, *A Comprehensive History of the Disciples of Christ* (New York, 1909). *See* also IDA WITHERS HARRISON, *History of the Christian Woman's Board of Missions, 1874-1919* (Lexington, Kentucky: privately printed, 1920), GRANT K. LEWIS, *A History of the American Christian Missionary Society* (St. Louis, 1937), and A. McLEAN, *A History of the Foreign Christian Missionary Society* (New York, 1919).

28 *See* W. R. WARREN, *The Life and Labors of Archibald McLean* (St. Louis, c. 1923). For typical exposition *see* A. McLEAN, *"Where the Book Speaks"* (New York, 1907).

29 Negro Disciples participate in the general International Convention and in the work of the various boards and agencies. Their own National Convention serves more particularly their (approximately) 50,000 members. The United Christian Missionary Society maintains two colleges for Negroes, Jarvis College at Hawkins, Texas, and Southern Christian Institute at Edwards, Mississippi.

30 The annual report of each of these boards appears in the current *Year Book of International Convention of Disciples of Christ* (*op. cit.*). A detailed study of the work of the agencies was reported in W. R. WARREN (ed.), *A Survey of Service* (St. Louis, 1928).

31 The mother of Edwin Markham was a member of the Christian Church in Oregon, and a poet. He was brought up among Disciples, being baptized at San José, California. He subsequently joined the Methodists and in later life became interested in Swedenborgianism.

32 The selection of preachers follows that made by EDGAR DEWITT JONES in a lecture, "Pulpit Princes of the Disciples of Christ," *Shane Quarterly* (School of Religion, Butler University, Indianapolis), October, 1951. The author of the present essay has taken the liberty of adding Dr. Jones' name to the list.

33 *See* J. S. LAMAR, *Memoirs of Isaac Errett*, 2 vols. (Cincinnati, 1893).

34 These magazines were *American Home Missionary* (1895-1918), *Business in Christianity* (1893-1918), *Christian Philanthropist* (1894-1918), *Missionary Intelligencer* (1887-1918), and *Missionary Tidings* (1883-1918).

35 For an account by a long-time associate who respected McGarvey but did not subscribe to his point of view, see W. C. MORROW, *"Brother McGarvey"* (St. Louis, 1940).

36 ALONZO WILLARD FORTUNE, *Thinking Things through with E. E. Snoddy* (St. Louis, 1940).

37 FINIS SCHUYLER IDLEMAN, *Peter Ainslie, Ambassador of Good Will* (Chicago, 1941).

38 For a statement on behalf of Disciples with reference to theological questions before the World Council, *see* W. E. GARRISON, "Response of the Disciples to Amsterdam," *Shane Quarterly*, October, 1950. This document was prepared as a representative expression rather than as a personal comment, and it had the approval of a significant group of leaders in the brotherhood.

39 Disciples have given significant leadership to the Federal Council of Churches (Jesse M. Bader), the International Council of Religious Education (Roy G. Ross), the Foreign Missions Conference (Emory Ross, M. Searle Bates), and to the continuing work of these agencies through the National Council of Churches; to the World Sunday School Association (Robert M. Hopkins); and to the World Council of Churches (Robert Tobias). (In fundamentalist circles, the journal of the National Association of Evangelicals, *United Evangelical Action,* is edited by a Disciple, James DeForest Murch.)

40 One reviewer has objected to the use of the term, "restorationists," as being invidious and misleading. No implications are intended in the use of the term other than to designate the persons holding the views described in these paragraphs. The term, "independents," often applied to them, is no more satisfactory, indicating a general tendency toward "direct support" missions and unwillingness to cooperate with the historic agencies. The term, "conservatives," is inaccurate, for many ardent supporters of the agencies and of ecumenical developments are also conservative in their theology. The term, "restorationists," comes conveniently to mind because of the fondness of those so denominated for the phrase, "the Restoration Movement," and for the slogan, "the restoration of primitive Christianity."

41 JAMES B. CARR, *The Foreign Missionary Work of the Christian Church* (privately printed, 1946) includes an account of many of these missionaries.

42 Founded September, 1925. (Published as *Facts*, January, 1922-August, 1925.) Published by the Christian Restoration Association, Cincinnati.

43 *Report of the Commission on Restudy of the Disciples of Christ* (Indianapolis: International Convention of Disciples of Christ, 1948).

BIBLIOGRAPHY

The Notes have been so written as to constitute a running biographical essay, indicating the most important titles as they bear upon the topics discussed. Two important bibliographical aids, both compiled by the curator of the Disciples of Christ Historical Society, should be mentioned here.

Furnishing a complete list of all known publications by persons belonging to the Disciples or Churches of Christ is CLAUDE E. SPENCER (comp.), *An Author Catalog of Disciples of Christ and Related Religious Groups* (Canton, Missouri: Disciples of Christ Historical Society, 1946).

A useful check-list of journals among the Disciples is found in CLAUDE E. SPENCER (comp.), *Periodicals of the Disciples of Christ and Related Religious Groups* (Canton, Missouri: Disciples of Christ Historical Society, 1943).

XXI

CHURCHES OF CHRIST

XXI

CHURCHES OF CHRIST

EARL WEST

HISTORICALLY, THE churches of Christ, claiming to be identified with the New Testament Church, and vigorously advocating a return to New Testament Christianity, have the same backgrounds as the "Disciples of Christ". Since 1906, when the federal census listed the two groups separately, each has gone its respective way following as consistently as possible those principles that have but tended to lead them farther apart. The story of these differences can best be told by an understanding of the historical processes that originated them.

As the morning of the nineteenth century dawned upon America, the rising sun saw a diversified religious panorama. Population centers were still spotted along the Atlantic seaboard, and the frontier stretched ominously down the Appalachian Mountains. Beyond were the far stretches of the west. By the beginning of the nineteenth century wagon trains and river boats were challenging the new area in ever increasing numbers. Log cabins were beginning to dot the hillsides as far west as the Mississippi, and here and there small forts were arising to offer but scant protection against the Indians.

This rugged frontier life offered the finest of soil into which to plant the seed of primitive Christianity. In times of hardship men turn to God, and the pioneer backwoodsman was no exception. He was in danger of cold, disease and constant attacks from the Indians. His work was painfully laborious, so from dawn till dark he worked, chopping trees, plowing his ground, making homespun clothing and preparing his food. He relied upon God, and read the Bible assiduously. On the cold winter nights around the fireplace, he read the "Good Book" to his children and impressed upon them the necessity of having faith in God. Schools were few but the pioneer taught his children to read, and the Bible was his textbook. The nineteenth century, perhaps more so than any other, came to be characterized as a Bible reading century. People who knew little else knew the Bible. Religion was the topic of conversation, and to be right with God was the sole ambition of a large host of people.

Yet the religious picture was somewhat complicated. The Methodist Church definitely had the vantage ground. The Revolutionary War had ended with the colonies regarding anything English definitely odious. However, the English Church was most popular in America before the Revolutionary War. The rebellion of the colonies against the political tyranny of England was hardly more determined than their rebellion against the religious. Already, in England, the great reformer, John Wesley, was working to reform the Church of England, and on this side of the Atlantic, where those followers were working in the Church of England, they had formed Wesleyan Societies. These groups were soon made up of the colonists distinctly. All pro-England colonists were in the Church of England, but the rest were identified with Wesley's followers. When on Christmas Day in Baltimore, 1784, these followers led by Francis Asbury broke with the English Church, they formed a new church now known as the Methodist Episcopal Church.

Protestantism, at the beginning of the nineteenth century, was largely colored by the thinking of John Calvin. It was the common belief that God had predestinated from eternity all who would be saved, and that society generally was made up of either the "elect" or "non-elect". To determine which one was, he must wait for an "experience", a "still small voice" or some climactic act of God to show that the penitent was of the "elect". Protestant thinking generally was colored by Calvinism which accounted for the success of large camp meetings, like that at Cane Ridge in Kentucky, and large movements, like the Great Awakening led by Jonathan Edwards.

Protestantism, too, was colored in the nineteenth century by deep denominational bigotry. Different religious parties were all too abundant on the American frontier. Prominent religious leaders in each denomination were vitriolic in their attacks upon others. Each insisted he was right, and that the Bible taught his particular kind of religious beliefs. Each denomination, therefore, insisted upon the authority of its creed. Religious bigotry, therefore, went hand in hand with religious partyism.

The earliest emphasis of Thomas Campbell and his more famous son, Alexander, (d. 1866), was on Christian Unity. The "Christian Association of Washington" which was established on August 17, 1809 by Thomas Campbell was in reality nothing more than a society for the promotion of Christian unity.[1] The *goal* to be achieved by this "restoration movement", as it came to be called, was the unity of all God's people. The *method* of achieving it was the restoration of primitive Christianity. It was held desirous that men should lay down all party names and be called Christians and Christians only. It was also held that men should renounce all human creeds and follow the Bible as their only authority in matters of faith and practice. The particular motto which Thomas Campbell coined was: "Where the Bible speaks, we speak; where the Bible is silent, we are silent". Only the form of the expression was new: the thought content was borrowed from William Chillingworth and Edward Stillingfleet. This motto was to become the battle-cry for the churches of Christ in the years ahead.

The need for a restoration of primitive Christianity was not new with either Thomas or Alexander Campbell. In this they were anticipated both in America and Europe. The Haldane brothers—James and Robert—rebelled against the cold formalism of the Church of Scotland and organized independent churches. One of their preachers, Grenville Ewing, organized

a theological school in Edinburgh. That Alexander Campbell
was influenced in his thinking by Ewing is quite evident. Another movement in Scotland was led by John Glas and Robert
Sandeman. They denied the value of creeds and confessions
of faith. Glas taught there were two classes of officers in the
New Testament Church: the "extraordinary" consisting of
apostles, prophets and evangelists; and the "ordinary", consisting of elders and deacons. Sandeman believed that faith
was simple assent to the testimony of Christ, advocated
the weekly observance of the Lord's Supper, and a plurality
of elders in one local congregation. Alexander Campbell's
indebtedness to these men he always acknowledged, but he
did deny being either a Sandemanian or a Glasite. He would
call no man on earth "father", to use a pet expression of his
own, meaning of course, that with him no man was an authority in religious matters.

The Campbells were also anticipated in America for forces
were at work on this side of the Atlantic twenty years before
the Campbells came, looking toward a purer form of Christianity. James O'Kelly, a temperamental Irish preacher among
the Wesleyan Societies in Virginia and North Carolina, looked
with disfavor at the organization of these societies into the
Methodist Episcopal Church. The crisis came when a General
Conference met in Baltimore on November 1, 1792 which led
to O'Kelly's withdrawal from the church, and with him four
other prominent men. This small group, meeting at Manakin-
town in Powhaton County, Virginia on Christmas Day, 1793
officially severed all relations with the Methodist Episcopal
Church, and took the name, "Republican Methodists". "Theirs
was to be a Republican-no slavery—glorious church, free from
all the evils of misgovernment".[2] Meeting at Old Lebanon in
Surry County, Virginia the next August, Rice Haggard, one of
their prominent leaders, stood up with his Bible and said:

> Brethren, this is a sufficient rule of faith and prac-
> tice. By it we are told that the disciples were called

Christians, and I move that henceforth and forever the followers of Christ be known as Christians simply.[3]

Soon the O'Kelly group devised what became known as the "Five Cardinal Principles of The Christian Church". These were:

1. The Lord Jesus Christ as the only Head of the Church.

2. The name Christian to the exclusion of all party and sectarian names.

3. The Holy Bible, or the Scriptures of the Old and New Testament our only creed, and a sufficient rule of faith and practice.

4. Christian character or vital piety, the only test of church fellowship and membership.

5. The right of private judgment, and the liberty of conscience, the privilege and duty of all.[4]

Here is a movement that was, in general, looking in the same direction the Campbells were later to move.

Elias Smith and Abner Jones, both working in New England, also were announcing restoration principles before the Campbells. Smith was led against some of the doctrines held by Protestantism as not in harmony with the New Testament. He accepted only the name Christian, and renounced the catechism, as "an invention of men". He convinced himself that the clergy opposed him because they had a system of their own invention contrary to the New Testament. Later he founded and edited a paper called, *The Herald of Gospel Liberty,* which he claimed was the first religious paper ever printed. The principles advocated by this periodical were the following: First, No head over the Church but Christ. Second, No confession of faith, articles of religion, rubric, canons, creeds, etc., but the New Testament. Third, No religious name but Christian.[5] Abner Jones is said to have established "the first free Christian Church in New England", the members of which called themselves just Christians.[6] The principles advocated by Jones, however, were not different from those proclaimed by Elias Smith.

But perhaps the most significant of the movements that anticipated Campbell was that led by Barton Warren Stone. Stone, a Presbyterian, was educated at the famous school of David Caldwell in North Carolina. He went with a wagon train to Nashville, Tennessee about 1798, and from thence to the Lexington region of Kentucky. Stone preached at the Concord meeting house, ten miles north east of Cane Ridge, near Paris, Kentucky. Kentucky was on the verge of a great revival motivated largely by James McGready, an enthusiastic Presbyterian evangelist. McGready had conducted great revivals in Logan County, and Stone was anxious to try them nearer home. Consequently, a great revival was conducted in August, 1801 at Cane Ridge with from twenty to thirty thousand in attendance.

Stone's thinking, however, was now troubling him. He found it difficult to reconcile the doctrine of man's total depravity with the command of God for the sinner to hear, believe and obey the gospel. Stone was led to believe that the gospel should be preached to all men, and that faith—the sinner's acceptance of that gospel—was a condition of salvation. It was twenty years, however, before Stone gave the subject of baptism thorough consideration and decided in favor of its necessity in the plan of salvation. For holding these views, however, Stone together with Robert Marshall, Richard McNemar, John Dunlavy, and John Thompson was expelled from the Washington Presbytery. Of his views at the time of his break, Stone writes in his autobiography,

> The distinguished doctrine preached by us, was, that God loved the world—the whole world, and sent His Son to save them, on condition that they believed on him—that the gospel was the means of salvation—but that this means would never be effectual to this

end, until believed and obeyed by us—that sinners were capable of understanding and believing this testimony, and of acting upon it by coming to the Saviour and obeying him and from him obtaining salvation and the Holy Spirit.[7]

After leaving the Presbyterian Church, Stone and his followers at first established a presbytery of their own, calling it the Springfield Presbytery. Their next step was to publish a document known as the "Apology of the Springfield Presbytery" in defense of their teaching. But in less than a year it occurred to this group that the very existence of the Springfield Presbytery "savored of a party spirit". They, therefore, dissolved the organization, and on June 28, 1804 isssued "The Last Will And Testament of The Springfield Presbytery", in which it was declared,

> *Imprimis.* We *will,* that this body die, be dissolved, and sink into union with the Body of Christ at large; for there is but one Body and One Spirit, even as we are called in one hope of our calling.[8]

For the next twenty years this movement which called for a return to original ground in Christianity swept down the Ohio valley as far west as the Mississippi River. Congregations sprang up in Ohio, Kentucky, Illinois, and Indiana and then later in Tennessee and states to the south. In 1826 Stone began publication of the *Christian Messenger.* In 1831 the Stone movement united with the "Reformers", as those of like-thought with Alexander Campbell were called. The meeting occurred at Lexington, Kentucky. "Raccoon" John Smith concluded the occasion and his speech by saying:

> Let us, then my brethren, be no longer Campbellites or Stoneites, New Lights or Old Lights, or any other kind of lights, but let us come to the Bible and to the Bible alone, as the only book in the world that can give us all the light we need.[9]

Commenting upon the meeting twelve years later, John Rogers wrote:

> No one ever thought that the Reformers, so called, had come over to us, or that we had gone over to them; that they were required to relinquish their opinions or we ours. We found ourselves contending for the same great principles of Christianity, and we resolved to unite our energies to harmonize the church, and save the world. . . I entered into it upon principle. I think immense good has grown out of it, that had it never taken place, our cause in Kentucky would be far in the rear of the position it now occupies.[10]

Thomas Campbell, a preacher in the Seceder Presbyterian Church in Ireland, left his native country early in 1807 because of illness to go to America. Upon landing at Philadelphia, the Synod of America sent him to western Pennsylvania to work under the Chartiers Presbytery. For the next several months Campbell fulfilled his ministerial duties by preaching according to monthly appointments in small country congregations. He was soon led, by the study of his New Testament, to see that the primitive church observed the Lord's Supper weekly, so Campbell proceeded to do the same. He also taught that creeds and confessions of faith were valueless. For this, he was called before the Chartiers Presbytery and thence before the Synod in Philadelphia. A series of trials followed, resulting in the deposition of Thomas Campbell. Concerning his belief then, Campbell wrote:

> With regard to faith I believe that the soul of man is the subject of it; the Divine Spirit is the author of it; the Divine Word the rule and reason of it; Christ and Him crucified the object of it; the Divine pardon, acceptance, and assistance, or grace here and glory hereafter, the direct, proper, and formal end of it. . .
> With respect to Confessions of Faith and Testimon-

ies I believe that the church has all the Divine warrant for such exhibitions of the truth, that our Confession and Testimony adduce for that purpose; and that it is lawful and warrantable to use them as terms of communion insofar as our testimony requires; in which sense I have never opposed them.[11]

For the next weeks after Campbell's suspension meetings were held in the houses of friends, at which time considerable discussion followed on the divided state of the religious world, and the fact that the only remedy seemed to be for all men to drop human creeds and go back solely to the Scriptures. On August 17, 1809 the "Christian Association of Washington" was formed, and before this group Thomas Campbell delivered the "Declaration and Address". This document is divided into three parts: First, the "Declaration", which states the purpose and plan of the organization. Second, the "Address", which is an analysis of the forces at work in the religious world that necessitate a restoration movement. Third, the "Appendix", which is designed to answer questions.

Three weeks after delivering this address, Thomas Campbell was joined by his family who had arrived safely from Ireland. He had many things to discuss with his son, Alexander. He was pleasantly surprised to find that his son, too, had grown tired of religious division, and was thinking along the same line of his father: a restoration of ancient Christianity as being the only answer to the world's religious ills. Alexander Campbell, upon studying carefully the "Declaration and Address", determined to spend his life advocating the principles that that document set forth. From henceforth, Thomas Campbell was to yield the dynamic leadership of the movement to his son.

Alexander Campbell now devoted himself to a life of careful, prayerful study of the Bible. Step by step he was led into a fuller knowledge of the word of God. Early in 1810, Thomas Campbell built a meeting house in the valley of the Brush Run and here on September 16, 1810 Alexander preached his first sermon. Late the next year Campbell turned his attention to the study of what the Bible taught on infant baptism, and discovered that it was not authorized by the word of God. A similar investigation of the popular practice of sprinkling led him to the conviction that immersion was the only proper baptism. It was ten years later, however, as Campbell was preparing for a debate on infant baptism with W. L. McCalla that he concluded that immersion in water was laid forth by the Scriptures as essential to salvation.

The practice of the Brush Run Church, of which Campbell was a member, to insist upon immersion for baptism, led to their being given an invitation by the Redstone Baptist Association to join that body. The Church was reluctant, knowing the fondness of the Baptists for creeds, but finally joined. Before this association on August 30, 1816 Campbell delivered his famous *Sermon on The Law,* setting forth the fact that the Law given at Mt. Sinai was given for the Jews, and was abrogated in the death of Christ, and that Christians now must live under the new covenant given by Christ. This sermon created an uneasy fellowship between the Association and the Brush Run church which finally resulted in a voluntary withdrawal by the congregation from the Association.

The decade between 1820-30 saw the Campbells pushing a strong aggressive campaign, punctuated by Campbell's three great religious debates—the Campbell-Walker Debate on Christian Baptism, the Campbell-McCalla Debate on Christian Baptism, and the Campbell-Owen Debate on Christian Evidences. In 1823 Campbell began the publication of the *Christian Baptist,* but for fear this name might attach itself to his brethren, he dropped the paper in 1830 in favor of a new publication which he called the *Millennial Harbinger.* Contrary to expectation in some quarters, the paper did not feature a thousand-year earthly reign conception, but only Campbell's belief that a purified Church must precede an endless era of the reign of righteousness and good will upon the earth.

However, a strong emphasis on prophecy was never a feature of Campbell's writings for he was far more practical minded.

In 1837 Campbell met Bishop John Purcell of Cincinnati in a debate on Roman Catholicism. Six years later he conducted his last major discussion with N. L. Rice on Christian Baptism and the work of the Holy Spirit. The establishment of the American Christian Missionary Society in 1849 set off a wave of internal controversy among the various congregations that grew with the passing of years, and finally resulted in a division between the churches of Christ and the Christian Church or Disciples of Christ.

Thomas Campbell, in announcing his famous motto, "Where the Bible Speaks, We speak; where the Bible is silent, we are silent" was believed to have meant that whatever institution, practice or belief was not authorized by the Scriptures should not be followed. On this basis of this motto, Campbell himself had rejected infant baptism, for there was no authority for it in the New Testament. Furthermore, the writings of Alexander Campbell in the *Christian Baptist* emphasized the all-sufficiency of the church of Christ for the work Christ intended and deprecated every human institution to do the work God gave the church. The church had grown rapidly up to 1849 without a Missionary Society, so why establish one? Moreover, a Missionary Society was unknown to the New Testament, for during primitive days all of the mission work that was done was accomplished by and through the church of Christ. Finally, it was urged that the establishment of such a society would be to set up an organization that would seek to control the churches, and the individual congregations would therefore lose their freedom. These, in the main, were the arguments used against the organization. It was felt that the establishment of the Society was a departure from apostolic Christianity, an abandonment of the earlier principles of the restoration movement, and by and large, an elevation of human wisdom over divine, for divine wisdom established no institution to do mission work other than the church. Tolbert Fanning, co-editor of the *Gospel Advocate* in 1857 wrote,

> The church, as we have often said, is Heaven's missionary society to a suffering world, and the ministers commissioned, sent out and supported by the church, are God's missionaries to call sinners to life. We have not been able to see the necessity of a missionary society beyond the church.[12]

It was ten years later before the question of instrumental music came up. Earlier in the restoration movement the instrument had not been used. The first known case of its use among the churches of Christ was with the church at Midway, Kentucky in 1859, but the objection was so strong that it was promptly withdrawn. By 1867, Benjamin Franklin, editor of the *American Christian Review,* then the most powerful weekly publication in the brotherhood, stated pointedly that out of nearly two thousand congregations less than ten were using the instrument in worship. But the next twenty-five years saw many congregations adopting both the use of the Missionary Society and the instrument of music, especially after the establishment of the *Christian Standard* in 1866 and the *Christian-Evangelist* in 1882 both of which strongly advocated these. Meanwhile, many congregations remained faithful to the earlier principles of the restoration and refused to introduce these "innovations", considering those who had done so as departing from the Scriptures in introducing practices for which they had no Bible authority. In the years ahead, the *Christian Standard* never relinquished its support of instrumental music in Christian worship but did temper somewhat its support of the missionary society. From the *Standard's* point of view the Society sought a dictatorial control over the local congregations, tended to foster the spirit of "liberalism" in religious thought, and led in the move to make the church another denomination among denominations.

But to return to the earlier days of the restoration movement, it should be remarked that opposition to the advocacy of the use of instrumental music and the missionary society was led in the main by the *American Christian Review* and the *Gospel Advocate*. The *Review* was established in 1856 by Benjamin Franklin in Cincinnati, Ohio, and was the most influential paper in the brotherhood until the death of its editor in 1878. John F. Rowe then edited the periodical until 1886, at which time it was purchased by Daniel Sommer who shortly afterward moved it to Indianapolis where it has since remained. An unfortunate personal difference occurred in 1886 between Rowe and Sommer which led to the establishment of the *Christian Leader* by Rowe. For the next several years the columns of both papers were filled with vitriolic attacks against the other. Their forces became divided, and in the area north of the Ohio River where they were located this fact doubtlessly contributed to the success of both the *Christian Standard* and the *Christian-Evangelist*. So intense was the *Leader's* and *Review's* opposition to the "digression" advocated by the *Standard* and the *Evangelist* that the former sought to overcome by adopting even greater extremes. Before long the *Review* concentrated most of its attack on the right of brethren to teach the Bible in Colleges. At various times in its history it objected to congregations having located preachers, using literature with which to teach the Bible, and the right of churches to conduct Bible classes. These latter extremes it has only sporadically dwelt upon. However, none of these "extremes" have characterized the churches of Christ as a whole, being in the main localized to a few congregations in the north.

The main opposition to "innovations" was led by the *Gospel Advocate* which paper continues to be published in Nashville, Tenn. The founders of the *Advocate* in 1855 were Tolbert Fanning, then president of Franklin College near Nashville, and William Lipscomb, one of the professors. Both men conducted the paper until the outbreak of the Civil War made further publication impossible. After the war, the paper was started again with Lipscomb's younger brother, David becoming editor. For a short time David Lipscomb was aided by Tolbert Fanning, but in 1870, he was joined by E. G. Sewell. For the next fifty years "Lipscomb & Sewell" were household names to members of the churches of Christ in the South. It is impossible to measure the influence of these two men in the church, although of the two, David Lipscomb was probably more influential. Few men have ever been found who had greater faith in God, and trusted more implicitly in the "way, the word, and the will of the Lord". He had no confidence in human wisdom as it applied to the church, and believed it to be the church's obligation to follow God without trying to improve upon the wisdom of God by adding the missionary society to do the *work* of the church or the instrument to do the *worship* of the church.

Early in the movement, other periodicals also spoke out against the instrument in worship. When Alexander Campbell was asked his views on the use of the instrument, he wrote in the *Millennial Harbinger*:

> The argument drawn from the Psalms in favor of instrumental music, is exceedingly opposite to the Roman Catholic, English Protestant, and the Scotch Presbyterian churches, and even to the Methodist communities. Their church having all the world in them— that is, all fleshly progeny of all the communicants, and being founded on the Jewish pattern of things— baptism being given to all born into the world of these politico-ecclesiastic communities—I wonder not, then, that an organ, fiddle, or a Jews' harp, should be requisite to stir up their carnal hearts, and work into ecstasy their animal souls, else 'hosannahs languish on their tongues and their devotions die'. And that all persons who have no spiritual discernment, taste or relish for

their spiritual meditations, for such aid is natural. Pure water from the flinty rock has no attractions for the mere toper or wine-bibber. A little alcohol, or genuine Cognac brandy, or good old Madeira, is essential to the beverage to make it truly refreshing. So to those who have no real devotion or spirituality in them, and whose animal nature flags under the oppression of church service, I think with Mr. G., that instrumental music would be only a desideratum, but an essential prerequisite to fire up their souls to even animal devotion. But I presume, to all spiritually-minded Christians such aids would be as a cowbell in a concert.[13]

From the year 1864 until it ceased publication in 1870, the *Millennial Harbinger* thrashed out the issue of instrumental music. From 1864-68 *Lard's Quarterly* also spoke out against it. This paper was edited by one of the first opponents of the instrument, Moses E. Lard. Still later, the *Apostolic Times,* edited by J. W. McGarvey, Moses E. Lard, L. B. Wilkes, W. H. Hopson, and Robert Graham. The *Times* occupied the middle-of-the-road on these issues, advocating the Missionary Society, but strongly opposing the use of the instrument. The untenableness of this position was soon evident and the "middle ground" slipped out of view.

By 1884 Austin McGary had established another periodical in Texas known as the *Firm Foundation.* The paper is still published in Austin, Texas and wields no small influence in the churches of Christ in the southwestern part of the nation.

At the present time, the *Christian Chronicle* of Abilene, Texas; the *Gospel Broadcast* of Dallas, Texas, and the more bellicose *Gospel Guardian* of Lufkin, Texas are among the major papers in the brotherhood. These, together with the *Gospel Advocate, Firm Foundation, American Christian Review,* and *Christian Leader* form the major group of brotherhood publications.[14]

David Lipscomb's thought was that it is the duty of Christians to teach the Bible in whatever capacity they may be found, be they doctors, bankers, lawyers, farmers or school teachers. This feeling has been widely shared by the brethren. Christians have established schools and have therefore added the study of the Bible to their curriculum. These are but private institutions and do not belong to the church. Among the major schools now operated by members of the churches of Christ are: Abilene Christian College at Abilene, Texas; Harding College at Searcy, Arkansas; David Lipscomb College at Nashville, Tennessee; and George Pepperdine College at Los Angeles, California. These are all four-year schools with the exception of George Pepperdine College which offers one year of graduate work in religion. The junior colleges include, Freed-Hardeman College at Henderson, Tennessee, and Florida Christian College at Tampa, Florida although the latter school does offer a four-year course in Bible only. Smaller schools on the high school level are also found in various places over the nation.

The Statistical Abstract for 1950 published by the U. S. Department of Commerce lists the churches of Christ as of 1947 having ten thousand congregations and 682,172 members. Members of the churches of Christ themselves put no confidence in these census reports for the reason that there is no central headquarters to make the individual congregations report. One who travels among the churches of Christ finds almost as many who did not report as those who did. The total number would undoubtedly be much nearer the one million mark than what is given in the census.

Although the churches of Christ have no Missionary Societies, they have become increasingly mission minded. Since 1892 they have maintained mission work in Japan, and have even established a college there known as Ibaraki Christian College. For many years preachers have been working in China, South Africa, the Philippine Islands, Korea, the Hawaiian Islands, Mexico, and Alaska. Since the last war the tempo of this mission work has greatly increased. In six years five strong congregations have been established in Germany, the work being done mainly in Frankfurt. A congregation now exists in Paris, France and several more have been planted in Italy. Churches of Christ in England and Australia have been in existence for many years but their existence cannot be credited to the work of churches of Christ in America.

Meanwhile, churches of Christ are being established in greatly increasing numbers in those areas of the United States where in the past they have been lacking—mainly in the midwest and New England. A nation-wide radio broadcast over a national hook-up is now being planned so that the possibilities for growth in the future seem almost unlimited.

NOTES AND BIBLIOGRAPHY

[1] ROBERT RICHARDSON, *Memoirs of Alexander Campbell* (Cincinnati, 1897).

[2] W. E. MacCLENNY, *Life of Jas. O'Kelly* (Indianapolis, Indiana, 1950), p. 116.

[3] J. PRESSLEY BARRETT, *The Centennial of Religious Journalism* (Dayton, Ohio, 1908), p. 264.

[4] MacCLENNY, *op. cit.*, pp. 121, 122.

[5] *Cf.* ELIAS SMITH, *The Life and Conversion of Elias Smith* (Portsmouth, N. H., 1816), p. 14.

[6] C. C. WARE, *Barton W. Stone* (St. Louis, 1932), p. 154.

[7] BARTON W. STONE, *Biography of Elder Barton Warren Stone* (Cincinnati, Ohio, 1847), p. 45.

[8] *Cf.* CHARLES A. YOUNG, *Historical Documents Advocating Christian Union* (Chicago, 1904), pp. 19-26.

[9] JOHN AUGUSTUS WILLIAMS, *Life of Elder John Smith* (Cincinnati, 1904), p. 454.

[10] C. C. WARE, *op. cit.*, p. 247.

[11] W. H. HANNA, *Thomas Campbell, Seceder, and Christian Union Advocate* (Cincinnati, 1935), pp. 45-47.

[12] TOLBERT FANNING, "Missions and Missionaries", *Gospel Advocate*, Vol. III, No. 5 (May, 1857), p. 130.

[13] ALEXANDER CAMPBELL, "Instrumental Music", *Millennial Harbinger*, Fourth Series, Vol. I, No. 10 (October, 1851), pp. 581, 582.

[14] For this history *see*, EARL WEST, *Search for the Ancient Order*, 2 Vols. (Indianapolis, Indiana, 1951).

XXII

THE CHURCH OF GOD
(ANDERSON, INDIANA)

XXII

THE CHURCH OF GOD (ANDERSON, INDIANA)

CHARLES EWING BROWN

Picking Out the Proper Labels

LET US suppose that "Shorty Smith" is a member of Congress. That is not his real name, and he does not really like it; but if you should put out his biography under the title Ambrose Augustine Smith, few people would buy the book, not knowing to whom this dignified title belonged.

The Church of God, Anderson, Indiana, is like that. We do not accept the title except for rough identification. Rather we are "the Church of God Reformation Movement"—not the only Christians in the world, but a movement in the universal Church. We believe that every true Christian in all the world, and even among the Saints in heaven, is a member of the Church of God. The regenerating touch of the finger of God—and that alone—makes him a member of the Church of God. We profess to be members of the Church of God purely and simply on the same basis as men and women everywhere claim to be Christians. When a person professes to be a Christian, people do not accuse him of fanatical exclusiveness. Christianity is such a broad religion that all men might profess it without seeming unduly narrow—and without denying a like right to their fellows.

This point will bear emphasis because it is almost completely misunderstood or ignored. We lay claim to the title Church of God just as a sailor lays claim to the sea. We believe that it is possible to set up a congregation so completely void of all organized restrictions that every Christian in the world may be regarded as a potential member thereof without a formal act of joining.

Think again of the sea. Every little gulf and inlet on all sea coasts of the earth is a part of the universal sea unless it is cut off by some sea wall that obstructs the tides of the ocean. So we believe that a little congregation out in the bushes anywhere may be a real Church of God and a gulf of the eternal sea of the universal Church if it has no barriers of creed and organization which exclude any other Christians whatsoever.

Therefore, in order to get the hard every day work of the church done, we do not organize the church as such, but we prefer to organize the particular work of the church which we seek to do. In the local congregation, we organize the Sunday School to teach religion in a systematic way. We organize various agencies to care for the church building and to carry on the work in every necessary way. In the same way we organize committees or boards to carry on the connectional work of the Christian community. We have colleges, a foreign missionary board, a home missionary board, a publication board, and whatever else is necessary now, or may become necessary in the future, in order to make possible for all the congregation's mutual participation in a cooperative program of social, moral and religious welfare for the help of mankind. In a similar way, our ministers are organized into state and regional ministerial assemblies covering most of the continental territory of the United States and of several foreign lands.

It is the belief of our people that this act of abstention from organizing the church as church is the indispensable prerequisite for recovering the unity of the church as it was known in New Testament times. Instead of believing that we have organized the one and only Church into which all Christians should come, we deny the possibility that any group of men can ever succeed in such a colossal undertaking.

Elaboration of this point is worth our time as our movement cannot be understood without this insight. Right or wrong, it is the clue to our history and to our reason for existence. It explains why we do not feel confused or embarrassed among a group of some six or eight churches of God, most of which organized as denominations long after we began our work in 1881. In fact, our doctrine of the church is in the foregoing respects quite unique, and it was never previously known in Church History since the Apostolic Age, except that it was adopted by the Friends or Quakers for a few months at the beginning of their work in the seventeenth century. However, the exigencies of their historical situation—such as their persecution by the State Church—made it seem not feasible for them to carry out at the time, and they soon dropped it.

The Reformation Before Luther

The Church of God Reformation Movement looks backward in history to the beginnings of democratic Christianity in Northern Italy, Southern France and Northern Spain as early as the eleventh century. This movement is commonly called after the Cathars, but David Schaff avers that there were no less than forty sects in this movement, most of whom were orthodox Christians. Driven underground by two great crusades, this movement of dissent from the ruling church of the age lived in secret for some five hundred years. In the fourteenth century, it appeared as the Lollard movement in England, whence it was carried to Bohemia by clerics in the train of Richard II of England. In Bohemia, it was promoted by John Hus (1373?-1415) and his followers where it kept alive a strong protest against the ancient church till after the rise of Luther. At the dawn of the sixteenth century Reformation, these hidden seeds of dissent against the old church began to sprout like grass in spring all over Europe. This movement became the third branch of the Reformation alongside of Lutheranism and the Reformed Church everywhere that evangelical Christianity was known. Known as Anabaptists, these democratic reformers were persecuted by Catholics and Protestants alike, but they became the precursors of the major part of American Protestantism. Ernest Sutherland Bates in his *The American Faith* credits the American doctrine of political freedom and the form of the American State to the influence of the spiritual democracy which prevailed in their conventicles for centuries. He calls them radical Christians, and defines radical Christians as those rejecting the church of the bishop on the one hand, and the church of the prince on the other. This radical Christianity grew out of a cry for a pure church which arose in religious circles in mediaeval times.

The Church of God Reformation movement also owes much to the great Pietistic revival which sprang up in Switzerland, Germany and Holland during the seventeenth century. This revival was a revolt against excessive dogma and ritual and a cry for warmth of individual religious experience. This Pietistic movement spread to the Wesleys in England, who added to it still another emphasis on entire sanctification. Both in its original form as revivalism, and with the added doctrine of sanctification, Pietism came to America and helped to shape the historic mold of the later Reformation Movement.[1]

The Cry for Unity

Another historic force that prepared the way for our work was the agitation for church unity that took various forms in the early nineteenth century. There was the movement in Ireland and Scotland which prepared the Campbells for their campaign for Christian unity in the early American scene. In 1825, Edward Cronin gathered a group (including John Nelson Darby) around him in Dublin, Ireland, and began an effort to realize Christian Unity which finally took the name of the Plymouth Brethren.

About this time the Rev. John Winebrenner was pastor of four congregations of the German Reformed Church in and near Harrisburg, Pennsylvania. Winebrenner became an ardent revivalist, and in his zeal he summoned the aid of neighboring Methodist preachers to help him in his work. This liberalism provoked resistance from his colleagues, and finally Winebrenner was expelled from his communion. He continued in his evangelistic efforts however, and with such success that finally he and his followers organized the Churches of God in North America in the year 1830. In 1942 the membership was 33,727. The movement was one more effort to solve the problem of sectarian division in the historic Christian church.

The Work of Daniel S. Warner

It is the belief of the Church of God Reformation that the spiritual insight into the nature of the church which originated the movement came not to one person alone but at least to a considerable number. In fact, the democracy of the movement has always been so marked that the usual glorification of leaders has been noticeably lacking in this work. Nevertheless, in order to put the story into coherent form, it is necessary to neglect many earnest workers and concentrate attention upon the few who were best known.

Of these, Daniel Sidney Warner undoubtedly stands first. Born in 1842 at Bristol (now Marshallville, Ohio), where his father kept a tavern, Warner moved with his family in 1863 to a farm in northwest Ohio, near the town of Montpelier, whence he went as a Union soldier to the Civil War. After his honorable discharge from the army, he became a country school teacher and took an active part in the fun and frolic of the social life of the countryside. About this time he became deeply perplexed by doubts and intellectual difficulties concerning religion.

Living in a community of Roman Catholics and Lutherans, he was not so familiar with revivalism as were many men who were later to become evangelical leaders; nevertheless, he was converted in a schoolhouse revival early in the year 1865, at the age of 23. Although Warner already had more than the average amount of education possessed by the leaders of his time, he enrolled as a student in Oberlin College the following autumn. He cut short his college course to begin preaching as a free-lance undenominational preacher. On September 5, 1867, he married Tamzen Ann Kerr, who bore him four children—a son and triplets—all of whom died in infancy. His wife died young, in 1872.

In October, 1872, D. S. Warner was licensed to preach by the West Ohio Eldership of the Churches of God (commonly called Winebrennerian). While in this ministry, he spent some time as a student in Vermillion College, Hayesville, Ohio. His library indicates scholarly tastes far outside the ordinary ranges of his time.

Warner labored in the various conferences of Ohio as pastor until May 23, 1873, when he was sent by the Board of Missions to the pioneer mission field of Southeastern Nebraska. He married, in 1874, a Miss Sarah Keller, who immediately went with him to Nebraska. In spite of incredible hardships and suffering, which undoubtedly shortened his life, Warner successfully preached at fourteen different stations and organized six new congregations in the two years of his stay in Nebraska. From Nebraska he returned to the regular work of the pastorate in his denomination in Ohio in 1875.

Doctrinal Conflicts

The present writer has carefully studied Warner's Manuscript Journals, and is struck with the sharpness and logic of his criticism of the Wesleyan doctrine of perfectionism or entire-sanctification. D. S. Warner rejected this doctrine vigorously for many years. It comes therefore as a surprise to learn that in the year 1877 he came to favor this doctrine. Accepting the theology, he finally professed the experience of entire-sanctification as taught by the National Association for the Promotion of Holiness. The Methodist Episcopal Church in America had received this doctrine from the Wesleys, and had preached it everywhere during its pioneer days. About the end of the Civil War, the doctrine began to lose its popularity in Methodism. At the same time it spread against opposition into other denominations. Ministers from various denominations (some excommunicated, some merely barred from their former pulpits) met and organized this Holiness Association. In the course of time, many Holiness Churches arose to furnish a field of labor for preachers of the holiness doctrine.

Warner immediately ran into a storm in his ecclesiastical relations. At last the General Eldership, on October 1, 1877, sustained charges against him for preaching holiness, but issued him a restricted license; but on January 30, 1878, the Standing Committee again heard charges against him for the same cause. They sustained these charges and withheld his license to preach among them.

In the meantime, a dissident body of the same church had been growing up in Indiana. They called themselves the North Indiana Eldership. Not all, but many of their members were favorable to holiness. They inaugurated a paper called *The Herald of Gospel Freedom* at Wolcottville, Indiana in 1878, of which I. W. Lowman was editor. Later, in the same year, Warner was elected associate editor in charge of a department on holiness.

In November, 1878, Warner moved to Rome City, Indiana. In February of the following year, Lowman moved the paper there, and on March 11, 1879, Warner bought a half interest in *The Herald of Gospel Freedom* from Lowman for $250.00. During all this time, Warner was laboring as a holiness evangelist, both among the brethren of the National Association and of the Eldership. On May 15, 1880, D. S. Warner's name appeared as sole editor of *The Herald of Gospel Freedom*. On December 23, 1880, the Board of Publication and the Standing Committee of the Northern Indiana Eldership voted to consolidate *The Herald of Gospel Freedom* and a small paper 8 months old, published by G. M. Haines in Indianapolis, Indiana, and called *The Pilgrim*. The first issue of the new paper was issued at Rome City, Indiana, January 1,

1881, and was called *The Gospel Trumpet*. On March 1, the third issue of this paper appeared published at Indianapolis, Indiana, whither Warner had removed. Warner bought Haines out in June, 1881, and remained editor of the paper until his death in December, 1895.

From Indianapolis, Indiana, the paper removed to Cardington, Ohio, in the Autumn of 1882. Remaining here till May, 1883, it then removed to Bucyrus, Ohio. Here Warner found friends and temporary success; but a small group of fanatics, gaining the support of his wife, tried to wrest the paper from his hands. At first, he almost yielded his consent, but when he finally refused to give it up, his wife left him and her little son forever. The terrible strain almost drove Warner insane for a few days, but kind friends comforted him, and finally he recovered his poise and went on with his work. His wife divorced him in an uncontested suit two years later. Warner remained unmarried until she died in 1893, after having remarried. His divorced wife died in May 24, 1893, and Warner married Frances Miller on August 12th of the same year.

In April of 1884, *The Gospel Trumpet* moved to Williamston, Michigan, where it remained until June, 1886, when it went to Grand Junction, Michigan, where Warner died in December, 1895. *The Gospel Trumpet* left Grand Junction, Michigan, June 28, 1896, to locate in Moundsville, West Virginia, where it remained until September 20, 1906, when it moved to Anderson, Indiana, where it has remained ever since. It developed into the official organ of the new movement. It is a church owned institution now handling a volume of two and a half to three million dollars worth of business yearly. *The Gospel Trumpet* paper has an annual circulation of some 29,000,—this besides the Sunday School literature and papers for children and youth.

Warner's New View of the Church

Up until after the time when he became editor of *The Gospel Trumpet,* Warner believed that the organization to which he belonged was the Church of God, because it was called by that name, and because it professed not to hold a human creed. As time passed his views developed. At last there came to him what he regarded as a divine illumination regarding the Church as a fellowship not amenable to human organizing. The greatest New Testament scholars had said that the New Testament community of believers was a fellowship and never an organized corporation. In the earliest times, the church had never distinguished between the visible and the invisible church. This distinction was unknown till the fourth century. The identity of the visible and invisible church was realized by maintaining an open fellowship free from bars of creedal or organizational restrictions, which would shut out any sincere Christian.

This view grew upon Warner to a point where he took dramatic action upon it: In October, 1881, at a little country church at Beaver Dam, Indiana, he and five other persons stepped out of the Northern Indiana Eldership into the open unorganized fellowship of all spiritual Christians throughout the world everywhere. That was the beginning of the Church of God Reformation Movement, which is not a church nor a sect, and not even an organization but merely an open fellowship of all Christians.

The idea was so new and fresh—so original—that Warner spent the rest of his life experimenting how to make it feasible in this world. Most of his associates admit that he made a series of little mistakes, just as is done by every successful and daring business man. But his total work was a brilliant success, and his central insight is shared today by a multitude of scholarly and able men who still labor at his task. The large majority of the ministers who share his vision today are college men, including many of the rank of Ph.D., and almost without exception these men find Warner's vision so appealing that no growth of mind and heart can ever make it seem small and narrow.

At the beginning, Warner was baffled by his opposition to all human organization. This prejudice hampered the work and consequently the growth of the movement. Gradually it dawned upon the fellowship that to organize the work of the church was a far different thing from trying to organize the church which is the Body of Christ. As this insight gained acceptance, the work has prospered beyond all former hopes.

The Social and Religious Backgrounds

Educated persons in the fellowship today understand clearly that God works within the social and historical framework of each generation of men. Such persons prefer to give a realistic rather than a fictitious picture of the multitudes of humble and earnest people who swarmed into the camp-meetings and tiny conventicles of Warner and his associates. Like the toiling multitudes who followed Wesley and other historic figures of the past, these people had given no hostages to fortune. They had nothing to lose. Not being social climbers, they had no fear of social stigma. One can get a picture of them by reading the journals of George Fox, and of Wesley. They were intense men like John Bunyan.

The theology of Warner and his co-workers was in regard to the plan of salvation (soteriology) exactly that of the Wesleys and the Wesleyan movement as modified by the holiness preachers on American soil. The discipline of the fellowship was the ascetic discipline handed down from the great Pietistic movement in Europe in the seventeenth century, sharpened, if possible, by the hard unremitting toil of the wilderness farms. Everything was forbidden that perhaps any evangelical church ever forbade: dancing, drinking, smoking and all forms of tobacco using, the theater, and all fine dress and extravagance —much like the early Friends.

The congregations were set up on a basis of fellowship in which they were theoretically independent like all congregational bodies; but from the beginning, congregations were more amenable to the influence of the associated ministerial groups than is true of most independent churches. There was no law about it. Custom made it so. Of recent years the ministers have taken advantage of the license to organize, and consequently, they have set up regional and state ministerial assemblies covering practically all the world wherever our congregations are found. Consequently, these ministerial assemblies actually exert influence upon the several congregations quite equal perhaps to that exercised by a presbytery or synod in the presbyterian system. So that, although congregational in polity, they have much of the coherence of congregational groups in the presbyterian system.

The Development of the Work

It will aid understanding of the history of the movement to bear in mind the stages of development through which it passed. At the beginning there was a small group of evangelists who went everywhere preaching the message. Gradually their number grew. No salaries were paid anywhere. Almost no church had a settled pastor. Such pastors as there were made their living by farming or other secular labor. Naturally there were no training schools of any kind. Any preacher who desired to give all his time to the ministry was obliged to travel in evangelistic work where all his support was "by faith." He must not even take up a collection of any kind.

From the beginning the same conditions prevailed at The Gospel Trumpet Company office. All the workers served without stated pay, and were supported by the free will offerings of the members sent in for the support of the work. Of course, the normal proceeds of the business were drawn upon for the maintenance of the workers, but so much free literature was sent out that for many years the income of the business hardly bore the expenses of the enterprise, and tens of thousands of dollars were contributed by adherents scattered over the country.

• Early Missionary Homes

At The Gospel Trumpet plant, a home was maintained where

unmarried workers lived during the years of free service which they gave to the publishing work. Generally, but not always, separate private homes were provided as homes for the married persons who worked at the Trumpet Office. Altogether these employees formed "the Trumpet Family." Almost from the beginning classes were formed in the "Trumpet Home" for the training of Christian workers in nearly all branches of learning which were judged to be useful in the promotion of their work. This programme was carried on for years, finally growing into a college and seminary.

In the same month in which Warner withdrew from the Northern Indiana Eldership of the Churches of God (Winebrennerian) another group of some twenty members led by J. C. Fisher and his wife Allie withdrew from the Northern Michigan Eldership of the same church and set up a congregation on the new order at Carson City, Michigan. J. C. Fisher became a colleague of Warner in the publication of *The Gospel Trumpet.*

Inasmuch as D. S. Warner exercised an active and energetic ministry in the holiness movement, he met many friends by that means. Others were drawn to him through reading his paper. Among these early workers were preachers from the Cole family in Missouri; first, Jeremiah, then Mary and George.

At the beginning the work was almost entirely a rural enterprise. Most of the preachers were farmers or farm workers, and they seemed to avoid the cities almost as if from fear. But D. S. Warner and his evangelistic company entered Denver, Colorado in 1888. J. W. Byers and his wife Jennie entered San Diego and Los Angeles, California, in 1890. In 1892, Warner began to advise the entrance of the workers into the city. A long list of evangelists invaded Chicago, Illinois, from 1883 on; but Gorham Tufts started the Open Door Mission in Chicago on January 10, 1895, and from that date the Reformation people have never ceased to hold public meetings in that city. In 1883, G. T. Clayton began preaching in Pittsburgh, Pennsylvania. In New York City, Charles James Blewitt, trained for the Presbyterian ministry in Columbia University (B.A.) and New York University (M.A.) and in Princeton and Union Theological seminaries, began preaching this message in 1897. The work has never ceased there since.

Missionary Homes

It soon became a custom to establish "Missionary Homes" in every city wherever possible. Here workers assembled who worked on the free will plan as was practiced at "the Trumpet Home." Academic training was a definite part of their program as a rule. In a big home as many as twenty workers would be housed. These would spend the morning in studies and classes, and canvass the neighborhood, or perhaps go afar in the city for spiritual visitation and to hold meetings in the afternoon and at night. Trainees of these Homes went out into general evangelistic work or into other forms of Christian service— perhaps as foreign missionaries.

These Homes vanished as rapidly as they came. About the beginning of World War I our people began to pour into the cities. Then we relaxed the most drastic of our ascetic practices and began to pay salaries to pastors. Almost in a month the "Homes" were turned over as residences of the pastor, and the workers disappeared. From that time the work of training was taken over by a Bible School at the Gospel Trumpet Office and Home which soon became Anderson College and Theological Seminary, and a similar institution developed into the Pacific Bible College at Portland, Oregon. The Gospel Trumpet Company began to pay set wages to its employees, and the old era passed—not without many a tear for the "good old days."

Outstanding Workers

"The Church of God Reformation Movement" was always extremely democratic. Plainness of dress, simplicity of behavior, and humility of life were its standards. All its workers were important, and none were granted any formal honor; nevertheless, for some fifty years its most influential place of leadership was in the office of the editor of *The Gospel Trumpet*. In the old days, before the ministers were organized into ministerial assemblies, the editor was the court of last resort in all kinds of controversies. No minister could be silenced whom he trusted, and no minister could enjoy recognition without his approval. As time passed the ministers organized Assemblies everywhere, and the present writer as editor at the time relinquished to the ministerial assemblies the sole right to determine the official standing of a minister. At the beginning also, the editor had sole charge of the Foreign Missionary work, and largely the Home Missionary work as well. Organization of the missionary boards took this duty and responsibility off his hands. In fact, the first editors carried officially at least almost the sole administrative responsibility of the business, educational and missionary work of the church, administered through their secretaries. As the work developed, these various responsibilities were gradually taken over by different officials or boards.

Enoch E. Byrum

When D. S. Warner, the first editor, died in December, 1895, an able assistant had been in training for eight years to take his place. Enoch E. Byrum (1861-1941) was reared on a farm in Randolph County in Southeast Indiana. He was educated in Ridgeville College, the Eastern Indiana Normal School, Valparaiso University (all of Indiana), and in Otterbein University (Ohio). Converted at the age of 15, he joined the United Brethren Church, but was won to the Reformation by his family, who were converted while he was away at college. On June 21, 1887, E. E. Byrum cut short his college studies to take up his work as co-publisher and assistant editor with D. S. Warner at Grand Junction, Michigan. His brother, Noah, then fifteen, followed him to the Trumpet Office. There Noah worked for thirty years before he ever received a pay check. E. E. Byrum became full editor at the death of Warner, and continued in the editorship until June, 1916, when he was followed by Frederick G. Smith, who was editor till June, 1930. At that time Charles E. Brown became editor, to be followed by Harold L. Phillips in June, 1951.

Early Leaders in the Work

Besides those named, A. J. Kilpatrick, an Ohio school teacher and veteran of the Union Army, was long a leading evangelist. Mrs. Sarah Smith, a well-to-do farm wife of Ohio, was very conspicuous in service; so were Sebastian Michels, A. B. Palmer and S. L. Speck of Michigan. B. E. Warren, also of Michigan, had a long career as song-writer and preacher. These all entered near the beginning of the work. A. J. Shelley of Michigan came in 1884. Following are the names of leaders and the dates of their accession to the movement: Wm. N. Smith and wife, 1883, Ohio; C. Z. Lindley, 1884, Iowa; Frederick Jacobson, 1884, Ill.; J. N. and George Howard, brothers, 1884, Ohio; Julia C. Myers, 1885, Missouri; J. P. Haner, 1886, Kansas; H. C. Wickersham, 1886, Indiana; Wm. G. Schell, 1886, Ohio; George Bolds, 1881, Missouri, was the father of a family whose children and grandchildren were long prominent; Wm. Hartman, 1887, was pastor in Kalamazoo, Michigan, for more than 50 years; John E. Roberts, 1887, Colorado; G. R. Achor, M. D., 1888, Kansas; A. B. Stanberry, 1888, Missouri; S. G. Bryant, M. D., 1890, Kansas; C. E. Orr, 1891, Indiana; A. L. Byers, song writer and editor, 1891, Illinois; H. M. Riggle and wife, Minnie, 1892; and A. T. Rowe, 1892, Pennsylvania; C. W. Naylor, 1893, Ohio; Willis M. Brown, 1895, Illinois.

The Spread of the Work

The work started in Beaver Dam, Indiana, and in Carson City, Michigan, almost simultaneously in October, 1881. From this date, swarms of evangelists began to traverse the midwestern states in wagons, buggies and on trains. They moved over Indiana, Michigan, Ohio, Illinois, Pennsylvania, Missouri, Colorado, Iowa, Nebraska. J. W. Byers went to California in 1890. Warner and his evangelistic company invaded the South in 1890. J. L. Green went to Oregon in 1893. F. N. Jacobson, C. H. and Mary Tubbs founded the work in the State of Washington in 1893. Having no settled pastors, the work was often temporary at first, so that it would die out and be started over again several times, but probably there was no State in which it completely died out from its beginning. At the present time (1952) there are congregations in every State of the Union, in the District of Columbia, and many foreign lands.

There are 1957 congregations in the U. S. and Canada, with 102,619 members, holding church property valued at $27,963,-220.76.

The Work in Foreign Lands

D. S. Warner is said to have been of Pennsylvania German descent. He studied German in college. Andrew Byers, a pioneer minister of Albany, Illinois, preached in both English and German, as did Mrs. Sarah Smith and many other of the pioneer preachers, including probably Warner himself. In March, 1893, *The Gospel Trumpet* began to publish two columns in German. About this time Max Dederer, said to be a product of the German universities, worked as a German translator in the Trumpet Office. On January 1, 1895, *The Gospel Trumpet* in German began to be issued semi-monthly from the office of the English Trumpet. Fred L. Hahn was the editor. This German paper was published by the Gospel Trumpet Company until September, 1928, when it was taken over by a German-American church committee and moved to York, Nebraska, where it is still issued.

In January, 1893, J. H. Rupert of Pennsylvania went to Hamburg, Germany. Hattie, his wife, soon followed him. Landing ignorant of German, Rupert was preaching in that language within three months. This was the beginning of a work in Germany which still continues strong. George Vielguth of Kansas went to Hamburg in 1901. Vielguth founded the work in Riga, Latvia, and in Quikborn, near Hamburg, Germany. In 1903, Karl Arbeiter joined him. They founded a permanent church in Essen. Other German-American preachers followed and they traveled far into East Prussia and the Caucasus in Russia, and founded churches in Russia, Poland, Austria, Hungary, Switzerland and Rumania. We had churches scattered far over that country before the Bolshevik Revolution. In Poland there were eight churches before World War II. These were all destroyed by the war. At present there are some forty-six congregations in West Germany. These all display uncommon zeal and energy. In fact, they are carrying on one of the greatest revival movements in Europe, but without any emotional sensationalism.

Dr. Ernst Kersten of Fritzlaar, Hessen, superintends a ministerial training college, and the Rev. G. Klabunde of Essen runs the church paper, *Evangeliums Posaune,* and pastors a congregation.

In January, 1893, G. R. Achot, M. D. and W. J. Henry landed in Liverpool, England. They were followed by John W. Daugherty, Lena L. Schoffner, J. H. Rupert and wife, and others. Much of their work has died out, but there is still a good congregation in Birkenhead, England, and another in Belfast, Ireland. The work in Switzerland grew out of the German work and comprises five congregations.

The Scandinavian Work

Thomas Nelson began publishing a Dano-Norwegian *Gospel Trumpet* in Muscatine, Iowa, in the year 1900. This grew into a Scandinavian publishing work at St. Paul, Minnesota, which published papers and literature in both Danish, Norwegian and Swedish, and scattered tons of literature among Scandinavian people in both America and Europe. Scandinavian congregations were raised up in North Dakota, Minnesota and surrounding states. About 1909 missionaries entered the

Scandinavian countries of Europe, but owing to the dying out of foreign language congregations in America, this work has not prospered. There are few churches in Denmark and Sweden at present. Work among the Greek-speaking people has followed a similar pattern. They have a publishing plant in Chicago, and a missionary in Athens.

Recent Developments

Almost the whole structure and nature of the work has changed within the last thirty-five years. Several causes induced or favored these changes. The old timers had a deadly fear of organization, but today the work is highly organized. Relaxation of the severe ascetic discipline, and the promotion of education and of youth work in general has transformed the movement almost into a youth movement. Emphasis has passed from doctrine to evangelism and religious education.

The organization of the ministerial assemblies has prepared the way for these changes. It has furnished instruments for democratic ownership and control of all the church's activities. The vast printing plant of the Gospel Trumpet Company was put in the hands of a publication board and placed under control of the General Ministerial Assembly. Under the able management of A. T. Rowe, from 1931 to 1950, it not only supplied the church with literature, but also provided funds for many other necessary purposes. The General Manager is Steele C. Smith; editor in chief, Harold Phillips.

In the old days, the Gospel Trumpet Company carried on the foreign missionary work under the editor's secretaries. This work began with a correspondence with a brilliant Indian Mohammedan student of Calcutta University, John A. D. Khan, in 1897. The Trumpet Company sent him 1000 pounds of literature, and two small presses. The same year Gorham Tufts visited him while in India on famine relief work. This beginning in India has never died out. In June, 1909, a committee was set up which finally grew into the Foreign Missionary Board which now carries on missionary work in Syria, Egypt, Kenya Colony, Africa, the West Indies, Costa Rica, Panama, Japan, India, and formerly in China. This board also gives aid to evangelization work in Greece and other parts of Europe. Swiss brethren are doing missionary work in Argentina and other parts of South America. Adam Miller is president and C. Lowery Quinn secretary.

The Board of Church Extension and Home Missions aids in dozens of evangelization and building projects in the States, and carries on missionary work in Alaska and Mexico, besides work among migrants and the neglected anywhere in America. W. H. Hunt is president and E. F. Adcock is secretary.

In 1932, Mrs. Nora Hunter organized the National Women's Home and Foreign Missionary Society. At present Ocie Perry is president and Clara L. Smith is secretary.

Anderson College and Theological Seminary

At the time when the Gospel Trumpet workers gave their services without salary, these workers occupied a large building not far from the plant. When these workers began to receive pay for their services, the Gospel Trumpet Company, under its then president, J. T. Wilson, set up a training school in this building. Gradually this school developed into an incorporated institution: The Anderson College and Theological Seminary. J. A. Morrison is president and Russel Olt, dean. Students number nearly one thousand, including part time students. More recently it has added a graduate school of theology under Earl Martin as dean.

A school which started in Spokane, Washington, in 1905, has grown into the Pacific Bible College of Portland, Oregon. A F. Gray is president and Otto Linn dean. Enrollment: 200.

The Alberta Bible Institute, Camrose, Alberta, Canada, H. C. Gardner, principal, also has added an accredited High School under the direction of W. G. Ewert.

In Anderson, Indiana, the Board of Christian Education, under T. Franklin Miller, executive secretary, awards as many as six thousand credits for leadership training per year. The youth work is under Tom A. Smith, director. A World Service Committee collected $730,000.00 in 1950.

NOTES

[1] In response to a specific inquiry of the editor as to special doctrines and practices, the author of this essay writes: "We practice immersion and feet-washing, the latter now much neglected—but we are hostile to premillennialism. The Holiness people took that from John Darby and the Plymouth Brethren after we got started." He adds that the general theology of the church is derived from the Wesleys and others.

BIBLIOGRAPHY

D. H. KROMMINGA, *The Millennium in the Church* (Grand Rapids, 1945).

ERNEST SUTHERLAND BATES, *The American Faith* (New York, 1940).

DAVID S. SCHAFF, *History of the Christian Church*, Vol. 5, Part I (New York, 1920).

WILLISTON WALKER, *A History of the Christian Church* (New York, 1918).

ALBERT HENRY NEWMAN, *A History of Anti-Pedobaptism* (Philadelphia, 1896).

A. L. BYERS, *Birth of a Reformation* (Anderson, Ind., 1921).

C. H. FORNEY, *History of the Churches of God* (Harrisburg, Pa., 1914).

D. S. WARNER'S Unpublished Journal.

HENRY C. WICKERSHAM, *A History of the Church* (Anderson, Ind., 1900).

ROBERT BARCLAY, *Apology* (Philadelphia, 1908).

Journal of George Fox (Friends Tract Association, London, 1891).

AXCHIE A. BOLITHO, *To the Chief Singer* (Anderson, Ind., 1942).

E. E. BYRUM, *Life Experiences* (Anderson, Ind., 1928).

Young People's Friend, Nov. 29, 1931; June 5, 1932; Oct. 23, 1932. (Sunday school paper for youth, published weekly—name of the paper now is *Youth.*)

AUBREY LELAND FORREST, "A Study of the Development of the Basic Doctrines and Institutional Patterns in the Church of God (Anderson, Ind.)" (Doctor of Philosophy thesis, University of Southern California).

INDEX

(*The Bibliographical Lists appended to each Chapter
are here not included.*)

Abilene Christian College—430
Abilene (Tex.)—429, 430
academic degrees—403
Academy, the (Schenectady, N. Y.)
—140
Achor, G. R.—449
Adams county (Indiana)—54
Adcock, E. F.—453
Advent Christian Church—384
*Advent Review and Sabbath Herald,
The*—375
Advent Source Collection—381
adventism, 371ff. *See* Seventh-Day
Adventists; Seventh-Day Baptists
affusion—53, 56. *See* sprinkling
African Methodist Episcopal Church
—327
African Methodist Episcopal Zion
Church—327
African Union First Coloured Meth-
odist Protestant Church—327
Ahnfelt, Oscar—259, 270
Ainslie, Peter—400, 404, 405
Akron University—346
Albany (N. Y.)—131, 132, 373
Alberta Bible Institute—453
Albright College—363
Albright, Jacob—355-357, 360, 362
Albright People, The Socalled—356
Alcazar—381
Aldersgate—325
Alfred (N. Y.)—199
alien immersion—198
All-Friends Conference—241
All-Young Friends Conference—242
Allegheny presbytery—218
Allen, Joseph H.—156
Allentown (Pa.)—303
American Association of Theological
Schools—403
American Baptist Association (Land-
markists)—197, 198

American Baptist Convention—190-
193, 198, 201, 203, 404
American Baptist Missionary Union—
190
American Baptist Foreign Mission
Society—191
American Baptist Home Mission
Society—189, 191
American Baptist Publication Society
—189
American Board of Commissioners for
Foreign Missions—78, 80, 175, 176
American Christian Missionary So-
ciety—396, 398, 425
American Christian Review—401,
426, 427, 429
American Church Missionary Society
—118
American Episcopal Church, *see* Prot-
estant Episcopal Church in the U. S.
of America
American Faith, The—438
American Friend, The—240
American Friends Fellowship Council
—241
American Friends Service Committee
—240-242
American Home Missionary Society
—80, 174, 175
American (Home) Missionary Society
(Ger. Ref. Church)—299
American Humanist Association—
161, 162
American Lutheran Church, the—
42, 43
American Lutheran Conference, the—
42
"American Lutheranism"—34
American Mennonite Brethren—63
American Millennial Association—384
American Missionary Association—
176

[455]

INDEX

[461]

INDEX

Emerson, James—317
Emerson, R. W.—150, 160
Emmons, Nathanael—173
Endicott, John—170, 171
English Reformation—95
Ephrata (Pa.)—285, 286
Ephrata Cloisters—285, 286
episcopacy—15, 94, 96, 99, 102, 103, 106, 107, 114, 121, 173, 209, 275, 326, 328, 357, 359, 364, 391; Methodist episcopacy—320. *See* bishop
Episcopal Church— *see* Protestant Episcopal Church in the U. S. of America. Also *see* Anglican Church; Church of England
Episcopalian, episcopal — 307, 319, 361, 372; Methodist—325; episcopal succession—20
episcopal polity—31, 71, 104, 121
episcopos—69
Epworth—313
Erasmus—27, 45, 153
Eric-Jansonists—*see* Jansonists
Errett, Isaac—400, 401, 405
Errors of the Trinity—153
Erskine College—211
Esbjörn, L. P.—38
Essays and Reviews—116
Essex Street Chapel—154
Ettinger, A.—359
Ettwein, J.—18
Evangelical and Reformed Church— 181; 295ff; doctrines—304ff; polity—306ff.
Evangelical Association, The—356
Evangelical Beacon, The—274
Evangelical Church—353ff., 362
Evangelical Congregational Church, the—362
Evangelical Free Church—269, 273, 274
"Evangelical Lutheran Church, The" —40
Evangelical Lutheran Church of America (Eielsen Synod)—42, 43
Evangelical Lutheran Joint Synod of Ohio and Other States—42
Evangelical Lutheran Joint Synod of Wisconsin and Other States—42
Evangelical Lutheran Synod of Iowa and Other States—42
Evangelical Mennonite Brethren—62, 63

Evangelical Mennonite Church—63
Evangelical Methodist Church—327
Evangelical Mission Covenant Church and the Free Churches of Swedish Background—249ff.
Evangelical movement—232-234, 236, 313, 315, 316
Evangelical National Foundation—253
Evangelical Press, the—360
Evangelical School of Theology—363
Evangelical Synod of North America —295, 299ff., 303, 307, 308
Evangelical Synod of the Northwest— 301
Evangelical Synodical Conference of N.A.—42
Evangelical Theological Seminary — 363
Evangelical Union—32, 36, 295, 299
Evangelical United Brethren Church— 353ff; doctrines—365ff; polity— 364ff.
Evangelicalism—106-108, 113, 114, 116-118, 124, 354
evangelism—201, 202, 232
Evangelist—400
Evangelisten—274
Evangeliums Posaune—451
Evanston Collegiate Institute—272
Evansville (Ind.)—301
Ewert, W. G.—453
Ewing, Grenville—417, 418
excommunication—37, 52
Ezel (Ky.)—213

Faith and Order—404
Falkner Swamp—296, 300
fall of man—337
Fanning, Tolbert—401, 426, 427
Faustus, Socinus—154
Federal census—415
Federal Council of Churches—19, 142, 302, 404
Federal religious census—398
feet washing—56, 59, 195-197, 286, 379, 454
Femme Osage (Mo.)—300
Ferm, Vergilius—1ff., 25ff.
Fey, H. E.—402
Finney, Charles J.—235
Finnish Apostolic Lutheran Church— 41

[463]

INDEX

General Conference (Ev. United Brethren)—365
General Conference (Friends)—233, 239, 242-244
General Conference Mennonite Church—55, 57, 58, 65
General Conference Mennonites—60, 63
General Conference (Meth.) — 323, 329, 330
General Conference (Seventh-Day Adventists)—376ff.
General Conventions (Episcopal)— 103, 104, 106, 112, 114, 115, 117, 119, 122, 123
General Council (Congregational)— 178, 179, 181
General Council (Evangelical and Ref. Church)—307
General Council (Lutheran)—35, 38
General Directory (Moravian)—16
General Ministerial Assembly (Church of God)—452
General Missionary Convention of the Baptist Denomination in the U. S. of America—189
General Rules (Methodist) —321, 322
General Six-Principle Baptists, The— 195
General Synod (Evangelical and Ref. Church)—306, 307
General Synod (Ref. Church)—133, 134, 138, 141, 143, 144, 299
General Synod (Lutheran) — 34-36, 38, 39, 260
General Synod (Moravian)—16
General Synod of the Associate Reformed Presbyterian Church—211
General Theological Seminary—106
General Tract Society (Baptist)—189
Genesee (N. Y.)—242
George Pepperdine College—430
Georgetown (Ky.)—402
Gerhard, John—32
German Evangelical Church Society of the West—300
German Ev. Lutheran Synod of Missouri, Ohio and Other States—37
German Evangelical Missionary Society—301
German language—358, 359

German Reformed Church—298, 354, 438
German Reformed Church in America —296, 297, 299
German Seventh-Day Baptists—200
German Valley (Ill.)—140
Germanna Ford (Va.)—296
Germantown (Pa.)—33, 53, 54, 200, 280, 287, 288
Gettysburg College—34
Gettysburg Theological Seminary—34, 35
Giffen, J. K.—216
gift of prophecy—378
Gilbert, N.—316
Gladden, Washington—179
Glas, John—390, 418
Gloria Dei Church—32
Gloucester (Mass.)—342, 343
Gnadenau (Kansas)—63
Gnesio-Lutherans—28
Goddard College—346
"God's Invasion Army"—272
Goebel, L. W.—302, 307
Gordon, Andrew—216
Gordon, G. A.—179
Gore, Charles—116
Goshen (Ind.)—65
Gospel Advocate—401, 426-429
Gospel Broadcast—429
Gospel Guardian—429
Gospel Herald—57
Gospel Messenger, The (Ch. of the Brethren)—288
Gospel Trumpet, The—442, 445-453
Gospel Visitor—288
Grabau, Johannes—32
grace, indiscriminate—29
Graham, Robert—429
Grand Junction (Mich.)—442, 448
Grand Rapids (Mich.)—144
Grand View (Luth.) Seminary—41
Gravois Settlement (Mo.)—300
Gray, A. F.—453
Great Awakening—75, 76, 156, 173, 189, 417. *See* Second Great Awakening
Great Second Advent Awakening— 371
Grebel, Conrad—51, 52, 60
Green, J. L.—450
Greenwood, John—169
Gregory, the Great—94

INDEX

Home Study Institute—382
Hood College—303
Hooker, Thomas—173
Hope College—140
Hopedale Fraternal Community—341
Hopkins, J. H., Jr.—114
Hopkins, Samuel—173
Hopkinsianism—143
Hopson, W. H.—429
Horizons—288
Horsch, John—64
Horstmann, J. H.—304
Howard, George—449
Howard, J. N.—449
Howard University—176
Hoy, W. E.—299
Hubberthorne, Richard—227
Hudson, Hendrik—131
Huguenots—70, 212
Hultman, J. A.—270
human dignity—149
humanism—151, 161, 162
Hungarian Churches—304
Hunt, Robert—98
Hunt, W. H.—453
Hunter, Mrs. Nora—453
Huntington, countess of—326
Hus, John—7, 437
Hussites—380
Huter, Jacob—60, 61
Hutterian Brethren—60, 61
Huyghens—155
Hymnal, the (Mission Covenant)—
    270
*Hymnal and Liturgies of the Moravian
    Church*—20
Hymnal of 1892 (Episcopal)—123
Hymnal of 1940, The (Episcopal)—
    123
hyper-Calvinism—196, 197

Icelandic Ev. Lutheran Synod in N. A.
    —42
Icelandic Lutherans—41ff.
Idea Fidei Fratrum—18
Idleman, F.—400
"Illinois Band"—174
Illinois College—174
immersion—53, 58, 59, 188, 198, 200,
    384, 389, 392, 393, 405, 424, 454.
    See trine immersion
Independent African Methodist Epis-

copal Church—327
Independent Board for Presbyterian
    Foreign Missions—85
Independent Yearly Meetings
    (Friends)—243, 244
Independents—187, 390
Indiana Central College—363
Indiana Yearly Meetings (Friends)—
    233, 243
Indianapolis—363, 399, 400, 427, 441,
    442
Indians, American—8, 10, 18, 33, 98,
    132, 141, 174, 176, 191, 227, 232,
    242, 303, 304, 314, 415
indulgences—26
Institutes of Calvin—30, 70
instrumental music—397, 398, 401,
    426-429
International Council of Congrega-
    tional Churches—179
International Convention of Disciples
    of Christ—399, 404-407
Iona monastery—94
"Iowa Band"—174
Iowa College—174
Iowa Synod—38
Ireland—71-73, 95, 210, 422, 438
Irish Conference (Methodist)—328
Irish-Scotch—*see* Scotch-Irish
Ironwood, Mich.—41

Jablonski, D. E.—20
Jacobson, F. N.—450
Jamaica, L. I.—73
James I—71
James II—97, 209
James, St.—228
Jamestown (Va.)—72, 97, 98
Janson, Eric—275
Jansonists—275
Janzen, Cornelius—63
Jefferson, Thomas—149, 154-156, 391
Jehovah's Witnesses—3
Jenkins, Burris—400
Jerusalem—384
Johns, J.—118
Johnson, Francis—169
Johnson, Samuel—100
Johnson C. Smith University—85
Johnstown (Pa.)—353
Jon Bjarnason Academy—42
Jones, Abner—391, 419, 420

INDEX

INDEX

Association of North America, the
—360
missions, Moravian—16ff.
Missionsvännen—269
Missouri Lutherans—32, 36ff., 40-
43
Missouri Synod—300
modernist controversy—*see* Fundamen-
talist-Modernist controversy
Mohammedanism—380
monastery—286
Monmouth College—217
Monongahela presbytery—218
Montgomery county (Pa.)—54
Montgomery, M. W.—275
Moody, D. L.—235, 262
Moody Bible Institute—-274
Moore, archbishop—105
Moore, Glenn—88
Moore, J. H.—288
Moore, R. C.—108
Moorehead, W. G.—219
Moravian Church, 7ff; doctrines —
11ff; missions—16ff; pioneer lead-
ers—18ff; polity—15ff; schools—
17; worship—14ff.
Moravian College and Theological
Seminary—15, 17
Moravian Daily Texts—20
Moravian Preparatory School—17
Moravian Seminary and College for
Women—17
Moravian, The—15
Moravians—251, 315
*Moravians, A World Wide Fellow-
ship, The*—19
Morrison, C. C.—400-402, 404
Morrison, J. A.—453
Morse, Kenneth—288
Mott, Lucretia—160
Moundsville (W. Va.)—442
Mt. Airy Theological Seminary—35
Muehlmeier, H. A.—298
Mueller, J. W.—307
Muhlenberg, Frederick—46
Muhlenberg, G. H. E.—46
Muhlenberg, Henry Melchior—32-35
Muhlenberg, Peter—46
Muhlenberg, W. A.—115, 117
Muhlenberg Memorial—115
Mullan, J. M.—308
Mumford, Stephen—199
Murray, John—342, 343, 347

musical instruments—*see* instrumental music
Muskingum College—217
Myers, Julia—449
mysticism—233

Naas, John—288
Nansemond county (Va.)—72
Naperville (Ill.)—363
Nashotah House—112
Nashville (Tenn.)—399, 400, 420,
427, 430
National Association for the Promo-
tion of Holiness—440, 441
National Baptist Convention of
America (negro)—194
National Baptist Convention of the
U. S. of America, Inc. (negro)—
194
National Council (Cong.)—178, 179
National Council (Episcopal)—122
National Council of the Churches of
Christ in the United States of
America—19, 43, 142, 145, 181,
193, 199, 201, 221, 339
National Covenant—209
National Lutheran, The—43
National Lutheran Council—43
National Synod of France (Presb.)—
70
Naylor, C. W.—449
Nazareth (Pa.)—9, 17
Nazareth Hall—17
Neenah (Wis.)—40, 41
Negro Baptists—193ff.
Negro Mission (Luth.)—43
Neillsville (Wis.)—304
Nelson, Clarence A.—265, 266
Nelson, Thomas, publishers—451
Nevin, J. W.—298
New Amsterdam—33, 131, 132, 137
New and United Meetings (Friends)
—244
New Brunswick (N. J.)—76, 103
New Brunswick Theological Seminary
—140
New Commentary on Acts—403
New Congregational Methodist
Church—327
New England—72, 75, 80, 88, 103,
104, 106, 110, 111, 149, 155,
170ff., 174ff., 188ff., 196, 199, 204,

INDEX

INDEX

Reading (Pa.)—363
real presence—117
Redstone Baptists Association—393, 424
Redstone presbytery—77
Reformat Usok Lapja—304
Reformed, the—8, 70, 96, 295, 298, 299, 354, 366, 372, 437
Reformed Church in America, The—131ff; 215; doctrines—137; membership—139; polity — 136, 138, 139
Reformed Church in the U. S.—295ff., 299, 301-304, 308
Reformed Church of Holland—297
Reformed Episcopal Church — 108, 114, 118ff.
Reformed Mennonites—55; Reformed Mennonite Church—64
Reformed Methodist Church—327
Reformed Methodist Union Episcopal Church—327
Reformed New Congregational Methodist Church—327
Reformed Presbyterian Church—210
Reformed Presbyterian Church in North America—210, 211
Reformed Presbyterian Church of North America—210, 211
Reformed Presbytery of North America—210
Reformed Protestant Dutch Church—139
Reformed United Brethren Church—361
Reformed Zion Union Apostolic Church—327
"Reformers"—421
Reformierte Kirche—135
Reforming Baptists—394
Regular Baptists—*see* General Association of Regular Baptist Churches (North)
Regular Baptists—196
Regulars (Old Lights)—189
Rehoboth (Md.)—73, 74
Reid, W. J., Sr.—219
Reimer, Claas—63
Reist, Hans—53
religious bigotry—417
Religious Telescope, The—359, 361, 363
Relly, James—342

"Relly-ites"—342
Reminiscences (Clark's)—110
Renaissance, the—152
Republican Methodists—391, 418
"Resettlement Congregation" (Moravian)—20
Restoration Herald—406
Restoration movement—405, 412, 417, 425-427
restorationism, term — 412; restorationists—405ff.
Revelation, 20:2—385
revelation, continuing—226, 230
"Reverend"—397
Rhinehart, W. R.—359
Rhodes, Benton—289
Rhodes, S. W.—374
Rhodes University (So. Af.)—404
Ribera—381
Rice, Luther—189
Rice, N. L.—396, 425
Richard II—437
Richards, G. W.—302, 308
Richmond (Ind.)—239, 240
"Richmond Declaration of Faith" (Friends)—239
Ridgeville College—448
Riggle, H. M.—449
Ris, Cornelis—65
Rising, F. S.—118, 119
ritual canon—117
ritualistic controversy—117
Riverside (N. J.)—10
Roberts, John E.—449
Robinson, John—170
Rochester (N. Y.)—39
Rogers, John—422
Rome City (Ind.)—441
Romeyn, D.—140
Rondthaler, E.—18, 19
Roosevelt, Theodore—212
Rosacrucians—286
Rosenius, C. O.—253-257, 259, 270, 272
Rowe, A. T.—449, 452
Rowe, J. F.—401, 427
Rudnerweide Mennonites—62
Rules of Dort—139
Runes, D. D.—3
Rupert, J. H.—450, 451
Rush, Benjamin—341
Russell, E.—234-236
Russell, R. M.—219

[475]

INDEX

INDEX